great soups for
EVERY DAY
of THE WEEK

WARM UP with hot bowls of soup, chili, chowder and stew this winter or whenever you feel like a hearty bowlful! With *Taste of Home's Big Book of Soup*, you'll find 544 recipes featuring everything from basic broth to elegant first-course soups that satisfy and impress.

Nothing beats a bowl brimming with soup on a chilly day to soothe the senses and warm your heart. *Taste of Home's Big Book of Soup* features old-fashioned favorites like Chicken Noodle Soup (page 5) and Easy Oven Stew (page 251). But it also includes recipes to "wow" family and guests alike.

When hot summer days have you staying away from the stove, select a cool soup to refresh and revive your family and guests. Use the bounty of your garden to brighten up an luncheon or picnic party with Gazpacho (page 285) or Succulent Strawberry Soup (page 270).

You'll also find more than 50 tips from experienced cooks and our Test Kitchen staff to help you discover new ways to enjoy soup. Plus, additional indexes will help you find just the recipe you need. See page 302 for the Index of Tips and for the Index by Chapter, and see page 307 for the Index by Major Ingredient & Cooking Method.

Taste of Home's Big Book of Soup is chock-full of treasured recipes from past issues of *Taste of Home* and its "sister" publications. Every recipe is a tried-and-true favorite of a fellow cook's family. And each one has been prepared and taste-tasted by our Test Kitchen home economists. That means you can make these recipes with confidence.

Book Editor: Beth Wittlinger

Senior Art Director: Linda Dzik

Executive Editor, Books: Heidi Reuter Lloyd

Senior Editor: Julie Schnittka

Food Editor: Janaan Cunningham

Proofreader: Julie Blume Benedict

Editorial Assistant: Barb Czysz

Graphic Art Associates: Ellen Lloyd, Monica Bergwall,
Niki Malmberg

Associate Food Editors: Coleen Martin, Diane Werner

Senior Recipe Editor: Sue A. Jurack

Recipe Editors: Janet Briggs, Mary King

Test Kitchen Director: Mark Morgan

Test Kitchen Home Economists: Peggy Fleming, Nancy Fridirici,
Tina Johnson, Ann Liebergen, Annie Rose, Pat Schmeling,
Wendy Stenman, Amy Welk-Thieding

Test Kitchen Assistants: Suzanne Kern, Rita Krajcir, Kris Lehman,
Sue Megonigle, Megan Taylor

Food Photographers: Rob Hagen, Dan Roberts, Jim Wieland

Set Stylists: Julie Ferron, Stephanie Marchese, Sue Myers,
Jennifer Bradley Vent

Associate Set Stylist: Melissa Haberman

Food Stylists: Sarah Thompson, Joylyn Trickel

Photographers Assistant: Lori Foy

Creative Director: Ardyth Cope

Senior Vice President, Editor in Chief: Catherine Cassidy

President: Barbara Newton

Chairman and Founder: Roy Reiman

Taste of Home Books
©2005 Reiman Media Group, Inc.
5400 S. 60th St., Greendale WI 53129
International Standard Book Number: 0-89821-460-2
International Standard Serial Number: 1535-2781
Printed in U.S.A.

For additional copies of this book, write *Taste of Home* Books,
P.O. Box 908, Greendale WI 53129. Or to order by credit card,
call toll-free 1-800/344-2560 or visit our Web site at
www.reimanpub.com.

table of CONTENTS

PICTURED ON THE COVER: Chicken Noodle Soup (page 5).

homemade BROTH
...the secret to spirit-warming soups!

Many great soups begin with a tasty broth or stock. The differences between stocks and broths are subtle. Broths are made from simmering meats, poultry, fish or vegetables. Stocks are made with bones (which may or may not have been roasted), meat and vegetables.

Broths have less body than stocks, which should be clear and free of grease. Stocks and broths may be used interchangeably for the recipes in this book.

Stock is often used as a base for making soups, gravies and sauces. It is an effective way to add flavor to dishes that call for broth. Making your own stock allows you to control the amount of salt (many store-bought broths are high in sodium).

By substituting stock or broth for water in recipes, you can inject a tasty boost into everyday foods like rice and pasta. And you can cut fat and calories by using stock instead of butter or oil to saute vegetables and meat.

Homemade Chicken Stock

Peppercorns and a handful of herbs add the perfect seasoning to this stock developed by our Test Kitchen home economists. To give it even more flavor, they first browned the chicken and sauteed the veggies.

        1 whole chicken (3 pounds)
        1 teaspoon canola oil
        2 medium carrots, cut into chunks
        1 medium onion, cut into chunks
        3 sprigs fresh parsley
        1 bay leaf
    1/2 teaspoon dried thyme
    1/4 teaspoon dried rosemary
    1/4 teaspoon whole peppercorns
 2-1/2 quarts cold water
        1 celery rib with leaves, cut into chunks

Cut chicken into parts, reserving back and neck. In a soup kettle, cook chicken breast halves in oil over medium heat until browned, about 5 minutes; remove and set aside. Cook remaining chicken pieces, including back and neck, in two batches until browned; set aside. In the same pan, saute the carrots and onion until onion is tender.

Place seasonings on a double thickness of cheesecloth; bring up corners of cloth and tie with kitchen string to form a bag.

Return chicken to the pan. Add cold water, celery and spice bag. Slowly bring to a boil over medium-low heat. Reduce heat; simmer, uncovered, for 30 minutes. Skim foam. Remove chicken breast halves from pan. Remove meat from bones; return bones to pan. Refrigerate chicken breast meat for another use.

Simmer stock, uncovered, 3-4 hours longer. Strain; discard the chicken, bones, vegetables and spice bag. Refrigerate for 8 hours or overnight. Remove fat from surface. **Yield:** about 2 quarts.

Italian Chicken Soup

pictured below

This satisfying soup gets its Italian flair from fennel, thyme, basil and orzo pasta. It comes from our Test Kitchen home economists.

    1   fennel bulb, chopped
  1/2   cup chopped onion
    2   teaspoons olive oil
    4   cups Homemade Chicken Stock
        (recipe on page 4)
    2   cups water
1-1/2   cups chopped carrots
    1   teaspoon salt
  1/4   teaspoon dried thyme
  1/4   teaspoon dried basil
  1/4   teaspoon pepper
    2   cups cubed cooked chicken breast
  1/2   cup uncooked orzo pasta
    2   tablespoons finely chopped fennel
        fronds

In a Dutch oven or soup kettle, saute fennel bulb and onion in oil until fennel is softened. Add the next seven ingredients. Bring to a boil. Reduce the heat; cover and simmer for 15 minutes.

Stir in chicken and orzo. Cover and cook for 20 minutes or until orzo is tender. Stir in fennel fronds. **Yield:** 4 servings.

Chicken Noodle Soup

pictured above and on front cover

You can prepare this comforting soup without the noodles, stir in the diced chicken and freeze. When ready to serve, simply defrost the soup, bring to a boil, add the noodles and cook as directed.

Diane Edgecomb, Humboldt, South Dakota

    1   broiler/fryer chicken (3 to 3-1/2
        pounds)
2-1/2   quarts water
    1   cup diced carrots
    1   cup diced celery
    1   tablespoon salt
    2   teaspoons chicken bouillon granules
  1/4   cup chopped onion
  1/4   teapoon dried marjoram
  1/4   teaspoon dried thyme
  1/8   teaspoon pepper
    1   bay leaf
1-1/2   cups uncooked fine noodles

In a large saucepan, place the first 11 ingredients. Bring to a boil; skim foam from broth. Reduce heat; cover and simmer for 1 to 1-1/2 hours or until chicken is tender.

Remove chicken from broth; allow to cool. Debone chicken; dice. Skim fat from broth; bring to a boil. Add noodles; cook until tender. Return chicken to pan; adjust salt to taste. Remove bay leaf before serving. **Yield:** 8-10 servings (2-1/2 quarts).

Simmer a Better Broth

For a more flavorful broth, use a high proportion of meat/bones and vegetables to water.

Be sure to use cold water when starting to make stock.

Bring the broth mixture to a boil slowly to help release more meat juices. An initial rapid boil tends to seal the juices into the meats.

During cooking time, if necessary, add just enough hot water to keep meat and vegetables covered.

3 Steps to Preparing Broth

1.
While the broth simmers (chicken is shown here), use a slotted spoon to skim foam from the surface. Skim frequently during the first 30 minutes, then as needed or every hour as the broth cooks.

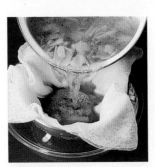

2.
To strain the broth, line a colander with two layers of cheesecloth and place in a large heat-resistant bowl. Gradually pour broth mixture into colander. Slowly lift colander from the bowl, letting broth drain.

3.
When ready to use the broth (beef is shown here), take chilled mixture from refrigerator and use a spoon to remove the hardened fat from the broth's surface. Discard the fat.

Homemade Beef Broth

Roasting soup bones in the oven first gives hearty beef flavor to this basic stock from our Test Kitchen home economists.

- 4 pounds meaty beef soup bones (beef shanks *or* short ribs)
- 3 medium carrots, cut into chunks
- 3 celery ribs, cut into chunks
- 2 medium onions, quartered
- 1/2 cup warm water
- 3 bay leaves
- 3 garlic cloves
- 8 to 10 whole peppercorns
- 3 to 4 sprigs fresh parsley
- 1 teaspoon *each* dried thyme, marjoram and oregano
- 3 quarts cold water

Place soup bones in a large roasting pan. Bake, uncovered, at 450° for 30 minutes. Add carrots, celery and onions. Bake 30 minutes longer; drain fat.

With a slotted spoon, transfer bones and vegetables to a soup kettle. Add warm water to the roasting pan; stir to loosen browned bits from the pan.

Transfer pan juices to kettle. Add seasonings and enough cold water just to cover. Slowly bring to a boil, about 30 minutes.

Reduce heat; simmer, uncovered, for 4-5 hours, skimming the surface as foam rises. If necessary, add hot water during the first 2 hours to keep ingredients covered.

Set beef bones aside until cool enough to handle. Remove meat from bones; discard bones and save meat for another use.

Strain broth, discarding the vegetables and seasonings. Refrigerate broth for 8 hours or overnight. Skim fat from surface. **Yield:** about 2-1/2 quarts.

Roast Beef Barley Soup

pictured above

Our Test Kitchen home economists share this recipe for a delicious soup brimming with tasty and colorful ingredients. It's so comforting on a crisp autumn day.

1/2 cup *each* chopped carrot, celery and
    onion
  1 tablespoon butter
  4 cups beef broth
  4 cups water
  2 cups chopped cooked roast beef
  1 can (14-1/2 ounces) diced tomatoes,
    undrained
    1 cup quick-cooking barley
1-1/2 teaspoons salt
  1/2 teaspoon pepper
  1/2 teaspoon dried basil
  1/2 teaspoon dried oregano
  1/2 cup frozen peas

In a soup kettle or Dutch oven, saute carrot, celery and onion in butter until tender, about 5 minutes. Add the broth, water, beef, tomatoes, barley, salt, pepper, basil and oregano; bring to a boil. Reduce heat; cover and simmer for 20 minutes, stirring occasionally. Add the peas. Simmer, uncovered, for 5 minutes. **Yield:** 12 servings (3 quarts).

"Soup *is the song of the* hearth... *and the* home."

comforting
CHICKEN
&TURKEY

and simmer for 1 hour. Add corn; cook 10 minutes longer. Top each serving with tortilla chips; sprinkle with cheese. **Yield:** 8 servings.

Southwestern Chicken Soup

pictured above

This hearty soup is one of my family's mainstays. So I often double the recipe and freeze some for future meals. The spices really liven up this filling soup.

Anne Smithson, Cary, North Carolina

    1 can (49-1/2 ounces) chicken broth
    1 can (14-1/2 ounces) crushed tomatoes,
       undrained
    1 can (14-1/2 ounces) diced tomatoes,
       undrained
    1 pound boneless skinless chicken
       breasts, cut into 1/2-inch cubes
    1 large onion, chopped
  1/3 cup minced fresh cilantro
    1 can (4 ounces) chopped green chilies
    1 garlic clove, minced
    1 teaspoon chili powder
    1 teaspoon ground cumin
  1/2 teaspoon dried oregano
  1/4 teaspoon cayenne pepper
    3 cups frozen corn, thawed
Baked tortilla chips
    1 cup (4 ounces) shredded Mexican
       cheese blend

In a large saucepan, combine the first 12 ingredients. Bring to a boil. Reduce heat; cover

Pasta Sausage Soup

Our family looks forward to a pot of soup every Saturday. This one ranks high at our house because the flavor is so good! The wonderful aroma of Italian seasonings simmering always brings folks to the table. The soup's nicely spiced, and the turkey sausage adds great flavor.

Janet Eggers, Pound, Wisconsin

1-1/2 pounds turkey Italian sausage links
    1 medium green pepper, cut
       into 1-inch strips
  1/2 cup chopped onion
    1 garlic clove, minced
    6 cups water
    1 can (28 ounces) diced tomatoes,
       undrained
    1 tablespoon sugar
    1 tablespoon Worcestershire sauce
    2 teaspoons chicken bouillon granules
    1 teaspoon salt
    1 teaspoon dried basil
    1 teaspoon dried thyme
2-1/2 cups uncooked bow tie pasta

Remove casings from sausage; cut links into 1/2-in. pieces. In a Dutch oven or soup kettle, cook sausage over medium heat for 5-7 minutes or until no longer pink.

Remove with a slotted spoon; drain, reserving 2 tablespoons drippings. In the drippings, saute the green pepper, onion and garlic for 4-5 minutes or until tender.

Add the water, tomatoes, sugar, Worcestershire sauce, bouillon, salt, basil, thyme and sausage. Bring to a boil; add pasta.

Reduce heat; simmer, uncovered, for 18-22 minutes or until pasta is tender. **Yield:** 10 servings (2-1/2 quarts).

Turkey Tomato Soup
pictured below

Turkey and tomatoes are high on my list of favorite foods. My husband grows the best tomatoes ever…and I made up this recipe to complement both ingredients. It's wonderful any time of year, but I prefer to make it when the tomatoes, green peppers, basil and garlic are all fresh from our garden.

Carol Brunelle, Ascutney, Vermont

  4 pounds tomatoes, seeded and chopped (about 8 large tomatoes)
  3 medium green peppers, chopped
  2 cans (14-1/2 ounces *each*) chicken broth
  1 can (14-1/2 ounces) vegetable broth
1-1/2 cups water
1-1/2 teaspoons beef bouillon granules
  2 garlic cloves, minced
  1 teaspoon dried oregano
  1 teaspoon dried basil
1/2 teaspoon pepper
  3 cups cubed cooked turkey
  3 cups cooked elbow macaroni
Minced fresh basil, optional

In a large saucepan or Dutch oven, combine the first 10 ingredients. Bring to a boil. Reduce heat; cover and simmer for 2 hours. Stir in turkey and macaroni; heat through. Garnish with fresh basil if desired. **Yield:** 12 servings (3 quarts).

Red Bean 'n' Sausage Soup

pictured below

We have many cold months in Idaho, and hearty soups served with hot rolls help warm us up. My mom got the recipe for this delicious soup—loaded with kidney beans, apples and turkey sausage—at a country restaurant in Lima, Montana.

Tami Christman, Soda Springs, Idaho

1 pound turkey Italian sausage links, casings removed
1 medium onion, diced
3 cups chicken broth
3 medium tart apples, peeled and chopped
1 can (14-1/2 ounces) crushed tomatoes, undrained
2 tablespoons cider vinegar
2 tablespoons chopped green pepper
2 tablespoons chopped sweet red pepper
2 tablespoons brown sugar
1/2 teaspoon seasoned salt
1/2 teaspoon ground mustard
1/4 teaspoon rubbed sage
1/4 teaspoon chili powder
1/4 teaspoon pepper
1 can (16 ounces) kidney beans, rinsed and drained

In a large saucepan or soup kettle, cook the sausage and onion over medium heat until meat is no longer pink; drain. Add the next 12 ingredients. Bring to a boil.

Reduce the heat; cover and simmer for 45 minutes, stirring occasionally. Add beans and heat through. **Yield:** 8 servings (2 quarts).

Creamy Chicken Rice Soup

I combined three recipes to come up with this take on the classic creamy chicken rice soup. I cut down on the butter, increased the vegetables and eliminated the half-and-half cream. This version is truly delicious.

Marge Wagner, Roselle, Illinois

1/2 cup chopped carrot
1/3 cup finely chopped onion
1/3 cup chopped celery
2 tablespoons butter
1/4 cup all-purpose flour
2 cans (14-1/2 ounces *each*) chicken broth
2 cups cooked long grain rice
1 cup cubed cooked chicken
1/2 teaspoon salt
1/4 teaspoon pepper
1/8 teaspoon garlic powder
1 cup 2% milk
2 tablespoons lemon juice
1 tablespoon white wine, optional

In a large saucepan, saute the carrot, onion and celery in butter until tender. Stir in flour until blended. Gradually stir in broth.

Add the rice, chicken, salt, pepper and garlic powder; bring to a boil. Reduce heat; cover and simmer for 10-15 minutes or until vegetables are tender. Reduce heat to low.

Stir in the milk, lemon juice and wine if desired. Cook and stir for 5 minutes or until heated through. **Yield:** 6 servings.

After-Thanksgiving Turkey Soup

As much as my family loves Thanksgiving, they look forward to this creamy soup using leftover turkey even more. It makes a big batch that we can enjoy for days.

Valorie Walker, Bradley, South Carolina

- 1 leftover turkey carcass (from a 12- to 14-pound turkey)
- 3 medium onions, chopped
- 2 large carrots, diced
- 2 celery ribs, diced
- 1 cup butter
- 1 cup all-purpose flour
- 2 cups half-and-half cream
- 1 cup uncooked long grain rice
- 2 teaspoons salt
- 1 teaspoon chicken bouillon granules
- 3/4 teaspoon pepper

Place turkey carcass in a soup kettle or Dutch oven and cover with water. Bring to a boil. Reduce heat; cover and simmer for 1 hour. Remove the carcass; cool. Set aside 3 qts. broth. Remove turkey from bones and cut into bite-size pieces; set aside.

In a soup kettle or Dutch oven, saute the onions, carrots and celery in butter until tender. Reduce heat; stir in flour until blended. Gradually add 1 qt. of reserved broth. Bring to a boil; cook and stir for 2 minutes or until thickened.

Add cream, rice, salt, bouillon, pepper, remaining broth and reserved turkey. Reduce heat; cover and simmer for 30-35 minutes or until rice is tender. **Yield:** 16 servings (about 4 quarts).

Roasted Chicken Noodle Soup
pictured above right

When the weather turns chilly around Reno, I stock my soup pot with this warmer-upper. The creamy, nicely seasoned broth is chock-full of tender chicken, potatoes, carrots and celery. There's old-fashioned goodness in every spoonful of this thick, nourishing soup!

Julee Wallberg, Reno, Nevada

- 1 cup chopped onion
- 1 cup chopped carrots
- 1 cup chopped celery
- 1 garlic clove, minced
- 2 teaspoons olive oil
- 1/4 cup all-purpose flour
- 1/2 teaspoon dried oregano
- 1/4 teaspoon dried thyme
- 1/4 teaspoon poultry seasoning
- 6 cups chicken broth
- 4 cups diced peeled uncooked potatoes
- 1 teaspoon salt
- 2 cups diced roasted chicken breast
- 2 cups uncooked yolk-free wide noodles
- 1 cup evaporated milk

In a Dutch oven or soup kettle, saute the onion, carrots, celery and garlic in oil for 5 minutes or until tender. Stir in the flour, oregano, thyme and poultry seasoning until blended; saute 1 minute longer.

Gradually add broth, potatoes and salt; bring to a boil. Reduce heat; cover and simmer for 15-20 minutes or until potatoes are tender.

Stir in the chicken and noodles; simmer for 10 minutes or until noodles are tender. Reduce heat. Stir in the milk; heat through (do not boil). **Yield:** 8 servings.

Spicy Chicken Tortilla Soup

This soup is as good as (if not better than) any kind I've had in a restaurant. I get so many compliments...I know you will, too!

Laura Johnson, Largo, Florida

>   1 large onion, chopped
>   2 tablespoons olive oil
>   1 can (4 ounces) chopped green chilies
>   2 garlic cloves, minced
>   1 jalapeno pepper, seeded and
>   chopped
>   1 teaspoon ground cumin
>   5 cups chicken broth
>   1 can (15 ounces) tomato sauce
>   1 can (14-1/2 ounces) diced tomatoes
>   with garlic and onion, undrained
>   3 cans (5 ounces *each*) white chicken,
>   drained
>   1/4 cup minced fresh cilantro
>   2 teaspoons lime juice
> Salt and pepper to taste
> Crushed tortilla chips
> Shredded Monterey Jack *or* cheddar cheese

In a large saucepan, saute onion in oil; add the chilies, garlic, jalapeno and cumin. Stir in the broth, tomato sauce and tomatoes. Bring to a boil. Reduce heat; stir in chicken. Simmer, uncovered, for 10 minutes.

Add the cilantro, lime juice, salt and pepper. Top with crushed tortilla chips and cheese. **Yield:** 7 servings.

Editor's Note: When cutting or seeding hot peppers, use rubber or plastic gloves to protect your hands. Avoid touching your face.

Brown Rice Turkey Soup
pictured above right

I don't recall where I got this recipe, but it's my all-time favorite turkey soup. Everyone who has tried it agrees. The sweet red pepper is what gives the soup its distinctive flavor.

Bobby Langley, Rocky Mount, North Carolina

>   1 cup diced sweet red pepper
>   1/2 cup chopped onion
>   1/2 cup sliced celery
>   2 garlic cloves, minced
>   2 tablespoons butter

>   3 cans (14-1/2 ounces *each*) chicken
>   broth
>   3/4 cup white wine *or* additional chicken
>   broth
>   1 teaspoon dried thyme
>   1/4 teaspoon pepper
>   2 cups cubed cooked turkey breast
>   1 cup instant brown rice
>   1/4 cup sliced green onions

In a Dutch oven, saute the red pepper, onion, celery and garlic in butter for 5-7 minutes or until vegetables are tender.

Add the broth, wine or additional broth, thyme and pepper. Bring to a boil. Reduce heat; cover and simmer for 5 minutes.

Stir in the turkey and rice. Bring to a boil; simmer, uncovered, for 5 minutes or until the rice is tender. Garnish with green onions. **Yield:** 5 servings.

Quick Turkey-Bean Soup

This recipe calls for canned beans, so cooking time is minimal. I make this soup mild and allow guests to add as much "heat" as they want with hot pepper sauce.

*Debbie Schermerhorn
Colorado Springs, Colorado*

Learn about Cilantro...

With its slightly sharp flavor, cilantro (also known as Chinese parsley) gives a distinctive flavor to many Mexican, Latin American and Oriental dishes.

Cilantro and other fresh herbs should be used promptly after purchase.

For short-term storage, immerse freshly cut stems in about 2 inches of water. Cover leaves loosely with a plastic bag and refrigerate for several days. Wash just before using.

---

    1   pound ground turkey
    2   garlic cloves, minced
    1   medium onion, chopped
    1   tablespoon vegetable oil
1-1/2   cups chopped celery
    1   medium green pepper, chopped
    1   medium sweet red pepper, chopped
    2   cans (14-1/2 ounces *each*) beef broth
    1   can (28 ounces) stewed tomatoes
    3   tablespoons tomato paste
  1/2   teaspoon cayenne pepper
  1/4   teaspoon dried basil
  1/4   teaspoon dried oregano
    2   cans (16 ounces *each*) kidney beans, rinsed and drained
    1   can (15 ounces) black beans, rinsed and drained
    1   can (15 ounces) pinto beans, rinsed and drained
    1   can (15-1/4 ounces) whole kernel corn, drained

In a soup kettle or Dutch oven over medium heat, cook turkey, garlic and onion in oil until meat is no longer pink; drain. Add celery and peppers; cook and stir for 2 minutes. Add broth, tomatoes, tomato paste, cayenne, basil and oregano; mix well.

Bring to a boil. Add beans and corn. Reduce heat; cover and simmer for 15 minutes. **Yield:** 14-16 servings (4 quarts).

Curried Chicken Rice Soup
pictured below

This is a terrific way to use up leftover chicken and cooked rice. With its mild curry and colorful chunks of carrot and celery, the thick mixture draws rave reviews every time I fix it.

Judie Anglen, Riverton, Wyoming

    2   large carrots, diced
    2   celery ribs, diced
    1   small onion, chopped
  3/4   cup butter
  3/4   cup all-purpose flour
    1   teaspoon seasoned salt
  1/2 to 1 teaspoon curry powder
    3   cans (12 ounces *each*) evaporated milk
    4   cups chicken broth
    2 to 3 cups cubed cooked chicken
    2   cups cooked long grain rice

In a large saucepan, saute carrots, celery and onion in butter for 2 minutes. Stir in flour, seasoned salt and curry until smooth. Gradually add milk. Bring to a boil; cook and stir for 2 minutes or until thickened. Gradually add broth. Stir in chicken and rice. Return to a boil.

Reduce heat; simmer, uncovered, for 10 minutes or until the vegetables are tender. **Yield:** 10-12 servings.

Soup Bar

pictured above

With all of its ingredients, this probably should be called "Surprise Soup" instead! Hearty, unique and fun to serve, it works especially well for large groups. I've prepared if for as many as 38 people by making a few adjustments to the recipe. Even children like it.

Lynn Conlon, Provo, Utah

4 cups chicken broth
2 cans (14-1/2 ounces *each*) stewed
    tomatoes
1 teaspoon chili powder
1 teaspoon garlic powder
1/4 teaspoon salt
1/8 teaspoon pepper
CONDIMENTS: 1 to 2 cups *each* of any of
    the following:
Shredded cheddar cheese
Frozen broccoli, carrots *and/or* cauliflower,
    thawed and chopped
Frozen corn *or* peas, thawed
Cubed cooked chicken, ham *or* sliced
    smoked sausage
Cooked crumbled bacon
Chopped fresh mushrooms
Minced fresh parsley
Cooked pasta *or* rice
Sour cream

In a medium kettle, combine the first six ingredients; bring to a boil. Reduce heat; cover and simmer for 30 minutes.

Meanwhile, arrange condiments in individual serving dishes. To serve, spoon desired condiments into soup bowl; top with hot soup. **Yield:** 6-8 servings.

Spicy Kielbasa Soup
pictured below

Red pepper flakes bring a little zip to this hearty soup that's full of good-for-you ingredients. Should you have any left over, this soup is great reheated, after the flavors have had time to blend. I like to serve steaming bowls of it with rye bread.

Carol Custer, Clifton Park, New York

    1/2 pound smoked turkey kielbasa, sliced
      1 medium onion, chopped
      1 medium green pepper, chopped
      1 celery rib with leaves, thinly sliced
      4 garlic cloves, minced
      2 cans (14-1/2 ounces *each*) chicken
        broth
      1 can (15-1/2 ounces) great northern
        beans, rinsed and drained

      1 can (14-1/2 ounces) stewed tomatoes,
        cut up
      1 small zucchini, sliced
      1 medium carrot, shredded
      1 tablespoon dried parsley flakes
    1/4 teaspoon crushed red pepper flakes
    1/4 teaspoon pepper

In a nonstick skillet, cook kielbasa over medium heat until lightly browned. Add the onion, green pepper, celery and garlic. Cook and stir for 5 minutes or until vegetables are tender.

Transfer to a slow cooker. Stir in the remaining ingredients. Cover and cook on low for 8-9 hours. **Yield:** 5 servings.

Texas Turkey Soup

I'm not really fond of soup, so I was a little hesitant to try this recipe. But after some adjustments over the years, I've come to love this one-of-a-kind turkey soup.

Betty Bakas, Lakehills, Texas

      2 quarts turkey broth
      4 cups cubed cooked turkey
      2 large white onions, halved
      2 celery ribs, sliced
      3 medium carrots, sliced
      1 cup *each* frozen corn, cut green beans
        and peas
      2 bay leaves
    1/2 to 1 teaspoon dried tarragon
    3/4 teaspoon garlic powder
    1/4 to 1/2 teaspoon hot pepper sauce
Salt and pepper to taste
  1-1/2 cups uncooked noodles
      1 tablespoon cornstarch
      1 tablespoon water

In a Dutch oven or soup kettle, combine broth, turkey, vegetables and seasonings; bring to a boil. Reduce heat; cover and simmer for 20-30 minutes or until vegetables are tender. Return to a boil; add noodles. Reduce heat; cover and simmer for 15-20 minutes or until noodles are tender.

Combine cornstarch and water until smooth; add to soup. Bring to a boil; boil for 2 minutes, stirring constantly. Remove bay leaves. **Yield:** 10-12 servings (3 quarts).

Low-Fat Chicken Dumpling Soup

pictured below

My husband was fooled with this low-fat recipe and I'm sure your family will be, too! A savory broth, hearty chunks of chicken and thick chewy dumplings provide plenty of comforting flavor.

Brenda White, Morrison, Illinois

    1 pound boneless skinless chicken
      breasts, cut into 1-1/2-inch cubes
    3 cans (14-1/2 ounces *each*) chicken
      broth
    3 cups water
    4 medium carrots, chopped
    1 medium onion, chopped
    1 celery rib, chopped
    1 teaspoon minced fresh parsley
  1/2 teaspoon salt
  1/4 teaspoon garlic powder
  1/4 teaspoon poultry seasoning
  1/4 teaspoon pepper
DUMPLINGS:
    3 egg whites
  1/2 cup 1% cottage cheese
    2 tablespoons water
  1/4 teaspoon salt
    1 cup all-purpose flour

In a large nonstick skillet coated with nonstick cooking spray, brown chicken. Add the broth, water, vegetables and seasonings. Bring to a boil. Reduce heat; simmer, uncovered, for 30 minutes.

Meanwhile, for dumplings, beat the egg whites and cottage cheese in a mixing bowl. Add water and salt. Stir in the flour; mix well.

Bring soup to a boil. Drop dumplings by tablespoonfuls onto the boiling soup. Reduce heat; cover and simmer for 15 minutes or until a toothpick inserted in dumplings comes out clean (do not lift cover while simmering). Serve immediately. **Yield:** 4 servings.

Barley Turkey Soup

Instead of using chicken broth, I frequently make homemade stock using the leftover holiday turkey. A steaming bowl of soup takes the chill out of winter.

Mrs. Warren Constans, Fruitland, Idaho

      2 quarts chicken broth
  1-1/2 cups diced celery
      1 cup medium pearl barley
      1 medium onion, diced
    3/4 cup diced carrots
    1/4 teaspoon salt
    1/2 teaspoon dried thyme
      1 bay leaf
    1/8 teaspoon ground allspice
    1/8 teaspoon pepper
Dash cayenne pepper
      2 cups cubed cooked turkey
    1/4 cup minced fresh parsley,
        optional

In a Dutch oven or soup kettle, combine the first 11 ingredients. Bring to a boil. Reduce heat; simmer, uncovered, for 30-40 minutes or until vegetables and barley are tender.

Stir in the turkey and parsley if desired; heat through. Discard the bay leaf before serving. **Yield:** 9 servings.

Oodles of Noodles Soup
pictured above

When my godchild was young, I often gave her a children's cookbook for her birthday or other special occasions. We'd plan an entire menu from the books, prepare the meal together and serve it to her family. This soup recipe was a favorite.

Lorri Reinhardt, Big Bend, Wisconsin

   3/4 **pound boneless skinless chicken breasts, cubed**
     2 **medium carrots, sliced**
     1 **small onion, chopped**
     2 **celery ribs, sliced**
     1 **garlic clove, minced**
     5 **cups water**
   1/4 **teaspoon pepper**
     2 **packages (3 ounces *each*) chicken ramen noodles**

In a large saucepan coated with nonstick cooking spray, saute the chicken, carrots, onion, celery and garlic until chicken is no longer pink. Add water, pepper and contents of seasoning packets from the noodles. Bring to a boil. Reduce heat; cover and simmer for 15-20 minutes or until carrots are tender.

Break noodles into pieces and add to soup; cover and cook for 3 minutes or until tender. **Yield:** 6 servings.

Lemony Turkey Rice Soup
pictured below

While growing up in Texas, I spent a lot of time helping my grandma cook. Lemon and cilantro add a deliciously different twist to turkey soup.

Margarita Cuellar, East Chicago, Indiana

     6 **cups chicken broth, *divided***
     1 **can (10-3/4 ounces) condensed cream of chicken soup, undiluted**
     2 **cups cooked rice**
     2 **cups diced cooked turkey**
   1/4 **teaspoon pepper**
     2 **tablespoons cornstarch**
   1/4 **to 1/3 cup lemon juice**
   1/4 **to 1/2 cup minced fresh cilantro**

In a large saucepan, combine 5-1/2 cups of broth, soup, rice, turkey and pepper. Bring to a boil; boil for 3 minutes.

In a small bowl, combine cornstarch and remaining broth until smooth. Gradually stir into hot soup. Cook and stir for 1-2 minutes or until thickened and heated through.

Remove from the heat; stir in lemon juice and cilantro. **Yield:** 8 servings (about 2 quarts).

Flower Garden Soup

pictured above

Fresh vegetables flavor traditional chicken soup in this bountiful blend created by our Test Kitchen staff. To add seasonal fun, just cut notches in the carrots and zucchini to make petals, slice the veggies, then simmer up bowls of blooms!

    6 medium carrots
    1 medium zucchini
    4 celery ribs, chopped
    1 medium onion, chopped
    8 cans (14-1/2 ounces *each*) chicken
       broth
    1 teaspoon dried basil
    1 teaspoon dried oregano
    4 cups cubed cooked chicken

Using a zest stripper or paring knife, cut a lengthwise strip on each carrot, forming a notch. Repeat at equal intervals around carrot. Repeat with zucchini. Cut carrots and zucchini into 1/4-in. slices; set zucchini aside.

In a Dutch oven or soup kettle, combine the carrots, celery, onion, broth, basil and oregano. Bring to a boil. Reduce heat; cover and simmer for 20-30 minutes or until vegetables are crisp-tender.

Add the chicken and reserved zucchini; simmer, uncovered, for 10 minutes or until the zucchini is tender. **Yield:** 8 servings (2 quarts).

Swedish Potato Dumpling Soup

Family and friends gather around our table throughout the year to enjoy good company and great food. As part of our Christmas Eve meal, I serve this hearty soup.

Margaret Peterson, Genoa, Nebraska

       1 broiler/fryer chicken (3-1/2 to 4
          pounds), cut up
    6-1/2 cups water
       2 teaspoons salt
       2 celery ribs, quartered
       1 medium carrot, quartered
       1 small onion, peeled
       4 whole peppercorns
       2 whole cloves
       2 whole allspice
       2 chicken bouillon cubes
       1 package (10 ounces) frozen green
          beans
       1 package (12 ounces) frozen noodles
    DUMPLINGS:
       2 medium potatoes, cooked and
          mashed (without added milk *or* butter)
       1 egg, beaten
       2 tablespoons half-and-half cream
       1 teaspoon sugar
     1/4 teaspoon salt
     1/2 cup all-purpose flour

In a 5-qt. soup kettle, combine the first 10 ingredients. Cover and bring to a boil. Reduce heat; simmer for 3 hours. Remove chicken; allow to cool. Strain broth, discarding vegetables and seasonings.

Add enough water to make 8 cups; return to kettle. Debone chicken and cut into chunks; add to kettle with beans and noodles. Bring to a boil; cook for 20 minutes.

For dumplings, mix potatoes, egg, cream, sugar and salt in a medium bowl. Gradually add flour to make a stiff batter (it should form a peak when spoon is lifted).

Drop by teaspoons into boiling soup. Cover and simmer for 3 minutes (do not lift lid while simmering). **Yield:** 12 servings (3 quarts).

Turkey Meatball Soup

pictured below

You don't need to cook the tender homemade meatballs or boil the egg noodles separately, so you can easily stir up this savory soup in no time.

Carol Losier, Baldwinsville, New York

  2 cans (14-1/2 ounces *each*) chicken broth
  1 celery rib with leaves, thinly sliced
  1 medium carrot, thinly sliced
1/4 cup chopped onion
  1 tablespoon butter
  1 egg, beaten
1/2 cup dry bread crumbs
  2 tablespoons dried parsley flakes
  1 tablespoon Worcestershire sauce
1/4 teaspoon pepper
1/2 pound lean ground turkey
  1 cup uncooked egg noodles

In a large saucepan, bring the broth, celery and carrot to a boil. Reduce heat; cover and simmer for 10 minutes. Meanwhile, in a small skillet, saute onion in butter until tender.

Transfer to a large bowl. Add the egg, bread crumbs, parsley, Worcestershire sauce and pepper. Crumble turkey over mixture and mix well. Shape into 1-in. balls.

Add meatballs to the simmering broth. Bring to a boil. Reduce heat; cover and simmer for 15 minutes or until meatballs are no longer pink. Add noodles. Cover and simmer for 5 minutes or until noodles are tender. **Yield:** 5 servings.

Chicken Tortilla Soup

pictured above

A few additions to canned cream of chicken soup provide the comforting flavor found in mock chicken dumpling soup. And you can't tell that the dumplings are actually tortilla strips. It goes from stovetop to tabletop in less than 30 minutes!

Carolyn Griffin, Macon, Georgia

  1 can (10-3/4 ounces) condensed cream of chicken soup, undiluted
  4 cups water
  2 cups cubed cooked chicken
  4 flour tortillas (6 inches), cut into 2-1/2-inch strips
Minced fresh parsley

In a 3-qt. saucepan, bring the soup and water to a boil. Stir in the chicken and tortilla strips; reduce heat to medium-low. Cook, uncovered, for 25-30 minutes, stirring occasionally. Sprinkle with parsley. **Yield:** 6 servings.

1-1/4 hours or until tender. Drain and reserve drippings. Skim fat. Cool chicken; debone and cut into chunks. Cover and refrigerate chicken. In a Dutch oven or soup kettle, bring chicken broth and reserved drippings to a boil. Add mushrooms, celery, carrots, onion and pepper; simmer for 30 minutes.

Meanwhile, for noodles, set aside 1/3 cup of flour. Combine salt and remaining flour in a bowl. Beat eggs, milk and oil; stir into dry ingredients. Sprinkle kneading surface with reserved flour; knead dough until smooth. Divide into thirds. Roll out each portion to 1/8-in. thickness; cut to desired width. Freeze two portions to use at another time.

Bring soup to a boil. Add one portion of noodles; cook for 7-9 minutes or until almost tender. Add chicken; heat through. **Yield:** 10 servings (2-3/4 quarts).

Best Chicken Noodle Soup
pictured above

For years, I worked at making a chicken soup that tasted just like my mother's. When I realized I couldn't, I decided to come up with my own recipe. It was an immediate hit! People enjoy the vegetables, noodles and rosemary.

Cheryl Rogers, Ames, Iowa

   1 tablespoon dried rosemary, crushed
   2 teaspoons garlic powder
   2 teaspoons pepper
   2 teaspoons seasoned salt
   2 broiler/fryer chickens (3 to 3-1/2 pounds *each*)
1-1/2 quarts chicken broth
2-1/4 cups sliced fresh mushrooms
  1/2 cup chopped celery
  1/2 cup sliced carrots
  1/2 cup chopped onion
  1/4 teaspoon pepper
NOODLES:
2-1/2 cups all-purpose flour, *divided*
   1 teaspoon salt
   2 eggs
   1 can (5 ounces) evaporated milk
   1 tablespoon olive oil

Combine the first four ingredients; rub over chickens. Place in an ungreased 13-in. x 9-in. x 2-in. baking pan. Cover and bake at 350° for

> "As a substitute for fresh celery, try freezing chopped celery leaves and using them later on when you make soups and casseroles."
>
> —*D.J. Shaske*
> *Peetz, Colorado*

Zesty Cheese Soup

My husband and I are retired, but I still look for shortcut recipes like the one I received from a great-niece. You'll likely have the majority of ingredients for this colorful soup in your pantry. To save time, I start warming the canned ingredients on the stove while I cube the cheese.

Modie Phillips, Lubbock, Texas

   1 can (15-1/4 ounces) whole kernel corn, drained

- 1 can (15 ounces) pinto beans, rinsed and drained
- 1 can (14-1/2 ounces) chicken broth
- 1 can (10 ounces) diced tomatoes and green chilies, undrained
- 1 can (10 ounces) premium chunk white chicken, drained
- 1 can (4-1/2 ounces) chopped green chilies
- 1 pound process cheese (Velveeta), cubed

Crushed tortilla chips, optional

In a 3-qt. saucepan, combine the first seven ingredients. Cook and stir until cheese is melted. Garnish with tortilla chips if desired. **Yield:** 6-8 servings (2 quarts).

Chicken Tarragon Soup

When the weather starts turning cooler, we like to sit down to dinner with this colorful rich soup. Add hot rolls and a salad, and you have a hearty meal.

Mary Wagner, Woodburn, Oregon

- 2 quarts chicken broth
- 2 cups cubed cooked chicken
- 1 jar (4 ounces) diced pimientos, undrained
- 1/4 cup chopped green onions
- 1 teaspoon dried tarragon
- 1/2 teaspoon salt
- 1/2 teaspoon pepper
- 2 chicken bouillon cubes
- 1/2 cup butter
- 1 cup all-purpose flour

In a soup kettle or Dutch oven, combine the first eight ingredients; bring to a gentle boil. In a small saucepan, melt butter. Stir in flour; cook and stir for 2 minutes.

Gradually add to boiling soup, stirring constantly until smooth. Return to a boil. Reduce heat; simmer, uncovered, for 15 minutes. **Yield:** 8-10 servings (2-1/2 quarts).

Cream of Wild Rice Soup

pictured below

Tender cubes of chicken, fresh vegetables and wild rice make this soup hearty enough for a meal. You can't beat the down-home comfort of a warm bowlful. I like to serve it with whole wheat rolls.

J. Beatrice Hintz, Neenah, Wisconsin

- 1 large onion, chopped
- 1 large carrot, shredded
- 1 celery rib, chopped
- 1/4 cup butter
- 1/2 cup all-purpose flour
- 8 cups chicken broth
- 3 cups cooked wild rice
- 1 cup cubed cooked chicken
- 1/4 teaspoon salt
- 1/4 teaspoon pepper
- 1 cup evaporated milk
- 1/4 cup snipped chives

In a large saucepan, saute the onion, carrot and celery in butter until tender. Stir in flour until blended. Gradually add broth. Stir in the rice, chicken, salt and pepper.

Bring to a boil over medium heat; cook and stir for 2 minutes or until thickened. Stir in milk; cook 3-5 minutes longer. Garnish with chives. **Yield:** 10 servings (2-1/2 quarts).

23

Souper Sources of Veggies

Nourishing soups are important for nutrition and good health. In fact, soups can provide a variety of vegetables and all of their nutrients in one meal.

And it's easy to bump up your consumption of vegetables...from making leftover soups using Thanksgiving turkey and veggies to cooking up hearty bowls of chili.

Fresh, frozen or canned vegetables provide many ingredients for a wonderful soup.

Sausage Soup

When I substituted turkey sausage for the pork sausage in my mother-in-law's recipe, we loved the result.

Sonya Atkins, Farmington, Missouri

> 1 pound bulk turkey breakfast sausage
> 1 cup chopped onion
> 3 cups water
> 2 chicken bouillon cubes
> 4 cups cubed peeled potatoes
> 1/2 teaspoon salt
> 1/4 teaspoon pepper
> 1/4 teaspoon dried sage
> 1 can (15-1/4 ounces) whole kernel corn, drained
> 1 can (15 ounces) cream-style corn
> 1-1/2 cups half-and-half cream *or* evaporated milk
> Chopped sweet red pepper

In a soup kettle or Dutch oven over medium heat, cook sausage and onion until sausage is no longer pink and onion is tender; drain. Add water and bouillon; bring to a boil. Add potatoes, salt, pepper and sage; return to a boil.

Reduce heat; cover and simmer for 25-30 minutes or until potatoes are tender. Stir in corn and cream; heat through. Garnish with red pepper. **Yield:** 10 servings (2-1/2 quarts).

Veggie Rice Soup

pictured below

My daughter relies on a boxed rice mix to get a head start on this rich and colorful soup. She likes to serve it to friends after football games in autumn, but it's a favorite with our family any time of year.

Janet Sawyer, Dysart, Iowa

> 1 package (6 ounces) chicken and wild rice mix
> 5 cups water
> 1 package (10 ounces) frozen chopped broccoli, thawed
> 1 medium carrot, shredded
> 2 teaspoons dried minced onion
> 1 can (10-3/4 ounces) condensed cream of chicken soup, undiluted
> 1 package (8 ounces) cream cheese, cubed
> 1/4 cup slivered almonds, optional

In a large saucepan, combine rice, contents of seasoning packet and water; bring to a boil. Reduce heat; cover and simmer for 10 minutes, stirring once.

Stir in the broccoli, carrot and onion. Cover and simmer for 5 minutes. Stir in soup and cream cheese. Cook and stir until cheese is melted. Stir in almonds if desired. **Yield:** 8 servings (about 2 quarts).

Matzo Ball Soup

My mother is of Russian descent and would make this for Friday night dinner while I was growing up. It's a very comforting soup that brings back many happy memories.

Bernice Polak, New Smyrna Beach, Florida

    1 broiler/fryer chicken (3-1/2 to 4
       pounds), cut up
    2 quarts water
    6 carrots, cut in half lengthwise, then
       into 2-inch pieces
    1 large onion, peeled
    2 celery ribs, cut in half
    2 sprigs fresh dill (3 inches)
MATZO BALLS:
    2 eggs
    1 cup matzo meal
    2 tablespoons chicken fat *or* shortening
    2 tablespoons minced fresh parsley
    2 teaspoons salt
Dash pepper
  1/2 to 1 cup cold water
    1 can (49 ounces) chicken broth
    2 teaspoons salt
  1/2 teaspoon pepper
    2 cups cooked noodles

Place chicken and water in an 8-qt. soup kettle. Cover and bring to a boil; skim fat. Add carrots, onion and celery. Fold dill in half and wrap many times with thread or dental floss; add to soup. Bring to a boil. Reduce heat to medium-low; cover but keep lid ajar and simmer for 2-1/2 hours.

Meanwhile, combine first six matzo ball ingredients in a medium bowl. Add enough water to make a thick pancake-like batter. Refrigerate for 2 hours (mixture thickens as it stands). Remove and discard onion, celery and dill from broth. Remove chicken and allow to cool; debone and cut into chunks. Skim fat from broth. Return chicken to kettle. Add canned broth, salt and pepper; bring to a boil. Reduce heat; cover and simmer.

To complete matzo balls, bring 4 qts. water to a boil in a 5-qt. Dutch oven. With very wet hands, form heaping teaspoonfuls of batter into balls. If mixture is too thin, stir in 1-2 tablespoons of matzo meal. Drop balls into boiling water. (They will sink when dropped but will rise in a few minutes.) Cook for 10 minutes. Remove with slotted spoon and add to simmering soup. Add noodles; heat through. **Yield:** 18 servings (4-1/2 quarts).

Turkey Barley Tomato Soup
pictured above

This low-calorie soup is so quick to prepare and tastes so good. It's a real stomach filler and warms us up on cold winter days.

Denise Kilgore, Lino Lakes, Minnesota

    1 pound lean ground turkey
  3/4 cup sliced *or* baby carrots
    1 medium onion, chopped
    1 celery rib, chopped
    1 garlic clove, minced
    1 envelope taco seasoning, *divided*
3-1/2 cups water
    1 can (28 ounces) Italian diced
       tomatoes, undrained
  3/4 cup quick-cooking barley
  1/2 teaspoon minced fresh oregano
       or 1/8 teaspoon dried oregano

In a Dutch oven, cook the turkey, carrots, onion, celery, garlic and 1 tablespoon taco seasoning over medium heat until meat is no longer pink. Stir in the water, tomatoes and remaining taco seasoning; bring to a boil.

Reduce heat; cover and simmer for 20 minutes. Add barley; cover and simmer for 15-20 minutes longer or until barley is tender. Stir in oregano. **Yield:** 6 servings.

Turkey Noodle Soup
pictured below

Homemade taste makes this chunky soup a favorite. We enjoy it with hot bread in winter and salad in summer.

Elaine Bickford, Las Vegas, Nevada

>   2 cans (14-1/2 ounces *each*) chicken broth
>   3 cups water
> 1-3/4 cups sliced carrots
>   1/2 cup chopped onion
>   2 celery ribs, sliced
>   1 package (12 ounces) frozen egg noodles
>   3 cups chopped cooked turkey
>   1 package (10 ounces) frozen peas
>   2 envelopes chicken gravy mix
>   1/2 cup cold water

In a large saucepan, bring the broth, water, carrots, onion and celery to a boil. Reduce heat; cover and simmer for 4-6 minutes or until vegetables are crisp-tender. Add the noodles. Simmer, uncovered, for 20 minutes or until noodles are tender.

Stir in turkey and peas. Combine gravy mixes and cold water until smooth; stir into the soup. Bring to a boil; cook and stir for 2 minutes or until thickened. **Yield:** 7 servings.

Chunky Chicken Soup
pictured above

Here's a satisfying soup that you'll find yourself serving year-round. Every spoonful is loaded with the fantastic flavor of chicken, celery, carrots and peas.

Kathy Both, Rocky Mountain House, Alberta

>   3 boneless skinless chicken thighs, cut into 1-inch pieces
>   1 cup sliced celery
>   1/2 cup chopped onion
>   2 tablespoons vegetable oil
>   6 cups chicken broth
> 1-1/2 cups sliced carrots
>   1 teaspoon dried thyme
>   1/2 teaspoon salt
>   1/4 teaspoon pepper
>   1/2 cup uncooked macaroni
> 1-1/2 cups frozen peas

In a 3-qt. saucepan, cook chicken, celery and onion in oil until chicken juices run clear. Add the broth, carrots, thyme, salt and pepper; bring to a boil.

Reduce heat; cover and simmer for 45 minutes or until the vegetables are tender. Stir in macaroni and peas. Cover and simmer for 15 minutes or until the macaroni is tender. **Yield:** 8 servings (2 quarts).

Chicken 'n' Veggie Soup

I need to eat low-fat, and my husband loves a good hearty soup, so this recipe fills the bill for both of us. My friends have raved over this soup, and all our grandchildren gobble up their vegetables this way.

Betty Kline, Panorama Village, Texas

3 quarts water
2 large carrots, sliced
1 cup chopped onion
3 celery ribs, sliced
2 cups broccoli florets
2 cups cauliflowerets
2 garlic cloves, minced
3 tablespoons chicken bouillon granules
3 tablespoons picante sauce
2-1/4 teaspoons minced fresh thyme *or* 3/4 teaspoon dried thyme
2-1/4 teaspoons minced fresh basil *or* 3/4 teaspoon dried basil
1 teaspoon minced fresh rosemary *or* 1/2 teaspoon dried rosemary, crushed
1/4 teaspoon cayenne pepper, optional
2 cups cubed cooked chicken breast
3-1/2 cups egg noodles, cooked and drained

In a large soup kettle, combine water, carrots, onion and celery. Bring to a boil. Reduce heat; cover and simmer for 20 minutes or until the vegetables are tender. Add the broccoli, cauliflower, garlic, bouillon, picante sauce and seasonings.

Cover and simmer for 20 minutes or until broccoli and cauliflower are tender. Add chicken and noodles. Cover and simmer for 5 minutes or until heated through. **Yield:** 12 servings (3 quarts).

Wild Rice Soup
pictured at right

Spending time in the kitchen has never been my hobby. When I got married and started a family, it became a necessity. This simple but satisfying soup makes me look like a fabulous cook!

Tracey Zeman, Zimmerman, Minnesota

3 cans (10-1/2 ounces *each*) condensed chicken broth
2 cups water

1/2 cup uncooked wild rice
1/2 cup sliced green onions
1/2 cup butter
3/4 cup all-purpose flour
3/4 teaspoon salt
1/2 teaspoon poultry seasoning
1/4 teaspoon pepper
2 cups half-and-half cream
2 cups cubed cooked chicken
1 jar (2 ounces) chopped pimientos, drained

In a large saucepan, combine the broth, water and rice; bring to a boil. Reduce heat; cover and simmer for 35-40 minutes or until the rice is tender.

In a medium saucepan, saute onions in butter over low heat. Stir in flour, salt, poultry seasoning and pepper. Cook, stirring constantly, until bubbly and thickened. Stir in cream; cook for 6 minutes or until mixture thickens slightly, stirring constantly.

Stir into the rice mixture. Add the chicken and pimientos; heat through. **Yield:** 6-8 servings (about 2 quarts).

fat. Reduce heat; cover and simmer 1-1/2 hours or until chicken is tender. Remove chicken; allow to cool. Add vegetables to broth; cook until tender. Debone chicken and cut into chunks; return to broth.

Meanwhile, for noodles, mix flour and salt in a medium bowl. Make a well in the center. Beat together the egg, water and oil; pour into well. Stir together, forming a dough. Turn dough onto a floured surface; knead 8-10 times. Roll into a 16-in. x 12-in. rectangle.

Combine filling ingredients; mix well. Sprinkle over dough to within 1/2 in. of edge; pat down. Moisten edges with water. Roll up jelly-roll style from long end; cut into 1/2-in. slices. Add noodles to gently boiling soup and cook for 6-8 minutes or until tender. **Yield:** 10 servings (2-1/2 quarts).

Chicken Soup with Stuffed Noodles
pictured above

Before retiring, I worked as a cook for 15 years. Now I spend lots of time in my kitchen preparing new, interesting food for the family. You'll love this rich, homey soup.

Jennifer Bucholtz, Kitchener, Ontario

        1 broiler/fryer chicken (3 to 3-1/2
          pounds), cut up
    2-1/2 quarts water
        2 teaspoons salt
      1/4 teaspoon pepper
        4 medium carrots, sliced
        2 celery ribs, sliced
        1 medium onion, diced
    NOODLES:
    1-1/4 cups all-purpose flour
        1 teaspoon salt
        1 egg
        5 tablespoons water
        1 teaspoon vegetable oil
    FILLING:
        2 eggs
    1-1/4 cups seasoned bread crumbs
        3 tablespoons butter, melted

Place chicken, water, salt and pepper in a large soup kettle. Cover and bring to a boil; skim

Chicken Gumbo

This makes a fresh-tasting, flavorful main dish that's sure to warm everyone right up. Gumbo is a thickened soup, and this recipe features a colorful mixture of traditional ingredients. Plus, it yields enough for a large group!

Willa Govoro, St. Clair, Missouri

        6 celery ribs, chopped
        3 medium green peppers, chopped
        3 medium onions, chopped
      3/4 cup butter
       10 quarts chicken broth
        7 cans (14-1/2 ounces *each*) diced
          tomatoes, undrained
        3 bay leaves
        2 tablespoons minced fresh parsley
        1 tablespoon pepper
        2 to 3 tablespoons garlic powder
        2 teaspoons salt
        2 cups uncooked long grain rice
       10 cups cubed cooked chicken
        6 cups cubed fully cooked ham
        1 package (16 ounces) frozen chopped
          okra
        2 pounds cooked small shrimp, peeled
          and deveined, optional

In a large soup kettle or kettles, saute celery, green peppers and onions in butter until tender. Add the next seven ingredients; bring to a boil. Stir in rice. Reduce heat; cover and simmer for 15-20 minutes or until rice is tender. Stir in chicken, ham, okra and shrimp. Simmer for 8-10 minutes or until shrimp turn pink and okra is tender. Discard bay leaves. **Yield:** 48 (1-cup) servings.

Turkey Soup With Slickers
pictured below

Our grandson calls this "bone soup" because I make it with Thanksgiving turkey bones! The recipe for slickers—half dumplings, half egg noodles—comes from my grandmother.

Christine Fleeman, Salem, Oregon

> 1 leftover turkey carcass (from a 14-pound turkey)
> 5 quarts water
> 1/2 cup chopped onion
> 1/2 cup chopped carrot
> 1/2 cup chopped celery
> 3 tablespoons dried parsley flakes
> 2 teaspoons salt
> 1/2 teaspoon pepper
> 2 bay leaves
> 1 egg
> 2-1/2 to 3 cups all-purpose flour
> 1/2 teaspoon dill weed
> 1/2 teaspoon poultry seasoning
> 1 cup frozen peas

Place the first nine ingredients in a Dutch oven or soup kettle. Bring to a boil; skim fat. Reduce heat; cover and simmer for 2 hours. Remove bay leaves. Remove carcass; allow to cool. Remove turkey from bones and cut into bite-size pieces; set aside.

Pour 1 cup of the broth into a bowl; add egg and beat. Stir in enough flour to form a stiff dough. Turn onto a floured surface; knead 8-10 times or until smooth. Divide dough in half; roll out each piece to 1/8-in. thickness. Cut into 2-in. x 1/4-in. strips. Add dill and poultry seasoning to remaining broth; bring to a gentle boil.

Drop slickers into broth; cover and cook for 30-35 minutes or until tender. Add peas and reserved turkey; heat through. **Yield:** 8-10 servings (2-1/2 quarts).

Rainy Day Soup

One rainy day a few years back, this comforting soup was served at a local arts and crafts bazaar. Now family members who are feeling under the weather request it.

Laine Fengarinas, Palm Harbor, Florida

> 1 pound ground turkey
> 1 can (46 ounces) V8 juice
> 1 jar (16 ounces) thick and chunky salsa
> 1 can (14-1/2 ounces) chicken broth
> 1 can (16 ounces) kidney beans, rinsed and drained
> 1 package (10 ounces) frozen mixed vegetables
> 4 cups shredded cabbage
> 1 cup chopped onion
> 1/2 cup cubed peeled potatoes
> 1/3 cup medium pearl barley

In a Dutch oven or soup kettle coated with nonstick cooking spray, cook turkey over medium heat until no longer pink; drain. Add all of the remaining ingredients; bring to a boil.

Reduce the heat; cover and simmer for 60-70 minutes or until the vegetables and barley are tender. **Yield:** 12 servings (3 quarts).

Bean, Chicken and Sausage Soup

pictured below

I found this recipe in a magazine and have tried different ingredients through the years. My husband thinks this is the best version yet. I hope you enjoy it, too!

Linda Johnson, Sevierville, Tennessee

- 1-1/2 pounds bulk Italian sausage
- 2 cups chopped onion
- 6 bacon strips, diced
- 2 quarts water
- 2 cans (14-1/2 ounces *each*) diced tomatoes, undrained
- 2 bay leaves
- 2 teaspoons garlic powder
- 1 teaspoon *each* dried thyme, savory and salt
- 1/2 teaspoon *each* dried basil, oregano and pepper
- 4 cups cubed cooked chicken
- 2 cans (15-1/2 ounces *each*) great northern beans, rinsed and drained

In a heavy 8-qt. Dutch oven or soup kettle, cook sausage, onion and bacon over medium heat until sausage is no longer pink; drain. Add water, tomatoes and seasonings. Cover and simmer for 30 minutes.

Add the chicken and beans. Simmer, uncovered, for 30-45 minutes. Remove bay leaves before serving. **Yield:** 18 servings (4-1/2 quarts).

"The night before I prepare a big kettle of soup, I chop and measure all the vegetables and refrigerate them in resealable plastic bags or in covered bowls. Next day, assembling the soup is a breeze!"

—Rose Boudreaux Bourg, Louisiana

Granny's Spicy Soup

My mother makes the best soups around and has become known to others as "The Soup Lady." When my kids ask me to make Granny's soup, I'm happy to oblige.

Rose Rose, Akron, Ohio

- 1 broiler/fryer chicken (3-1/2 to 4 pounds), cut up
- 2 quarts water
- 4 to 5 celery ribs with leaves, diced
- 2 medium carrots, diced
- 1 large onion, diced
- 1 to 1-1/2 teaspoons pickling spices
- 1-1/2 teaspoons salt
- 4 chicken bouillon cubes
- 1/4 teaspoon pepper
- 1 cup uncooked noodles

Place chicken and water in a large soup kettle. Cover and bring to a boil; skim fat. Reduce heat; cover and simmer for 2 hours or until chicken falls off bone. Strain broth; return to kettle. Allow chicken to cool; debone and cut into chunks. Skim fat from broth. Return chicken to broth along with celery, carrots and onion.

Place pickling spices in a tea ball or cheesecloth bag; add to soup. Bring to a boil. Reduce heat; cover and simmer for 1 hour. Remove spices; add salt, bouillon, pepper and noodles. Cook for 10-15 minutes or until noodles are tender. **Yield:** 12 servings (about 3 quarts).

Editor's Note: The soup gets its name from the pickling spices, not from being hot.

Chicken Soup for Two
pictured above

I love eating a big bowl of this colorful fresh-tasting soup on a winter's day. What a great way to warm up!

Ruth Wimmer, Bland, Virginia

> 2 cups chicken broth
> 1 cup fresh *or* frozen corn
> 1 small celery rib, chopped
> 1 small carrot, chopped
> 1 small onion, chopped
> 1 cup cubed cooked chicken
> 1/2 cup canned diced tomatoes
Salt and pepper to taste

In a saucepan, combine the first five ingredients. Bring to a boil. Reduce heat; cover and simmer for 25-30 minutes or until vegetables are tender. Stir in the chicken, tomatoes, salt and pepper; heat through. **Yield:** 2 servings.

Hearty Chicken Noodle Soup
pictured at right

I'm grateful that my mother taught me to make these wonderful old-fashioned noodles, which were a big favorite of mine when I was growing up. They give the soup delightful flavor.

Cindy Renfrow, Sussex, New Jersey

> 1 stewing chicken (about 6 pounds), cut up
> 2 quarts water
> 1 large onion, quartered
> 1 cup chopped fresh parsley
> 1 celery rib, sliced
> 5 chicken bouillon cubes
> 5 whole peppercorns
> 4 whole cloves
> 1 bay leaf
> 2 teaspoons salt
> 1/2 teaspoon pepper
Dash dried thyme
> 2 medium carrots, thinly sliced
NOODLES:
> 1-1/4 cups all-purpose flour
> 1/2 teaspoon salt
> 1 egg
> 2 tablespoons milk

In a large kettle, combine first 12 ingredients; bring to a boil. Reduce heat; cover and simmer for 2-1/2 hours or until chicken is tender. Remove chicken from broth; cool. Debone chicken; cut into chunks. Strain broth and skim fat; return to kettle. Add chicken and carrots.

For noodles, mix flour and salt in a medium bowl. Make a well in center. Beat egg and milk; pour into well. Stir together, forming a dough. Turn dough onto a floured surface; knead 8-10 times. Roll into a 12-in. x 9-in. rectangle. Cut into 1/2-in. strips; cut strips into 1-in. pieces.

Bring soup to a simmer; add noodles. Cover and cook for 12-15 minutes or until noodles are tender. **Yield:** 10-12 servings.

Tex-Mex Chicken Soup

pictured below

We keep busy here on our ranch. So I'm always looking for dishes that can be prepared in a hurry but are still filling and tasty. This quick and easy soup is a real winner.

MayDell Spiess, Industry, Texas

1/2 cup chopped onion
2 garlic cloves, minced
1 tablespoon vegetable oil
4 cups chicken broth
3 cups cubed cooked chicken
3 medium zucchini, sliced
1 can (14-1/2 ounces) diced tomatoes, undrained
1 can (11 ounces) whole kernel corn, drained
1 can (8 ounces) tomato sauce
1/2 cup salsa
2 teaspoons ground cumin
1 teaspoon salt
3/4 teaspoon pepper
1/2 teaspoon dried oregano
Shredded cheddar cheese, optional
Tortilla chips, optional

In a 4-qt. soup kettle, saute onion and garlic in oil until tender. Add the next 11 ingredients; bring to a boil. Reduce heat; cover and simmer for 30 minutes. If desired, top individual servings with cheese and serve with tortilla chips. **Yield:** 12 servings (3 quarts).

Grandma's Chicken 'n' Dumpling Soup

pictured below left

I've enjoyed making this rich soup for over 30 years. Every time I serve it, I remember my grandma, who was very special to me and was known as a great cook.

Paulette Balda, Prophetstown, Illinois

      1 broiler/fryer chicken (3-1/2 to 4 pounds), cut up
2-1/4 quarts cold water
      5 chicken bouillon cubes
      6 whole peppercorns
      3 whole cloves
      1 can (10-3/4 ounces) condensed cream of chicken soup, undiluted
      1 can (10-3/4 ounces) condensed cream of mushroom soup, undiluted
1-1/2 cups chopped carrots
      1 cup fresh *or* frozen peas
      1 cup chopped celery
      1 cup chopped peeled potatoes
   1/4 cup chopped onion
1-1/2 teaspoons seasoned salt
   1/4 teaspoon pepper
      1 bay leaf
DUMPLINGS:
      2 cups all-purpose flour
      4 teaspoons baking powder
      1 teaspoon salt
   1/4 teaspoon pepper
      1 egg, beaten
      2 tablespoons butter, melted
   3/4 to 1 cup milk
Snipped fresh parsley, optional

Place chicken, water, bouillon, peppercorns and cloves in an 8-qt. Dutch oven or soup kettle. Cover and bring to a boil; skim fat. Reduce heat; cover and simmer 1-1/2 hours or until chicken is tender. Strain broth; return to kettle.

Allow chicken to cool; debone and cut into chunks. Skim fat from broth. Return chicken to kettle with soups, vegetables and seasonings; bring to a boil. Reduce heat; cover and simmer for 1 hour. Uncover; increase heat to a gentle boil. Remove bay leaf.

For dumplings, combine dry ingredients in a medium bowl. Stir in egg, butter and enough milk to make a moist stiff batter. Drop by teaspoonfuls into soup. Cover and cook without lifting the lid for 18-20 minutes. Sprinkle with parsley if desired. **Yield:** 12 servings (3 quarts).

Soup Making Tips

Since everyone likes different levels of salt in soup, add only a portion of the salt called for in a recipe at the beginning of the cooking process. When the soup is nearly ready to be served, taste it and adjust the salt or allow others to salt their own soup bowls.

Also, if family members are watching their fat intake, you may want to skim the fat from broths before adding ingredients to complete the soup. For example, refer to that step in Grandma's Chicken 'n' Dumpling Soup (recipe above left).

Spicy Chicken Rice Soup

This zippy chicken and rice soup is brimming with flavor and color. For a change of pace, I garnish steaming bowls of it with crispy fried tortilla strips and some shredded pepper Jack cheese.

Elaine Grover, Santa Maria, California

      4 cups chicken broth
      2 cups cubed cooked chicken
      2 celery ribs, chopped
      2 medium carrots, chopped
      1 medium green pepper, chopped
      1 medium onion, chopped
   1/3 cup uncooked long grain rice
   1/4 cup minced fresh cilantro
   1/2 teaspoon dried oregano
   1/2 teaspoon salt
   1/2 teaspoon pepper
   1/4 teaspoon ground cumin
   1/8 to 1/4 teaspoon crushed red pepper flakes

In a large saucepan, combine all ingredients. Bring to a boil. Reduce heat; cover and simmer for 20-25 minutes or until rice and vegetables are tender. **Yield:** 6 servings.

Chicken Soup With Spaetzle

Bay leaves boost the flavor in this wonderful soup recipe. My family loves the homemade spaetzle, which is pretty simple to make. I enjoy making this recipe often.

Elaine Lange, Grand Rapids, Michigan

  1 broiler/fryer chicken (2 to 3 pounds), cut into pieces
  2 tablespoons vegetable oil
  2 quarts chicken broth
  2 bay leaves
  1/2 teaspoon dried thyme
  1/4 teaspoon pepper
  1 cup sliced carrots
  1 cup sliced celery
  3/4 cup chopped onion
  1 garlic clove, minced
  1/3 cup medium pearl barley
  2 cups sliced fresh mushrooms
SPAETZLE:
1-1/4 cups all-purpose flour
  1/8 teaspoon baking powder
  1/8 teaspoon salt
  1 egg, lightly beaten
  1/4 cup water
  1/4 cup milk

In a large kettle or Dutch oven, brown chicken pieces in oil. Add the broth, bay leaves, thyme and pepper. Simmer until chicken is tender. Cool broth and skim off fat. Skin and bone chicken and cut into bite-size pieces; return to broth along with carrots, celery, onion, garlic and barley. Bring to a boil. Reduce heat; cover and simmer for 35 minutes. Add mushrooms and simmer 8-10 minutes longer. Remove bay leaves.

Combine first three spaetzle ingredients in a small bowl. Stir in egg, water and milk; blend well. Drop batter by 1/2 teaspoonfuls into simmering soup. Cook for 10 minutes. **Yield:** 8-10 servings (2-1/2 quarts).

Turkey Wild Rice Soup
pictured below

An area turkey grower shared this recipe with me. A rich and smooth soup, it makes great use of two Minnesota resources—turkey and wild rice. Be prepared to serve seconds!

Terri Holmgren, Swanville, Minnesota

  1 medium onion, chopped
  2 celery ribs, diced
  2 carrots, diced
  1/2 cup butter
  1/2 cup all-purpose flour
  4 cups chicken *or* turkey broth
  2 cups cooked wild rice
  2 cups half-and-half cream
  2 cups diced cooked turkey
  1 teaspoon dried parsley flakes

1/2 teaspoon salt
1/4 teaspoon pepper

In a large kettle or Dutch oven, saute onion, celery and carrots in butter until onion is transparent. Reduce heat. Blend in flour and cook until bubbly. Gradually add chicken broth, stirring constantly. Bring to a boil; boil for 1 minute.

Reduce heat; add wild rice, cream, turkey, parsley, salt and pepper; simmer for 20 minutes. **Yield:** 10-12 servings (about 3 quarts).

Mom's Tomato Vegetable Soup

I developed this vegetable-based soup from a recipe my mom made when I was a child. Its robust down-home taste brings back wonderful memories of growing up on the farm.

Sandra Davis, Brownsville, Tennessee

1 broiler/fryer chicken (3 to 3-1/2 pounds), cut up
8 cups water
1 celery rib, halved
1 medium onion, halved
3 medium potatoes, peeled and cut into 1/2-inch cubes
2 cups tomato juice
1 can (16 ounces) mixed vegetables, drained
1 can (15-1/2 ounces) black-eyed peas, rinsed and drained
1 can (14-1/2 ounces) stewed tomatoes
1/2 cup chopped onion
2-1/2 teaspoons salt
1 teaspoon pepper
1/2 pound ground beef
1 can (15 ounces) cream-style corn

In an 8-qt. soup kettle, place chicken, water, celery and onion. Cover and bring to a boil; skim fat. Reduce heat; cover and simmer for 1-1/2 hours or until chicken falls off the bones. Strain broth and skim fat; return broth to kettle. Add the next eight ingredients. Debone the chicken and cut into chunks; return to kettle. Bring to a boil.

Meanwhile, in a medium skillet, cook beef over medium heat until no longer pink; drain and add to soup. Reduce heat; cover and simmer for 1 hour. Stir in corn; cook, uncovered, for 30 minutes, stirring occasionally. **Yield:** 18 servings (4-1/2 quarts).

Peasant Soup for One
pictured above

In mere minutes this hearty soup simmers on the stovetop to perfection, yet it tastes like it cooked for hours.

Kay Harris, Amarillo, Texas

1 boneless skinless chicken breast half (4 ounces), cubed
1/4 cup chopped onion
1 small potato, cubed
1 small carrot, sliced
1 cup chicken broth
1 garlic clove, minced
1/4 teaspoon dried tarragon, crushed
1/8 teaspoon salt
Dash pepper
2 teaspoons chopped fresh parsley

Coat a saucepan with nonstick cooking spray; brown chicken over medium-high heat. Add the next eight ingredients; bring to a boil.

Reduce heat. Cover and simmer for 20-25 minutes or until vegetables are tender. Sprinkle with parsley. **Yield:** 1 serving.

Chicken Wild Rice Soup

pictured above

I'm originally from Minnesota, where wild rice grows in abundance and is very popular in recipes. This soup has been part of our Christmas Eve menu for years. To save time, I cook the chicken and wild rice and cut up the vegetables the day before.

Virginia Montmarquet, Riverside, California

2 quarts chicken broth
1/2 pound fresh mushrooms, chopped

1 cup finely chopped celery
1 cup shredded carrots
1/2 cup finely chopped onion
1 teaspoon chicken bouillon granules
1 teaspoon dried parsley flakes
1/4 teaspoon garlic powder
1/4 teaspoon dried thyme
1/4 cup butter
1/4 cup all-purpose flour
1 can (10-3/4 ounces) condensed cream of mushroom soup, undiluted
1/2 cup dry white wine *or* additional chicken broth
3 cups cooked wild rice
2 cups cubed cooked chicken

In a large saucepan, combine the first nine ingredients. Bring to a boil. Reduce heat; cover and simmer for 30 minutes.

In a soup kettle or Dutch oven, melt butter. Stir in flour until smooth. Gradually whisk in broth mixture. Bring to a boil; cook and stir for 2 minutes or until thickened.

Whisk in soup and wine or broth. Add the rice and chicken; heat through. **Yield:** 14 servings (3-1/2 quarts).

Quick Chicken Dumpling Soup

Although we were on a tight budget when I was a youngster, we always had good food. This comforting soup with soft dumplings was one of Mom's mainstays.

Brenda Risser, Willard, Ohio

    2 cans (10-3/4 ounces *each*) condensed
       cream of chicken soup, undiluted
3-1/3 cups milk, *divided*
1-2/3 cups biscuit/baking mix

In a 3-qt. saucepan, combine soup and 2-2/3 cups of milk. Bring to a boil over medium heat; reduce heat.

In a bowl, combine biscuit mix with remaining milk just until blended. Drop by rounded tablespoons onto simmering soup. Cook, uncovered, for 10 minutes.

Cover and simmer 10-12 minutes longer or until dumplings test done (do not lift lid while simmering). Serve immediately. **Yield:** 4 servings.

Harvest Turkey Soup
pictured at right

The recipe for this super soup evolved over the years. I've been diabetic since I was 12, so I've learned to use herbs and spices to make dishes like this taste terrific. It also has a colorful blend of vegetables.

Linda Sand, Winsted, Connecticut

    1 turkey carcass (from a 12-pound
      turkey)
    5 quarts water
    2 large carrots, shredded
    1 cup chopped celery
    1 large onion, chopped
    4 chicken bouillon cubes
    1 can (28 ounces) stewed tomatoes
3/4 cup fresh or frozen peas
3/4 cup long grain rice
    1 package (10 ounces) frozen chopped
      spinach
    1 tablespoon salt
3/4 teaspoon pepper
1/2 teaspoon dried marjoram
1/2 teaspoon dried thyme

Place the turkey carcass and water in a Dutch oven or soup kettle; bring to a boil. Reduce heat; cover and simmer for 1-1/2 hours. Remove carcass; allow to cool. Remove turkey from bones and cut into bite-size pieces; set aside. Strain broth. Add carrots, celery, onion and bouillon; bring to a boil. Reduce heat; cover and simmer for 30 minutes.

Add the tomatoes, peas, rice, spinach, salt, pepper, marjoram, thyme and reserved turkey. Return to a boil; cook, uncovered, for 20 minutes or until rice is tender. **Yield:** 22 servings (5-1/2 quarts).

Meatball Alphabet Soup

pictured below

Bite-size meatballs made from ground turkey perk up this fun alphabet soup. A variety of vegetables accents the rich tomato broth that is nicely seasoned with herbs. Our Test Kitchen staff came up with the recipe.

> 1 egg, lightly beaten
> 2 tablespoons quick-cooking oats
> 2 tablespoons grated Parmesan cheese
> 1/4 teaspoon garlic powder
> 1/4 teaspoon Italian seasoning
> 1/2 pound lean ground turkey
> 1 cup chopped onion
> 1 cup chopped celery
> 1 cup chopped carrots
> 1 cup diced peeled potatoes
> 1 tablespoon olive oil
> 2 garlic cloves, minced
> 4 cans (14-1/2 ounces *each*) chicken broth
> 1 can (28 ounces) diced tomatoes, undrained
> 1 can (6 ounces) tomato paste
> 1/4 cup minced fresh parsley
> 1 teaspoon dried basil
> 1 teaspoon dried thyme
> 3/4 cup uncooked alphabet pasta

In a bowl, combine the first five ingredients. Crumble turkey over mixture and mix well. Shape into 1/2-in. balls. In a nonstick skillet, brown meatballs in small batches over medium heat until no longer pink. Remove from the heat; set aside.

In a large saucepan or Dutch oven, saute the onion, celery, carrots and potatoes in oil for 5 minutes or until crisp-tender. Add garlic; saute 1 minute longer. Add the broth, tomatoes, tomato paste, parsley, basil and thyme; bring to a boil. Add pasta; cook for 5-6 minutes.

Reduce heat; add meatballs. Simmer, uncovered, for 15-20 minutes or until vegetables are tender. **Yield:** 9 servings.

Cheesy Tortilla Soup

My daughter came up with this dish when trying to duplicate a soup she sampled at a restaurant.

LaVonda Owen, Marlow, Oklahoma

> 1 envelope chicken fajita marinade mix
> 4 boneless skinless chicken breast halves, diced
> 2 tablespoons vegetable oil
> 1/2 cup chopped onion
> 1/4 cup butter
> 1/3 cup all-purpose flour
> 2 cans (14-1/2 ounces *each*) chicken broth
> 1/3 cup canned diced tomatoes with chilies
> 1 cup cubed process cheese (Velveeta)
> 1-1/2 cups (6 ounces) shredded Monterey Jack cheese, *divided*
> 1-1/2 cups half-and-half cream
> Guacamole
> 1/2 cup shredded cheddar cheese
> Tortilla chips

Prepare fajita mix according to package directions; add chicken and marinate as directed. In a medium skillet, cook chicken in oil until juices run clear; set aside.

In a 3-qt. saucepan, cook onion in butter until tender. Stir in flour and cook for 1 minute. Stir in broth; cook and stir until thickened and bubbly. Add tomatoes, process cheese and 1 cup Monterey Jack; cook and stir until cheese melts. Stir in cream and chicken; heat through but do not boil.

Spoon into bowls. Garnish with guacamole, cheddar cheese, remaining Monterey Jack and tortilla chips. **Yield:** 8 servings (2 quarts).

Chicken Vegetable Soup

pictured above

Recipes have to pass three tests for me to use them: they must taste good, be nutritious and come together easily. This soup scores high on all three counts!

Connie Thomas, Jensen, Utah

    1 can (28 ounces) diced tomatoes, undrained
    2 cups chicken broth
    2 cups cubed cooked chicken breast
    1 cup frozen corn
    2 celery ribs with leaves, chopped
    1 can (6 ounces) tomato paste
1/4 cup dried lentils, rinsed
    1 tablespoon sugar
    1 tablespoon Worcestershire sauce
    2 teaspoons dried parsley flakes
    1 teaspoon dried marjoram

In a slow cooker, combine the tomatoes, broth, chicken, corn, celery, tomato paste, lentils, sugar, Worcestershire sauce, parsley and marjoram.

Cover and cook on low for 6-8 hours or until the celery and lentils are tender. **Yield:** 8 servings (2 quarts).

Broccoli Wild Rice Soup

pictured below

I love soup and serve it often. This is my favorite recipe, which I received from my sister. It tastes delicious, is made quickly and freezes well.

Martha Pollack, Mainville, Ohio

    5 cups water
    1 package (6 ounces) long grain and wild rice mix
    1 can (10-3/4 ounces) cream of chicken soup, undiluted
1-1/2 cups milk
    1 package (8 ounces) cream cheese, cubed
1/4 teaspoon salt
    1 package (10 ounces) frozen chopped broccoli, thawed
    1 large carrot, shredded
1/4 cup sliced almonds, toasted

In a large saucepan, combine the water and rice mix with contents of seasoning packet; bring to a boil. Reduce heat; cover and simmer for 20 minutes.

Add the soup, milk, cream cheese and salt; stir until cheese is melted. Add broccoli and carrot; cook over medium-low heat for 5-6 minutes or until vegetables and rice are tender. Garnish with almonds. **Yield:** 6 servings.

Editor's Note: This recipe was tested with Uncle Ben's Original Long Grain and Wild Rice Mix.

Mexican Chicken Soup

pictured below

This zesty dish is loaded with chicken, corn and black beans in a mildly spicy red broth. As a busy mom of three young children, I'm always looking for dinner recipes that can be prepared in the morning. The kids love the taco-like taste of this easy soup.

Marlene Kane, Lainesburg, Michigan

1-1/2	pounds boneless skinless chicken breasts, cubed
2	teaspoons canola oil
1/2	cup water
1	envelope taco seasoning
1	can (32 ounces) V8 juice
1	jar (16 ounces) salsa
1	can (15 ounces) black beans, rinsed and drained
1	package (10 ounces) frozen corn, thawed
6	tablespoons cheddar cheese
6	tablespoons sour cream
2	tablespoons chopped fresh cilantro

In a large nonstick skillet, saute chicken in oil until no longer pink. Add water and taco seasoning; simmer until chicken is well coated. Transfer to a slow cooker.

Add V8 juice, salsa, beans and corn; mix well. Cover and cook on low for 3-4 hours or until heated through. Serve with cheddar cheese, sour cream and cilantro. **Yield:** 6 servings.

Chicken and Dumpling Soup

Our five kids are grown and live away from the farm, but they visit often with their families. So I stay in practice in the kitchen! I frequently serve this soup for Sunday dinner.

Joey Ann Mostowy, Bruin, Pennsylvania

6	pieces bone-in chicken
1-1/2	quarts water
2	celery ribs, cut into chunks
1	medium onion, cut into chunks
1/2	cup diced green pepper
1	garlic clove, minced
1	tablespoon minced fresh dill
1	teaspoon salt
1/2	teaspoon pepper
1	can (10-3/4 ounces) condensed cream of potato soup, undiluted
1	can (10-3/4 ounces) condensed cream of chicken soup, undiluted
1	package (10 ounces) frozen mixed vegetables, thawed
1	tube (7-1/2 ounces) refrigerated buttermilk biscuits

In a soup kettle or Dutch oven, combine the first nine ingredients; bring to a boil. Reduce heat; cover and simmer for 50-60 minutes or until chicken is tender. Remove chicken; allow to cool. Debone and cut into chunks; set aside. Strain broth and set aside.

In a large saucepan, combine soups. Gradually add broth, stirring constantly. Add mixed vegetables and chicken; cook over medium heat for 20-30 minutes or until vegetables are tender.

On a floured board, pat biscuits to 1/4-in. thickness; cut into 1/4-in. strips. Bring soup to boil; drop in strips. Cover and cook for 15-18 minutes. **Yield:** 8-10 servings (2-1/2 quarts).

Cream of Broccoli Soup

Frozen vegetables make this a quick soup to stir up. Turkey ham lends a hearty flavor with less fat.

Eileen Claeys, Long Grove, Iowa

- 1 package (10 ounces) frozen chopped broccoli
- 3/4 cup finely chopped cooked turkey ham
- 1/2 cup water
- 1/4 cup frozen cut green beans
- 1 tablespoon chopped onion
- 2 tablespoons all-purpose flour
- 1 cup milk
- 1/3 cup cubed process cheese (Velveeta)

In a large saucepan, combine the first five ingredients; cover and cook over medium heat until vegetables are tender, about 5 minutes (do not drain).

Combine flour and milk until smooth; gradually add to the vegetable mixture. Bring to a boil; boil for 1-2 minutes, stirring constantly. Remove from the heat. Stir in cheese; cover and let stand until melted, about 5 minutes. Stir before serving. **Yield:** 3 servings.

> 66 The secret ingredient in my broccoli soup recipe is the instant mashed potato flakes I like to add with the milk and butter in order to thicken it. 99
>
> —*Jane Lee Boyd Cameron, West Virginia*

Curly Noodle Soup
pictured above right

Diners will ladle out praises all around the table when you serve this flavorful soup. My husband and three sons can't get enough of it. I created this recipe for a dinner I hosted for a group of friends. The main course was Italian, and I needed a good soup, so I converted a favorite tortilla soup recipe by substituting pasta and adding different seasonings.

Maxine Pierson, San Ramon, California

- 1 pound boneless skinless chicken breasts, cut into 1/2-inch pieces
- 1 large onion, chopped
- 4 celery ribs, sliced
- 2 medium carrots, sliced
- 4 garlic cloves, minced
- 2 tablespoons butter
- 2 tablespoons olive oil
- 1/4 cup all-purpose flour
- 1 teaspoon dried basil
- 1/2 teaspoon dried oregano
- 1/8 teaspoon pepper
- 3 cans (14-1/2 ounces *each*) chicken broth
- 1 can (14-1/2 ounces) diced tomatoes, undrained
- 6 ounces uncooked tricolor spiral pasta

In a large saucepan or Dutch oven, saute the chicken, onion, celery, carrots and garlic in butter and oil for 5 minutes. Stir in the flour, basil, oregano and pepper until blended. Gradually add broth and tomatoes. Bring to a boil.

Reduce heat; cover and simmer for 1 hour. Return to a boil; stir in the pasta. Reduce heat; simmer, uncovered, for 12-15 minutes or until the pasta is tender. **Yield:** 9 servings.

In a bowl, combine biscuit mix, cornmeal and 1/2 cup of cheese; stir in milk. Drop by heaping tablespoonfuls onto the simmering soup. Cover and cook for 12-15 minutes or until dumplings are firm.

Sprinkle with remaining cheese; cover and simmer 1 minute longer or until the cheese is melted. Serve immediately. **Yield:** 6-8 servings (2-1/2 quarts).

Vegetable Noodle Soup

This creamy soup is great on a cold winter day. I created it when I didn't have all the ingredients for broccoli soup. I like this combo even better.

Judie Peters, Camden, Indiana

> 3-1/2 cups milk
> 1 package (16 ounces) frozen California-blend vegetables
> 1/2 cup cubed process cheese (Velveeta)
> 1 envelope chicken noodle soup mix

In a large saucepan, bring milk to a boil. Stir in vegetables and return to a boil. Reduce heat; cover and simmer for 6 minutes.

Stir in cheese and soup mix. Return to a boil. Reduce heat. Simmer, uncovered, for 5-7 minutes or until the noodles are tender and the cheese is melted, stirring occasionally. **Yield:** 5-6 servings.

Southwestern Turkey Dumpling Soup

pictured above

Here's a Western twist on traditional turkey dumpling soup. I especially like this recipe because it's fast and easy.

Lisa Williams, Steamboat Springs, Colorado

> 1 can (15 ounces) tomato sauce
> 1 can (14-1/2 ounces) diced tomatoes, undrained
> 1-3/4 cups water
> 1 envelope chili seasoning
> 3 cups diced cooked turkey *or* chicken
> 1 can (16 ounces) kidney beans, rinsed and drained
> 1 can (15 ounces) black beans, rinsed and drained
> 1 can (15-1/4 ounces) whole kernel corn, drained
> 1-1/2 cups biscuit/baking mix
> 1/2 cup cornmeal
> 3/4 cup shredded cheddar cheese, *divided*
> 2/3 cup milk

In a Dutch oven, combine the first five ingredients; bring to a boil. Reduce heat; cover and simmer for 10 minutes, stirring occasionally. Add beans and corn.

> 66 My recipe for Turkey, Barley 'n' Veggie Soup also freezes well for up to 3 months. So you can enjoy it again later. 99
>
> —*Betty Kleberger Florissant, Missouri*

Turkey, Barley 'n' Veggie Soup

pictured below

This satisfying soup has an interesting blend of flavors...and it's good for you, too. It's a great way to use up leftover holiday turkey.

Betty Kleberger, Florissant, Missouri

      2 cans (one 40-1/2 ounces, one 14-1/2 ounces) chicken broth
      4 cups cubed cooked turkey
      2 medium carrots, halved and thinly sliced
      1 large potato, peeled and cubed
      2 cups frozen cut green beans
      1 medium green pepper, chopped
      1 celery rib, chopped
      3 garlic cloves, minced
  1/2 cup uncooked medium pearl barley
      2 bay leaves
      1 teaspoon dried thyme
      1 teaspoon rubbed sage
  1/2 teaspoon salt

In a Dutch oven or soup kettle, combine all of the ingredients. Bring to a boil. Reduce heat; simmer, uncovered, for 45-55 minutes or until barley and vegetables are tender. Discard bay leaves. **Yield:** 10 servings (3 quarts).

Comforting Chicken Noodle Soup

pictured above

A good friend made us this rich, comforting soup after the birth of our son. It was such a help to have dinner taken care of until I was back on my feet. This yummy dish is so simple to fix that now I give a pot of it (along with the recipe) to other new mothers.

Joanna Sargent, Sandy, Utah

      2 quarts water
      8 chicken bouillon cubes
  6-1/2 cups uncooked wide egg noodles
      2 cans (10-3/4 ounces *each*) condensed cream of chicken soup, undiluted
      3 cups cubed cooked chicken
      1 cup (8 ounces) sour cream
  Minced fresh parsley

In a large saucepan, bring water and bouillon to a boil. Add noodles; cook, uncovered, until tender, about 10 minutes. Do not drain.

Add soup and chicken; heat through. Remove from the heat; stir in sour cream. Sprinkle with the parsley. **Yield:** 10-12 servings (about 2-1/2 quarts).

" **Soup** puts the heart at **ease** and **eliminates** tension. "

bountiful
BEEF & GROUND BEEF

Beef Vegetable Soup

pictured above

This nicely seasoned soup tastes so good. It's convenient, too, since it simmers all day in the slow cooker.

Jean Hutzell, Dubuque, Iowa

        1 pound ground beef
        1 medium onion, chopped
    1/2 teaspoon salt
    1/4 teaspoon pepper
        3 cups water
        3 medium potatoes, peeled and cut
            into 3/4-inch cubes
        1 can (14-1/2 ounces) Italian diced
            tomatoes, undrained
        1 can (11-1/2 ounces) V8 juice
        1 cup chopped celery
        1 cup sliced carrots
        2 tablespoons sugar
        1 tablespoon dried parsley flakes
        2 teaspoons dried basil
        1 bay leaf

In a nonstick skillet, cook beef and onion over medium heat until meat is no longer pink; drain. Stir in salt and pepper.

Transfer to a 5-qt. slow cooker. Add the remaining ingredients. Cover and cook on low for 9-11 hours or until vegetables are tender. Discard bay leaf before serving. **Yield:** 7 servings.

Reuben Soup

When we're lucky (or have been good—I'm not certain which!), this soup is served in the staff cafeteria at school. The cooks have served it for years, and it remains a winner. I'm sure it will be a hit with your family.

Mary Lindell, Sanford, Michigan

    1/2 cup chopped onion
    1/2 cup sliced celery
        2 tablespoons butter
        1 cup chicken broth
        1 cup beef broth
    1/2 teaspoon baking soda
        2 tablespoons cornstarch
        2 tablespoons water
    3/4 cup sauerkraut, rinsed and drained
        2 cups half-and-half cream
        2 cups chopped cooked corned beef
        1 cup (4 ounces) shredded Swiss cheese
Salt and pepper to taste
Rye croutons, optional

In a large saucepan, saute onion and celery in butter until tender. Add broth and baking soda. Combine cornstarch and water; add to pan. Bring to a boil; boil for 2 minutes, stirring occasionally. Reduce heat.

Add sauerkraut, cream and corned beef; simmer and stir for 15 minutes. Add cheese; heat until melted. Add salt and pepper. Garnish with croutons if desired. **Yield:** about 6 servings (1-1/2 quarts).

Sweet-and-Sour Beef Cabbage Soup

This soup has been a favorite of mine from a local restaurant for years. The owner said many people have requested the recipe, so I'm happy to share it with you.

Mae Lavan, Chicago, Illinois

        2 quarts water
    3/4 cup diced cooked roast beef
        1 cup chopped onion
        1 cup chopped tomato
    1/2 cup shredded cabbage
    1/2 cup sliced celery
    1/3 cup chopped carrot

1 cup sugar
1/2 cup cider vinegar
1/4 cup burgundy, optional
2 tablespoons browning sauce
2 tablespoons Worcestershire sauce
2 teaspoons tomato sauce
6 beef bouillon cubes
1/2 teaspoon garlic powder
1/4 teaspoon dried thyme
Salt and pepper to taste
2 tablespoons all-purpose flour
2 tablespoons vegetable oil

In a Dutch oven, combine all ingredients except flour and oil. Bring to a boil over medium heat. Reduce heat; simmer, uncovered, until vegetables are tender.

Combine flour and oil until well blended; stir into the soup. Simmer until slightly thickened. Serve hot. **Yield:** 8-10 servings (2-3/4 quarts).

> "You can substitute one-third to one-half of the water in many of your vegetable-based soup recipes with V8 juice. It adds a richer and more robust flavor."
>
> —*Taste of Home Test Kitchen Staff*

Garden Minestrone Soup
pictured at right

Here's the perfect soup to put all those vegetables to good use! It's great for a light meal served with a salad and warm bread. Take it to a potluck and watch people go back for seconds.

Lana Rutledge, Shepherdsville, Kentucky

1 beef chuck roast (4 pounds)
1 gallon water
2 bay leaves
2 medium onions, diced

2 cups sliced carrots
2 cups sliced celery
1 can (28 ounces) diced tomatoes, undrained
1 can (15 ounces) tomato sauce
1/4 cup chopped fresh parsley
Salt and pepper to taste
4 teaspoons dried basil
1 teaspoon garlic powder
2 packages (9 ounces *each*) frozen Italian *or* cut green beans
1 package (16 ounces) frozen peas
2 cans (15-1/2 ounces *each*) kidney beans, rinsed and drained
2 boxes (7 ounces *each*) shell macaroni, cooked and drained
Grated Parmesan cheese, optional

Place beef roast, water and bay leaves in a large kettle or Dutch oven; bring to a boil. Reduce heat; cover and simmer until meat is tender, about 3 hours. Remove meat from broth; cool. Add onions, carrots and celery to broth; cook for 20 minutes or until vegetables are tender.

Cut meat into bite-size pieces; add to broth. Add tomatoes, tomato sauce, parsley, seasonings, Italian or green beans, peas and kidney beans. Cook until vegetables are done, about 10 minutes. Add macaroni and heat through. Remove bay leaves. Ladle into soup bowls; sprinkle with Parmesan cheese if desired. **Yield:** about 40 servings (10 quarts).

Hamburger Garden Soup

pictured above

On our four acres in the country, we have a large garden and raise our own steer. The only thing I need to buy for this soup is the garlic!

Alma Grady, Falls Creek, Pennsylvania

1 pound ground beef
1 cup chopped onion
1 garlic clove, minced
4 medium tomatoes, chopped *or* 1 can (28 ounces) diced tomatoes, undrained
2 cups fresh *or* frozen corn
2 cups water

3 tablespoons minced fresh parsley *or* 1 tablespoon dried parsley flakes
2 tablespoons minced fresh basil *or* 2 teaspoons dried basil
2 tablespoons minced fresh thyme *or* 2 teaspoons dried thyme
1-1/2 teaspoons minced fresh rosemary *or* 1/2 teaspoon dried rosemary, crushed
1 teaspoon salt
1/2 teaspoon pepper

In a large saucepan, cook the beef, onion and garlic over medium heat until meat is no longer pink; drain. Add the remaining ingredients; bring to a boil. Reduce heat; simmer, uncovered, for 30 minutes or until heated through. **Yield:** 5 servings.

Stroganoff Soup

My husband and I share a love for all kinds of soup and came up with this delicious recipe together. It really does taste like beef Stroganoff.

Karen Shiveley, Springfield, Minnesota

- 1/2 pound sirloin steak *or* beef tenderloin, cut into thin strips
- 1/2 cup chopped onion
- 1 tablespoon butter
- 2 cups water
- 1-1/2 cups milk
- 1/4 cup tomato paste
- 2 teaspoons beef bouillon granules
- 1 can (8 ounces) mushroom stems and pieces, drained
- 1 teaspoon salt
- 1/8 teaspoon pepper
- 1 can (12 ounces) evaporated milk
- 1/3 cup all-purpose flour
- 2 cups cooked wide egg noodles
- 1/2 cup sour cream

In a 3-qt. saucepan over medium heat, cook beef and onion in butter until meat is browned. Stir in water, milk, tomato paste and bouillon. Add mushrooms, salt and pepper; bring to a boil. Reduce heat; cover and simmer for 20-30 minutes or until meat is tender.

Combine evaporated milk and flour; stir until smooth. Gradually add to soup, stirring constantly. Bring to a boil; boil for 2 minutes, stirring constantly. Add noodles and heat through. Remove from the heat; stir in sour cream. **Yield:** 6 servings.

> "Be creative with Hamburger Garden Soup. For example, try adding shredded carrots or frozen mixed vegetables. To make a more filling soup, add pasta or rice."
>
> —*Taste of Home Test Kitchen Staff*

Mushroom Barley Soup
pictured above

A few years ago, a friend at work shared the recipe for this wonderful soup. With beef, barley and vegetables, it's hearty enough to be a meal.

Lynn Thomas, London, Ontario

- 1-1/2 pounds boneless beef chuck, cut into 3/4-inch cubes
- 1 tablespoon vegetable oil
- 2 cups finely chopped onion
- 1 cup diced carrots
- 1/2 cup sliced celery
- 1 pound fresh mushrooms, sliced
- 2 garlic cloves, minced
- 1/2 teaspoon dried thyme
- 1 can (14-1/2 ounces) beef broth
- 1 can (14-1/2 ounces) chicken broth
- 2 cups water
- 1/2 cup medium pearl barley
- 1 teaspoon salt
- 1/2 teaspoon pepper
- 3 tablespoons chopped fresh parsley

In a Dutch oven or soup kettle, brown meat in oil. Remove meat with a slotted spoon and set aside. Saute onion, carrots and celery in drippings over medium heat until tender, about 5 minutes. Add mushrooms, garlic and thyme; cook and stir for 3 minutes. Add broths, water, barley, salt and pepper.

Return meat to pan; bring to a boil. Reduce heat; cover and simmer for 1-1/2 to 2 hours or until the barley and meat are tender. Add parsley. **Yield:** about 11 servings (2-3/4 quarts).

49

Easy Beef Goulash

pictured above

I found the recipe for this stovetop goulash several years ago in an old cookbook. It really hits the spot with warm home-baked bread from the bread machine and a dish of cold applesauce.

Phyllis Pollock, Erie, Pennsylvania

1-1/2 cups uncooked spiral pasta
    1 pound boneless beef sirloin steak, cut into 1/8-inch-thick strips
    1 tablespoon canola oil
    1 medium onion, chopped
    1 medium green pepper, chopped
    1 can (14-1/2 ounces) diced tomatoes, undrained
1-1/2 cups water
    1 cup beef broth
1-1/2 teaspoons red wine vinegar
    1 to 2 teaspoons paprika
    1 teaspoon sugar
  1/2 teaspoon salt
  1/4 teaspoon caraway seeds
  1/4 teaspoon pepper
    2 tablespoons all-purpose flour
  1/4 cup cold water

Cook pasta according to package directions. Meanwhile, in a large nonstick skillet, stir-fry beef in oil for 4-5 minutes or until browned. Add onion and green pepper; cook and stir for 2 minutes. Stir in tomatoes, water, broth, vinegar and seasonings. Bring to a boil. Reduce heat; cover and simmer for 15 minutes.

In a small bowl, combine flour and cold water until smooth. Add to the skillet. Bring to a boil; cook and stir for 2 minutes or until thickened. Drain the pasta and stir into the beef mixture. **Yield:** 6 servings.

Vegetable Beef Soup

pictured below

Your crew will chase away winter's chill with a spoon when you cook up this hearty soup. It has such a rich flavor…and it's full of nutritious vegetables and chunks of tender steak.

Brigitte Schultz, Barstow, California

    1 pound boneless beef sirloin steak, cut into 1/2-inch cubes
  1/4 teaspoon pepper, *divided*
    2 teaspoons olive oil
    2 cans (14-1/2 ounces *each*) beef broth
    2 cups cubed peeled potatoes
1-1/4 cups water
    2 medium carrots, sliced
    1 tablespoon onion soup mix
    1 tablespoon dried basil

1/2 teaspoon dried tarragon
2 tablespoons cornstarch
1/2 cup white wine *or* additional beef broth

Sprinkle steak with 1/8 teaspoon pepper. In a Dutch oven, brown steak in batches in oil over medium heat. Add the broth, potatoes, water, carrots, onion soup mix, basil, tarragon and remaining pepper; bring to a boil. Reduce heat; cover and simmer for 20-25 minutes or until vegetables are tender.

In a small bowl, combine the cornstarch and wine or additional broth until smooth; stir into soup. Bring to a boil; cook and stir for 2 minutes or until thickened. **Yield:** 7 servings.

Hamburger Soup

Folks always comment on the great blend of spices and the hearty addition of cabbage in this soup.

Terry Dunn, Kenai, Alaska

1 pound ground beef *or* turkey
1 large onion, chopped
4 large potatoes, peeled and cubed
4 large carrots, grated
4 celery ribs, chopped
1/2 small head cabbage, shredded
1/4 cup uncooked long grain rice
1 quart water
1 can (28 ounces) diced tomatoes, undrained
1 can (8 ounces) tomato sauce
1 can (16 ounces) kidney beans, rinsed and drained
2 bay leaves
1 teaspoon dried basil
1 teaspoon dried thyme
3/4 teaspoon pepper
1/2 teaspoon dill weed
1 to 2 teaspoons salt

In a Dutch oven or soup kettle, cook meat and onion over medium heat until meat is no longer pink; drain. Add all of remaining ingredients; bring to a boil. Reduce heat and simmer, uncovered, for 2-3 hours. Remove bay leaves before serving. **Yield:** 14 servings (3-1/2 quarts).

Country Cabbage Soup

pictured below

My mother-in-law, who is a wonderful cook, has shared many recipes with me, including this one. Beef and tomatoes go nicely with cabbage, onion and celery.

Vicky Catullo, Youngstown, Ohio

2 pounds ground beef
2 cans (28 ounces *each*) stewed tomatoes
1 medium head cabbage, shredded
2 large onions, chopped
6 celery ribs, chopped
Salt and pepper to taste

In a large saucepan or Dutch oven, cook beef over medium heat until no longer pink; drain. Add the tomatoes, cabbage, onions and celery; bring to a boil.

Reduce heat; simmer, uncovered, for 25 minutes or until the vegetables are tender. Add salt and pepper. **Yield:** 12-14 servings (3-1/4 quarts).

Hearty Vegetable Soup

pictured below

When we come in from playing in the snow, I serve this hearty soup. It is so warming and satisfying!

Nancy Soderstrom, Roseville, Minnesota

- 1 beef chuck roast (2-1/2 to 3 pounds)
- 4 quarts water
- 1 cup medium pearl barley
- 1-1/2 cups chopped onion
- 1-1/2 cups chopped celery
- 1 tablespoon salt
- 1 teaspoon pepper
- 1 can (28 ounces) diced tomatoes, undrained
- 1-1/2 cups chopped carrots
- 1 package (16 ounces) frozen mixed vegetables
- 1/4 cup minced fresh parsley
- 1/2 teaspoon dried basil
- 1/4 teaspoon dried thyme
- 1/4 teaspoon garlic salt

Place roast in a large Dutch oven or soup kettle. Add water, barley, onion, celery, salt and pepper; bring to a boil. Reduce heat; cover and simmer for 1 hour and 15 minutes or until meat is tender. Remove meat; cool. Cut into bite-size pieces. Skim fat from broth.

Add beef and remaining ingredients; bring to a boil. Reduce heat; cover and simmer for 45 minutes or until vegetables are tender. **Yield:** 15-20 servings (6 quarts).

Beef Wild Rice Soup

I tasted this thick and hearty soup at a food fair I helped judge. It didn't earn a ribbon, but I thought it was a real winner. The original recipe called for uncooked wild rice, but instead I use a quick-cooking rice blend.

Kathy Herink, Gladbrook, Iowa

- 1 pound ground beef
- 2 cups chopped celery
- 2 cups chopped onion
- 3 cups water
- 1 can (14-1/2 ounces) chicken broth
- 1 can (10-3/4 ounces) condensed cream of mushroom soup, undiluted
- 1 package (6.75 ounces) quick-cooking long grain and wild rice mix
- 5 bacon strips, cooked and crumbled

In a 3-qt. saucepan, cook the beef, celery and onion over medium heat until beef is no longer pink and vegetables are tender; drain.

Add water, broth, soup and rice with contents of the seasoning packet. Bring to a boil. Reduce heat; cover and simmer for 5 minutes. Garnish with bacon. **Yield:** 8 servings (about 2 quarts).

Shaker Herb 'n' Meatball Soup

Filling soups like this make it easy to get through cold New England winters. The meatballs are extra-easy because they cook in the soup...there's no need for browning beforehand.

Carolyn Milke, North Canton, Connecticut

- 2 quarts beef broth
- 2 cans (14-1/2 ounces *each*) diced tomatoes, undrained
- 3 medium potatoes, peeled and cubed
- 3 medium carrots, sliced
- 1 cup shredded cabbage
- 1 large onion, chopped
- 1/2 cup chopped fresh parsley
- 6 whole peppercorns
- 1/2 teaspoon dried marjoram
- 1/2 teaspoon celery seed
- 1/2 teaspoon dried thyme
- 1/8 teaspoon ground cumin
- 1/2 cup soft bread crumbs
- 1 egg, beaten
- 1 teaspoon Worcestershire sauce

1/4 teaspoon salt
1/8 teaspoon pepper
1 pound lean ground beef

In a Dutch oven or soup kettle, combine the first 12 ingredients; bring to a boil. Reduce heat; cover and simmer for 1 hour.

In a bowl, combine the bread crumbs, egg, Worcestershire sauce, salt and pepper. Crumble beef over mixture and mix well. Shape into 1-in. balls; drop into soup.

Cover and simmer for 2 hours or until meatballs are no longer pink. **Yield:** 12-14 servings (3-1/2 quarts).

Dilly Beef Barley Soup

My mother and grandmother were wonderful cooks who taught me to create foods that were both attractive and full-flavored. This soup from Mom meets those requirements nicely.

Phyllis Kramer, Little Compton, Rhode Island

3/4 cup dried baby lima beans
1/2 cup dried yellow split peas
1/2 cup dried green split peas
4 medium carrots, sliced
4 celery ribs, sliced
3 quarts water
2 pounds boneless beef short ribs, cut into 1-inch cubes
2 medium onions, chopped
3/4 cup medium pearl barley
5 chicken bouillon cubes
4 medium potatoes, peeled and cubed
1 tablespoon chopped fresh dill *or* 1 teaspoon dill weed
1-1/2 teaspoons salt
1/4 teaspoon pepper

In a Dutch oven or soup kettle, combine the beans, peas, carrots, celery and water; bring to a boil. Reduce heat; cover and simmer for 1-1/2 hours. Add the beef, onions, barley and bouillon; bring to a boil. Skim foam.

Reduce heat; cover and simmer for 2 hours or until meat and beans are tender. Add potatoes and simmer for 20 minutes. Add dill, salt and pepper; cook for 5 minutes. **Yield:** 15 servings (3-3/4 quarts).

Stuffed Roast Pepper Soup

pictured above

After sampling a similar soup at a summer resort, my daughter and I invented this version. Using a colorful variety of peppers makes it especially appealing.

Betty Vig, Viroque, Wisconsin

2 pounds ground beef
1/2 medium onion, chopped
6 cups water
8 beef bouillon cubes
2 cans (28 ounces *each*) diced tomatoes, undrained
2 cups cooked rice
2 teaspoons salt
1/2 teaspoon pepper
1/2 teaspoon paprika
3 medium green, yellow *or* sweet red peppers seeded and chopped

In a large Dutch oven or soup kettle, cook beef and onion over medium heat until the meat is no longer pink and the onion is tender; drain.

Add bouillon cubes, tomatoes, rice and seasonings. Bring to a boil; reduce heat and simmer, covered, for 1 hour.

Add chopped peppers; cook, uncovered, for 10-15 minutes or just until tender. **Yield:** 14-16 servings (4 quarts).

53

Cabbage Zucchini Borscht

I know my family will get a hearty, healthy meal when I serve this soup. There are so many good vegetables to stir in!

Agatha Wiebe, Winkler, Manitoba

 1 meaty beef soup bone
 2 quarts water
 4 cups shredded cabbage
 2 cups cubed peeled potatoes
 2 cups sliced carrots
 2 cups diced peeled tomatoes
 1 onion, chopped
 1/2 cup chopped fresh parsley
 2 tablespoons dill weed
 1 tablespoon anise seed, tied in a
   cheesecloth bag
 1-1/2 teaspoons salt
 1/2 teaspoon pepper
 2 cups chopped cooked beets
 3 cups shredded zucchini

Place soup bone and water in a Dutch oven or soup kettle; bring to a boil. Reduce heat and simmer, uncovered, for 40-45 minutes. Skim off fat. Add cabbage, potatoes, carrots, tomatoes, onion, parsley, dill, anise seed, salt and pepper.

Simmer, uncovered, 2-1/2 to 3 hours. Remove meat from soup bone; discard bone and add meat to soup. Stir in beets and zucchini. Simmer 15-20 minutes longer or until zucchini is tender. Remove anise seed before serving. **Yield:** 12-14 servings (4 quarts).

Hungarian Goulash

pictured above

With tender beef and a rich flavorful sauce, this entree is an old favorite.

Joan Rose, Langley, British Columbia

 1 pound beef stew meat, cut
   into 1-inch cubes
 1 pound lean boneless pork, cut
   into 1-inch cubes
 2 large onions, thinly sliced
 2 tablespoons vegetable oil
 2 cups water
 2 tablespoons paprika
 1/2 teaspoon salt
 1/2 teaspoon dried marjoram
 1 tablespoon all-purpose flour
 1 cup (8 ounces) sour cream
Hot cooked noodles

In a large skillet over medium heat, brown beef, pork and onions in oil; drain. Add the water, paprika, salt and marjoram; bring to a boil. Reduce heat; cover and simmer for 1-1/2 hours or until meat is tender.

Just before serving, combine flour and sour cream until smooth; stir into meat mixture. Bring to a boil over medium heat; cook and stir for 1-2 minutes or until thickened and bubbly. Serve over noodles. **Yield:** 6-8 servings.

What's the Difference?

Goulash, a traditional Hungarian dish, was originally served as a thick soup. It is now more commonly served as a stew.

Borscht is a bright red Polish and Russian soup, and its original base was the cow parsnip. Today, borscht is a beetroot soup that is made with meat stock, cabbage and potatoes and other root vegetables.

Unstuffed Pepper Soup
pictured above

One of my sisters gave me the recipe for this quick-and-easy soup that tastes just like stuffed green peppers. The thick hearty mixture is chock-full of good stuff. Plus, the aroma produced while it's cooking is wonderful.

Evelyn Kara, Brownsville, Pennsylvania

1-1/2 pounds ground beef
   3 large green peppers, chopped
   1 large onion, chopped
   2 cans (14-1/2 ounces *each*) beef broth
   2 cans (10-3/4 ounces *each*) condensed tomato soup, undiluted
   1 can (28 ounces) crushed tomatoes, undrained
   1 can (4 ounces) mushroom stems and pieces, drained
1-1/2 cups cooked rice

In a Dutch oven or large saucepan, cook the beef, green peppers and onion over medium heat until meat is no longer pink; drain.

Stir in the broth, soup, tomatoes and mushrooms. Bring to a boil. Reduce heat; cover and simmer for at least 30 minutes, stirring occasionally. Add rice and heat through. **Yield:** 10 servings.

55

Zesty Vegetable Beef Soup

pictured below

My family loves to come to the table for hot homemade biscuits and a bowl of this flavorful filling soup. They rave over how good it tastes. A friend shared the recipe with me.

Brenda Wood, Portage la Prairie, Manitoba

BROTH:
    2 quarts water
    3 pounds beef short ribs with bones
    1 large onion, quartered
    2 medium carrots, quartered
    2 celery ribs, quartered
    8 whole allspice
    2 bay leaves
    1 tablespoon salt
 1/2 teaspoon pepper
SOUP:
    1 quart V8 juice
    3 celery ribs, sliced
    2 medium potatoes, peeled and cubed
    2 medium carrots, sliced
    1 medium onion, diced
    2 teaspoons Worcestershire sauce
 1/2 teaspoon hot pepper sauce
 1/2 teaspoon dried oregano
 1/2 teaspoon dried basil
 1/4 teaspoon chili powder
    1 cup uncooked noodles

In a Dutch oven or soup kettle, bring broth ingredients to a boil. Reduce heat; cover and simmer for 2 hours or until meat is tender. Remove ribs; allow to cool. Skim fat and strain broth; discard vegetables and seasonings. Remove meat from bones and cut into bite-size pieces; return to broth.

Add the first 10 soup ingredients; bring to a boil. Reduce heat; cover and simmer for 1 hour or until vegetables are tender. Stir in noodles. Return to a boil; cook, uncovered, for 15 minutes or until the noodles are tender. **Yield:** 12-14 servings (3-3/4 quarts).

Goulash Soup

I found this recipe in a church cookbook and modified it slightly so it tastes just like the goulash soup we had while visiting Germany. It's now become a favorite at our house.

Lois Teske, Buckley, Illinois

1-1/2 pounds lean beef stew meat, cut
        into 1-inch cubes
    2 pounds beef soup bones
    1 quart fresh tomatoes, peeled and
        chopped
    1 medium onion, chopped
    4 large potatoes, peeled and diced
    6 carrots, sliced
    3 celery ribs, sliced
    3 cups chopped cabbage
    3 tablespoons Worcestershire sauce
    2 to 4 teaspoons salt
 1/2 teaspoon pepper
    3 tablespoons minced fresh parsley

In a large kettle or Dutch oven, cover stew meat and soup bones with water. Simmer, covered, about 2 hours or until meat is tender. Remove meat from bones; strain broth and discard bones. Return broth and meat to kettle.

Add the next nine ingredients. Simmer, covered, about 1 hour or until vegetables are tender. Sprinkle with parsley. **Yield:** about 16 servings (4 quarts).

Cheesy Meatball Soup

pictured below

Meat, potatoes and other vegetables make this rich-tasting soup a meal-in-one. Process cheese sauce makes it taste like a cheeseburger. I serve this soup with a nice crusty loaf of French bread.

Ione Sander, Carlton, Minnesota

  1 egg
  1/4 cup dry bread crumbs
  1/2 teaspoon salt
  1 pound ground beef
  2 cups water
  1 cup diced celery
  1 cup whole kernel corn
  1 cup cubed peeled potatoes
  1/2 cup sliced carrot
  1/2 cup chopped onion
  2 beef bouillon cubes
  1/2 teaspoon hot pepper sauce
  1 jar (16 ounces) process cheese sauce

In a bowl, combine egg, bread crumbs and salt. Crumble beef over mixture and mix well. Shape into 1-in. balls. In a large saucepan, brown meatballs; drain. Add the water, celery, corn, potatoes, carrot, onion, bouillon and hot pepper sauce; bring to a boil.

Reduce heat; cover and simmer for 25 minutes or until meat is no longer pink and potatoes are tender. Stir in the cheese sauce; heat through. **Yield:** 4-6 servings.

Simple Taco Soup

pictured above

We first sampled this chili-like soup at a church dinner. It's a warming dish on a cold day, and since it uses packaged seasonings and several cans of vegetables, it's a snap to prepare.

Glenda Taylor, Sand Springs, Oklahoma

  2 pounds ground beef
  1 envelope taco seasoning mix
1-1/2 cups water
  1 can (15-3/4 ounces) mild chili beans
  1 can (15-1/4 ounces) whole kernel corn, drained
  1 can (15 ounces) pinto beans, rinsed and drained
  1 can (14-1/2 ounces) stewed tomatoes
  1 can (10 ounces) diced tomatoes with green chilies
  1 can (4 ounces) chopped green chilies, optional
  1 envelope ranch salad dressing mix

In a Dutch oven or large kettle, cook beef over medium heat until no longer pink; drain. Add taco seasoning and mix well. Stir in remaining ingredients.

Simmer, uncovered, for 15 minutes or until heated through, stirring occasionally. **Yield:** 6-8 servings (about 2 quarts).

Three's-a-Charm Shamrock Soup

pictured above

There's no better way to use up leftover corned beef, cabbage and potatoes than to make a hearty soup. This second-time-around meal is one of my best.

Deborah McMurtrey, Estes Park, Colorado

- 6 celery ribs, chopped
- 4 medium carrots, sliced
- 2 cups cubed peeled potatoes
- 5 cups water
- 3 cups cubed cooked corned beef
- 2 cups chopped cooked cabbage
- 1 teaspoon dill weed
- 1 teaspoon salt
- 1 teaspoon seasoned salt
- 1/2 teaspoon white pepper

In a large soup kettle, bring the celery, carrots, potatoes and water to a boil. Reduce heat; cover and simmer until vegetables are tender, about 20 minutes.

Stir in the remaining ingredients. Cover and simmer for 15-20 minutes or until heated through. **Yield:** 10 servings (2-1/2 quarts).

Tortellini Vegetable Soup

pictured below

Tomatoes, carrots, green beans, potatoes, corn and celery are the perfect complements to convenient frozen tortellini in this heartwarming soup. Add a crusty loaf of bread and a green salad, and dinner is ready in no time.

Deborah Hutchinson, Enfield, Connecticut

- 1 large onion chopped
- 2 celery ribs, chopped
- 2 tablespoons vegetable oil
- 2 cans (14-1/2 ounces *each*) beef broth
- 1 cup *each* frozen corn, sliced carrots and cut green beans
- 1 cup diced uncooked potatoes
- 1 teaspoon dried basil
- 1 teaspoon dried thyme
- 1/2 teaspoon minced chives
- 2 cans (14-1/2 ounces *each*) diced tomatoes, undrained
- 2 cups frozen beef *or* cheese tortellini

In a Dutch oven or soup kettle, saute the onion and celery in oil. Add the broth, corn, carrots, beans, potatoes, basil, thyme and chives; bring to a boil. Reduce heat; cover and simmer for 10-15 minutes or until potatoes are tender.

Add the tomatoes and tortellini. Simmer, uncovered, for 4-5 minutes or until tortellini is heated through. **Yield:** 10 servings (2-1/2 quarts).

Oriental Friendship Soup

After we completed our chores, Mom would warm us up with lots of hot soup. My love of soup continues today.

Cyndi Stanton, Wellsville, New York

      1 large onion, thinly sliced
      2 tablespoons vegetable oil
1-1/2 pounds sirloin steak, thinly sliced
      1 cup sliced celery
      2 cans (14-1/2 ounces *each*) beef broth
      1 tablespoon cornstarch
      2 tablespoons soy sauce
      1 can (14 ounces) chop suey vegetables, drained
      2 cups cooked fine egg noodles
      1 package (10 ounces) fresh spinach, torn
  1/4 teaspoon pepper
Chow mein noodles, optional

In a Dutch oven or soup kettle, saute onion in oil until tender. Remove and set aside. In the same pan, stir-fry beef, a few slices at a time, until no longer pink. Add celery; stir-fry for 2-4 minutes or until crisp-tender. Return onion and meat to pan. Add broth.

In a small bowl, combine cornstarch and soy sauce; mix well. Add to pan. Bring to a boil; cook and stir for 2 minutes or until bubbly. Stir in vegetables, egg noodles, spinach and pepper; heat through. Garnish with chow mein noodles if desired. **Yield:** 6 servings.

Beefy Tomato Soup

Beef and macaroni add heartiness to this soup, which is very nicely seasoned, too!

Patricia Staudt, Marble Rock, Iowa

      1 pound ground beef
      1 quart tomato juice
      3 cups water
  3/4 cup uncooked elbow macaroni
      1 envelope onion soup mix
  1/4 teaspoon chili powder

In a large saucepan, cook beef over medium heat until no longer pink; drain. Add the remaining ingredients. Bring to a boil. Reduce heat; simmer, uncovered, for 15-20 minutes or until macaroni is tender. **Yield:** 8 servings.

Zucchini Beef Soup
pictured above

I make this wonderful garden-fresh soup as soon as my homegrown zucchini is plentiful. I often double the recipe and freeze some to enjoy later.

Betty Claycomb, Alverton, Pennsylvania

  1/2 pound ground beef
      2 celery ribs, thinly sliced
  1/3 cup chopped onion
  1/2 cup chopped green pepper
      1 can (28 ounces) diced tomatoes, undrained
      3 medium zucchini, cubed
      2 cups water
1-1/2 teaspoons Italian seasoning
      1 teaspoon salt
      1 teaspoon beef bouillon granules
  1/2 teaspoon sugar
Pepper to taste
Shredded Parmesan cheese, optional

In a large saucepan, cook beef, celery, onion and green pepper over medium heat until meat is no longer pink and vegetables are tender; drain. Stir in tomatoes, zucchini, water, Italian seasoning, salt, bouillon, sugar and pepper.

Bring to a boil. Reduce heat; cover and simmer for 20-25 minutes or until the zucchini is tender. Garnish with Parmesan cheese if desired. **Yield:** 6 servings.

Old-World Tomato Soup

pictured below

This hearty soup has been in our family for four generations, and I've never seen another recipe like it. Each spoonful brings back memories.

Linda Pandolfo, East Haddam, Connecticut

3 quarts water
4 beef short ribs (about 2 pounds)
2 to 3 meaty soup bones (about 2 pounds)
1 can (28 ounces) whole tomatoes, undrained
3 celery ribs, halved
1 large onion, quartered
1/2 cup chopped fresh parsley, *divided*
1 tablespoon salt
1-1/2 teaspoons pepper
4 carrots, cut into 1-inch pieces
2 parsnips, peeled and quartered
2 cups (16 ounces) sour cream
1/2 cup all-purpose flour
1/2 teaspoon ground nutmeg, optional
1 package (8 ounces) egg noodles, cooked and drained

In a large kettle, combine the water, ribs, soup bones, tomatoes, celery, onion, 1/4 cup parsley, salt and pepper. Cover and simmer for 2 hours.

Add the carrots and parsnips. Cover and simmer for 1 hour or until the meat and vegetables are tender.

With a slotted spoon, remove meat, bones and vegetables. Strain broth and skim off fat; return all but 1 cup broth to kettle. Set reserved broth aside. Remove meat from the bones; dice and return to kettle. Discard celery and onion. Cut parsnips, carrots and tomatoes into 1/2-in. pieces and return to kettle. Add remaining parsley.

In a bowl, combine sour cream, flour, nutmeg if desired and reserved broth; stir into soup. Add noodles. Cook and stir until thickened and heated through (do not boil). **Yield:** 16-20 servings.

Hearty Meatball Soup

A little bit of this thick and hearty soup goes a long way, so it's terrific to take to potlucks. My husband and I enjoy this on cold winter nights.

Janice Thompson, Lansing, Michigan

2 eggs
1 cup soft bread crumbs
1 teaspoon salt
1/2 teaspoon pepper
1 pound lean ground beef
1 pound ground pork
1/2 pound ground turkey
4 cups beef broth
1 can (46 ounces) tomato juice
2 cans (14-1/2 ounces *each*) stewed tomatoes
8 cups shredded cabbage
1 cup thinly sliced celery
1 cup thinly sliced carrots
8 green onions, sliced
3/4 cup uncooked long grain rice
2 teaspoons dried basil
3 tablespoons minced fresh parsley
2 tablespoons soy sauce

In a bowl, combine the eggs, bread crumbs, salt and pepper. Crumble meat over mixture and mix well. Shape into 1-in. balls.

In a soup kettle, bring broth to a boil. Carefully add the meatballs. Add the tomato juice, tomatoes, vegetables, rice and basil. Cover and simmer for 30 minutes.

Add the parsley and soy sauce. Simmer, uncovered, for 10 minutes or until meatballs are no longer pink and vegetables are tender. **Yield:** 22-24 servings (5-3/4 quarts).

Potluck Pasta Soup

In an attempt to duplicate a soup served at an Italian restaurant, I came up with this recipe.

Marilyn Foss, Beavertown, Ohio

  1-1/2 pounds ground beef
     2 quarts water
     2 cans (14-1/2 ounces *each*) Italian
       stewed tomatoes
     2 cups diced carrots
  1-1/2 cups diced celery
     1 cup chopped onion
     1 can (8 ounces) tomato sauce
     1 envelope onion soup mix
     1 tablespoon sugar
     1 teaspoon Italian seasoning
     2 garlic cloves, minced
     2 bay leaves
   1/2 teaspoon pepper
     3 cups cooked elbow macaroni
     1 can (15 ounces) garbanzo beans,
       rinsed and drained
   1/2 cup chopped green pepper

In a soup kettle or Dutch oven, cook beef over medium heat until no longer pink; drain. Add water, tomatoes, carrots, celery, onion, tomato sauce, soup mix and seasonings; bring to a boil.

Reduce heat; simmer, uncovered, for 1 hour. Stir in macaroni, beans and green pepper; heat through. Discard bay leaves before serving.
Yield: 20 servings (5 quarts).

Beef Barley Soup
pictured above

This soup is a meal in itself. I like to serve it with thick slices of homemade bread.

Jan Spencer, McLean, Saskatchewan

     2 pounds beef short ribs with bones
     5 cups water
     1 can (14-1/2 ounces) diced tomatoes,
       undrained
     1 medium onion, chopped
     1 to 1-1/2 teaspoons salt
   1/8 teaspoon pepper
     2 cups sliced carrots
     1 cup sliced celery
     1 cup chopped cabbage
   2/3 cup quick-cooking pearl barley
   1/4 cup minced fresh parsley

In a soup kettle, combine ribs, water, tomatoes, onion, salt and pepper; bring to a boil over medium heat. Reduce heat; cover and simmer for 1-1/2 to 2 hours or until meat is tender. Remove the ribs and cool. Skim fat. Remove meat from bones and cut into bite-size pieces; return to broth.

Add carrots, celery and cabbage; bring to a boil. Reduce heat; cover and simmer 15 minutes. Add barley; return to a boil. Reduce heat; cover and cook 10-15 minutes or until barley and vegetables are tender. Add parsley.
Yield: 8 servings (2 quarts).

> ❝ To reduce preparation time when making Potluck Pasta Soup, chop the carrots, celery and onion early in the day or even the night before. Store in separate plastic bags in the refrigerator. ❞
>
> —*Marilyn Foss*
> *Beavertown, Ohio*

Zesty Tortilla Soup

Our family enjoys Mexican food, and we especially find this soup appealing. It has just the right amount of zip without being overwhelming.

Tammy Leiber, Navasota, Texas

     1 medium onion, chopped
     2 garlic cloves, minced
     2 tablespoons vegetable oil
     2 pounds beef stew meat, cut
       into 1-inch cubes
     2 cups water
     1 can (14-1/2 ounces) stewed tomatoes
     1 can (10 ounces) diced tomatoes with
       green chilies, undrained
     1 can (10-3/4 ounces) condensed
       tomato soup, undiluted
     1 can (10-1/2 ounces) beef broth
     1 can (10-1/2 ounces) chicken broth
     1 tablespoon Worcestershire sauce
     1 teaspoon ground cumin
     1 teaspoon chili powder
     1 teaspoon salt
     1 teaspoon lemon-pepper seasoning
   1/2 teaspoon hot pepper sauce
    10 corn tortillas (6 inches)
Shredded cheddar cheese, sour cream and
   sliced green onions, optional

In a Dutch oven or soup kettle, saute onion and garlic in oil until onion is tender. Add next 13 ingredients; bring to a boil. Reduce heat. Cover; simmer for 1-1/2 hours or until beef is tender.

Tear tortillas into bite-size pieces; add to soup. Simmer, uncovered, for 10 minutes; let stand for 5 minutes. Garnish individual servings with

cheese, sour cream and onions if desired. **Yield:** 10 servings (2-1/2 quarts).

Pizza Soup

pictured above

My kids first sampled this soup in the school cafeteria. They couldn't stop talking about it, so I knew I had to get the recipe!

Penny Lanxon, Newell, Iowa

     1 pound ground beef
     2 cans (26 ounces each) condensed
       tomato soup, undiluted
 6-1/2 cups water
     1 jar (28 ounces) spaghetti sauce
     1 tablespoon Italian seasoning
     2 cups (8 ounces) shredded cheddar
       cheese
Additional shredded cheddar cheese,
   optional

In a soup kettle or Dutch oven, cook beef over medium heat until no longer pink; drain. Add the soup, water, spaghetti sauce and Italian seasoning; bring to a boil. Reduce heat; simmer, uncovered, for 15 minutes.

Add cheese; cook and stir until melted. Garnish with additional cheese if desired. **Yield:** 16 servings (4 quarts).

> "
> Make Pizza Soup a more complete and satisfying meal by serving it with grilled cheese or sub sandwiches. "
>
> —*Taste of Home Test Kitchen Staff*

Beef Minestrone

Beef, vegetables, rice and seasonings are wonderful in this meaty minestrone.

Ann Lape, Richmondville, New York

    1 pound ground round
    1 cup chopped onion
    6 cups water
    1 cup cubed peeled potatoes
    1 cup chopped tomatoes
    1 cup shredded cabbage
    1 cup chopped carrots
  1/2 cup chopped celery
  1/4 cup uncooked long grain rice
  1/2 teaspoon dried basil
  1/2 teaspoon dried thyme
    1 bay leaf
  1/4 teaspoon pepper
    5 teaspoons grated Parmesan

In a Dutch oven, cook meat and onion over medium heat until meat is no longer pink and onion is tender; drain.

Add the next 11 ingredients; bring to a boil. Reduce heat; cover and simmer for 1 hour. Discard bay leaf. Sprinkle each serving with 1/2 teaspoon of Parmesan. **Yield:** 10 servings.

Quick Beef Noodle Soup

This takes minutes but tastes like it simmered all day. It's great any day of the week.

Margery Bryan, Royal City, Washington

    1 pound ground beef
  1/2 cup chopped onion
    2 cans (14-1/2 ounces *each*) Italian stewed tomatoes
    2 cans (10-1/2 ounces *each*) beef broth
    1 can (16 ounces) mixed vegetables, drained
    1 teaspoon dried oregano
  1/2 teaspoon salt
  1/4 teaspoon pepper
    1 cup uncooked medium egg noodles

In a Dutch oven or soup kettle, cook beef and onion over medium heat until meat is no longer pink; drain. Add next six ingredients. Bring to a boil; add noodles.

Reduce heat to medium-low; cover and cook for 10-15 minutes or until the noodles are done. **Yield:** 6-8 servings (2 quarts).

Hearty Taco Soup

pictured below

If you need a meal in a hurry, this fast recipe fills the bill! When I have time, I like to make bread bowls to serve the soup in—it makes for a unique presentation and a hearty main dish!

Nancy Wilkes, Preston, Idaho

    1 pound ground beef
  1/4 cup chopped onion
    2 cups fresh corn
    1 can (14-1/2 ounces) diced tomatoes, undrained
    1 can (16 ounces) kidney beans, rinsed and drained
    1 can (8 ounces) tomato sauce
    1 envelope taco seasoning
Corn chips, shredded cheddar cheese *and/or* sour cream, optional

In a large saucepan, cook ground beef and onion over medium heat until the meat is no longer pink; drain. Add the corn, tomatoes, beans, tomato sauce and taco seasoning.

Cover; simmer for 15 minutes, stirring occasionally. Serve with chips, cheese and/or sour cream if desired. **Yield:** 4-6 servings (1-1/2 quarts).

63

Barley Peasant Soup

Barley brightens the broth of this soup. Shared by the National Barley Foods Council, this recipe makes a savory supper or lunch.

 1 pound beef stew meat, cut into 1/2- to 3/4-inch cubes
 1 tablespoon olive oil
 2 cups chopped onion
 1 cup sliced celery
 2 garlic cloves, minced
 5 cups water
 5 cups beef broth
 2 cups sliced carrots
 1-1/2 cups medium pearl barley
 1 can (15 ounces) garbanzo beans, rinsed and drained
 1 can (15 ounces) kidney beans, rinsed and drained
 4 cups sliced zucchini
 3 cups diced plum tomatoes
 2 cups chopped cabbage
 1/4 cup snipped fresh parsley
 1 teaspoon dried thyme
 1-1/2 teaspoons Italian seasoning
Salt and pepper to taste
Grated Parmesan cheese, optional

In a large saucepan or Dutch oven, brown meat in oil. Add onion, celery and garlic. Cook until beef is no longer pink. Add water and broth; bring to a boil. Add carrots and barley. Reduce heat; cover and simmer for 45-60 minutes or until barley is tender.

Add beans, zucchini, tomatoes, cabbage, parsley and seasonings; simmer 15-20 minutes or until vegetables are tender. Top individual bowls with Parmesan cheese if desired. **Yield:** 16-20 servings (5 quarts).

Beefy Tomato Pasta Soup

pictured below

If you're a fan of Italian fare, you'll like this chunky combination. I enjoy this satisfying soup, and it's easier to fix than lasagna.

Nancy Rollag, Kewaskum, Wisconsin

 1 pound ground beef
 2 medium green peppers, cut into 1-inch chunks
 1 medium onion, cut into chunks
 2 garlic cloves, minced
 5 to 6 cups water
 2 cans (14-1/2 ounces *each*) Italian diced tomatoes, undrained
 1 can (6 ounces) tomato paste
 1 tablespoon brown sugar
 2 to 3 teaspoons Italian seasoning
 1 teaspoon salt
 1/4 teaspoon pepper
 2 cups uncooked spiral pasta
Croutons, optional

In a Dutch oven or soup kettle, cook the beef, green peppers, onion and garlic over medium heat until meat is no longer pink; drain. Add the water, tomatoes, tomato paste, brown sugar, Italian seasoning, salt and pepper.

Bring to a boil. Add pasta. Cook for 10-14 minutes or until pasta is tender, stirring occasionally. Serve with croutons if desired. **Yield:** 10 servings (about 2-1/2 quarts).

Taco Bean Soup
pictured above

Just as tasty and fun to eat, this soup is chock-full of taco-goodness. It's a wonderful mix of flavors!

Roxanne Barone, Billings, Montana

2 pounds ground beef
1 medium onion, finely chopped
1 can (28 ounces) tomatoes
1 can (15 ounces) tomato sauce
1 cup water
1 can (15 ounces) pinto beans, rinsed and drained
1 can (15-1/4 ounces) whole kernel corn, drained
1 envelope taco seasoning mix
Shredded cheddar cheese, sliced avocado, chopped tomato and corn chips, optional

In a Dutch oven, cook beef and onion over medium heat until meat is no longer pink; drain. Puree the tomatoes in their liquid; add to pan with tomato sauce, water, beans, corn and taco seasoning. Bring to a boil. Reduce heat and simmer for 5 minutes.

If desired, top each serving with cheese, avocado and tomato, and serve with chips. **Yield:** 10 servings (2-1/2 quarts).

65

Ground Beef 'n' Noodle Soup

This savory specialty combines ground beef with onions, celery and carrots. It's a wonderful soup to make any day of the week.

Judy Brander, Two Harbors, Minnesota

      1-1/2 pounds ground beef
        1/2 cup *each* chopped onion, celery
             and carrot
          7 cups water
          1 envelope au jus mix
          2 tablespoons beef bouillon granules
          2 bay leaves
        1/8 teaspoon pepper
      1-1/2 cups uncooked egg noodles

In a large saucepan or Dutch oven, cook beef, onion, celery and carrot over medium heat until meat is no longer pink and vegetables are tender; drain. Add water, au jus mix, bouillon, bay leaves and pepper; bring to a boil. Stir in the noodles.

Boil, uncovered, for 15 minutes or until noodles are tender, stirring occasionally. Discard bay leaves before serving. **Yield:** 8 servings (2 quarts).

Beef Tortellini Soup

Because of its rich spicy flavor, this soup has been a favorite in our home for years. I think you'll agree the tortellini adds an interesting twist.

Tammy Nadeau, Presque Isle, Maine

          1 pound ground beef
          7 cups beef broth
          2 cans (14-1/2 ounces *each*) stewed
             tomatoes
        3/4 cup ketchup
        3/4 cup thinly sliced carrots
        3/4 cup thinly sliced celery
        3/4 cup finely chopped onion
          1 tablespoon dried basil
      1-1/2 teaspoons seasoned salt
          1 teaspoon sugar
        1/4 teaspoon pepper
          4 bay leaves
      1-1/2 cups dried cheese-filled tortellini
             Grated Parmesan cheese, optional

In a Dutch oven or soup kettle, cook beef over medium heat until no longer pink; drain. Add the next 11 ingredients; bring to a boil. Reduce heat; cover and simmer for 30 minutes. Add

tortellini; cook for 20-30 minutes or until tender. Remove bay leaves. Garnish individual servings with Parmesan cheese if desired. **Yield:** 10-12 servings (3-1/4 quarts).

South-of-the-Border Soup
pictured below

Cooking and creating new recipes are favorite pastimes of mine. This is an original recipe that earned me first place in the Wisconsin Beef cookoff some years ago!

Lynn Ireland, Lebanon, Wisconsin

          1 egg
        1/4 cup dry bread crumbs
        1/2 teaspoon salt
        1/4 teaspoon pepper
          1 pound ground beef
          1 jar (16 ounces) picante sauce
          1 can (15-1/4 ounces) whole kernel corn,
             drained
          1 can (15 ounces) black beans, rinsed
             and drained
          1 can (14-1/2 ounces) diced tomatoes,
             undrained
      1-1/4 cups water

In a bowl, combine the first four ingredients. Crumble beef over mixture and mix well. Shape into 1-in. balls. In a large saucepan, brown meatballs; drain. Add the picante sauce, corn, beans, tomatoes and water; bring to a boil.

Reduce heat; cover and simmer for 20 minutes or until the meat is no longer pink. **Yield:** 8 servings (2 quarts).

Roast Beef Soup

If your family's like mine, you have to disguise leftovers in order for anyone to eat them! This special soup turns leftovers into a lively meal.

Kathy Jensen, Edmonds, Washington

2 pounds cooked roast beef, cut into 1-inch cubes
1-1/4 cups chopped onion
2 tablespoons vegetable oil
4-1/2 cups water
1 jar (12 ounces) au jus gravy
1 cup leftover beef gravy *or* 1 can (10-1/4 ounces) beef gravy
1 envelope brown gravy mix
2 bay leaves
1/4 teaspoon garlic salt
1/4 teaspoon pepper
1/4 teaspoon hot pepper sauce
1 cup dried lentils, rinsed
1 cup leftover cooked vegetables *or* 1 cup frozen vegetables

In a 3-qt. saucepan, saute beef and onion in oil until onion is tender. Add the next eight ingredients; cover and simmer for 1 hour. Stir in lentils; cover and simmer for 30 minutes.

Add the vegetables; cover and simmer for 10 minutes or until the lentils and vegetables are tender. Remove bay leaves. **Yield:** 6-8 servings (2 quarts).

Mixed Bean Soup
pictured above right

Guests and family alike praise this soup and always ask for seconds.

Arlene Hilman, Cawston, British Columbia

1 package (12 ounces) mixed dried beans
2 quarts water
1/2 pound ground beef, cooked and drained
1 can (14-1/2 ounces) diced tomatoes, undrained
1 cup chopped celery
1 tablespoon salt

1 teaspoon dried parsley flakes
2 garlic cloves, minced
1 teaspoon dried thyme
2 bay leaves
Pepper to taste

Place beans in a large saucepan or Dutch oven; add enough water to cover by 2 in. Bring to a boil; boil for 2 minutes. Remove from the heat; cover and let stand for 1 hour. Drain and discard liquid. Add 2 qts. water to the beans; bring to a boil. Cover and simmer for 30 minutes.

Add remaining ingredients; bring to a boil. Reduce heat; cover and simmer for 1-1/2 to 2 hours or until beans are tender. Discard bay leaves before serving. **Yield:** 10 servings (2-1/2 quarts).

> "The nicest thing about Mixed Bean Soup is that any variation of dried beans can be used."
>
> —*Arlene Hilman Cawston, British Columbia*

Forgotten Minestrone

I sprinkle servings of this soup with Parmesan cheese and offer garlic bread on the side. It's a snap to make in the slow cooker.

Marsha Ransom, South Haven, Michigan

   1 pound lean beef stew meat
   6 cups water
   1 can (28 ounces) diced tomatoes, undrained
   1 beef bouillon cube
   1 medium onion, chopped
   2 tablespoons minced dried parsley
2-1/2 teaspoons salt
1-1/2 teaspoons ground thyme
  1/2 teaspoon pepper
   1 medium zucchini, thinly sliced
   2 cups finely chopped cabbage
   1 can (16 ounces) garbanzo beans, drained
   1 cup uncooked small elbow *or* shell macaroni
  1/4 cup grated Parmesan cheese, optional

In a slow cooker, combine beef, water, tomatoes, bouillon, onion, parsley, salt, thyme and pepper. Cover and cook on low for 7-9 hours or until meat is tender.

Add zucchini, cabbage, beans and macaroni; cook on high, covered, 30-45 minutes more or until the vegetables are tender. Sprinkle individual servings with Parmesan cheese if desired. **Yield:** 8 servings.

Southwestern Vegetable Soup

In addition to being a teacher, I'm a mother of three. So this quick and easy soup is perfect for my busy schedule. A real plus is that my family loves it!

Nancy Chumbley, Argyle, Texas

   2 pounds ground beef
   1 medium onion, chopped
   2 cans (15 ounces *each*) chili beans, undrained
   2 cans (14-1/2 ounces *each*) beef broth
   1 can (15-1/2 ounces) hominy, rinsed and drained

   1 can (15-1/4 ounces) whole kernel corn, drained
   1 can (14-1/2 ounces) Mexican-style stewed tomatoes
   1 can (10 ounces) diced tomatoes and green chilies, undrained
   1 can (4 ounces) chopped green chilies

In a Dutch oven or soup kettle, cook beef and onion over medium heat until meat is no longer pink; drain. Add remaining ingredients; bring to a boil. Reduce heat; cover and simmer for 15 minutes. **Yield:** 12-14 servings (3-1/2 quarts).

Scotch Broth
pictured above

I make up big pots of this hearty soup to freeze in plastic containers. Then I can bring out one or two containers at a time. I heat the frozen soup in a saucepan on low all morning. By lunchtime, it's hot and ready to serve!

Ann Main, Moorefield, Ontario

   2 pounds meaty beef soup bones
   2 quarts water
   6 whole peppercorns
1-1/2 teaspoons salt
   1 cup chopped carrots
   1 cup chopped turnips
   1 cup chopped celery

1/2 cup chopped onion
1/4 cup medium pearl barley

In a large kettle, combine soup bones, water, peppercorns and salt. Cover and simmer for 2-1/2 hours or until the meat easily falls from the bones. Remove meat from bones; dice meat and discard bones. Strain broth; skim off fat.

Combine broth, meat and remaining ingredients. Bring to a boil. Reduce heat; cover and simmer about 1 hour or until vegetables and barley are tender. **Yield:** 6-8 servings (2 quarts).

Veggies 'n' Beef Soup

This quick and colorful soup goes together in minutes. Even my husband—who admits he's no cook—makes it on occasion.

Agnes Bierbaum, Gainesville, Florida

1/2 **pound ground beef**
2 **cups water**
1 **can (14-1/2 ounces) stewed tomatoes**
1 **package (10 ounces) frozen mixed vegetables**
1 **can (8 ounces) tomato sauce**
1 **envelope onion soup mix**
1/2 **teaspoon sugar**

In a saucepan over medium heat, cook beef until no longer pink; drain. Add the remaining ingredients; bring to a boil.

Reduce heat; cover and simmer for 10-15 minutes or until the vegetables are tender. **Yield:** 6 servings.

Cheeseburger Soup

pictured at right

A local restaurant serves a similar soup but wouldn't share their recipe with me. So I developed my own, modifying a recipe for potato soup. I was really pleased at how good this all-American soup turned out.

Joanie Shawhan, Madison, Wisconsin

1/2 **pound ground beef**
3/4 **cup chopped onion**
3/4 **cup shredded carrots**

3/4 cup diced celery
1 teaspoon dried basil
1 teaspoon dried parsley flakes
4 tablespoons butter, *divided*
3 cups chicken broth
4 cups diced peeled potatoes (1-3/4 pounds)
1/4 cup all-purpose flour
8 ounces process cheese (Velveeta), cubed (2 cups)
1-1/2 cups milk
3/4 teaspoon salt
1/4 to 1/2 teaspoon pepper
1/4 cup sour cream

In a 3-qt. saucepan, cook beef over medium heat until no longer pink; drain and set aside. In the same saucepan, saute onion, carrots, celery, basil and parsley in 1 tablespoon butter until vegetables are tender, about 10 minutes.

Add broth, potatoes and beef; bring to a boil. Reduce heat; cover and simmer for 10-12 minutes or until potatoes are tender.

Meanwhile, in a small skillet, melt remaining butter. Add flour; cook and stir for 3-5 minutes or until bubbly. Add to soup; bring to a boil. Cook and stir for 2 minutes. Reduce heat to low. Add cheese, milk, salt and pepper; cook and stir until cheese melts. Remove from the heat; blend in sour cream. **Yield:** 8 servings (2-1/4 quarts).

Beefy Ramen Soup

pictured above

Take advantage of convenience items to prepare this hearty soup in a hurry. Bowls of the chunky mixture are chock-full of ground beef, noodles and vegetables.

Arlene Lynn, Lincoln, Nebraska

    1 **pound ground beef**
    1 **can (46 ounces) V8 juice**
    1 **envelope onion soup mix**
    1 **package (3 ounces) beef ramen noodles**
    1 **package (16 ounces) frozen mixed vegetables**

In a large saucepan, cook beef over medium heat until no longer pink; drain. Stir in the V8 juice, soup mix, contents of noodle seasoning packet and mixed vegetables.

Bring to a boil. Reduce heat; simmer, uncovered, for 6 minutes or until vegetables are tender. Return to a boil; stir in noodles. Cook for 3 minutes or until noodles are tender. **Yield:** 8 servings.

Rich Onion Beef Soup

When you're in the mood for soup that's big on beef flavor, reach for this robust recipe.

Nina Hall, Citrus Heights, California

      2 cups thinly sliced onions
      1 tablespoon butter
      2 cups cubed cooked lean beef
      2 cans (14-1/2 ounces *each*) beef broth
      3 tablespoons all-purpose flour
  1/2 teaspoon ground mustard
  1/2 teaspoon sugar
  1/2 cup dry red wine *or* additional beef
          broth
      1 teaspoon browning sauce

In a large saucepan, cook onions in butter over medium-low heat for 15-20 minutes or until tender and golden brown, stirring occasionally. Add beef and broth. Bring to a boil. Reduce heat; cover and simmer for 10 minutes.

In a small bowl, combine the flour, mustard and sugar; stir in wine or additional broth and browning sauce until smooth. Stir into soup. Bring to a boil; cook and stir for 1-2 minutes or until slightly thickened. **Yield:** 5 servings.

Cheesy Vegetable Soup

My husband doesn't care much for tomatoes, so I created this recipe that features lots of delicious cheese. We enjoy bowlfuls with fresh-from-the-oven corn bread.

Robin Counce, Arvada, Colorado

  1-1/2 pounds ground beef
      1 medium onion, chopped
      4 medium potatoes, peeled and cubed
      1 cup chopped carrots
      1 cup *each* frozen corn, peas and cut
          green beans
      4 cups water
      1 can (46 ounces) V8 juice
      2 pounds process cheese (Velveeta),
          cubed

In a soup kettle or Dutch oven, cook beef and onion over medium heat until meat is no longer pink; drain and set aside. Add vegetables and water to the kettle; bring to a boil.

Reduce heat; cover and simmer for 15-20 minutes or until vegetables are tender. Add V8 juice

and the beef mixture; heat through. Add cheese; cook and stir until melted. **Yield:** 16 servings (4 quarts).

Tortellini Soup
pictured below

This soup is unbelievably fast to make. For a creamy variation, I sometimes substitute cream of mushroom soup for the French onion soup.

Marsha Farley, Bangor, Maine

      1 pound ground beef
  3-1/2 cups water
      1 can (28 ounces) diced tomatoes,
          undrained
      1 can (10-1/2 ounces) condensed French
          onion soup, undiluted
      1 package (9 ounces) frozen cut green
          beans
      1 package (9 ounces) refrigerated
          cheese tortellini
      1 medium zucchini, chopped
      1 teaspoon dried basil

In a large saucepan, cook beef over medium heat until no longer pink; drain. Add the remaining ingredients; bring to a boil. Cook, uncovered, for 5 minutes or until heated through. **Yield:** 6-8 servings.

Creole Soup

pictured above

Special seasonings set this flavorful soup apart from any others I've tried. It makes a big batch, so it's perfect when feeding a crowd. Plus, the leftovers freeze well.

Del Mason, Martensville, Saskatchewan

  1 pound ground beef
  1 medium onion, finely chopped
  2 quarts water
  1 can (28 ounces) diced tomatoes, undrained
  3 cups shredded cabbage
  3 cups cubed peeled potatoes
  1 can (15-1/2 ounces) pork and beans
  1 can (11-1/8 ounces) condensed Italian tomato soup, undiluted
  1 can (4 ounces) mushroom stems and pieces, undrained
  1 cup sliced carrots
  1 cup chopped green pepper
  1 cup frozen peas
  3 celery ribs with leaves, finely chopped
  3 chicken bouillon cubes
  2 tablespoons dried parsley flakes
  1 teaspoon *each* Cajun seasoning, chili powder, Creole seasoning, pepper and crushed red pepper flakes
  1 bay leaf

In a soup kettle or Dutch oven, cook beef and onion over medium heat until meat is no longer pink; drain. Add the remaining ingredients; bring to a boil.

Reduce heat; simmer, uncovered, for 25 minutes or until vegetables are tender. Discard bay leaf before serving. **Yield:** 18 servings (4-1/2 quarts).

Easy Vegetable Soup

pictured below

We like to eat this tasty soup with tortilla chips. Canned tomatoes and beans and frozen vegetables give you a head start when preparing this recipe.

Jan Sharp, Blue Springs, Missouri

  1 pound ground beef
  1 medium onion, chopped
  1 can (28 ounces) diced tomatoes, undrained
  1 package (16 ounces) frozen vegetable blend of your choice
  1 can (16 ounces) kidney beans, undrained
  1 can (14-1/2 ounces) beef broth
  1 envelope taco seasoning
  1 garlic clove, minced
Shredded cheddar cheese, optional

In a large saucepan or Dutch oven, cook beef and onion over medium heat until meat is no longer pink; drain.

Add the tomatoes, vegetables, beans, broth, taco seasoning and garlic; bring to a boil. Reduce heat; simmer, uncovered, for 10 minutes. Garnish with cheese if desired. **Yield:** 10-12 servings (2-3/4 quarts).

Italian Wedding Soup
pictured at right

I'm not sure where the name of this soup originated, but my aunt in Pennsylvania shared the recipe with me. Even in our hot Florida climate, this soup always satisfies. Family and friends frequently ask me to prepare it.

Nancy Ducharme, Deltona, Florida

    1 egg
3/4 cup grated Parmesan *or* Romano
     cheese
1/2 cup dry bread crumbs
    1 small onion, chopped
3/4 teaspoon salt, *divided*
1-1/4 teaspoons pepper, *divided*
1-1/4 teaspoons garlic powder, *divided*
    2 pounds ground beef
    2 quarts chicken broth
1/3 cup chopped spinach
    1 teaspoon onion powder
    1 teaspoon dried parsley flakes
1-1/4 cups cooked medium shell pasta

In a bowl, combine the egg, cheese, bread crumbs, onion, 1/4 teaspoon salt, 1/4 teaspoon pepper and 1/4 teaspoon garlic powder. Crumble beef over mixture and mix well. Shape into 1-in. balls.

In a soup kettle or Dutch oven, cook the meatballs over medium heat until no longer pink; drain. Add the broth, spinach, onion powder, parsley, and remaining salt, pepper and garlic powder; bring to a boil. Reduce heat; simmer, uncovered, for 5 minutes. Stir in pasta; heat through. **Yield:** 12 servings (3 quarts).

Gingersnap Goulash

A friend shared this authentic recipe with me years ago. I think you'll enjoy the extra spice from the addition of gingersnaps. It wonderfully captures the flavor of sauerbraten.

Diane Hoffman, Brunswick, Nebraska

1-1/2 pounds beef stew meat, cut
     into 1-inch cubes
    2 quarts water
    1 cup chopped onion
  12 gingersnap cookies, crumbled
    2 tablespoons Worcestershire sauce
    2 tablespoons brown sugar
    1 teaspoon salt
1/4 teaspoon pepper
    1 bottle (14 ounces) ketchup

In a Dutch oven or soup kettle, brown the meat. Add the next seven ingredients and bring to a boil. Reduce heat; cover and simmer for 1 hour or until meat is tender. Add ketchup; cover and simmer for 1 hour, stirring occasionally. **Yield:** 8-10 servings (2-1/2 quarts).

"One **whiff** of a savory **aromatic** soup makes **appetites** come to **attention**."

appealing
PORK

Cajun Corn Soup

pictured below

I found this recipe years ago and substituted Cajun stewed tomatoes for a bolder taste. Now I prepare this dish for out-of-state guests who want to taste some Cajun food. Everyone who tries it gives it high marks. Plus, it's easy to prepare.

Sue Fontenot, Kinder, Louisiana

    1 cup chopped onion
    1 cup chopped green pepper
    6 green onions, sliced
  1/2 cup vegetable oil
  1/2 cup all-purpose flour
    3 cups water
    1 can (14-1/2 ounces) Cajun-style
      stewed tomatoes
    2 cups chopped peeled tomatoes
    1 can (6 ounces) tomato paste
    2 packages (16 ounces *each*) frozen
      whole kernel corn
    3 cups cubed cooked ham
1-1/2 pounds fully cooked smoked sausage,
      sliced
  1/8 teaspoon cayenne pepper *or* to taste
Salt to taste
Hot pepper sauce to taste

In a large kettle or Dutch oven, saute onion, green pepper and green onions in oil until tender, about 5 minutes. Add flour and cook until bubbly. Add water, stewed and chopped tomatoes and tomato paste; mix well.

Stir in the corn, ham, sausage, cayenne pepper, salt and hot pepper sauce. Bring to a boil, stirring frequently. Reduce heat; simmer, uncovered, for 1 hour, stirring occasionally. **Yield:** 12-14 servings.

Canadian Bacon Potato Soup

Canadian bacon adds a hint of smoky flavor to this hearty soup that my husband loves. It doesn't have the typical butter and heavy cream you'll find in many potato soups, but it's still rich and satisfying.

Cheryl Morgan, Dover, Minnesota

    2 medium onions, chopped
    4 medium potatoes, peeled and
      quartered
    2 cups chicken broth
    1 can (12 ounces) evaporated milk
    5 slices (3 ounces) Canadian bacon,
      chopped
    1 packet butter-flavored granules
  1/4 teaspoon salt
  1/8 teaspoon pepper
    7 tablespoons sour cream
  1/3 cup minced chives

In a large saucepan or Dutch oven coated with nonstick cooking spray, saute onions until tender. Add potatoes and broth; bring to a boil. Reduce heat; cover and simmer for 20-25 minutes or until potatoes are very tender. Set aside 1 cup potato mixture.

Puree remaining mixture in batches in a blender or food processor; return to the pan. Stir in the milk, Canadian bacon, butter-flavored granules, salt, pepper and reserved potato mixture. Heat through (do not boil). Garnish each serving with 1 tablespoon sour cream; sprinkle with chives. **Yield:** 7 servings.

Editor's Note: This recipe was tested with Butter Buds mix.

Hearty Minestrone
pictured above

This main dish gets its flavor from Italian sausage. Plus, it uses up a bounty of zucchini.

Donna Smith, Victor, New York

- 1 pound bulk Italian sausage
- 2 cups sliced celery
- 1 cup chopped onion
- 6 cups chopped zucchini
- 1 can (28 ounces) diced tomatoes, undrained
- 1-1/2 cups chopped green pepper
- 1-1/2 teaspoons Italian seasoning
- 1-1/2 teaspoons salt
- 1 teaspoon dried oregano
- 1 teaspoon sugar
- 1/2 teaspoon dried basil
- 1/4 teaspoon garlic powder

In a large saucepan, cook the sausage over medium heat until no longer pink. Remove with a slotted spoon to paper towel to drain, reserving 1 tablespoon of drippings.

Saute celery and onion in the drippings for 5 minutes. Add sausage and remaining ingredients; bring to a boil. Reduce heat; cover and simmer for 20-30 minutes or until the vegetables are tender. **Yield:** 9 servings.

Sauerkraut Soup

pictured at right

The medley of tomato, sauerkraut and smoked sausage gives this soup old-world flavor. It's enjoyable to make and serve, especially during these cold months.

Jean Marie Cornelius, Whitesville, New York

>   1 pound smoked Polish sausage, cut into 1/2-inch pieces
>   5 medium potatoes, peeled and cubed
>   2 medium onions, chopped
>   2 carrots, cut into 1/4-inch slices
>   3 cans (14-1/2 ounces *each*) chicken broth
>   1 can (32 ounces) sauerkraut, rinsed and drained
>   1 can (6 ounces) tomato paste

In a large saucepan or Dutch oven, combine sausage, potatoes, onions, carrots and chicken broth; bring to a boil.

Reduce heat; cover and simmer for 30 minutes or until potatoes are tender. Add sauerkraut and tomato paste; mix well. Return to a boil. Reduce heat; cover and simmer 30 minutes longer.

If a thinner soup is desired, add additional water or chicken broth. **Yield:** 8-10 servings (2-1/2 quarts).

Company's Coming Soup

This soup is great for entertaining because it can be assembled ahead and left to simmer. Plus, with fresh bread and salad, it's a satisfying meal that won't leave anyone hungry.

Roberta McHam, Hurst, Texas

>   1 pound (about 2 cups) dried 10-bean mix
>   2 quarts water
>   3 cups diced fully cooked ham
>   1 teaspoon salt
>   1/2 teaspoon pepper
>   1 can (10 ounces) diced tomatoes and green chilies, undrained
>   1 large onion, chopped

>   1/4 cup lemon juice
>   1 teaspoon garlic powder

Place beans and enough water to cover in a Dutch oven or soup kettle. Bring to a boil; boil for 2 minutes. Remove from the heat; let stand for 1 hour. Drain beans and discard liquid.

Return beans to kettle; add water, ham, salt and pepper. Bring to a boil. Reduce heat; cover and simmer for 60-70 minutes or until the beans are tender.

Add remaining ingredients; cover and simmer for 30 minutes or until onion is tender. **Yield:** 10-12 servings (3 quarts).

Basque Vegetable Soup

pictured at right

This is a hearty soup widely served here, especially at the many restaurants specializing in Basque cuisine. It's a nice way to use the abundant vegetables that are available this time of year. Give it a try this harvest season.

Norman Chegwyn, Richmond, California

3/4 pound Polish sausage, sliced
     1 broiler/fryer chicken (2 to 3 pounds)
     8 cups water
     2 leeks, sliced
     2 carrots, sliced
     1 large turnip, peeled and cubed
     1 large onion, chopped
     1 large potato, peeled and cubed
     1 garlic clove, minced
1-1/2 teaspoons salt
   1/2 teaspoon pepper
     1 tablespoon snipped fresh parsley
     1 teaspoon dried thyme
     1 cup shredded cabbage
     2 cups cooked navy or great northern
       beans

In a skillet, cook the sausage until done. Drain on paper towels; set aside. In a large Dutch oven, cook chicken in water until juices run clear. Remove chicken; let cool. Strain broth and skim off fat. Return the broth to Dutch oven.

Add leeks, carrots, turnip, onion, potato, garlic, salt, pepper, parsley and thyme. Bring to a boil. Reduce heat; cover and simmer for 30 minutes.

Meanwhile, remove chicken from bones and cut into bite-size pieces; add to the Dutch oven. Add cabbage, beans and cooked sausage. Simmer, uncovered, for about 30 minutes or until vegetables are tender. **Yield:** 10-12 servings.

Zippy Potato Soup
pictured above

This savory soup has a lot of substance, especially for the men in the family. We enjoy brimming bowls all winter long.

Clara Lee Parsons, Terre Haute, Indiana

   3/4 pound sliced bacon, diced
     1 medium onion, chopped
     8 to 10 potatoes, peeled and cut into
       chunks
     1 medium carrot, grated
     5 cups water
     1 can (12 ounces) evaporated milk
     2 tablespoons butter
4-1/2 teaspoons minced fresh parsley
     2 teaspoons Worcestershire sauce
   1/2 teaspoon ground mustard
   1/2 teaspoon ground nutmeg
   1/4 teaspoon salt
   1/8 to 1/4 teaspoon cayenne pepper

In a large skillet, cook bacon and onion; drain and set aside. In a soup kettle or Dutch oven, cook the potatoes and carrot in water for 20 minutes or until tender (do not drain).

Stir in the remaining ingredients and the bacon mixture. Cook for 10 minutes or until heated through. **Yield:** 14 servings (3-1/2 quarts).

kale, cream and sausage to soup; heat through (do not boil). **Yield:** 8 servings (2 quarts).

Sausage Kale Soup

pictured above

This zesty soup is sure to become a favorite with your guests. The spicier the seasoning in the sausage, the better the soup.

Nancy Dyer, Grove, Oklahoma

    1 pound uncooked Italian sausage links
  3/4 cup chopped onion
    1 bacon strip, diced
    2 garlic cloves, minced
    2 cups water
    1 can (14-1/2 ounces) chicken broth
    2 cups diced potatoes
    2 cups thinly sliced fresh kale *or* spinach
  1/3 cup heavy whipping cream

Place the sausages in an ungreased 15-in. x 10-in. x 1-in. baking pan; pierce casings. Bake at 300° for 20-25 minutes or until fully cooked. Drain; set aside to cool.

Meanwhile, in a saucepan, saute onion and bacon for 3 minutes or until onion is tender. Add garlic; saute for 1 minute. Add water, broth and potatoes; bring to a boil.

Reduce heat; cover and simmer for 20 minutes or until potatoes are tender. Cut sausages in half lengthwise, then into 1/4-in. slices. Add

Pasta Meatball Soup

pictured below

When time is tight, I whip up this soup. It has many things I have around the house, including pasta, prepared spaghetti sauce, canned vegetables and frozen meatballs. The chunky mixture simmers only a few minutes before it's ready to be ladled into bowls.

Beverly Menser, Madisonville, Kentucky

      1 cup uncooked spiral *or* shell pasta
     32 frozen Italian meatballs (about 1
        pound), thawed
      2 cans (14-1/2 ounces *each*) chicken
        broth
      1 can (28 ounces) diced tomatoes,
        undrained
  1-1/2 cups frozen sliced carrots, thawed
      1 can (16 ounces) kidney beans, rinsed
        and drained
      1 jar (14 ounces) meatless spaghetti
        sauce
      1 jar (4-1/2 ounces) sliced mushrooms,
        drained
      1 cup frozen peas

Cook pasta according to package directions. Meanwhile, combine the remaining ingredients in a soup kettle or Dutch oven.

Bring to a boil; cover and simmer for 5 minutes. Drain pasta and add to the soup; heat through. **Yield:** 10 servings (3 quarts).

Spaghetti Soup

With spaghetti sauce, noodles and Italian seasonings, this soup tastes like spaghetti! It's so easy, even our daughter can make it by herself.

Laura Braun, Appleton, Wisconsin

- 2 pounds bulk Italian sausage
- 1 cup chopped onion
- 1 garlic clove, minced
- 2 cans (14-1/2 ounces *each*) beef broth
- 1 jar (30 ounces) spaghetti sauce
- 1 can (15 ounces) sliced carrots, drained
- 1 can (14-1/2 ounces) Italian flat beans, drained
- 1 cup water
- 1 teaspoon Italian seasoning
- 1 teaspoon dried basil
- 3-1/2 cups cooked macaroni
- Grated Parmesan *or* shredded mozzarella cheese, optional

In a large saucepan or Dutch oven over medium heat, cook the sausage, onion and garlic until meat is no longer pink; drain.

Add the broth, spaghetti sauce, carrots, beans, water, Italian seasoning and basil; bring to a boil. Reduce heat; cover and simmer for 10-15 minutes.

Just before serving, add the macaroni and heat through. Garnish with cheese if desired. **Yield:** 12-14 servings (3 quarts).

Ham and Vegetable Soup
pictured above right

The basis for this soup's broth conveniently comes from canned bean soup. Everyone who tries this comments on how nicely the ham blends with the vegetables.

Helen Peterson, Rives Junction, Michigan

- 2 pounds smoked ham shanks
- 4 medium carrots, sliced
- 1 cup thinly sliced celery
- 1 medium onion, chopped
- 2 quarts water
- 2-1/2 cups diced unpeeled red potatoes
- 1 cup *each* frozen corn, peas and cut green beans
- 1 can (11-1/2 ounces) condensed bean and bacon soup, undiluted
- 1/4 teaspoon pepper

Place first five ingredients in a Dutch oven or soup kettle; bring to a boil. Reduce heat; cover and simmer for 2-1/2 hours or until meat falls off the bones. Add potatoes and vegetables; bring to a boil. Reduce heat; cover and simmer for 1 hour.

Remove shanks; allow to cool. Remove meat from bones and cut into bite-size pieces; discard bones.

Return meat to kettle. Stir in soup and pepper; heat through. **Yield:** 14-16 servings (4 quarts).

Italian Peasant Soup
pictured above

My father shared this recipe with me, and I use it whenever I need a satisfying, healthy meal. Loaded with sausage, chicken, beans and spinach, the quick soup is nice for special occasions, too.

Kim Knight, Hamburg, Pennsylvania

1 pound Italian sausage links, casings removed and cut into 1-inch slices
2 medium onions, chopped
6 garlic cloves, chopped
1 pound boneless skinless chicken breasts, cut into 1-inch cubes
2 cans (15 ounces *each*) cannellini *or* white kidney beans, rinsed and drained
2 cans (14-1/2 ounces *each*) chicken broth
2 cans (14-1/2 ounces *each*) diced tomatoes, undrained
1 teaspoon dried basil
1 teaspoon dried oregano
6 cups fresh spinach leaves, chopped
Shredded Parmesan cheese, optional

In a Dutch oven or soup kettle, cook sausage over medium heat until no longer pink; drain. Add onions and garlic; saute until tender. Add chicken; cook and stir until no longer pink. Stir in beans, broth, tomatoes, basil and oregano.

Cook, uncovered, for 10 minutes. Add the spinach and heat just until wilted. Serve with Parmesan cheese if desired. **Yield:** 11 servings (2-3/4 quarts).

Cabbage Sausage Soup

pictured below

We grow 300 acres of cabbage on the Lewis Taylor Farms. My wife, our two daughters and I eat lots of that leafy crop. This hearty, savory soup showcases cabbage in a pretty tomato broth.

Bill Brim, Tifton, Georgia

1 pound bulk Italian sausage
1 large onion, chopped
2 garlic cloves, minced
7 cups chopped cabbage (about 1-1/2 pounds)
4 cans (28 ounces *each*) diced tomatoes, undrained
2 teaspoons dried basil

2 teaspoons brown sugar
1 teaspoon dried oregano
1 bay leaf
3/4 teaspoon minced fresh rosemary *or* 1/4 teaspoon dried rosemary, crushed
1/2 teaspoon salt
1/8 teaspoon pepper

In a Dutch oven or soup kettle, cook sausage, onion and garlic over medium heat until meat is no longer pink. Add cabbage; cook and stir for 3-5 minutes or until cabbage is crisp-tender.

Stir in the remaining ingredients. Bring to a boil. Reduce heat; cover and simmer for 30-35 minutes or until cabbage is tender. Discard bay leaf before serving. **Yield:** 16 servings (4 quarts).

Cauliflower Pork Soup

This recipe was given to me by a friend several years ago. Everyone enjoys it, even my husband, who typically doesn't care for cauliflower.

Loretta Wohlenhaus, Cumberland, Iowa

1 pound ground pork
1 small head cauliflower, broken into florets
2 cups water
1/2 cup chopped onion
2 cups milk, *divided*
1/4 cup all-purpose flour
2 cups (8 ounces) shredded sharp cheddar cheese
1/2 teaspoon salt
1/8 teaspoon pepper
Chopped chives, optional

In a skillet, cook pork over medium heat until no longer pink; drain and set aside. In a large kettle or Dutch oven, cook cauliflower in water for 10 minutes or until tender. Do not drain. Add pork, onion and 1-1/4 cups milk to cauliflower.

In a small bowl, combine flour and remaining milk until smooth; stir into cauliflower mixture. Bring to a boil; boil and stir for 2 minutes. Remove from heat; add cheese, salt and pepper, stirring until cheese melts. Garnish with chives if desired. **Yield:** 6-8 servings (2 quarts).

Sunday Gumbo

pictured at right

With sausage, chicken and shrimp plus rice, a medley of vegetables and the heat of cayenne, this soup is one my husband and I enjoy for dinner many Sunday evenings. It's wonderful with crusty bread.

Debbie Burchette, Summitville, Indiana

    1 pound Italian sausage links, sliced
    1 pound boneless skinless chicken
      breasts, cubed
    3 tablespoons vegetable oil
    1 medium sweet red pepper, chopped
    1 medium onion, chopped
    3 celery ribs, chopped
    1 teaspoon dried marjoram
    1 teaspoon dried thyme
  1/2 teaspoon garlic powder
  1/2 teaspoon cayenne pepper
    3 cans (14-1/2 ounces *each*) chicken
      broth
  2/3 cup uncooked brown rice
    1 can (14-1/2 ounces) diced tomatoes,
      undrained
    1 pound uncooked medium shrimp,
      peeled and deveined
    2 cups frozen sliced okra

In a Dutch oven, brown sausage and chicken in oil. Remove with a slotted spoon and keep warm. In the drippings, saute red pepper, onion and celery until tender.

Stir in the seasonings; cook for 5 minutes. Stir in the broth, rice and sausage mixture; bring to a boil. Reduce heat; cover and simmer for 20-25 minutes or until rice is tender.

Stir in tomatoes, shrimp and okra; cook for 10 minutes or until shrimp turn pink, stirring occasionally. **Yield:** 16 servings (about 4 quarts).

Split Pea and Ham Soup

Not a winter goes by that I don't fix at least one batch of this traditional pea soup. It's a hot and filling meal that really warms up my family.

Lucille Schreiber, Gleason, Wisconsin

    1 pound (about 2 cups) dried green
      split peas
    7 cups water
    1 teaspoon vegetable oil
    1 teaspoon salt
    2 cups diced fully cooked ham
    2 cups chopped carrots
    1 cup chopped celery
    1 cup chopped onion
    1 cup diced peeled potato
  1/2 teaspoon garlic powder
  1/2 teaspoon pepper
  1/4 cup chopped fresh parsley

In a Dutch oven or soup kettle, bring peas, water, oil and salt if desired to a boil. Reduce heat; cover and simmer for 2 hours, stirring occasionally.

Add the next seven ingredients; cover and simmer for 30 minutes or until the vegetables are tender. Stir in parsley. **Yield:** 8-10 servings (2-3/4 quarts).

Canadian Cheese Soup

pictured at right

My family loves Canadian bacon but few dishes call for this pork product. Everyone was thrilled the first time I offered this succulent soup.

Jolene Roudebush, Troy, Michigan

3 cups chicken broth
4 medium potatoes, peeled and diced
2 celery ribs, diced
1 medium carrot, diced
1 small onion, diced
6 ounces Canadian bacon, trimmed and diced
2 tablespoons butter
2 tablespoons all-purpose flour
1 cup milk
2 cups (8 ounces) shredded cheddar cheese
1/8 teaspoon pepper

In a Dutch oven or soup kettle, combine the first five ingredients; bring to a boil. Reduce heat; cover and simmer for 20 minutes or until vegetables are very tender. With a potato masher, mash vegetables several times. Add bacon; continue to simmer.

Meanwhile, melt butter in a small saucepan; stir in the flour and cook, stirring constantly, for 1 minute. Gradually whisk in milk.

Bring to a boil; boil and stir for 2 minutes (mixture will be thick). Add to vegetable mixture, stirring constantly.

Remove from the heat; add cheese and pepper. Stir just until cheese is melted. **Yield:** 8 servings (2 quarts).

Creamed Cabbage Soup

Here's a delicious use of the ham and cabbage combination. A thick and hearty soup combined with subtle flavors, it is a favorite meal on our table during the winter months.

Laurie Harms, Grinnell, Iowa

2 cups chicken broth
1 medium onion, diced
1 cup diced celery
1 medium head cabbage, shredded
1 carrot, diced
1/4 cup butter
3 tablespoons all-purpose flour
1 cup milk
2 cups half-and-half cream
2 cups diced fully cooked ham
1-1/2 teaspoons salt
1/4 teaspoon pepper
1/2 teaspoon dried thyme
Chopped fresh parsley

In a large kettle, combine broth and vegetables. Cover and simmer until vegetables are tender, about 20 minutes.

In a saucepan, melt butter; stir in flour. Gradually add milk and cream; cook and stir until thickened. Stir into vegetable mixture.

Add the ham, salt, pepper and thyme; heat through. Garnish with parsley. **Yield:** 6-8 servings (2 quarts).

Creamy Ham and Asparagus Soup

pictured above

Like most country cooks, I often bake a large ham so that I can use leftovers in tasty dishes like this. Fresh asparagus is wonderful in this soup's creamy broth.

Maurine Kent, Kilgore, Texas

1-1/2 cups fresh asparagus pieces
    1 medium carrot, julienned
    2 tablespoons butter
    3 small white onions, quartered
    2 tablespoons all-purpose flour
    1 cup milk
    1 cup chicken broth
    1 cup cubed fully cooked ham
    1 jar (2-1/2 ounces) sliced mushrooms, drained
    1 cup half-and-half cream
Salt and pepper to taste
Grated Parmesan cheese, optional
Chopped fresh parsley, optional

Place asparagus in a saucepan with enough water to cover; cook until crisp-tender. Drain and set aside.

In a heavy saucepan, saute carrot in butter for 3-5 minutes; add onions and saute 2 minutes longer or until tender.

Stir in flour; gradually add milk. Bring to a boil; boil and stir for 2 minutes. Add broth, ham, mushrooms and reserved asparagus.

Reduce heat; add cream. Heat through but do not boil. Add salt and pepper. Garnish with Parmesan cheese and parsley if desired. **Yield:** 4 servings.

Black-Eyed Pea Soup

Since we raise our own pigs, I like to use ground pork in this zesty soup. But I've used ground beef with equally good results. Green chilies give this dish some Southwestern flair.

Mary Lou Chernik, Taos, New Mexico

1-1/2 pounds ground pork
    1 large onion, chopped
    2 garlic cloves, minced
    3 cans (15-1/2 ounces *each*) black-eyed peas, rinsed and drained
    2 cups water
    1 can (14-1/2 ounces) stewed tomatoes
    1 can (10 ounces) diced tomatoes and green chilies
    1 can (4 ounces) chopped green chilies
    1 tablespoon beef bouillon granules
    1 tablespoon molasses
    1 teaspoon Worcestershire sauce
  1/2 teaspoon salt
  1/4 teaspoon pepper
  1/4 teaspoon ground cumin

In a large soup kettle or Dutch oven, cook the pork, onion and garlic over medium heat until meat is no longer pink; drain.

Stir in the remaining ingredients; bring to a boil. Reduce heat; cover and simmer for 45 minutes. **Yield:** 12 servings (about 3 quarts).

Italian Zucchini Soup

pictured below

This recipe was given to me by my neighbor. Nice and simple, it's a good way to use a lot of your zucchini and other garden vegetables. It freezes well and is great to have on hand on a cold winter day.

Clara Mae Chambers, Superior, Nebraska

    1 pound bulk Italian sausage
    1 cup chopped onion
    2 cups chopped celery
    1 medium green pepper, chopped
    2 to 4 tablespoons sugar
    2 teaspoons salt
  1/2 teaspoon dried basil
  1/2 teaspoon dried oregano
  1/2 teaspoon pepper
    1 quart canned tomatoes, cut up
    4 cups diced zucchini
Grated Parmesan cheese, optional

In a Dutch oven, cook sausage and onion over medium heat until meat is no longer pink; drain. Add the next eight ingredients; cover and simmer for 1 hour.

Stir in zucchini and simmer for 10 minutes. Sprinkle with grated Parmesan cheese if desired. **Yield:** 2 quarts.

Add the pepperoni, red and green peppers, mushrooms, garlic, sage, basil, oregano, salt and pepper. Cover and simmer for 10 minutes or until vegetables are tender.

Ladle soup into ovenproof bowls. Top each with a slice of bread and sprinkle with mozzarella cheese.

Broil 4 in. from the heat until the cheese is melted and bubbly. **Yield:** 10 servings (about 2-1/2 quarts).

French Bread Pizza Soup

pictured above

This robust soup is a family favorite, and it's a big hit with my canasta group as well. I top each bowl with a slice of toasted bread and cheese, but you can have fun incorporating other pizza toppings such as cooked sausage.

Jackie Brossard, Kitchener, Ontario

> 2 cans (14-1/2 ounces *each*) diced tomatoes, undrained
> 2 cans (10-3/4 ounces *each*) condensed tomato soup, undiluted
> 2-1/2 cups water
> 1 package (3-1/2 ounces) sliced pepperoni, quartered
> 1 medium sweet red pepper, chopped
> 1 medium green pepper, chopped
> 1 cup sliced fresh mushrooms
> 2 garlic cloves, minced
> 1/2 teaspoon rubbed sage
> 1/2 teaspoon dried basil
> 1/2 teaspoon dried oregano
> Salt and pepper to taste
> 10 slices French bread, toasted
> 1-1/2 cups (6 ounces) shredded mozzarella cheese

In a Dutch oven or soup kettle, bring the tomatoes, soup and water to a boil. Reduce heat; cover and simmer for 15 minutes. Mash with a potato masher.

Ham and Chicken Gumbo

I've always enjoyed spending time in the kitchen and worked as a home economist for a utility company in the 1940s. With two kinds of meat, this gumbo makes a hearty supper.

Jean Leonard, Farmington, New Mexico

> 6 bacon strips, cut into 1/2-inch pieces
> 3/4 cup chopped onion
> 2 garlic cloves, minced
> 1 cup diced fully cooked ham
> 1/2 cup diced cooked chicken
> 2 cups frozen cut okra
> 1 can (14-1/2 ounces) diced tomatoes, undrained
> 2 cups chicken broth
> 1 teaspoon Worcestershire sauce
> 1/4 teaspoon salt
> 8 drops hot pepper sauce
> Hot cooked rice

In a large skillet, cook bacon just until crisp. Add onion and cook, stirring constantly, until bacon is crisp and onion is soft. Add the garlic, ham and chicken; cook for 2 minutes, stirring constantly.

Stir in the okra, tomatoes and broth; bring to a boil. Reduce the heat; cover and simmer for 30 minutes.

Add the Worcestershire sauce, salt and hot pepper sauce. Serve the gumbo over rice. **Yield:** 4 servings.

Best-Ever Potato Soup

pictured below

You'll be surprised at the taste of this rich, cheesy concoction—it's not a typical potato soup. I came up with the recipe after enjoying baked potato soup at one of our favorite restaurants. I added bacon, and we think that makes it even better.

Coleen Morrissey, Sweet Valley, Pennsylvania

      6 bacon strips, diced
      3 cups cubed peeled potatoes
      1 can (14-1/2 ounces) chicken broth
      1 small carrot, grated
  1/2 cup chopped onion
      1 tablespoon dried parsley flakes
  1/2 teaspoon *each* celery seed, salt and
         pepper
      3 tablespoons all-purpose flour
      3 cups milk
      8 ounces process cheese (Velveeta),
         cubed
      2 green onions, thinly sliced, optional

In a large saucepan, cook bacon until crisp; drain. Add potatoes, broth, carrot, onion, parsley, celery seed, salt and pepper. Cover and simmer until potatoes are tender, about 15 minutes.

Combine flour and milk until smooth; add to soup. Bring to a boil; boil and stir for 2 minutes.

Add cheese; stir until cheese is melted and the soup is heated through. Garnish with green onions if desired. **Yield:** 8 servings (2 quarts).

Confetti Soup

I created this recipe when I was trying to think of something new and interesting to serve my family. They never cared much for vegetables until they tried this delicious soup.

Nancy Olson, Belgrade, Minnesota

      1 cup diced carrots
      1 cup diced rutabaga
  1/2 cup chopped celery
  1/2 cup broccoli florets
  1/2 cup cauliflowerets
  1/2 cup chopped onion
      3 tablespoons water
      3 tablespoons butter, optional
      1 cup cubed process cheese (Velveeta)
      1 cup frozen whole kernel corn
  1/2 cup frozen peas
  1/2 cup diced fully cooked ham
      5 cups milk
  1-1/2 teaspoons salt
  1/2 teaspoon pepper
  1/4 teaspoon sugar

In a microwave-safe 3-qt. baking dish, combine carrots, rutabaga, celery, broccoli, cauliflower, onion, water and butter if desired.

Cover and microwave on high for 14 minutes or until vegetables are just tender, stirring three times during cooking.

Stir in cheese, corn, peas and ham; cover and let stand for 1 minute. Add the milk, salt, pepper and sugar.

Cover and microwave on medium-high, stirring three times, for 8-10 minutes or until cheese is melted and soup is heated through (do not boil). **Yield:** 8 servings (2 quarts).

Zucchini Sausage Soup

pictured below

I've received numerous 4-H cooking awards in past years and often cook for the family...much to my mom's delight!

Lindsay Gibson, New Springfield, Ohio

       12 ounces pork breakfast sausage links
        1 cup chopped celery
      1/2 cup chopped onion
        1 pound zucchini, sliced
        3 cans (14-1/2 ounces *each*) stewed
           tomatoes
        1 can (14-1/2 ounces) chicken broth
        2 teaspoons garlic powder
        1 teaspoon salt
      1/2 teaspoon dried oregano
      1/2 teaspoon Italian seasoning
      1/2 teaspoon sugar
      1/4 teaspoon dried basil
        1 medium green pepper, chopped

Cut sausage into 1/4-in. slices; brown in a Dutch oven or soup kettle. Add celery and onion; saute until tender. Drain.

Stir in the next nine ingredients. Bring to a boil; reduce heat and simmer for 35 minutes. Add green pepper and simmer for 10 minutes. **Yield:** 6-8 servings (2 quarts).

Mock Minestrone

Don't let the number of ingredients in this recipe fool you. The bulk of the items are combined all at once and simmered, making this a no-fuss favorite.

Jorja Hutton, Sturgeon Bay, Wisconsin

        2 pounds bulk Italian sausage
        1 large onion, chopped
        1 garlic clove, minced
        6 cups water
        1 jar (30 ounces) chunky spaghetti sauce
        2 cans (10-3/4 ounces *each*) condensed
           beef broth, undiluted
        1 can (15 ounces) garbanzo beans,
           rinsed and drained
        1 package (10 ounces) frozen chopped
           spinach, thawed and squeezed dry
        1 cup diced zucchini
        1 cup thinly sliced carrots
    1-1/2 teaspoons dried basil
      1/2 teaspoon pepper
        4 cups cooked pasta
Grated Parmesan cheese, optional

In a Dutch oven or soup kettle, cook sausage, onion and garlic over medium heat until sausage is no longer pink and onion is tender; drain. Stir in the next nine ingredients.

Simmer for 20 minutes. Add pasta and heat through. Garnish with cheese if desired. **Yield:** 20-22 servings (5-1/2 quarts).

Quick Wild Rice Soup

While my mother helped out on the family farm, I took over in the kitchen and have been cooking ever since. I often serve this soup with a loaf of warm bread.

Jane Meyer, Linn, Kansas

       10 bacon strips
        1 medium onion, chopped
        1 box (6-3/4 ounces) quick-cooking long
           grain and wild rice mix
        2 cans (10-3/4 ounces *each*) condensed
           cream of potato soup, undiluted
        4 cups milk
        2 cups cubed process cheese (Velveeta)

2 teaspoons garlic powder
2 teaspoons Worcestershire sauce
1/2 teaspoon onion powder
1/4 teaspoon pepper
Dash Liquid Smoke, optional
1 cup (8 ounces) sour cream
Shredded cheddar cheese

Peel and dice the baked potatoes; set aside. In a Dutch oven or soup kettle, cook the bacon over medium heat until crisp. Using a slotted spoon, remove to paper towels. Drain, reserving 1-1/2 teaspoons drippings.

Add the soups, milk, garlic powder, Worcestershire sauce, onion powder, pepper, Liquid Smoke if desired and reserved potatoes to the drippings.

Cook, uncovered, for 10 minutes or until heated through, stirring occasionally. Stir in sour cream; cook for 1-2 minutes or until heated through (do not boil). Garnish with cheddar cheese and bacon. **Yield:** 10 servings (2-1/2 quarts).

In a large skillet, cook bacon until crisp; remove to paper towels to drain. Reserve 1 teaspoon drippings; saute onion in drippings.

In a large kettle or Dutch oven, cook rice according to package directions; stir in soup, milk, cheese and onion. Crumble eight strips of bacon; add to soup.

Cook and stir over low heat until cheese is melted. Crumble remaining bacon and sprinkle over soup. **Yield:** 6-8 servings (2-1/2 quarts).

Creamy Potato Soup
pictured above

I came up with this comforting soup when I was crunched for time and wanted to use up leftover baked potatoes. Since then, it has become a mealtime staple. Its wonderful aroma always gets cheers from my husband when he arrives home from work.

Julie Smithouser, Colorado Springs, Colorado

3 to 4 medium baking potatoes, baked
5 bacon strips, diced
2 cans (10-3/4 ounces *each*) condensed cream of potato soup, undiluted
1 can (10-3/4 ounces) condensed cheddar cheese soup, undiluted
3-1/2 cups milk

Oven-Baked Bean Soup

When I know I have a busy day ahead of me, I reach for this recipe. I just pop this soup in the oven early in the day and have a delicious ready-to-eat meal all set for supper.

Delores Anderson, Woodburn, Oregon

1 pound dried navy beans
1-1/4 pounds fully cooked ham, diced
3 quarts water
2 cans (8 ounces *each*) tomato sauce
1 cup *each* diced onion, celery and carrot
2 teaspoons chili powder
2 teaspoons salt
1 teaspoon dried marjoram
1/4 teaspoon pepper

Combine all ingredients in a 6-qt. ovenproof Dutch oven. Cover and bake at 350° for 4-1/2 to 5 hours or until beans are tender. **Yield:** 14-18 servings (4-1/2 quarts).

appealing PORK

Baked Potato Soup
pictured above

This recipe was given to me by a dear friend with whom I taught school. She came to Texas from Michigan, and I from Oklahoma. Her entire family has become very special to me. I think of them whenever I make this rich savory soup.

Loretha Bringle, Garland, Texas

> 2/3 cup butter
> 2/3 cup all-purpose flour
> 7 cups milk
> 4 large baking potatoes, baked, cooled, peeled and cubed (about 4 cups)

> 4 green onions, sliced
> 12 bacon strips, cooked and crumbled
> 1-1/4 cups shredded cheddar cheese
> 1 cup (8 ounces) sour cream
> 3/4 teaspoon salt
> 1/2 teaspoon pepper

In a large soup kettle or Dutch oven, melt the butter. Stir in flour; heat and stir until smooth. Gradually add milk, stirring constantly until thickened. Add potatoes and onions.

Bring to a boil, stirring constantly. Reduce heat; simmer for 10 minutes. Add remaining ingredients; stir until cheese is melted. Serve immediately. **Yield:** 8-10 servings (2-1/2 quarts).

92

Hearty Ham Borscht

I like to keep a big pot of this borscht simmering on the stove during busy times on the farm. That way, folks can dip into the kettle when they have a chance to sit down for a quick meal.

Joanne Kukurudz, River Hills, Manitoba

> 1 meaty ham bone *or* 2 smoked ham hocks
> 6 cups water
> 2 cups diced fully cooked ham
> 3 cups chopped cooked beets
> 1 can (14 ounces) pork and beans
> 1 can (10-3/4 ounces) condensed tomato soup, undiluted
> 1 cup frozen peas
> 1 cup chopped carrots
> 1 cup frozen cut green beans
> 1 medium onion, chopped
> 2 to 3 tablespoons snipped fresh dill *or* 1 tablespoon dill weed
>
> Sour cream, optional

Place ham bone and water in a Dutch oven or soup kettle; bring to a boil. Reduce heat; cover and simmer for 1-1/2 hours.

Remove ham bone; allow to cool. Remove meat from bone and cut into bite-size pieces; discard bone. Return meat to kettle.

Add the ham, beets, pork and beans, soup, peas, carrots, beans, onion and dill. Cover and simmer for 45 minutes or until vegetables are tender. Garnish with sour cream if desired. **Yield:** 12-14 servings (3-1/2 quarts).

Kielbasa Bean Soup

pictured at right

I usually make a double batch of this meaty vegetable soup and freeze some in serving-size containers. It makes a nice meal for hectic days or unexpected guests.

Emily Chaney, Penobscot, Maine

> 4-1/2 cups water
> 2 cans (14-1/2 ounces *each*) diced tomatoes, undrained

> 1 can (16 ounces) kidney beans, rinsed and drained
> 1 can (15-1/2 ounces) great northern beans, rinsed and drained
> 1 can (15 ounces) garbanzo beans *or* chickpeas, rinsed and drained
> 2 medium green peppers, chopped
> 2 medium onions, chopped
> 2 celery ribs, chopped
> 1 medium zucchini, sliced
> 2 teaspoons chicken bouillon granules
> 2 garlic cloves, minced
> 2-1/2 teaspoons chili powder
> 2 teaspoons dried basil
> 1-1/2 teaspoons salt
> 1/2 teaspoon pepper
> 2 bay leaves
> 3/4 pound fully cooked kielbasa *or* Polish sausage, halved lengthwise and sliced

In a soup kettle or Dutch oven, combine the first 16 ingredients. Bring to a boil. Reduce heat; cover and simmer for 1 hour. Add sausage and heat through. Discard bay leaves. **Yield:** 12 servings (about 3 quarts).

Spicy Zucchini Soup

pictured at right

My files are overflowing with recipes I keep meaning to try. So when I encountered a bumper crop of zucchini, I finally reached for this recipe. We look forward to it each summer.

Catherine Johnston, Stafford, New York

1 pound bulk Italian sausage
3 cans (28 ounces *each*) diced tomatoes, undrained
3 cans (14-1/2 ounces *each*) beef broth
2 pounds zucchini, diced
2 medium green peppers, diced
2 cups thinly sliced celery
1 cup chopped onion
2 teaspoons Italian seasoning
1 teaspoon dried basil
1 teaspoon dried oregano
1 teaspoon salt
1/2 teaspoon sugar
1/4 teaspoon pepper
1/4 teaspoon garlic powder
3 cups cooked macaroni

In a Dutch oven or soup kettle, cook sausage over medium heat until no longer pink; drain. Add the tomatoes, broth, zucchini, green peppers, celery, onion and seasonings; bring to a boil.

Reduce heat; cover and simmer for 1-1/4 to 1-1/2 hours or until vegetables are tender. Add macaroni; heat through. **Yield:** 14-16 servings (4 quarts).

Hearty Tortellini Soup

Once you brown the sausage, it's a snap to throw in the other ingredients and let them simmer. Frozen tortellini is added minutes before serving for a savory soup that tastes like you spent hours making it.

Diana Laubon, Minerva, Ohio

3 uncooked Italian sausage links (1/2 to 3/4 pound)
1 quart water
2 cans (14-1/2 ounces *each*) Italian stewed tomatoes

1 can (10-1/2 ounces) condensed French onion soup, undiluted
2 cups broccoli coleslaw mix
1 cup frozen cut green beans
2 cups frozen cheese tortellini
Grated Parmesan cheese, optional

Cut sausage into 3/4-in. pieces; brown in a Dutch oven or soup kettle. Drain. Add water, tomatoes, soup, coleslaw mix and beans; bring to a boil. Reduce heat; cover and simmer for 20-25 minutes or until vegetables are tender.

Uncover; add tortellini. Cook for 3-5 minutes or until pasta is tender. Garnish with Parmesan cheese if desired. **Yield:** 10-12 servings (about 3 quarts).

Editor's Note: Broccoli coleslaw mix may be found in the produce section of most grocery stores.

Garden Vegetable Soup

This soup is packed with energy, yet has a nice, mild flavor. The recipe makes a whole gallon, but don't worry about leftovers—like most soups, it's great reheated!

Kelly Rettiger, Emporia, Kansas

1-1/2 cups chopped onion
1 cup chopped leeks

- 1 garlic clove, minced
- 1 tablespoon vegetable oil
- 8 cups chicken broth
- 8 cups cubed peeled potatoes
- 4 carrots, sliced
- 2 cups diced turnips
- 2 cups sliced mushrooms
- 6 ounces spinach, cut into thin strips
- 1 pound smoked Polish sausage, thinly sliced and browned
- 1 package (8 ounces) pasta wheels, cooked and drained
- 1/2 teaspoon salt
- 1/4 teaspoon pepper
- Grated Parmesan cheese, optional

In a large soup kettle or Dutch oven, cook onion, leeks and garlic in oil until tender, about 5 minutes. Add chicken broth, potatoes, carrots, turnips and mushrooms.

Cover and cook over low heat until vegetables are tender, about 30-40 minutes. Add spinach and sausage; cook for 10 minutes. Add pasta, salt and pepper; heat through. Serve with Parmesan cheese if desired. **Yield:** 16 servings (1 gallon).

Jiffy Jambalaya

My husband and I make this nicely spiced combination when we're pressed for time.

Carolyn Gubser, Waukesha, Wisconsin

- 1 medium onion, chopped
- 1/2 cup chopped green pepper
- 2 tablespoons vegetable oil
- 1 pound fully cooked kielbasa *or* Polish sausage, cut into 1/4-inch slices
- 1 can (28 ounces) diced tomatoes, undrained
- 1/2 cup water
- 1 tablespoon sugar
- 1 teaspoon paprika
- 1/2 teaspoon dried thyme
- 1/2 teaspoon dried oregano
- 1/4 teaspoon garlic powder
- 3 drops hot pepper sauce
- 1-1/2 cups uncooked instant rice

In a skillet, saute onion and green pepper in oil until tender. Stir in the sausage, tomatoes, water, sugar and seasonings. Bring to a boil; add the rice. Cover and cook for 5 minutes or until the rice is tender. **Yield:** 6 servings.

Carrot Cheese Soup

pictured below

I thought this sounded like a compatible mix of ingredients when I read the recipe for the first time—and it is delicious. It's a pretty color and makes a hearty soup to serve during the winter months.

Terese Snyder, Marquette, Michigan

- 2 to 3 tablespoons butter
- 2 tablespoons all-purpose flour
- 1 medium carrot, diced
- 2 green onions, sliced
- 2 tablespoons diced fully cooked ham
- 2 cups hot chicken broth
- 1/3 cup shredded cheddar cheese
- 1 tablespoon minced fresh parsley
- 1/8 teaspoon pepper
- Dash hot pepper sauce

In a saucepan, melt the butter; stir in flour until smooth. Cook and stir over medium heat for 2 minutes.

Add carrot, onions and ham; cook and stir for 1 minute. Gradually add broth. Bring to a boil; boil and stir for 2 minutes.

Add the cheese, parsley, pepper and hot pepper sauce; heat until the cheese is melted and the vegetables are tender. **Yield:** 2 servings.

appealing PORK

Parmesan Potato Soup

pictured above

Even my husband, who's not much of a soup eater, and our two boys likes this recipe. With crusty bread and a salad, it's a satisfying meal.

Tami Walters, Kingsport, Tennessee

  4 medium baking potatoes (about 2 pounds)
3/4 cup chopped onion
1/2 cup butter
1/2 cup all-purpose flour
1/2 teaspoon dried basil
1/2 teaspoon seasoned salt
1/4 teaspoon celery salt
1/4 teaspoon garlic powder
1/4 teaspoon onion salt
1/4 teaspoon pepper
1/4 teaspoon rubbed sage
1/4 teaspoon dried thyme
4-1/2 cups chicken broth
  6 cups milk
3/4 to 1 cup grated Parmesan cheese
 10 bacon strips, cooked and crumbled

Pierce potatoes with a fork; bake in the oven or microwave until tender. Cool, peel and cube; set aside.

In a large Dutch oven or soup kettle over medium heat, saute onion in butter until tender. Stir in flour and seasonings. Gradually add broth, stirring constantly. Bring to a boil; cook and stir for 2 minutes.

Add potatoes; return to a boil. Reduce heat; cover and simmer for 10 minutes. Add milk and cheese; heat through. Stir in bacon. **Yield:** 10-12 servings.

Navy Bean Soup

My kids can't resist their grandmother's bean soup. A touch of nutmeg sets it apart from all other kinds.

Melissa Stuchlik, Lincolnville, Kansas

    1 pound dried navy beans
    2 quarts water
1-1/2 to 2 pounds smoked ham hocks
    1 cup chopped onion
  1/4 cup chopped fresh parsley
1-1/2 teaspoons salt
    1 teaspoon dried basil
  1/2 teaspoon dried oregano
  1/2 teaspoon pepper
  1/4 teaspoon ground nutmeg
    1 bay leaf
    2 cups thinly sliced carrots
    1 cup chopped celery
  3/4 cup mashed potato flakes

Place beans and enough water to cover in a Dutch oven or soup kettle. Bring to a boil; boil for 2 minutes. Remove from the heat; let stand for 1 hour. Drain beans and discard liquid.

Return beans to kettle; add water, ham hocks, onion, parsley and seasonings. Bring to a boil. Reduce heat; cover and simmer for 1 hour or until beans are tender.

Add carrots, celery and potato flakes; mix well. Cover and simmer for 30 minutes or until vegetables are tender.

Remove bay leaf. Remove ham hocks; allow to cool. Remove meat from bones and cut into bite-size pieces. Discard bones. Return meat to kettle; heat through. **Yield:** 12-14 servings (3-1/2 quarts).

Creamy Wild Rice Soup

pictured below

Whenever I make this soup in the morning, it's gone by evening. Friends and family alike rave about the unbeatable combination of down-home flavors. I can't count the number of requests I've had for the recipe!

Patricia Batchelder, Fond du Lac, Wisconsin

    3/4 cup uncooked wild rice
      1 tablespoon vegetable oil
      1 quart water
    1/2 teaspoon salt
      1 medium onion, chopped
      1 celery rib, sliced
      1 medium carrot, sliced
    1/2 cup butter
    1/2 cup all-purpose flour
      3 cups chicken broth
      2 cups half-and-half cream
      1 cup diced fully cooked ham
    1/2 teaspoon dried rosemary
    1/4 teaspoon pepper

In a soup kettle or Dutch oven over medium heat, saute rice in oil for 5 minutes. Add water and salt; bring to a boil.

Reduce heat; cover and simmer for 35 minutes (rice will not be completely cooked). Drain, reserving 1-1/2 cups cooking liquid; set rice and liquid aside separately.

In the same kettle, saute onion, celery and carrot in butter until onion is transparent. Reduce heat; stir in flour and cook until bubbly.

Gradually add broth and cooking liquid; stirring constantly. Bring to a boil; boil for 2 minutes, stirring constantly.

Add cream, ham, rosemary, pepper and rice. Reduce heat; cover and simmer for 30-35 minutes or until rice is tender. **Yield:** 8 servings (2 quarts).

Potato and Cabbage Soup

I can trace this recipe back to my great-grandmother whose parents were potato farmers in Ireland. Although I include ham in my soup, my grandmother didn't...especially during the Depression. It's a filling soup that's wonderful with homemade bread.

Pat Rimmel, Ford City, Pennsylvania

      1 large onion, chopped
      2 tablespoons butter
    10 cups water
      6 cups chopped cabbage
      4 cups diced peeled potatoes
      3 tablespoons chicken bouillon
        granules
    1/2 teaspoon coarsely ground pepper
    1/2 teaspoon dried minced garlic
      4 cups cubed fully cooked ham

In a large saucepan or Dutch oven, saute onion in butter until tender. Add the water, cabbage, potatoes, bouillon, pepper and garlic.

Cover and simmer for 20-25 minutes or until potatoes are tender. Stir in ham; heat through. **Yield:** 12-14 servings (about 3-1/2 quarts).

"Do you have a **kinder**, more adaptable **friend** in the world of food than **soup**?"

satisfying
MEATLESS

30-Minute Minestrone
pictured above

This simple, chunky soup has a beefy broth that is seasoned nicely. Spinach adds a refreshing difference.

Betty Claycomb, Alverton, Pennsylvania

  2 medium carrots, chopped
  1 cup chopped cabbage
  1 celery rib, thinly sliced
  1 small onion, chopped
  1 garlic clove, minced
  2 teaspoons vegetable oil
  3 cups water
  1 can (14-1/2 ounces) Italian stewed *or* diced tomatoes, undrained
  3 beef bouillon cubes
  1 cup torn fresh spinach
  2/3 cup cooked elbow macaroni
  1/4 teaspoon pepper

In a 3-qt. saucepan, saute carrots, cabbage, celery, onion and garlic in oil for 5 minutes. Add water, tomatoes and bouillon; bring to a boil.

Reduce heat. Simmer, uncovered, for 20-25 minutes or until vegetables are tender. Stir in spinach, macaroni and pepper; heat through. **Yield:** 5 servings.

Asparagus Soup

Each spring, my husband takes our dogs and searches for wild asparagus. He's been so successful that I finally developed this recipe.

Betty Jones, Kohler, Wisconsin

      1 cup chopped onion
      6 green onions, sliced
      3 tablespoons butter
  1-1/2 cups sliced fresh mushrooms
      1 pound fresh asparagus, cut into 1/2 inch pieces
      1 can (49-1/2 ounces) chicken broth
    1/2 cup chopped fresh parsley
    1/2 teaspoon salt
    1/2 teaspoon dried thyme
    1/4 teaspoon pepper
    1/8 teaspoon cayenne pepper
      2 cups cooked wild rice
      3 tablespoons cornstarch
    1/3 cup water

In a 3-qt. saucepan, saute onions in butter for 4 minutes. Add mushrooms and cook until tender. Add asparagus, broth and seasonings; cover and simmer for 30 minutes. Add rice.

Dissolve cornstarch in water; stir into soup. Bring to a boil; boil for 2 minutes, stirring constantly. **Yield:** 8-10 servings (2-1/4 quarts).

Basil Tomato Soup

Corn dresses up this quick and easy tomato soup. My husband and two sons—who don't always care for soup—like this as much as I do. It's a great way to use up tomatoes.

Alice Culberson, Kingsport, Tennessee

    1/2 cup uncooked small shell pasta
    3/4 cup chopped red onion
    3/4 cup diced celery
      3 garlic cloves, minced
      4 teaspoons olive oil
    3/4 cup fresh *or* frozen corn, thawed
  4-1/2 cups vegetable broth
      1 to 2 tablespoons minced fresh basil leaves
    3/4 teaspoon salt
    1/8 teaspoon pepper
      6 medium firm tomatoes, peeled, seeded and chopped

Cook pasta according to package directions; drain and set aside. In a large saucepan, saute the onion, celery and garlic in oil for 8-10 minutes or until tender.

Add corn; saute for 2 minutes. Add broth, basil, salt and pepper. Bring to a boil. Reduce heat; cover and simmer for 15 minutes. Stir in pasta and tomatoes; heat through. **Yield:** 7 servings.

Broccoli Cheese Soup
pictured below

This soup has basic ingredients, but it tastes so good. The green broccoli florets and the brilliant orange carrots make this creamy soup a colorful addition to any table.

Evelyn Massner, Oakville, Iowa

2 cups sliced carrots
1 cup sliced celery
2 cups broccoli florets
1-1/2 cups chopped onion
1/2 cup butter
3/4 cup all-purpose flour
1 can (10-1/2 ounces) condensed chicken broth, undiluted
1 quart milk
1/2 pound process cheese (Velveeta), cubed

In a large saucepan, bring 2 qts. water to a boil. Add carrots, celery and broccoli; cover and boil for 5 minutes.

Meanwhile, in a large saucepan, saute onion in butter. Add flour and stir to make smooth paste. Gradually add chicken broth and milk. Cook until mixture thickens, about 8-10 minutes.

Add the carrots, celery and broccoli; heat through. Add cheese; heat until cheese is melted and vegetables are tender. **Yield:** 6-8 servings (2 quarts).

Cauliflower-Cheese Soup

We use this rich and filling soup as a meal in itself. Accompanied by a salad and rolls, it makes a fine luncheon. It also makes a very nice prelude to a dinner menu when you entertain.

Angel Berube, Prince George, British Columbia

1 medium head cauliflower, broken into florets (about 5 cups)
2/3 cup chopped onion
1/4 cup butter
1/4 cup all-purpose flour
2 cups chicken broth
2 cups half-and-half cream
1/2 teaspoon Worcestershire sauce
3/4 teaspoon salt
1 cup (4 ounces) shredded cheddar cheese
Minced fresh chives *or* parsley

In a saucepan, cook cauliflower in enough water to cover until tender. Drain and reserve liquid; set aside.

In the same saucepan, saute onion in butter until tender. Add flour; cook and stir until bubbly. Add broth; bring to a boil over medium heat. Reduce heat and stir in 1 cup cooking liquid, cream and Worcestershire sauce. Stir in cauliflower and salt.

Remove from the heat. Add cheese and stir until melted. Sprinkle with chives or parsley. **Yield:** 6-8 servings (2 quarts).

Curried Pumpkin Soup

pictured below

I whipped up this satisfying soup last Thanksgiving for my family, and everyone was crazy about it! Even my brother, who is one of the pickiest eaters I know, asked for seconds.

Kimberly Knepper, Euless, Texas

   1/2 pound fresh mushrooms, sliced
   1/2 cup chopped onion
     2 tablespoons butter
     2 tablespoons all-purpose flour
   1/2 to 1 teaspoon curry powder
     3 cups vegetable broth
     1 can (15 ounces) solid-pack pumpkin
     1 can (12 ounces) evaporated milk
     1 tablespoon honey
   1/2 teaspoon salt
   1/4 teaspoon pepper
   1/4 teaspoon ground nutmeg
Fresh or frozen chives, optional

In a large saucepan, saute the mushrooms and onion in butter until tender. Stir in the flour and curry powder until blended. Gradually add the broth. Bring to a boil; cook and stir for 2 minutes or until thickened.

Add the pumpkin, milk, honey, salt, pepper and nutmeg; heat through. Garnish with chives if desired. **Yield:** 7 servings.

Squash Tortellini Soup

This soup is fast, flavorful and good for you. Packaged cheese tortellini meets colorful summer squash, fresh spinach and shredded carrots in every eye-appealing bowl.

Chris Snyder, Boulder, Colorado

    5 cups chicken broth
3-1/2 cups shredded carrots (about 10
      ounces)
    1 cup chopped yellow summer squash
    3 cups torn fresh spinach
    1 package (9 ounces) refrigerated
      cheese tortellini

In a large saucepan, combine the broth, carrots and squash. Bring to a boil. Reduce heat; simmer, uncovered, for 3 minutes. Stir in spinach and tortellini. Cover and cook for 5 minutes or until tortellini is heated through. **Yield:** 7 servings.

Summer Soup

An overabundant garden led to this recipe! As the vegetable crop changes with the seasons, so can the soup.

Carrie Sherrill, Forestville, Wisconsin

    2 medium potatoes, peeled and sliced
    2 medium carrots, sliced
    1 cup green beans, cut into 1/2-inch
      pieces
    2 garlic cloves, minced
    1 small onion, finely chopped
    2 tablespoons butter
  1/4 cup all-purpose flour
    1 can (14-1/2 ounces) chicken broth
1-1/2 cups milk
    1 teaspoon dried basil
  1/4 teaspoon pepper
  1/4 teaspoon salt

In a saucepan, cook potatoes, carrots and beans in water to cover until tender, about 10 minutes. Drain. In a soup kettle or Dutch oven, saute garlic and onion in butter until tender. Stir in flour until bubbly.

Gradually add chicken broth, milk and seasonings. Cook, stirring occasionally, until thickened. Add vegetables; heat through. **Yield:** 4 servings (about 1 quart).

Garden Tomato Soup
pictured above

"Delicious" and "filling" are the words used to describe this soup whenever I've served it to friends. It makes a tasty lunch alone or with a sandwich.

Frances McFarlane, Winnipeg, Manitoba

    1 cup chopped celery
    1 small onion, chopped
    1 medium carrot, shredded
    1 small green pepper, chopped
  1/4 cup butter
4-1/2 cups chicken broth, *divided*
    4 cups chopped peeled tomatoes
      (about 7 medium)
    2 teaspoons sugar
  1/2 teaspoon curry powder
  1/2 teaspoon salt
  1/4 teaspoon pepper
  1/4 cup all-purpose flour

In a 3-qt. saucepan, saute celery, onion, carrot and green pepper in butter until tender. Add 4 cups broth, tomatoes, sugar, curry, salt and pepper; bring to a boil. Reduce heat; simmer, uncovered, for 20 minutes.

In a small bowl, stir flour and remaining broth until smooth. Gradually stir into tomato mixture; bring to a boil. Cook and stir until thickened and bubbly, about 2 minutes. **Yield:** 6 servings (1-3/4 quarts).

Country Mushroom Soup

pictured above

The big fresh-mushroom flavor of this soup sets it apart from other recipes I've tried. After preparing this family favorite for guests, I frequently get recipe requests.

Elsie Cathrea, Elmira, Ontario

- 1/4 cup butter
- 1/4 cup all-purpose flour
- 2 cups chicken broth
- 1/2 teaspoon salt
- 1/4 teaspoon pepper
- 1 to 2 bay leaves
- 2/3 cup finely chopped celery
- 1/4 cup finely chopped onion
- 3 tablespoons vegetable oil
- 4 to 5 cups sliced fresh mushrooms (about 1 pound)
- 2/3 cup half-and-half cream *or* milk

In a 2-qt. saucepan, melt butter; stir in flour until smooth. Gradually stir in broth until smooth. Add salt, pepper and bay leaves. Simmer, uncovered, for 15 minutes, stirring occasionally.

Meanwhile, in another saucepan, saute the celery and onion in oil until tender. Add mushrooms; cook and stir until tender. Add to broth mixture; bring to a boil. Reduce heat; simmer, uncovered, for 15 minutes, stirring occasionally. Add cream; heat through. Discard bay leaves. **Yield:** 4 servings.

Herbed Vegetable Soup

You'll get garden-fresh flavor in every spoonful of this satisfying soup. Basil and rosemary accent the veggies nicely.

Carol Jean Lopez, Westwood, Massachusetts

- 3 cups finely shredded cabbage
- 1 package (16 ounces) frozen cut green beans
- 2 celery ribs, thinly sliced
- 2 medium carrots, thinly sliced
- 2 small zucchini, chopped
- 1 small onion, chopped
- 3 cups tomato juice
- 2 teaspoons chicken bouillon granules
- 1 teaspoon salt-free seasoning blend
- 1/2 teaspoon dried basil
- 1/4 teaspoon dried rosemary, crushed

In a large saucepan, combine the first seven ingredients; bring to a boil. Reduce heat; cover and cook for 15 minutes or until vegetables are tender. Add the bouillon, seasoning blend, basil and rosemary; bring to a boil. Reduce heat; cover and simmer for 10 minutes. **Yield:** 8 servings.

Onion Soup for Two

pictured below

I adapted a basic recipe to copy the onion soup served at my favorite restaurant. No matter what my entree, I always ordered the soup.

Now I can make it at home. It's a meal in itself or an impressive beginning to a full-course meal.

Barbara Brunner, Steelton, Pennsylvania

 2 medium onions, chopped
 1 teaspoon sugar
 6 tablespoons butter, *divided*
 1 tablespoon all-purpose flour
 1/8 teaspoon pepper
Dash ground nutmeg
 2-1/2 cups beef broth
 2 tablespoons grated Parmesan cheese
 2 slices French bread (1 inch thick)
 4 slices provolone cheese

In a saucepan, saute onions and sugar in 3 tablespoons of butter until golden brown. Stir in the flour, pepper and nutmeg until blended. Gradually stir in broth. Bring to a boil; cook and stir for 2 minutes. Reduce heat; cover and simmer for 30 minutes. Stir in the Parmesan cheese.

Meanwhile, in a skillet, melt remaining butter; add bread. Cook until golden brown on both sides. Ladle soup into two ovenproof bowls. Place a slice of cheese in each bowl; top with bread and remaining cheese. Bake at 375° for 10 minutes or until the cheese is bubbly. **Yield:** 2 servings.

Swiss-Topped Cauliflower Soup

pictured above right

Since I came across this recipe a few years ago, it's become my husband's favorite soup. With fresh bread, we enjoy this as a hearty supper in winter.

C.C. McKie, Chicago, Illinois

 2 medium onions
 4 whole cloves
 4 cups water
 2 cans (10-1/2 ounces *each*) condensed chicken broth, undiluted
 3 medium leeks (white portion only), sliced
 3 medium carrots, sliced
 1 teaspoon salt
 1 teaspoon dried marjoram
 1/2 teaspoon celery seed
 1/2 teaspoon ground nutmeg
 1/4 teaspoon white pepper
 1 medium head cauliflower, broken into florets and thinly sliced (about 6 cups)
 1 tablespoon cornstarch
 1/2 cup heavy whipping cream
 2 egg yolks, beaten
 1/2 pound sliced Swiss cheese, cut into 4-inch x 1/2-inch strips

Quarter one onion; stuff the cloves into the second onion. In a large saucepan, combine water and broth; add onions, leeks, carrots and seasonings. Bring to a boil.

Reduce heat; cover and simmer for 15 minutes. Add cauliflower; simmer, uncovered, for 30 minutes or until vegetables are tender. Remove from the heat.

In a bowl, combine cornstarch and cream until smooth. Stir in egg yolks. Stir a small amount of hot soup into cream mixture; return all to the pan, stirring constantly. Simmer, uncovered, for 15 minutes. Discard the whole onion.

Ladle soup into individual ramekins. Top with cheese strips. Broil 4-6 in. from the heat for 3-5 minutes or until the cheese is bubbly. Serve immediately. **Yield:** 6-8 servings.

Broccoli Potato Soup

pictured below

I rely on a few handy ingredients to make canned soup taste just like homemade. The creamy mixture that results is hearty with chunks of broccoli and potato.

Barbara Baker, Valparaiso, Indiana

> 2 cups broccoli florets
> 1 small onion, thinly sliced
> 1 tablespoon butter
> 1 can (10-3/4 ounces) condensed cream of potato soup, undiluted
> 1 cup milk
> 1/2 cup water
> 3/4 teaspoon minced fresh basil
>   or 1/4 teaspoon dried basil
> 1/4 teaspoon pepper
> 1/3 cup shredded cheddar cheese

In a large saucepan, saute broccoli and onion in butter until tender. Stir in soup, milk, water, basil and pepper; heat through.

Add the shredded cheddar cheese and stir until the cheese is melted. **Yield:** 4 servings.

Tomato Leek Soup

This recipe was given to me years ago from a friend in Australia. We're a family that loves soup, and this recipe is one of our favorites.

Lois McAtee, Oceanside, California

> 3 leeks, finely sliced
> 5 cups chicken broth
> 2 pounds fresh tomatoes, peeled and chopped
> 1 teaspoon minced fresh basil
>   or 1/4 teaspoon dried basil
> 1/2 teaspoon lemon pepper
> 1/4 teaspoon salt

In a saucepan, bring the leeks and broth to a boil. Boil for 5 minutes. Add the tomatoes.

Reduce the heat; simmer for 10 minutes. Stir in the basil, lemon pepper and salt. **Yield:** 6-8 servings (2 quarts).

Creamy Tomato Soup

My husband, who doesn't like tomato soup, really likes this rich and creamy version. It's easy, but it tastes like you put a lot of work into it. When I share it with co-workers, everyone loves it.

Marie Keyes, Cheney, Washington

> 1 medium onion, chopped
> 2 tablespoons butter
> 2 cans (14-1/2 ounces *each*) diced tomatoes, undrained
> 2 cans (10-3/4 ounces *each*) condensed tomato soup, undiluted
> 1-1/2 cups milk
> 1 teaspoon sugar
> 1/2 to 1 teaspoon dried basil
> 1/2 to 1 teaspoon paprika
> 1/8 to 1/4 teaspoon garlic powder
> 1 package (8 ounces) cream cheese, cubed

In a saucepan, saute onion in butter until tender. Stir in tomatoes, soup, milk, sugar, basil, paprika and garlic powder. Bring to a boil.

Reduce heat; cover and simmer for 10 minutes. Stir in cream cheese until melted. Serve immediately. **Yield:** 8 servings (2 quarts).

Summer's Bounty Soup

pictured below

Lots of wonderfully fresh-tasting vegetables are showcased in this chunky soup. It's a great way to use up summer's excess produce. And it's so versatile—you can add or delete just about any vegetable.

Victoria Zmarzley-Hahn
Northampton, Pennsylvania

4 medium tomatoes, chopped
2 medium potatoes, peeled and cubed
2 cups halved fresh green beans
2 small zucchini, cubed

1 medium yellow summer squash, cubed
4 small carrots, thinly sliced
2 celery ribs, thinly sliced
1 cup cubed peeled eggplant
1 cup sliced fresh mushrooms
1 small onion, chopped
1 tablespoon minced fresh parsley
1 tablespoon salt-free garlic and herb seasoning
4 cups V8 juice

Combine all ingredients in a 5-qt. slow cooker. Cover and cook on low for 7-8 hours or until the vegetables are tender. **Yield:** 12-14 servings (about 3-1/2 quarts).

Broccoli-Cauliflower Cheese Soup

Even people who aren't particularly fond of broccoli and cauliflower can't resist this tempting soup. On busy days, you'll appreciate its ease of preparation.

Janet Hall, Pleasant Valley, Iowa

>   3 quarts water
>   8 chicken bouillon cubes
> 2-1/2 cups diced peeled potatoes
>   1 cup chopped celery
>   1/2 cup chopped onion
>   2 packages (10 ounces *each*) frozen chopped broccoli
>   1 package (16 ounces) frozen cauliflowerets
>   2 cans (10-3/4 ounces *each*) condensed cream of chicken soup, undiluted
>   1 pound process cheese (Velveeta), cubed
>   1/2 teaspoon dried thyme
>   1/4 teaspoon pepper

In a soup kettle or Dutch oven, combine the first five ingredients; cook over medium heat for about 20 minutes or until vegetables are tender. Add broccoli and cauliflower; cook over medium heat for 10 minutes.

Stir in the soup, cheese, thyme and pepper; simmer for 20 minutes, stirring occasionally. **Yield:** 18-20 servings (about 5-1/2 quarts).

Creamy Vegetable Soup
pictured above

I came up with this soup after tasting a similar version at a restaurant. My family just loves it!

Audrey Nemeth, Mount Vernon, Maine

>   1 large onion, chopped
>   1/4 cup butter
>   3 medium sweet potatoes, peeled and chopped
>   3 medium zucchini, chopped
>   1 bunch broccoli, chopped
>   2 quarts chicken broth
>   2 medium potatoes, peeled and shredded
>   2 teaspoons salt
>   1 teaspoon pepper
>   1 teaspoon celery seed
> 1 to 2 teaspoons ground cumin
>   2 cups half-and-half cream

In a large kettle, saute onion in butter until transparent but not browned. Add the sweet potatoes, zucchini and broccoli; saute lightly for 5 minutes or until crisp-tender.

Stir in broth; simmer for a few minutes. Add potatoes and seasonings; cook another 10 minutes or until vegetables are tender. Stir in cream and heat through. **Yield:** 12-16 servings (4 quarts).

> " I buy large amounts of fresh broccoli, wash it, blanch it in boiling water for a couple minutes and freeze it in freezer bags. It always tastes garden-fresh! "
>
> *—Tamra Harrington*
> *Scottsdale, Arizona*

Hearty Potato Soup
pictured below

I love our lifestyle here in Idaho's potato country. My favorite potato soup originally called for heavy cream and bacon fat, but I've trimmed down the recipe.

Gladys DeBoer, Castleford, Idaho

  6 medium potatoes, peeled and sliced
  2 medium carrots, diced
  6 celery ribs, diced
  2 quarts water
  1 medium onion, chopped
  6 tablespoons butter
  6 tablespoons all-purpose flour
  1 teaspoon salt
1/2 teaspoon pepper
1-1/2 cups milk

In a large kettle, cook potatoes, carrots and celery in water until tender, about 20 minutes. Drain, reserving the liquid and setting the vegetables aside.

In the same kettle, saute onion in butter until soft. Stir in flour, salt and pepper; gradually add milk, stirring constantly until thickened. Gently stir in cooked vegetables.

Add 1 cup or more of reserved cooking liquid until soup is desired consistency. **Yield:** 8-10 servings (about 2-1/2 quarts).

Tomato and Creamy Mushroom Soup

This soup recipe came about while I was experimenting with the goodies from my garden...I serve it often to my family, especially in the winter. We live in the country and raise horses, and I just love looking out my kitchen window at these fine animals as I cook!

Bonnie Hawkins, Woodstock, Illinois

  1 pound fresh mushrooms, thinly
    sliced
  6 tablespoons butter, *divided*
  2 medium onions, minced
  1 garlic clove, minced
  2 medium carrots, chopped
  3 celery ribs, finely chopped
  3 tablespoons all-purpose flour
  8 cups beef broth
  2 medium tomatoes, peeled, seeded
    and chopped
  1 can (15 ounces) tomato sauce
  1 teaspoon salt
1/2 teaspoon pepper
  3 tablespoons minced fresh parsley
Sour cream, optional

In a large kettle or Dutch oven, saute mushrooms in 4 tablespoons butter until tender. Remove mushrooms; set aside.

In the same kettle, saute onions, garlic, carrots and celery in remaining butter until tender. Stir in flour until smooth.

Add the broth, tomatoes, tomato sauce, salt, pepper and half of the mushrooms. Simmer, covered, about 30 minutes.

Add the minced fresh parsley and remaining mushrooms; simmer 5 minutes longer or until heated through. Garnish each serving with a dollop of sour cream if desired. **Yield:** about 12 servings (3 quarts).

Fresh Tomato Soup

pictured below

This can be put together in no time. When tomato season is here, you'll find me making this pretty and pleasing soup often.

Marilyn De Zort, Fairfield, Montana

　　　1 cup chopped onion
　1/4 cup butter
　　　3 pounds fresh tomatoes, peeled,
　　　　 seeded and chopped
　　　2 tablespoons tomato paste
　　　1 tablespoon sugar
　　　1 teaspoon salt
　　　1 teaspoon dried basil
　1/2 teaspoon dried thyme
　1/4 teaspoon pepper
　1/4 cup all-purpose flour
　　　4 cups chicken broth, *divided*
　　　1 cup heavy whipping cream

In a 3-qt. saucepan over medium heat, saute onion in butter until tender. Add tomatoes, tomato paste, sugar, salt, basil, thyme and pepper. Simmer 10 minutes, stirring occasionally.

Combine flour and 3/4 cup broth; form a smooth paste. Add to tomato mixture with remaining broth. Bring to a boil; boil for 2 minutes, stirring constantly.

Reduce heat; cover and simmer for 30 minutes or until tomatoes are tender. Remove from the heat. Stir in cream; serve immediately. **Yield:** 4-6 servings.

Mushroom 'n' Barley Soup

This soup is a variation on one I found years ago. We love it!

Laura Christensen, Bountiful, Utah

　　　6 cups sliced fresh mushrooms
　　　2 large onions, chopped
　　　1 cup chopped celery
　　　1 cup chopped carrots
　　　5 cups water, *divided*
　　　4 cups cooked medium pearl barley
　　　4 cups beef broth
　　　4 teaspoons Worcestershire sauce
1-1/2 teaspoons salt
　　　1 teaspoon dried basil
　　　1 teaspoon dried parsley flakes
　　　1 teaspoon dill weed
　　　1 teaspoon dried oregano
　1/2 teaspoon salt-free seasoning blend
　1/2 teaspoon dried thyme
　1/2 teaspoon garlic powder

In a Dutch oven or soup kettle, combine the mushrooms, onions, celery, carrots and 1 cup water. Cook and stir over medium-high heat until vegetables are tender. Add remaining ingredients; bring to a boil. Reduce heat; cover and simmer for 1 hour. **Yield:** 10 servings.

Rosy Potato Soup

Parsley and paprika delicately season this distinctive soup.

Holly Youngers, Cunningham, Kansas

　　　1 large onion, chopped
　3/4 cup chopped celery
　　　3 tablespoons butter
　　　1 tablespoon all-purpose flour
　1/2 to 3/4 teaspoon salt
　　　3 cups milk
　　　3 medium potatoes, peeled, cooked
　　　　 and sliced (2-1/2 cups)
　　　1 tablespoon minced fresh parsley
　　　1 tablespoon paprika

In a large saucepan, saute onion and celery in butter until tender. Stir in flour and salt until blended. Gradually add milk.

Bring to a boil; cook and stir for 2 minutes or until thickened and bubbly. Reduce heat. Add the potatoes, parsley and paprika; heat through. **Yield:** 5 servings.

Minestrone Soup

pictured above

Brimming with a harvest of garden bounty, this quick-to-fix soup is fresh-tasting and nutritious. The tomato-based broth is chock-full of everything from carrots and zucchini to garbanzo beans and elbow macaroni.

Heather Ryan, Brown Deer, Wisconsin

4 medium carrots, chopped
1 medium zucchini, sliced
1/4 cup chopped onion
1 garlic clove, minced
1 tablespoon olive oil
2 cans (14-1/2 ounces each) vegetable broth
3 cups V8 juice
1 can (15 ounces) garbanzo beans or chickpeas, drained
1 can (14-1/2 ounces) diced tomatoes, undrained
1 cup frozen cut green beans
1/2 cup uncooked elbow macaroni
1 teaspoon dried basil
1 tablespoon minced fresh parsley

In a Dutch oven, cook the carrots, zucchini, onion and garlic in oil for 7 minutes or until the onion is tender. Add the next seven ingredients. Bring to a boil. Reduce heat; simmer, uncovered, for 15 minutes. Stir in parsley. Cook 5 minutes longer or until macaroni is tender. **Yield:** 8 servings.

111

Cauliflower Soup

pictured below

Cauliflower and carrots share the stage in this cheesy soup that's sure to warm you up on the chilliest of nights. We like it with hot pepper sauce; however, it can be omitted with equally tasty results.

Debbie Ohlhausen, Chilliwack, British Columbia

- 1 medium head cauliflower, broken into florets
- 1 medium carrot, shredded
- 1/4 cup chopped celery
- 2-1/2 cups water
- 2 teaspoons chicken bouillon granules
- 3 tablespoons butter
- 3 tablespoons all-purpose flour
- 3/4 teaspoon salt
- 1/8 teaspoon pepper
- 2 cups milk
- 1 cup (4 ounces) shredded cheddar cheese
- 1/2 to 1 teaspoon hot pepper sauce, optional

In a large saucepan, combine the cauliflower, carrot, celery, water and bouillon. Bring to a boil. Reduce heat; cover and simmer for 12-15 minutes or until the vegetables are tender (do not drain).

In another large saucepan, melt butter. Stir in the flour, salt and pepper until smooth. Gradually add milk. Bring to a boil over medium heat; cook and stir for 2 minutes or until thickened.

Reduce the heat. Stir in the cheese until melted. Add hot pepper sauce if desired. Stir into the cauliflower mixture. **Yield:** 8 servings (about 2 quarts).

Creamy Onion Soup

I enjoy inviting people into my home to sample flavorful foods like this creamy soup. You'll find it's a nice twist on the traditional version.

Minnie Paulson, Stanley, North Dakota

- 8 medium onions, thinly sliced
- 1/3 cup butter
- 2 tablespoons all-purpose flour
- 1 teaspoon salt
- 1/2 teaspoon pepper
- 8 cups chicken broth
- 1 cup (8 ounces) sour cream
- 1/2 cup milk
- 12 slices French bread (1 inch thick), toasted
- 1 cup (4 ounces) shredded mozzarella cheese

In a large kettle or Dutch oven, saute onions in butter until tender. Sprinkle with flour, salt and pepper; cook and stir for 1 minute.

Gradually add broth. Bring to a boil; cook and stir for 2 minutes. Reduce heat; simmer, uncovered, for 30 minutes.

Combine sour cream and milk. Stir into soup; heat through (do not boil). Place a slice of toasted bread in each soup bowl; ladle soup over bread. Sprinkle with mozzarella cheese. **Yield:** 12 servings.

Chunky Asparagus Soup

This recipe was handed down from my great-grandmother. I've modified it a little, but it remains a treasure from the past. My family never tires of it at asparagus time.

Vivian Heffner, Windsor, Pennsylvania

  2 pounds fresh asparagus, chopped
  1 small onion, chopped
  1 garlic clove, minced
  2 tablespoons butter
1/2 to 1 teaspoon curry powder
  1 jar (4 ounces) sliced mushrooms, drained
  1 tablespoon diced pimientos
  1 quart chicken broth
  1 can (12 ounces) evaporated milk
1/2 pound process cheese (Velveeta), cut into 1-inch cubes

In a large saucepan, saute asparagus, onion and garlic in butter for 8-10 minutes or until tender. Add the curry powder; simmer 5 more minutes.

Add mushrooms and pimientos. Stir in chicken broth and milk. Heat through, but do not boil. Add cheese cubes and stir until melted. **Yield:** 8-10 servings (2-1/2 quarts).

No-Fuss Potato Soup

pictured above

For a busy-day supper, my family loves to have big, steaming, delicious bowls of this soup, along with fresh bread from our bread machine.

Dotty Egge, Pelican Rapids, Minnesota

  6 cups cubed peeled potatoes
  5 cups water
  2 cups chopped onion
1/2 cup chopped celery
1/2 cup thinly sliced carrots
1/4 cup butter
  4 teaspoons chicken bouillon granules
  2 teaspoons salt
1/4 teaspoon pepper
  1 can (12 ounces) evaporated milk
  3 tablespoons chopped fresh parsley
Snipped chives, optional

In a large slow cooker, combine the first nine ingredients. Cover and cook on high for 7 to 8 hours or until the vegetables are tender.

Add milk and parsley; mix well. Cover and cook 30-60 minutes longer or until heated through. Garnish with chives if desired. **Yield:** 8-10 servings (about 3 quarts).

Slow-Cooker Tips

When using a slow cooker, as in No-Fuss Potato Soup, keep in mind the following tips:

To speed up cooking time on most slow cooker recipes, including soups and stews, follow the general rule that 1 hour on high is equal to 2 hours on low.

To warm up rolls or slices of bread to go with a soup or stew, wrap them in foil and set them in the covered cooker right on top of the hot, cooked soup or stew for a few minutes.

satisfying MEATLESS

Taco Twist Soup

pictured above

I lighten up this soup recipe by substituting black beans for the ground beef originally called for...and by topping off bowlfuls with reduced-fat sour cream and cheese. Spiral pasta adds a fun twist.

Colleen Zertler, Cedar Falls, Wisconsin

      1 medium onion, chopped
      2 garlic cloves, minced
      2 teaspoons olive oil
      3 cups beef broth *or* vegetable broth
      1 can (15 ounces) black beans, rinsed
         and drained
      1 can (14-1/2 ounces) diced tomatoes
  1-1/2 cups picante sauce
      1 cup uncooked spiral pasta
      1 small green pepper, chopped
      2 teaspoons chili powder
      1 teaspoon ground cumin
    1/2 cup shredded cheddar cheese
      3 tablespoons sour cream

In a large saucepan, saute onion and garlic in oil until tender. Add the broth, beans, tomatoes, picante sauce, pasta, green pepper and seasonings. Bring to a boil, stirring frequently.

Reduce heat; cover and simmer for 10-12 minutes or until pasta is tender, stirring occasion-ally. Serve with cheese and sour cream. **Yield:** 6 servings.

Southern Garden Soup

I created this recipe as a way to combine all of my family's favorite produce into one dish. No matter how much I make, this soup never lasts long around our house.

Leslie Owens, Poplar Bluff, Missouri

  6-1/4 cups water, *divided*
      5 chicken bouillon cubes
      2 cups cauliflowerets
    1/2 cup small boiling onions
      2 pounds fresh asparagus, cut
         into 1/2-inch pieces
      1 can (8 ounces) sliced water chestnuts,
         drained
      1 cup chopped fresh spinach
    1/2 cup chopped chives
    1/2 teaspoon dried marjoram
    1/2 teaspoon salt
  1/8 to 1/4 teaspoon pepper
    1/8 teaspoon ground nutmeg
      3 tablespoons cornstarch

In a 3-qt. saucepan, bring 6 cups water and bouillon to a boil. Add cauliflower and onions; cover and cook for 5 minutes. Add the next eight ingredients; cover and cook for 5 minutes or until asparagus is tender.

Dissolve cornstarch in remaining water; stir into soup. Bring to a boil; boil for 2 minutes, stir-ring constantly. Serve immediately. **Yield:** 8-10 servings (2-1/4 quarts).

Pumpkin Vegetable Soup

This golden-toned soup is wonderfully warming on crisp autumn days. Unlike most creamy pumpkin soups, this one is especially hearty, with additional vegetables such as potatoes, carrots and corn. For fun autumn flair, serve the soup in hollowed-out pumpkin shells.

Joan Conover, Easton, Pennsylvania

1 large onion, chopped
2 tablespoons butter
4 cups chicken broth
2 medium potatoes, peeled and cubed
2 large carrots, chopped
2 celery ribs, chopped
1 cup cooked fresh *or* frozen lima beans
1 cup fresh *or* frozen corn
1 can (15 ounces) solid-pack pumpkin
1/2 teaspoon salt
1/4 teaspoon white pepper
1/4 teaspoon ground nutmeg

In a large saucepan, saute onion in butter until tender. Add the broth, potatoes, carrots, celery, lima beans and corn. Bring to a boil. Reduce heat; cover and simmer for 25-30 minutes or until vegetables are tender.

Stir in the pumpkin, salt, pepper and nutmeg. Cook 5-10 minutes longer or until soup is heated through. **Yield:** 7 servings.

Carrot Zucchini Soup
pictured below

Here's an easy way to get kids to eat their vegetables. Carrots were never my family's favorite, but with this delicious soup, they hardly know they're eating them.

Joanne Novellino, Bayville, New Jersey

"In fall, I wash, dry and freeze bunches of parsley in plastic bags. Later, I chop off what I need for soups and return the rest to the freezer."

—*Eunice Stoen*
Decorah, Iowa

2 small onions
2 cups water
1/2 pound carrots, cut into 1-inch pieces
1/8 teaspoon celery salt
1/8 teaspoon pepper
2 cups diced zucchini (3 to 4 medium)
1-1/2 teaspoons olive oil
1-1/2 teaspoons butter
1/2 cup diced seeded peeled tomatoes
2/3 cup evaporated milk
2 tablespoons minced fresh parsley

Chop one onion; set aside. Quarter the other onion and place in a 3-qt. saucepan. Add the water, carrots, celery salt and pepper; bring to a boil. Reduce heat; cover and simmer for 20 minutes or until carrots are tender.

Transfer to a blender or food processor; cover and process until pureed. Return to the pan.

In a skillet, saute the zucchini and chopped onion in oil and butter until tender; add to carrot mixture. Stir in tomatoes.

Cover and simmer for 10 minutes or until tomatoes are tender. Stir in milk and parsley; heat through. **Yield:** 2-4 servings.

115

satisfying MEATLESS

Summer Vegetable Soup

pictured above

This vegetable soup is chock-full of garden goodness, from zucchini and green beans to celery and potato, but it's the turmeric that gives it a tasty new twist.

Edith Ruth Muldoon, Baldwin, New York

  1 small onion, quartered and thinly sliced
  1 tablespoon olive oil
  4 cups chicken broth
  1 cup sliced zucchini
  1 can (15-1/2 ounces) navy beans, rinsed and drained
  1/2 cup diced peeled red potato
  1/2 cup cut fresh green beans (2-inch pieces)
  1/2 cup chopped peeled tomato
  1/4 teaspoon pepper
  1/8 teaspoon ground turmeric
  1/4 cup chopped celery leaves
  2 tablespoons tomato paste

In a large saucepan, saute onion in oil until tender. Add the next eight ingredients. Bring to a boil. Reduce heat; cover and simmer for 20-30 minutes or until vegetables are tender. Stir in celery leaves and tomato paste. Cover and let stand for 5 minutes before serving. **Yield:** 4 servings.

Knoephla Soup

While I was growing up, my mom would make this traditional German soup. It tasted so good on chilly fall days. Knoephla (pronounced nip-fla) Soup is still a warm and comforting meal for my family.

Lorraine Meyers, Willow City, North Dakota

      1/2 cup butter
        3 medium potatoes, peeled and diced
        1 small onion, grated
        3 cups milk
    1-1/2 quarts water
        6 teaspoons chicken bouillon granules
   KNOEPHLA:
    1-1/2 cups all-purpose flour
        1 egg, beaten
        5 to 6 tablespoons milk
      1/2 teaspoon salt

In a large skillet, melt butter; cook potatoes and onion for 20-25 minutes or until tender. Add milk; heat through but do not boil. Set aside. In a soup kettle or Dutch oven, bring water and bouillon to a boil.

Meanwhile, combine knoephla ingredients to form a stiff dough. Roll into a 1/2-in. rope. Cut into 1/4-in. pieces and drop into boiling broth. Reduce heat; cover and simmer for 10 minutes. Add the potato mixture; heat through. **Yield:** 8-10 servings (2-1/2 quarts).

Pot o' Gold Potato Soup

This golden soup may not be what you expect to find at the end of the rainbow, but you'll treasure its rich flavor. Our Test Kitchen staff came up with this delightful recipe.

      3/4 cup chopped celery
      3/4 cup chopped onion
      1/4 cup butter
        2 cans (14-1/2 ounces *each*) chicken broth
    2-1/3 cups mashed potato flakes
    1-1/2 cups milk
      1/2 cup cubed process cheese (Velveeta)
      3/4 teaspoon garlic salt
      1/8 to 1/4 teaspoon chili powder
      1/2 cup sour cream

In a 3-qt. saucepan, saute celery and onion in butter for 2-3 minutes. Stir in broth; bring to boil. Reduce heat. Add potato flakes; cook and stir for 5-7 minutes. Add milk, cheese, garlic salt and chili powder.

Cook and stir until cheese is melted. Just before serving, add sour cream and heat through (do not boil). **Yield:** 6 servings.

Swiss-Barley Mushroom Soup

In this recipe, hearty barley and rich Swiss cheese add a flavorful twist to traditional mushroom soup. You'll find one batch of this filling soup goes a long way.

Germaine Stank, Pound, Wisconsin

      1/2 pound fresh mushrooms, sliced
      1/2 cup chopped onion
      1/2 cup butter, melted
      1/2 cup all-purpose flour
        3 cups water
      1/2 cup quick-cooking barley
        3 chicken bouillon cubes
        3 cups milk
        2 cups (8 ounces) shredded Swiss cheese
        2 tablespoons Worcestershire sauce
        1 tablespoon dried parsley flakes
      1/4 teaspoon pepper

In a 3-qt. saucepan, saute mushrooms and onion in butter until tender. With a slotted spoon, transfer mushrooms and onion to a bowl; set aside.

Stir flour into pan drippings; cook over medium heat until lightly browned. Stir in water until smooth. Add barley; bring to a boil. Reduce heat; simmer, uncovered, stirring constantly, for 15 minutes or until barley is tender.

Add bouillon, milk, cheese, Worcestershire sauce, parsley and pepper; cook and stir until bouillon is dissolved and cheese is melted. Add the mushroom mixture; heat through. **Yield:** 6 servings.

Broccoli Soup

pictured below

After a full day of work, I like to make a supper that's quick and easy. This wonderful soup can be made with ingredients purchased at any grocery store.

Joyce McDowell, Winchester, Ohio

>   3 cups or 2 cans (14-1/2 ounces each)
>   chicken broth
>   1 large bunch broccoli, chopped
>   (about 5 cups)
> 1-1/2 cups chopped onion
>   3 bay leaves
>   6 tablespoons butter
>   7 tablespoons all-purpose flour
>   3 cups milk
> Salt and pepper to taste

In a saucepan, bring chicken broth to a boil. Add broccoli, onion and bay leaves. Reduce heat and simmer until broccoli is tender; remove bay leaves.

Meanwhile, in another saucepan, melt butter. Stir in flour to make a smooth paste. Gradually stir in milk. Cook over medium heat until mixture is hot and thickened, stirring occasionally.

Add 1 cup of broccoli stock to milk mixture; stir until well blended. Gradually add remaining broccoli stock to milk mixture. Heat and stir until well-blended. Season with salt and pepper. **Yield:** 6 servings.

Winter Vegetable Soup

Folks always seem to ask for the recipe whenever I make this flavorful filling soup. And they're surprised to learn that refried beans are a major ingredient!

Gertrude Vinci, Reno, Nevada

>   1 cup chopped celery
> 1/2 cup chopped onion
>   1 garlic clove, minced
>   2 tablespoons olive oil
> 1-1/2 quarts water
>   1 can (14-1/2 ounces) diced tomatoes,
>   undrained
>   3 medium potatoes, peeled and cubed
>   2 medium carrots, diced
>   1 cup chopped cabbage
>   3 tablespoons minced fresh parsley
>   2 teaspoons brown sugar
> 1-1/4 teaspoons salt
>   1 teaspoon dried marjoram
> 1/2 teaspoon dried rosemary, crushed
> 1/4 teaspoon pepper
> 1/8 teaspoon cayenne pepper
>   2 cans (16 ounces each) refried beans
>   with green chilies
>   1 can (16 ounces) kidney beans, rinsed
>   and drained
> Hot cooked macaroni

In a Dutch oven or soup kettle, saute celery, onion and garlic in oil for 7 minutes or until tender. Add the next 12 ingredients; bring to a boil. Reduce heat; cover and simmer for 40 minutes. Stir in beans.

Cover and simmer for 20 minutes or until vegetables are tender. Serve over macaroni. **Yield:** 12-16 servings (4 quarts).

Creamy-Cheesy Cauliflower Soup

My aunt always made this smooth rich-tasting soup for me when I came to visit. I could smell it simmering as soon as I arrived. I think of her whenever I have a bowlful.

Heather Kasprick, Keewatin, Ontario

>   1 medium head cauliflower, broken
>   into florets
>   2 cans (10-3/4 ounces each) condensed
>   cream of chicken soup, undiluted

1 can (10-3/4 ounces) condensed
    cheddar cheese soup, undiluted
1 can (14-1/2 ounces) chicken broth
2 cups milk

Place cauliflower in a saucepan with 1 in. of water; bring to a boil. Reduce heat; cover and simmer for 5-10 minutes or until crisp-tender.

Meanwhile, in another saucepan, combine soups, broth and milk; heat through. Drain the cauliflower; stir into soup. **Yield:** 9 servings.

Rich French Onion Soup
pictured above

When entertaining guests, I bring out this savory soup while we're waiting for the main course. It's simple to make—just saute the onions early in the day and let the soup simmer until dinnertime. In winter, big bowls of it make a warming supper with a salad and biscuits.

Linda Adolph, Edmonton, Alberta

  6 large onions, chopped
1/2 cup butter
  6 cans (10-1/2 ounces *each*) condensed
    beef broth, undiluted

1-1/2 teaspoons Worcestershire sauce
   3 bay leaves
  10 slices French bread, toasted
Shredded Parmesan and mozzarella cheeses

In a large skillet, saute onions in butter until crisp-tender. Transfer to an ungreased 5-qt. slow cooker. Add the broth, Worcestershire sauce and bay leaves.

Cover and cook on low for 5-7 hours or until the onions are tender. Discard bay leaves. Top each serving with French bread and cheeses. **Yield:** 10 servings.

Mixed Vegetable Soup

This recipe is so flexible, you can use whatever veggies you have on hand. But this combination is really my favorite.

Lucille Franck, Independence, Iowa

  2 small carrots, grated
  2 celery ribs, chopped
  1 small onion, chopped
1/2 cup chopped green pepper
1/4 cup butter
  2 cans (14-1/2 ounces *each*) chicken
    broth, *divided*
  2 cans (14-1/2 ounces *each*) diced
    tomatoes, undrained
  1 tablespoon sugar
1/4 teaspoon pepper
1/4 cup all-purpose flour

In a 3-qt. saucepan, saute the carrots, celery, onion and green pepper in butter until tender. Reserve 1/2 cup chicken broth.

Add the tomatoes, sugar, pepper and remaining broth to pan; bring to a boil. Reduce the heat; cover and simmer for 20 minutes.

Combine flour and reserved broth until smooth; gradually add to soup. Bring to a boil; cook and stir for 2 minutes. **Yield:** 8 servings (2 quarts).

Russian Borscht

With beets, carrots, cabbage and tomatoes, this recipe is great for gardeners like myself. Not only is it delicious, its bright crimson color is eye-catching on the table.

Ginny Bettis, Montello, Wisconsin

>   2 cups chopped fresh beets
>   2 cups chopped carrots
>   2 cups chopped onion
>   4 cups beef broth
>   1 can (16 ounces) diced tomatoes, undrained
>   2 cups chopped cabbage
>   1/2 teaspoon salt
>   1/2 teaspoon dill weed
>   1/4 teaspoon pepper
> Sour cream, optional

In a 3-qt. saucepan, combine beets, carrots, onion and broth; bring to a boil. Reduce heat; cover and simmer for 30 minutes. Add tomatoes and cabbage.

Cover and simmer for 30 minutes or until cabbage is tender. Stir in salt, dill and pepper. Top each serving with sour cream if desired. **Yield:** 8 servings (2 quarts).

French Onion Soup

pictured above

I like to carry on a special holiday tradition that always includes this soup. This version has a slightly sweet flavor that makes it unique.

Lise Thomson, Magrath, Alberta

>   6 cups thinly sliced onions
>   1 tablespoon sugar
>   1/2 teaspoon pepper
>   1/3 cup vegetable oil
>   6 cups beef broth
>   8 slices French bread (3/4 inch thick), toasted
>   1/2 cup shredded Parmesan *or* Swiss cheese

In a Dutch oven or soup kettle over medium-low heat, cook onions, sugar and pepper in oil for 20 minutes or until onions are caramelized, stirring frequently. Add the broth; bring to a boil. Reduce heat; cover and simmer for 30 minutes. Ladle soup into ovenproof bowls.

Top each with a slice of French bread; sprinkle with cheese. Broil until cheese is melted. Serve immediately. **Yield:** 8 servings.

Excess Soup Solutions

Often, you make soup from leftovers. But what can you do with leftover soup?

Soup freezes well in family size portions. So you can enjoy it later, or you can make something new. For example, you can use leftover cream of mushroom soup with sauteed chicken breasts. Make a new entree by simmering them together and serving it over pasta.

If your soup has too many veggie ingredients and little broth, strain out a few spoonfuls to use as a filling for meat pies or quiche.

Rosemary Mushroom Soup

The pungent, piney fragrance and flavor of rosemary really adds spark to this tasty soup. I hope you enjoy it!

Sandra Burrows, Coventry, Connecticut

> 1 cup sliced fresh mushrooms
> 2 garlic cloves, minced
> 1/4 cup butter
> 1 can (10-3/4 ounces) condensed cream of mushroom soup, undiluted
> 1 cup half-and-half cream
> 1 tablespoon minced fresh rosemary *or* 1 teaspoon dried rosemary, crushed
> 1/2 teaspoon paprika
> 2 tablespoons minced chives

In a large saucepan, saute mushrooms and garlic in butter until tender. Stir in the mushroom soup, cream, rosemary and paprika; heat through but do not boil. Sprinkle with chives. **Yield:** 3 servings.

Minestrone in Minutes

I found this recipe in a magazine years ago and adapted it to suit my family's taste. It tastes especially good accompanied by oven-fresh garlic bread.

Susan Herman-Havens, Beggs, Oklahoma

> 1 can (14-1/2 ounces) beef broth
> 1 can (14-1/2 ounces) diced tomatoes, undrained
> 1 tablespoon chopped fresh parsley
> 1 teaspoon dried basil
> 1 garlic clove, minced
> Pinch sugar
> 1/4 cup uncooked macaroni
> 2 cups frozen peas, thawed
> 1/2 cup frozen green beans, thawed
> Grated Parmesan cheese, optional

In a 2-qt. saucepan, combine the first six ingredients; bring to a boil. Add macaroni; cover and cook for 10 minutes or until macaroni is tender. Stir in peas and beans. Cook for 3 minutes. Garnish with Parmesan cheese if desired. **Yield:** 4 servings.

Creamy Monterey Jack Soup
pictured below

This mild comforting soup can be made in a matter of minutes. Served as a first course, it upgrades any meal from so-so to wow!

Shannette Matlock, Louisville, Kentucky

> 2-1/2 cups water
> 1 medium tomato, chopped
> 1 can (4 ounces) chopped green chilies
> 1 can (12 ounces) evaporated milk
> 1 can (10-3/4 ounces) condensed cream of onion soup, undiluted
> 1 can (10-3/4 ounces) condensed cream of potato soup, undiluted
> 1/8 teaspoon garlic salt
> 8 ounces bulk Monterey Jack cheese, cut into 1-inch cubes

In a large saucepan, combine the water, tomato and chilies. Bring to a boil; boil for 5 minutes. Stir in milk, soups and garlic salt.

Cook and stir over medium heat until heated through. Place cheese cubes in serving bowls; ladle hot soup over cheese. **Yield:** 6 servings.

1/4 cup chopped onion
1 garlic clove, minced
2 teaspoons olive oil
1-1/2 cups chicken broth
2 medium tomatoes, peeled, seeded and chopped
1 teaspoon fresh oregano
or 1/4 teaspoon dried oregano
3 tablespoons uncooked couscous
1/8 teaspoon salt

In a saucepan, saute onion and garlic in oil until tender. Add the broth, tomatoes and oregano. Bring to a boil.

Reduce heat; cover and simmer for 20-25 minutes or until tomatoes are tender. Remove from the heat; stir in couscous and salt. Let stand for 5 minutes. **Yield:** 2 servings.

Cheesy Onion Soup
pictured above

I made a few adjustments to make this savory soup rich, buttery and cheesy.

Janice Pogozelski, Cleveland, Ohio

1 large onion, chopped
3 tablespoons butter
3 tablespoons all-purpose flour
1/2 teaspoon salt
Pepper to taste
4 cups milk
2 cups (8 ounces) shredded Colby-Monterey Jack cheese
Seasoned salad croutons
Grated Parmesan cheese, optional

In a large saucepan, saute the onion in butter. Stir in the flour, salt and pepper until blended. Gradually add milk. Bring to a boil; cook and stir for 2 minutes or until thickened. Stir in Colby-Monterey Jack cheese until melted. Serve with croutons and Parmesan cheese if desired. **Yield:** 6 servings.

Tomato Couscous Soup

I like this simple soup because the fresh tomato flavor really stands out. It's a favorite at our house alongside a toasted cheese sandwich.

Joyce Woldt, Waupaca, Wisconsin

Broccoli Noodle Soup

My husband's aunt shared the recipe for this creamy soup, which tastes like you spent all day cooking. It's very filling with a salad and bread. We spoon the leftovers over baked potatoes.

Trinity Nicholas, Mt. Carbon, West Virginia

1 package (10 ounces) frozen chopped broccoli
2 ounces angel hair pasta, broken into small pieces
1/4 cup butter
1 tablespoon all-purpose flour
1 cup water
3/4 cup milk
1/8 teaspoon pepper
6 ounces process cheese (Velveeta), cubed
1/2 cup sour cream

Cook both the broccoli and pasta according to package directions; drain. In a large saucepan, melt butter; stir in flour until smooth. Gradually stir in the water, milk and pepper until blended. Bring to a boil; cook and stir for 2 minutes or until thickened.

Reduce heat; stir in cheese until melted. Stir in the broccoli, pasta and sour cream; heat through (do not boil). **Yield:** 4-5 servings.

Italian Vegetable Soup

pictured below

One night when my husband and I needed a quick supper, I threw together this satisfying soup using only what we had on hand. It's a family favorite, and it's good for us, too!

Margaret Glassic, Easton, Pennsylvania

- **2 cans (14-1/2 ounces *each*) chicken broth**
- **1 medium potato, peeled and cubed**
- **1 medium onion, chopped**
- **1 medium carrot, chopped**
- **1 celery rib, chopped**
- **1/2 cup frozen peas**
- **1 bay leaf**
- **1 teaspoon Italian seasoning**
- **1/8 teaspoon pepper**
- **1/2 cup small shell pasta, cooked and drained**
- **1 can (14-1/2 ounces) diced tomatoes, undrained**

In a large saucepan, combine the first nine ingredients. Bring to a boil. Reduce heat; cover and simmer for 15-20 minutes or until vegetables are crisp-tender.

Add pasta and tomatoes; heat through. Discard bay leaf before serving. **Yield:** 6 servings.

Egg Dumpling Soup

This simple recipe makes for a warm and filling soup. The dumplings are easy to mix together and taste wonderful.

Mary Lou Christman, Norwich, New York

> 6 cups chicken broth
> 1 cup finely chopped celery
> 3 tablespoons minced fresh parsley
> 2 eggs
> 2/3 cup all-purpose flour
> 1 to 2 tablespoons milk
> Pepper to taste

In a 4-qt. saucepan, bring broth, celery and parsley to a boil. Meanwhile, in a small bowl, beat eggs. Beat in flour and enough milk to form a mixture the consistency of cake batter. Drop by teaspoonfuls into boiling broth.

Reduce heat to medium-low; cover and simmer for 10-15 minutes or until dumplings are light and not gummy. Season with pepper. **Yield:** 4-6 servings (1-3/4 quarts).

Cream of Cauliflower Soup

pictured above

This mildly cheesy cauliflower soup is one of my favorites. My two sons and husband enjoy it, too. I make it often in summer, although it's good anytime.

Karen Brown, West Lafayette, Ohio

> 1/3 cup green onions (tops only)
> 2 tablespoons butter
> 2 tablespoons all-purpose flour
> 1/2 teaspoon salt
> 2 cups chicken broth
> 1 package (10 ounces) frozen cauliflower, thawed and chopped
> 2 cups milk
> 1-1/2 cups (6 ounces) shredded cheddar cheese
> 2 tablespoons dry sherry, optional
> 1 tablespoon minced chives

In a saucepan, saute onions in butter until tender. Stir in flour and salt until blended. Gradually add broth. Bring to a boil; cook and stir for 2 minutes or until thickened. Reduce heat.

Add cauliflower; simmer for 2 minutes. Add the milk and cheese; cook and stir until cheese is melted. Stir in sherry if desired. Garnish with chives. **Yield:** 6 servings.

Low-Fat Potato Soup

My husband was surprised to learn that I make this soup low in fat when I use fat-free milk and reduced-fat cheese.

Natalie Warf, Spring Lake, North Carolina

> 1-3/4 cups diced peeled potatoes
> 1 medium onion, chopped
> 1/4 cup chopped celery
> 1 can (14-1/2 ounces) chicken broth
> 1/8 teaspoon pepper
> 3 tablespoons cornstarch
> 1 can (12 ounces) evaporated milk, *divided*
> 1 cup (4 ounces) shredded cheddar cheese

In a large saucepan, combine the potatoes, onion, celery, broth and pepper. Bring to a boil. Reduce heat; cover and simmer for 15-18 minutes or until vegetables are tender. Combine cornstarch and 1/4 cup milk until smooth; stir into potato mixture. Add the remaining milk.

Bring to a boil; cook and stir for 2 minutes or until thickened. Remove from the heat. Stir in cheese until melted. **Yield:** 5 servings.

Tomato Green Bean Soup

pictured below

When I can't get homegrown tomatoes and green beans, I've found that frozen beans and canned tomatoes (or even stewed tomatoes) work just fine. Served with warm breadsticks, this soup is a complete meal. My husband and I enjoy it as a meatless dish, but you could also add cooked chicken or ham.

Bernice Nolan, Granite City, Illinois

- 1 cup chopped onion
- 1 cup chopped carrots
- 2 teaspoons butter
- 6 cups chicken broth
- 1 pound fresh green beans, cut into 1-inch pieces
- 1 garlic clove, minced
- 3 cups diced fresh tomatoes
- 1/4 cup minced fresh basil *or* 1 tablespoon dried basil
- 1/2 teaspoon salt
- 1/4 teaspoon pepper

In a large saucepan, saute onion and carrots in butter for 5 minutes. Stir in the broth, beans and garlic; bring to a boil.

Reduce heat; cover and simmer for 20 minutes or until vegetables are tender. Stir in the tomatoes, basil, salt and pepper. Cover and simmer 5 minutes longer. **Yield:** 9 servings.

Spinach 'n' Tortellini Soup

I like to top bowls of this tasty soup with a little grated Parmesan cheese. Then I serve it with crusty bread to round out the meal.

Donna Morgan, Hend, Tennessee

- 2 garlic cloves, minced
- 1 tablespoon butter
- 3 cans (14-1/2 ounces *each*) chicken broth *or* vegetable broth
- 1 package (9 ounces) refrigerated cheese tortellini
- 1 package (10 ounces) frozen chopped spinach, thawed and squeezed dry
- 1 can (14-1/2 ounces) diced tomatoes with green chilies, undrained

In a saucepan, saute the garlic in butter until tender. Stir in the broth. Bring to a boil. Add tortellini; cook for 5-6 minutes or until tender. Stir in the spinach and tomatoes; heat through. **Yield:** 5 servings.

Sweet Potato Minestrone

The sweet potatoes add a delightful flavor to the more traditional minestrone recipe. My family can never get enough of this soup!

Helen Vail, Glenside, Pennsylvania

- 4 cans (14-1/2 ounces *each*) beef broth
- 3 cups water
- 2 medium sweet potatoes, peeled and cubed
- 1 medium onion, chopped
- 4 garlic cloves, minced
- 2 teaspoons Italian seasoning
- 6 cups shredded cabbage
- 1 package (7 ounces) small pasta shells
- 2 cups frozen peas

In a soup kettle or Dutch oven, combine beef broth, water, potatoes, onion, garlic and Italian seasoning; bring to a boil. Reduce heat; cover and simmer for 10 minutes. Return to a boil.

Add the cabbage, pasta and peas; cook for 8-10 minutes or until the pasta and vegetables are tender. **Yield:** 14 servings (about 3-1/2 quarts).

125

Savory Cheese Soup
pictured above

This delicious soup recipe was shared by a friend and instantly became a hit with my husband. Its big cheese flavor blends wonderfully with the flavor of the vegetables.

Dee Falk, Stromsburg, Nebraska

1/4 cup chopped onion
3 tablespoons butter
1/4 cup all-purpose flour
1/4 teaspoon salt
1/8 teaspoon pepper
1/8 teaspoon garlic powder
2 cups milk

1 can (14-1/2 ounces) chicken broth
1/2 cup shredded carrots
1/2 cup finely chopped celery
1-1/2 cups (6 ounces) shredded cheddar cheese
3/4 cup shredded mozzarella cheese
Fresh *or* dried chives, optional

In a large saucepan, saute onion in butter until tender. Add flour, salt, pepper and garlic powder; stir until smooth. Gradually add milk; cook and stir over medium heat until thickened and bubbly.

Meanwhile, bring chicken broth to a boil in a small saucepan. Add carrots and celery; simmer for 5 minutes or until vegetables are tender. Add to milk mixture and stir until blended. Add cheeses. Cook and stir until melted (do not boil). Garnish with chives if desired. **Yield:** about 4 servings.

Slow-Cooked Vegetable Soup

You just have to try this hearty soup for its unique blend of flavors and beautiful appearance. With all the rich foods served during the holidays, it's nice to serve this soup loaded with fiber and vitamins.

Christina Till, South Haven, Michigan

       3/4 cup chopped onion
       1/2 cup chopped celery
       1/2 cup chopped green pepper
         2 tablespoons olive oil
         1 large potato, peeled and diced
         1 medium sweet potato, peeled and diced
         1 to 2 garlic cloves, minced
         3 cups chicken broth *or* water
         2 medium fresh tomatoes, chopped
         1 can (16 ounces) kidney beans, rinsed and drained
         1 can (15 ounces) garbanzo beans *or* chickpeas, rinsed and drained
         2 teaspoons soy sauce
         1 teaspoon paprika
       1/2 teaspoon dried basil
       1/4 teaspoon salt
       1/4 teaspoon ground turmeric
         1 bay leaf
Dash cayenne pepper

In a large skillet, saute the onion, celery and green pepper in oil until crisp-tender. Add the potato, sweet potato and garlic; saute 3-5 minutes longer.

Transfer to a 5-qt. slow cooker. Stir in the remaining ingredients. Cover and cook on low for 9-10 hours or until vegetables are tender. Discard bay leaf before serving. **Yield:** 12 servings (about 3 quarts).

Four-Onion Soup
pictured below

This mellow, rich-tasting onion soup is topped with toasted French bread and melted cheese.

Margaret Adams, Pacific Grove, California

         1 medium yellow onion
         1 medium red onion
         1 medium leek (white portion only)
         5 green onions with tops
         1 garlic clove, minced
         2 tablespoons butter
         2 cans (14-1/2 ounces *each*) beef broth
         1 can (10-1/2 ounces) beef consomme
         1 teaspoon Worcestershire sauce
       1/2 teaspoon ground nutmeg
         1 cup (4 ounces) shredded Swiss cheese
         6 slices French bread (3/4 inch thick), toasted
         6 tablespoons grated Parmesan cheese

Slice all onions 1/4 in. thick. In a 3-qt. saucepan over medium-low heat, saute onions and garlic in butter for 15 minutes or until tender and golden, stirring occasionally. Add next four ingredients; bring to a boil. Reduce heat; cover and simmer for 30 minutes.

Sprinkle 1 tablespoon of Swiss cheese in the bottom of six ovenproof 8-oz. bowls. Ladle hot soup into bowls. Top with bread. Sprinkle with remaining Swiss cheese and Parmesan cheese. Broil until cheese melts. Serve immediately. **Yield:** 6 servings.

127

Cheesy Broccoli Soup

pictured below

This creamy soup goes together in a flash because it uses frozen chopped broccoli and process cheese. Plus, it's easy to warm up for another time!

Jo Maasberg, Farson, Wyoming

> 2 cups water
> 1 teaspoon chicken bouillon granules
> 1 package (16 ounces) frozen chopped broccoli, thawed
> 1 medium onion, chopped
> 1/4 cup butter
> 3 tablespoons all-purpose flour
> 1 cup milk
> 1 pound process cheese (Velveeta), cubed

In a large saucepan, bring water and bouillon to a boil. Add broccoli. Reduce heat; cover and simmer for 3-4 minutes or until crisp-tender. Drain, reserving 3/4 cup liquid.

In another large saucepan, saute onion in butter until tender. Whisk in flour until blended. Add the milk and cheese. Cook over medium-low heat until cheese is melted, stirring frequently. Stir in broccoli and reserved cooking liquid. **Yield:** 4 servings.

Marvelous Mushroom Soup

pictured at right

Soup is on top of the list of things I love to cook. I've used this recipe as a beginning course to a meal and as a Sunday supper with hot rolls and butter.

Beverly Rafferty, Winston, Oregon

> 1/2 pound fresh mushrooms, sliced
> 1 large onion, finely chopped
> 1 garlic clove, minced
> 1/2 teaspoon dried tarragon
> 1/4 teaspoon ground nutmeg
> 3 tablespoons butter
> 1/4 cup all-purpose flour
> 2 cans (14-1/2 ounces *each*) beef broth
> 1 cup (8 ounces) sour cream
> 1/2 cup half-and-half cream
> 1/2 cup evaporated milk
> 1 teaspoon lemon juice

Dash hot pepper sauce
Salt and pepper to taste

In a Dutch oven or soup kettle, saute the mushrooms, onion, garlic, tarragon and nutmeg in butter until vegetables are tender. Stir in flour until smooth. Gradually add broth; bring to a boil, stirring constantly.

Reduce heat to low; slowly add sour cream. Cook and stir until smooth. Stir in cream and milk. Add lemon juice, hot pepper sauce, salt and pepper. Heat through (do not boil). **Yield:** 6 servings.

Sunset Tomato Soup

The secret to the beautiful orange color of this chunky soup I created is the mix of garden-fresh yellow tomatoes, red plum tomatoes and carrots.

Emily Beebe, Stoughton, Wisconsin

> 4 medium carrots, sliced
> 1 medium onion, chopped
> 1 tablespoon olive oil
> 3 to 4 large yellow tomatoes, peeled and coarsely chopped
> 4 plum tomatoes, peeled and coarsely chopped
> 1 can (14-1/2 ounces) chicken broth *or* vegetable broth

2 cups seasoned croutons
1-1/3 cups shredded mozzarella cheese

In a 3-qt. microwave-safe dish, combine the first eight ingredients. Cover and microwave at 50% power for 25-30 minutes or until onions are tender. Ladle hot soup into four microwave-safe bowls. Top with croutons and cheese.

Cover with waxed paper; microwave on high for 1 minute or until cheese is melted. Serve immediately. **Yield:** 4 servings.

Editor's Note: This recipe was tested in an 850-watt microwave.

Tomato Mushroom Consomme

A family friend gave me this recipe. Fresh mushrooms and seasonings really dress up canned consomme. I like to serve it alongside a sandwich for a complete meal.

Kris Countryman, Joliet, Illinois

2 cups sliced fresh mushrooms
1/4 cup snipped fresh dill
1 tablespoon butter
1 can (10-1/2 ounces) condensed beef consomme, undiluted
1 can (10-3/4 ounces) condensed tomato soup, undiluted
2 cups water
1/4 cup sliced green onions
1/4 cup chopped fresh parsley
1 teaspoon lemon juice

In a saucepan, saute the mushrooms and dill in butter for 5 minutes or until the mushrooms are tender.

Add all of the remaining ingredients; bring to a boil. Reduce heat; cover and simmer for 5 minutes. **Yield:** 4 servings.

1/2 teaspoon salt
1/4 teaspoon pepper
1-1/2 teaspoons snipped fresh dill *or* 3/4 teaspoon dill weed

In a Dutch oven or large kettle, saute carrots and onion in oil until onion is tender. Add the tomatoes, broth, salt and pepper. Bring to a boil.

Reduce heat; simmer, uncovered, for 45-60 minutes or until liquid is slightly reduced. Stir in dill; simmer 15 minutes longer. **Yield:** 4 servings.

Microwave French Onion Soup

Enjoy the taste and comfort of this classic soup through the convenience of microwave cooking. It's a recipe that I turn to time and again. After one spoonful, you'll understand why.

Mina Dyck, Boissevain, Manitoba

3 cups boiling water
1 can (14-1/2 ounces) beef broth
3 tablespoons butter
2 teaspoons beef bouillon granules
1 teaspoon Worcestershire sauce
1/8 teaspoon salt
1/8 teaspoon pepper
3 cups thinly sliced onions

"To feel **safe** and **warm** on a cold night,
all you really need is **soup**."

special CREAMED SOUPS & BISQUES

Potato Cheese Soup

pictured at right

My father was Swiss, so cheese has been a basic food in our family as long as I can remember. With its big cheese taste, you'll want to prepare this soup often.

Carol Smith, New Berlin, Wisconsin

  3 medium potatoes (about 1pound),
    peeled and quartered
  1 small onion, finely chopped
  1 cup water
  1 teaspoon salt
  3 cups milk
  3 tablespoons butter, melted
  2 tablespoons all-purpose flour
  2 tablespoons minced fresh parsley
1/8 teaspoon white pepper
  1 cup (4 ounces) shredded Swiss cheese

In a saucepan, bring potatoes, onion, water and salt to a boil. Reduce heat; cover and simmer until potatoes are tender. Do not drain; mash slightly. Stir in milk.

In a small bowl, blend butter, flour, parsley and pepper; stir into the potato mixture. Cook and stir over medium heat until thickened and bubbly. Remove from heat; add cheese and stir until almost melted. **Yield:** 6 servings (1-1/2 quarts).

Spinach Potato Soup

I first made this fresh-tasting soup for a school potluck on St. Patrick's Day. It was a hit, and now I make it throughout the year.

Lois McAtee, Oceanside, California

  3 cups milk
  1 can (15 ounces) sliced potatoes,
    drained
  1 package (10 ounces) frozen creamed
    spinach, thawed
1/2 teaspoon dried basil
1/2 to 3/4 teaspoon garlic salt

Combine all ingredients in a saucepan. Bring to a boil. Reduce heat; cover and simmer for 15 minutes. Cool slightly.

Transfer mixture to a blender; cover and process until small pieces of potato remain. Return to the pan and heat through. **Yield:** 4-6 servings.

Peppery Sweet Potato Soup

Roasted jalapeno and red peppers plus garlic accent the delicate sweet potato flavor in this golden soup. The recipe is from my grandmother, who loved making soups that were fast, easy and great-tasting. My family always asks for seconds.

Suzan Wiener, Spring Hill, Florida

  1 jalapeno pepper
  2 medium sweet red peppers
  5 garlic cloves
  1 teaspoon olive oil
  5 cups chicken broth
  4 cups cold mashed sweet potatoes
    (prepared without milk *or* butter)
1/2 teaspoon salt
  1 cup milk

Broil whole jalapeno and red peppers 4 in. from the heat until the skins blister, about 7 minutes. With tongs, rotate peppers a quarter turn. Broil and rotate until all sides are blistered and blackened. Immediately place peppers in a bowl; cover with plastic wrap.

Let stand for 15-20 minutes. Peel off and discard charred skin; remove stems and seeds. Finely chop peppers.

Place garlic on a double thickness of heavy-duty foil; drizzle with oil. Wrap foil around garlic. Bake at 425° for 15-20 minutes. Cool for 10-15 minutes. Squeeze softened garlic from skins into a small bowl and mash.

In a large saucepan or soup kettle, combine the peppers, garlic, broth, sweet potatoes and salt. Bring to a boil. Reduce heat; simmer, uncovered, for 25 minutes, stirring occasionally. Stir in milk; heat through. Cool slightly.

Process soup in batches in a blender or food processor until smooth; return all to the pan and heat through. **Yield:** 10 servings (2-1/2 quarts).

Editor's Note: When cutting or seeding hot peppers, use rubber or plastic gloves to protect your hands. Avoid touching your face.

> " For a lighter version of a cream-based soup, I substitute evaporated skim milk for the heavy whipping cream or half-and-half cream. "
>
> —*Leslie Rintz*
> *Newton, New Jersey*

Butternut Squash Bisque
pictured at right

I'm always improvising on recipes. For this one, I started with a basic creamed vegetable soup, and then added roasted squash and leeks for a distinctive taste. This soup is a great way to get folks to eat veggies. They only know how wonderful it tastes and pretty it looks!

Dianna Wacasey, Houston, Texas

  1 **medium butternut squash, peeled, seeded and cut into 1-inch cubes (about 4 cups),** *divided*
1/2 **cup orange juice**
1/3 **cup packed brown sugar**

  1 **cinnamon stick (3 inches)**
  1 **cup sliced leeks (white portion only)**
  1 **medium tart apple, peeled and chopped**
1/2 **cup chopped onion**
1/4 **cup butter**
  4 **cups chicken broth**
1/3 **cup heavy whipping cream**
Salt and pepper to taste
  1 **tablespoon olive oil**

In a roasting pan, toss 3 cups of squash, orange juice and brown sugar; add cinnamon. Cover and bake at 450° for 30-40 minutes or until squash is tender. Discard cinnamon; drain squash, reserving cooking liquid. Set squash and liquid aside.

In a Dutch oven, saute leeks, apple and onion in butter until tender. Add broth; bring to a boil. Stir in cooked squash; cook for 5 minutes. Add cream, salt and pepper; heat through. Cool slightly.

In a blender or food processor, process soup in batches until smooth. Return all to the pan; heat through (do not boil). Cut remaining squash into 1/4-in. cubes. In a skillet, saute squash cubes in oil and reserved cooking liquid until squash is tender and liquid has evaporated. Ladle soup into bowls. Garnish with squash cubes. **Yield:** 6 servings.

Apple Squash Soup
pictured above

This is a new twist on an old favorite—pumpkin soup. I add a little ginger and sage to apples and squash to make this creamy soup. My family loves it when autumn rolls around.

Crystal Ralph-Haughn, Bartlesville, Oklahoma

1 large onion, chopped
1/2 teaspoon rubbed sage
2 tablespoons butter
1 can (14-1/2 ounces) chicken broth

3/4 cup water
2 medium Granny Smith *or* other tart apples, peeled and finely chopped
1 package (12 ounces) frozen mashed squash, thawed
1 teaspoon ground ginger
1/2 teaspoon salt
1/2 cup milk

In a saucepan, saute onion and sage in butter for 3 minutes or until tender. Add the broth, water and apples; bring to a boil. Reduce heat; cover and simmer for 12 minutes. Add the squash, ginger and salt; return to a boil. Reduce heat; simmer, uncovered, for 10 minutes. Cool until lukewarm.

Process in batches in a blender or food processor until smooth; return to pan. Add milk; heat through. (Do not boil.) **Yield:** 5 servings.

Spinach Garlic Soup

During the years I owned and operated a deli, this was one of the most popular soups I served.

Marilyn Paradis, Woodburn, Oregon

> 1 package (10 ounces) fresh spinach, trimmed and coarsely chopped
> 4 cups chicken broth
> 1/2 cup shredded carrots
> 1/2 cup chopped onion
> 8 garlic cloves, minced
> 1/3 cup butter
> 1/4 cup all-purpose flour
> 3/4 cup heavy whipping cream
> 1/4 cup milk
> 1/2 teaspoon pepper
> 1/8 teaspoon ground nutmeg

In a 5-qt. Dutch oven, bring spinach, broth and carrots to a boil. Reduce heat; simmer 5

Carrots in the Kitchen

When you're purchasing carrots to use in your cooking, make sure to select firm, bright-orange carrots. They should be free of cracks or dry spots. You can store your carrots in a plastic bag in the refrigerator for up to 2 weeks.

As a fun topper to warm bowls of soup, try using grated carrots. For example, set aside extra grated carrot from Spinach Garlic Soup (shown above) to use on each bowl. Or use grated carrots as a garnish instead of cheese. It adds color without the calories!

minutes, stirring occasionally. Remove from the heat; cool to lukewarm.

Meanwhile, in a skillet, saute onion and garlic in butter until onion is soft, about 5-10 minutes. Add flour; cook and stir over low heat for 3-5 minutes. Add to spinach mixture.

Puree in small batches in a blender or food processor until finely chopped. Place in a large saucepan. Add cream, milk, pepper and nutmeg; heat through but do not boil. **Yield:** 4-6 servings.

Tomato Bisque

This quick-and-easy recipe earned me a blue ribbon at a local fair. I hope it wins raves at your table, too.

Mrs. B.B. Mallory, Irving, Texas

> 2 cans (14-1/2 ounces *each*) diced tomatoes, undrained
> 2 beef bouillon cubes
> 1 tablespoon sugar
> 1 to 2 teaspoons salt
> 1 teaspoon onion powder
> 1 bay leaf
> 1/4 teaspoon dried basil
> 1/4 teaspoon white pepper
> 1/2 cup butter
> 1/3 cup all-purpose flour
> 4 cups milk

In a saucepan, combine the first eight ingredients; bring to a boil. Reduce heat; simmer, uncovered, for 30 minutes. Remove bay leaf; press mixture through sieve and set aside.

In a large saucepan, melt butter; blend in flour until smooth and bubbly. Gradually stir in milk. Bring to a boil over medium heat, stirring constantly; cook for 2 minutes.

Reduce the heat. Gradually stir in the tomato mixture until smooth; heat through. **Yield:** 8-10 servings.

Savory Leek Soup

pictured above

There's no mistaking that savory is the main herb seasoning this rich and creamy soup. It has a wonderful aroma.

Eleanor Davis, Pittsburgh, Pennsylvania

> 4 medium leeks (white portion only), chopped
> 1/2 cup minced chives
> 1/2 cup butter
> 4 cups chicken broth
> 2 cups mashed potatoes (prepared with milk and butter)
> 2 tablespoons minced fresh savory *or* 2 teaspoons dried savory
> 3 cups half-and-half cream
> Salt and pepper to taste

In a large saucepan, saute leeks and chives in butter until tender. Add the broth, potatoes and savory; bring to a boil. Reduce heat; simmer, uncovered, for 8-10 minutes. Cool slightly.

Process in batches in a blender or food processor until smooth; return to pan. Stir in the cream, salt and pepper; heat through. **Yield:** 8-10 servings.

Mushroom Bisque

Parsley stars as an ingredient in this tasty bisque. It adds just the right flavor combination with the mushrooms.

Emily Chaney, Penobscot, Maine

> 1/2 pound fresh mushrooms, sliced
> 1 medium onion, sliced
> 1 cup minced fresh parsley
> 1/4 cup butter
> 1 tablespoon all-purpose flour
> 1 can (14-1/2 ounces) beef broth
> 1 cup (8 ounces) sour cream

In a large saucepan, saute mushrooms, onion and parsley in butter until tender. Stir in flour until blended; gradually add broth. Bring to a boil; cook and stir for 2 minutes or until thickened. Cool slightly.

Transfer to a blender; cover and process until pureed. Return to pan. Stir in sour cream; heat through, stirring occasionally (do not boil). **Yield:** 4 servings.

Mashed Potato Soup

You won't recognize the leftover mashed potatoes in this excellent-tasting soup. Topped with chives, it's especially good on chilly fall evenings.

Dorothy Bateman, Carver, Massachusetts

> 1 tablespoon chopped onion
> 1 tablespoon butter
> 2 cups milk
> 1-1/2 cups mashed potatoes (prepared with milk and butter)
> 1/2 teaspoon salt
> 1/8 teaspoon celery salt
> 1/8 teaspoon pepper
> 1 tablespoon minced fresh *or* dried chives

In a saucepan, saute the onion in butter until tender. Add milk, potatoes, salt and celery salt and pepper; heat through. Garnish with chives. **Yield:** 3 servings.

Pumpkin Soup

pictured below

While it looks elegant and is an appealing addition to a holiday meal, this creamy soup is so simple to make. My husband was skeptical at first, but after one bowl, he asked for second helpings!

Elizabeth Montgomery, Taylorville, Illinois

   1/2 cup finely chopped onion
     2 tablespoons butter
     1 tablespoon all-purpose flour
     2 cans (14-1/2 ounces *each*) chicken broth
     1 can (15 ounces) solid-pack pumpkin
     1 teaspoon brown sugar
   1/4 teaspoon salt
   1/8 teaspoon pepper
   1/8 teaspoon ground nutmeg
     1 cup heavy whipping cream

In a large saucepan, saute onion in butter until tender. Remove from the heat; stir in flour until smooth. Gradually stir in the broth, pumpkin, brown sugar, salt, pepper and nutmeg; bring to a boil.

Reduce heat and simmer for 5 minutes. Add cream; cook for 2 minutes or until heated through. **Yield:** 6 servings.

Coming to Terms

Creamed soups and bisques may seem similar, but they're not identical:

Bisques are thick, rich pureed soups made with seafood, poultry or vegetables.

Creamed soups are pureed soups with a smooth, silky texture. They frequently use a single vegetable, such as asparagus or carrot. They may be thickened with flour or potatoes and can be made without cream.

Zucchini Bisque

I like to serve this soup as a first course for special dinners. It is nice and light, pretty in color and very appetizing with its blend of flavors.

Marjorie Beck, Sonora, California

     1 medium onion, diced
   1/2 cup butter
 2-1/2 cups shredded zucchini
 2-1/2 cups chicken broth
   1/2 teaspoon dried basil
   1/2 teaspoon salt
   1/2 teaspoon pepper
   1/4 teaspoon ground nutmeg
     1 cup half-and-half cream

In a large saucepan, saute onion in butter. Add zucchini and chicken broth. Simmer, covered, for about 15 minutes; add seasonings.

Puree on low in a blender. Return to pan; stir in cream and heat through. **Yield:** 4-5 servings (5 cups).

Tomato Dill Bisque

pictured at right

My family really enjoys this soup when we make it from our garden tomatoes. When those tomatoes are plentiful, I make a big batch (without mayonnaise) and freeze it. Then we can enjoy it even after the garden is gone for the season.

Susan Breckbill, Lincoln Univ., Pennsylvania

    2 medium onions, chopped
    1 garlic clove, minced
    2 tablespoons butter
    2 pounds tomatoes, peeled and
      chopped
  1/2 cup water
    1 chicken bouillon cube
    1 teaspoon sugar
    1 teaspoon dill weed
  1/2 teaspoon salt
  1/4 teaspoon pepper
  1/2 cup mayonnaise, optional

In a large saucepan, saute onions and garlic in butter until tender. Add tomatoes, water, bouillon, sugar and seasonings. Cover and simmer 10 minutes or until tomatoes are tender. Remove from heat; cool.

Puree in a blender or food processor. Return to saucepan. If a creamy soup is desired, stir in mayonnaise. Cook and stir over low heat until heated through. Serve warm. **Yield:** 5 servings (5 cups).

Creamy Squash Soup

You can simmer this smooth full-flavored soup using whatever winter squash is available. I like to serve it with rolls, fruit and cheese.

Gayle Lewis, Yucaipa, California

    3 bacon strips
    1 cup finely chopped onion
    2 garlic cloves, minced
    2 cups mashed cooked winter squash
    2 tablespoons all-purpose flour
    1 can (12 ounces) evaporated milk,
      divided
    3 cups chicken broth
  1/2 teaspoon curry powder
  1/2 teaspoon salt

  1/4 teaspoon pepper
  1/8 teaspoon ground nutmeg
Sour cream, optional

In a saucepan or Dutch oven, cook bacon until crisp; crumble and set aside. Drain all but 1 tablespoon drippings; saute onion and garlic in drippings until tender.

In a blender or food processor, puree squash, flour, 1/3 cup milk and onion mixture; add to pan. Add broth, curry powder, salt, pepper, nutmeg and remaining milk; bring to a boil over medium heat. Boil for 2 minutes.

Top servings with a dollop of sour cream if desired. Sprinkle with bacon. **Yield:** 6-8 servings.

Spinach Bisque

When my grandchildren were only 3 years old, they tried this yummy soup at a local restaurant and fell in love with it, so I immediately asked for the recipe. They still call it Yummy Soup.

Mary Lou Allaman, Kirkwood, Illinois

    5 packages (10 ounces *each*) frozen
      chopped spinach, thawed and well
      drained
    3 cups half-and-half cream
    3 packages (8 ounces *each*) cream
      cheese, cubed
    1 can (14-1/2 ounces) chicken broth

1 cup (4 ounces) shredded cheddar
   cheese
3/4 cup grated Parmesan cheese
2 garlic cloves, minced
1 teaspoon salt
1/2 teaspoon pepper

In a Dutch oven or soup kettle, combine spinach and cream. Cover and cook over medium-low heat until heated through.

Add remaining ingredients. Cook, uncovered, stirring constantly, until cheese is melted and soup is hot. **Yield:** 14 servings (3-1/2 quarts).

Asparagus Cress Soup

pictured below

Here's a refreshing soup that combines two spring treats—asparagus and watercress. Serve it as the first course to a special meal with family or friends.

Teresa Lillycrop, Puslinch, Ontario

3/4 cup chopped green onions
1/4 cup butter
3 tablespoons all-purpose flour
2-1/2 cups chicken broth
1-1/2 pounds fresh asparagus, cut
   into 1-inch pieces
1/2 bunch watercress, stems removed
   (about 1 cup, lightly packed)
1-1/2 cups half-and-half cream

3/4 teaspoon salt
1/4 teaspoon white pepper
1/8 teaspoon cayenne pepper
Sour cream

In a large saucepan, saute onions in butter 3-4 minutes or until soft. Stir in flour to form a smooth paste. Cook for 2 minutes. Gradually stir in broth and bring to a boil.

Add asparagus and watercress; cover and simmer 5-7 minutes or until vegetables are tender. Cool.

Puree soup in a blender or food processor until smooth. Return to saucepan; stir in half-and-half cream. Heat over low to serving temperature (do not boil).

Season with salt, white pepper and cayenne. Garnish each serving with a dollop of sour cream. **Yield:** 6 servings.

Acorn Squash Soup

The recipe for this thick and creamy soup was given to me by a fellow squash lover. The attractive rich yellow soup is especially enjoyable during the cool nights of Indian summer.

Dorrene Butterfield, Lincoln, Nebraska

1 small onion, chopped
1/4 cup chopped celery
2 tablespoons butter
2 tablespoons all-purpose flour
1 teaspoon chicken bouillon granules
1/2 teaspoon dill weed
1/4 teaspoon curry powder
Dash cayenne pepper
2 cups chicken broth
1 can (12 ounces) evaporated milk
3 cups mashed cooked acorn squash
Salt and pepper to taste
5 bacon strips, cooked and crumbled

In a large saucepan, saute the onion and celery in butter. Stir in flour, bouillon, dill, curry and cayenne until blended. Gradually add broth and milk. Bring to a boil; cook and stir for 2 minutes. Add the squash, salt and pepper; heat through.

In a blender, process the soup in batches until smooth. Pour into bowls; garnish with bacon. **Yield:** 6 servings.

Crab Bisque

pictured above

This hearty chowder has a creamy broth that's swimming with tasty chunks of crab and crunchy corn.

Sherrie Manton, Folsom, Louisiana

1 celery rib, thinly sliced
1 small onion, chopped
1/2 cup chopped green pepper
3 tablespoons butter
2 cans (14-3/4 ounces *each*) cream-style corn
2 cans (10-3/4 ounces *each*) condensed cream of potato soup, undiluted
1-1/2 cups milk
1-1/2 cups half-and-half cream
2 bay leaves
1 teaspoon dried thyme
1/2 teaspoon garlic powder
1/4 teaspoon white pepper
1/8 teaspoon hot pepper sauce
3 cans (6 ounces *each*) crabmeat, drained, flaked and cartilage removed

In a large saucepan or soup kettle, saute celery, onion and green pepper in butter until tender. Add the next nine ingredients; mix well.

Stir in crab; heat through. Discard bay leaves.

Transfer to a freezer container; cover and freeze for up to 3 months.

To use frozen soup: Thaw in the refrigerator; place in a saucepan and heat through. **Yield:** 10 servings.

Curried Zucchini Soup

This soup, a recipe given to me by one of my daughters-in-law, is a special treat when used from the freezer on a cold winter's day. It calls to mind memories of the zucchini summer that was—and gives hope of the zucchini summer yet to be!

Ruth McCombie, Etobicoke, Ontario

      2 pounds zucchini, sliced (about 4 medium)
      5 green onions, chopped
      4 cups chicken broth
      1 to 2 tablespoons butter, optional
1-1/2 teaspoons curry powder
      1 teaspoon salt
   1/8 teaspoon cayenne pepper

In a large saucepan or Dutch oven, combine all ingredients. Simmer, covered, until zucchini is soft, about 15 minutes.

Puree in batches in a blender on low speed; return to pan and heat through. **Yield:** 6-8 servings (2 quarts).

Cream of Carrot Soup

I came up with this yummy soup when I was in a hurry one day and we needed something hot to eat. It's versatile, too. You can substitute most any vegetable with excellent results.

Ruth Andrewson, Leavenworth, Washington

   4 cups chicken broth
   4 large carrots, cut into chunks
1/2 cup heavy whipping cream
   1 teaspoon sugar

In a saucepan, bring broth and carrots to a boil. Reduce heat; simmer, uncovered, until carrots are tender, about 15 minutes. Cool slightly.

In a blender, cover and process soup in small batches until smooth; return to the pan. Stir in cream and sugar; heat through. **Yield:** 5 servings.

Creamy Tomato Bisque
pictured below

This rich, creamy bisque has a wonderful old-fashioned flavor. It makes a nice accompaniment to any meal.

Cathy Fulton, Hazlet, New Jersey

   2 cups water
   4 chicken bouillon cubes
   1 can (14-1/2 ounces) diced tomatoes, undrained
1/2 cup chopped celery
   2 tablespoons chopped onion
   2 medium fresh tomatoes, peeled and diced
1/4 cup butter
   3 tablespoons all-purpose flour
   2 cups half-and-half cream
1/3 to 1/2 cup sherry, optional

In a large saucepan, bring first five ingredients to a boil. Reduce heat; cover and simmer for 15-20 minutes or until vegetables are tender. Cool. Puree mixture in a food processor or blender; set aside.

In the same saucepan, saute fresh tomatoes in butter for 5 minutes. Stir in flour to make a smooth paste. Gradually add cream and stir over low heat until thickened.

Stir in pureed mixture and sherry if desired. **Yield:** about 8 servings (2 quarts).

special **CREAMED SOUPS & BISQUES**

Cream of Asparagus Soup

My best friend and I enjoy this smooth soup so much we knew we had to share it. Pepper gives it zip.

Hilda Magnuson, Whittier, California

        1   medium onion, chopped
        1   garlic clove, minced
        3   cups cut fresh asparagus (1-inch pieces)
    2-1/2   cups chicken broth
      1/8   teaspoon crushed red pepper flakes
        3   ounces cream cheese, cubed
        2   tablespoons sour cream
        1   tablespoon snipped fresh dill *or* 1 teaspoon dill weed
      1/2   teaspoon ground nutmeg

In a large saucepan coated with nonstick cooking spray, saute onion and garlic until tender. Add asparagus, broth and red pepper flakes. Bring to a boil. Reduce heat; cover and simmer for 10-15 minutes or until asparagus is tender.

Place a third of the mixture in a blender; add cream cheese, sour cream and dill. Cover and process until smooth; return to pan. Cook over medium heat until heated through. Sprinkle with nutmeg. **Yield:** 4 servings.

Pantry Tomato Soup

A few handy pantry items create this fresh-tasting tomato soup. It's super easy...and oh-so-good!

Gail Westing, Landfall, Minnesota

        1   can (8 ounces) tomato sauce
        1   tablespoon butter
  1/8 to 1/4   teaspoon onion powder
    Dash pepper
        2   cups milk

In a saucepan, combine the first four ingredients. Bring to a simmer over medium heat. Gradually stir in milk; cook and stir until heated through (do not boil). **Yield:** 2 servings.

Butternut Boats

pictured below

This thick and creamy soup became a part of my recipe collection, thanks to my grown daughter, Jane. We share recipes back and forth all the time. This one, we both agree, is a real treat! (To make it extra fun, our home economists suggest using the squash shells as serving bowls.)

Evelyn Bentley, Ames, Iowa

        3   small butternut squash (about 1-1/2 pounds *each*)
        4   large leeks (white portion only), sliced
        1   teaspoon dried thyme
        5   tablespoons butter
        3   cups chicken broth
    1-1/4   teaspoons salt
      1/2   teaspoon pepper
      1/2   cup sour cream, optional
    Chopped chives *or* parsley

Cut squash in half; remove and discard seeds. Place with cut side down in a greased 13-in. x 9-in. x 2-in. baking pan. Add 1/4 in. of water to pan. Cover and bake at 375° for 40 minutes or until tender. Scoop out pulp, leaving about a 1/4-in. shell. Set shells and pulp aside.

In a large saucepan, saute leeks and thyme in butter until tender. Add pulp, broth, salt and pepper; simmer for 20 minutes.

Remove from the heat; cool slightly. Puree in a blender; return to pan and heat through. Spoon into squash shells.

Place sour cream in a heavy-duty resealable plastic bag; cut a small hole in the corner of the bag. If desired, pipe a coil of sour cream over squash filling.

Beginning at the center, use a toothpick to draw right angles across the piped lines about 1/2 in. apart. Sprinkle with chives. **Yield:** 6 servings.

Broccoli Nutmeg Soup
pictured at right

This thick and creamy soup has wonderful broccoli flavor with just a hint of nutmeg. It's delicious!

Marion Tipton, Phoenix, Arizona

    4 cups chicken broth
    2 to 2-1/2 pounds broccoli, cut into
      florets
  1/2 cup chopped green onions
    1 tablespoon olive oil
  1/4 cup all-purpose flour
    1 teaspoon salt
  1/4 teaspoon ground nutmeg
  1/8 teaspoon pepper
    1 cup half-and-half cream

In a large saucepan, bring the broth to a boil; add broccoli. Reduce heat; cover and simmer until tender, about 10 minutes.

Meanwhile, in a small skillet, saute onions in oil until tender; stir into broth. Remove from the heat; cool 10-15 minutes. Puree in small batches in a blender or food processor until smooth. Return all to the saucepan; set aside.

In a bowl, combine flour, salt, nutmeg and pepper. Slowly add cream, stirring constantly. Gradually stir into broccoli mixture.

Return to the heat; cook over medium heat until heated through, stirring occasionally. **Yield:** 4 servings.

Carrot Leek Soup

This is a tasty way to get a serving of vegetables. The leek, carrots and potatoes are wonderfully seasoned in a nice creamy soup.

Norma Meyers, Huntsville, Arkansas

    1 medium leek, thinly sliced
    4 teaspoons butter
    6 medium carrots, sliced
    2 medium potatoes, peeled and cubed
    3 cans (14-1/2 ounces *each*) chicken
      broth
    2 cups milk
  1/8 teaspoon pepper

In a large saucepan, saute leek in butter until tender. Add the carrots, potatoes and broth; bring to a boil. Reduce heat; cover and simmer until vegetables are tender. Cool to room temperature.

Remove vegetables with a slotted spoon to a blender or food processor. Add enough cooking liquid to cover; blend until smooth. Return to pan. Stir in milk and pepper; heat through. **Yield:** 10 servings.

Fresh Pumpkin Soup

pictured above

*This appealing soup harvests the fall flavors of
just-picked pumpkins and tart apples...and is
sure to warm you up on a crisp autumn day.
Top the creamy puree with a sprinkling of
toasted pumpkin seeds.*

Jane Shapton, Portland, Oregon

  8 **cups chopped fresh pumpkin
    (about 3 pounds)**
  4 **cups chicken broth**
  3 **small tart apples, peeled and chopped**

  1 **medium onion, chopped**
  2 **tablespoons lemon juice**
  2 **teaspoons minced fresh gingerroot**
  2 **garlic cloves, minced**
1/2 **teaspoon salt**
TOASTED PUMPKIN SEEDS:
 1/2 **cup pumpkin seeds**
  1 **teaspoon canola oil**
1/8 **teaspoon salt**

In a slow cooker, combine the first eight ingredients; mix well. Cover and cook on low for 8-
10 hours or until the pumpkin and apples are
tender.

Meanwhile, toss pumpkin seeds with oil and salt. Spread in an ungreased 15-in. x 10-in. x 1-in. baking pan. Bake at 250° for 50-60 minutes or until golden brown. Set aside.

Cool the pumpkin mixture slightly; process in batches in a blender or food processor. Transfer to a large saucepan; heat through. Garnish with toasted pumpkin seeds. **Yield:** 9 servings.

Zesty Tomato Soup

When some friends stopped by unexpectedly, my husband, Phil, came up with this fast-to-fix soup that tastes homemade. Two easy ingredients give canned soup just the right amount of zip.

JoAnn Gunio, Franklin, North Carolina

  2 cans (10-3/4 ounces *each*) condensed tomato soup, undiluted
2-2/3 cups water
  2 teaspoons chili powder
Oyster crackers *or* shredded Monterey Jack cheese, optional

In a saucepan, combine the first three ingredients; heat through. Garnish with crackers or cheese if desired. **Yield:** 4-5 servings.

Spicy Seafood Bisque
pictured at right

This spicy soup, featuring shrimp, crabmeat and tomatoes, gets its zip from hot pepper sauce and cayenne pepper. It's easy to prepare and dresses up any meal. Of all the recipes I've borrowed from my mom, this soup is the one that I've made most often.

Kevin Weeks, North Palm Beach, Florida

1/2 cup chopped onion
1/2 cup chopped celery
  2 tablespoons butter
  4 cups chicken broth
  3 cups tomato juice
  1 can (14-1/2 ounces) diced tomatoes, undrained
  1 tablespoon Worcestershire sauce

  1 teaspoon seafood seasoning
  1 teaspoon dried oregano
1/2 teaspoon garlic powder
1/2 teaspoon hot pepper sauce
1/4 teaspoon cayenne pepper
  1 bay leaf
1/2 cup uncooked small shell pasta *or* elbow macaroni
  1 pound uncooked medium shrimp, peeled and deveined
  1 can (6 ounces) crabmeat, drained, flaked and cartilage removed

In a large saucepan, saute the onion and celery in butter until tender. Add broth, tomato juice, tomatoes, Worcestershire sauce and seasonings; bring to a boil. Reduce heat; cover and simmer for 20 minutes.

Discard the bay leaf. Add pasta to the soup; cook, uncovered, until tender. Add the shrimp and crab; simmer 5 minutes longer or until the shrimp turn pink. **Yield:** 10-12 servings (about 3 quarts).

145

Zippy Tomato Soup

Quick to fix and eat, this soup gets a little heat from cayenne pepper. My family enjoys warm bowls topped with parsley.

Ardith Morton, Merriman, Nebraska

- 2 quarts tomato juice
- 1 beef bouillon cube
- 1 tablespoon dried minced onion
- 1/2 teaspoon dried basil
- 1/4 teaspoon dried oregano
- 1/4 teaspoon garlic powder
- 1/8 teaspoon cayenne pepper
- 2 tablespoons minced fresh parsley

Combine the first seven ingredients in a 3-qt. saucepan; bring to a boil. Reduce heat; cover and simmer for 5 minutes. Add parsley. Serve immediately. **Yield:** 8 servings (2 quarts).

Broccoli and Crab Bisque

Since our son is a broccoli grower, our friends keep supplying us with recipes using broccoli. To this family favorite, we add a tossed salad, rolls, fruit and cookies.

Dorothy Child, Malone, New York

- 1 cup sliced leeks (white part only)
- 1 cup sliced fresh mushrooms
- 1 cup fresh broccoli florets
- 1 garlic clove, minced
- 1/4 cup butter
- 1/4 cup all-purpose flour
- 1/4 teaspoon dried thyme, crushed
- 1/8 teaspoon pepper
- 1 bay leaf
- 2 cans (10-1/2 ounces *each*) condensed chicken broth, undiluted
- 1 cup half-and-half cream
- 3/4 cup shredded Swiss cheese
- 1 package (6 ounces) frozen crabmeat, thawed, drained and flaked

In a saucepan, cook leeks, mushrooms, broccoli and garlic in butter until broccoli is crisp-tender. Remove from the heat; blend in flour and seasonings. Stir in broth and cream.

Cook and stir until mixture comes to a boil and is thickened; cook 1 minute. Add cheese; stir until melted. Add crabmeat and heat through; do not boil. Remove bay leaf before serving. **Yield:** 4-5 servings (5 cups).

Butternut Squash Soup
pictured above

This deep golden soup is as pretty as it is yummy. If you'd like, you can intensify the garlic flavor by adding an extra bulb. The garlic is what really flavors this soup.

Lynn Proudfoot, Huntington, Connecticut

- 3 pounds unpeeled butternut squash, halved and seeded
- 2 large unpeeled onions
- 1 small garlic bulb
- 1/4 cup olive oil
- 2 tablespoons minced fresh thyme *or* 2 teaspoons dried thyme
- 3 to 3-1/2 cups chicken broth
- 1/2 cup heavy whipping cream
- 3 tablespoons minced fresh parsley
- 1/2 teaspoon salt
- 1/4 teaspoon pepper

Fresh thyme sprigs, optional

Cut squash into eight large pieces. Place cut side up in a 15-in. x 10-in. x 1-in. baking pan. Cut 1/4 in. off tops of onion and garlic bulbs (the end that comes to a closed point).

Place cut side up in baking pan. Brush with oil; sprinkle with thyme. Cover tightly and bake at 350° for 1-1/2 to 2 hours or until vegetables are very tender. Uncover and let stand until lukewarm. Remove peel from squash and onions; remove soft garlic from skins.

Combine vegetables, broth and cream. Puree in small batches in a blender or food processor until smooth; transfer to a large saucepan.

Add parsley, salt and pepper; heat through (do not boil). Garnish with thyme if desired. **Yield:** 8 servings (2 quarts).

Tomato Dill Soup
pictured below

Most often, I make this soup ahead and keep it in the fridge. It's particularly good to take out and heat up with tuna or grilled cheese sandwiches, hard rolls or a salad.

Patty Kile, Greentown, Pennsylvania

> 1 medium onion, thinly sliced
> 1 garlic clove, minced
> 2 tablespoons vegetable oil
> 1 tablespoon butter
> 1/2 teaspoon salt
> Pinch pepper
> 3 large tomatoes, sliced
> 1 can (6 ounces) tomato paste
> 1/4 cup all-purpose flour
> 2 cups water, *divided*
> 3/4 cup heavy whipping cream, whipped
> 1 to 2 tablespoons finely minced fresh dill *or* 1 to 2 teaspoons dill weed

In a large saucepan over low heat, cook onion and garlic in oil and butter until tender. Add salt, pepper and tomatoes; cook over medium-high heat for 3 minutes. Remove from the heat and stir in tomato paste.

In a small bowl, combine flour and 1/2 cup of water; stir until smooth. Stir into saucepan. Gradually stir in remaining water until smooth; bring to a boil over medium heat. Cook and stir for 2 minutes.

Place mixture in a sieve over a bowl. With the back of a spoon, press vegetables through the sieve to remove seeds and skin; return puree to the pan.

Add cream and dill; cook over low heat just until heated through (do not boil). **Yield:** 4 servings (1 quart).

Carrot-Rice Soup

Great soup can be made in less than 30 minutes, and this recipe is proof!

Anneliese Deising, Plymouth, Michigan

> 3 leeks (white part only), thinly sliced
> 2 tablespoons butter
> 3 medium carrots, grated
> 6 cups chicken broth
> 3/4 cup cooked long grain rice
> 1/4 teaspoon ground mace
> Dash pepper
> 3/4 cup heavy whipping cream
> Additional grated carrots, optional

In a 3-qt. saucepan, saute leeks in butter for 1 minute. Add carrots and cook 1 minute longer. Stir in the broth, rice, mace and pepper; bring to a boil.

Reduce the heat; cover and cook for 15 minutes or until the rice and carrots are tender. Cool slightly.

Puree in batches in a blender; return to pan. Add cream; heat through but do not boil. Garnish with carrots if desired. **Yield:** 6 servings.

Creamy Carrot Soup

pictured above

When I serve this creamy soup, people are amazed by the bright carrot color. A hint of rosemary adds a nice spark.

Grace Yaskovic, Branchville, New Jersey

1 cup chopped onion
1/4 cup butter
4-1/2 cups sliced carrots (1/4 inch thick)
1 large potato, peeled and cubed
2 cans (14-1/2 ounces *each*) chicken broth
1 teaspoon ground ginger
2 cups heavy whipping cream
1 teaspoon crushed dried rosemary
1/2 teaspoon salt
1/8 teaspoon pepper

In a 5-qt. Dutch oven, saute onion in butter until tender. Add the carrots, potato, broth and ginger. Cover and cook over medium heat for 30 minutes or until vegetables are tender. Cool 15 minutes.

Puree in small batches in a blender or food processor until smooth. Return all to the saucepan; add cream, rosemary, salt and pepper. Cook over low heat until heated through. **Yield:** 6-8 servings (2-1/2 quarts).

Easy Seafood Bisque

I've always enjoyed seafood bisque at restaurants and one day decided to try my hand at a homemade version. Everyone says this is one of the better recipes they've tasted.

Cindy Rogowski, Lancaster, New York

- 1/2 cup chopped onion
- 1 tablespoon butter
- 1 can (10-3/4 ounces) condensed cream of celery soup, undiluted
- 1 can (10-3/4 ounces) condensed cream of shrimp soup, undiluted
- 1 package (8 ounces) imitation crabmeat, chopped
- 2-1/4 cups milk
- 1 teaspoon chicken bouillon granules
- 1/2 teaspoon dried parsley flakes
- 1/4 teaspoon garlic powder
- 1/4 teaspoon dried marjoram
- 1/4 teaspoon pepper

In a 3-qt. saucepan, saute onion in butter until tender. Stir in remaining ingredients. Cover and cook over medium-low heat for 20 minutes or until heated through, stirring occasionally. **Yield:** 4-5 servings.

Creamy Asparagus Soup

This asparagus soup tastes like spring. Pureed to a smooth and creamy texture, the soup is nicely seasoned with thyme...and is sure to please asparagus lovers.

Adele Long, Sterling Heights, Michigan

- 2 green onions, chopped
- 1 garlic clove, minced
- 1 tablespoon butter
- 2 cans (14-1/2 ounces *each*) chicken broth *or* vegetable broth
- 1 pound fresh asparagus, trimmed and cut into 1-inch pieces
- 1/2 teaspoon salt
- 1/2 to 3/4 teaspoon dried thyme
- 1/8 teaspoon pepper
- 1 bay leaf
- 2 tablespoons all-purpose flour
- 3 tablespoons water
- 1/4 cup sour cream
- 1 teaspoon grated lemon peel

In a large saucepan, saute onions and garlic in butter. Add the broth, asparagus, salt, thyme, pepper and bay leaf. Bring to a boil.

Reduce heat; cover and simmer for 8-10 minutes or until asparagus is tender. Drain asparagus, reserving cooking liquid. Discard bay leaf. Cool slightly.

In a food processor, combine asparagus and 1/2 cup cooking liquid; cover and process until smooth. Return pureed asparagus and remaining cooking liquid to pan.

Combine flour and water until smooth; stir into soup. Bring to a boil; cook and stir for 1-2 minutes or until thickened. Garnish each serving with sour cream and lemon peel. **Yield:** 4 servings.

Accenting with Herbs...

Fresh herbs can make a dish a feast for the eyes as well as the taste buds! The blossoms of many herbs are edible and can be a lovely accompaniment to dishes, especially if the herbs are part of the recipe.

Pair herbs with different textures, colors and leaf sizes. For example, big gray-green velvety sage leaves are an interesting contrast to tiny delicate dark-green oregano or thyme leaves.

Make an eye-catching border on individual bowls of soup by chopping chives and sprinkling them just around the edge of the dish.

Quick Pea Soup

This brightly colored, fresh-tasting soup is one of our daughter's favorites. She purees it in the blender in just seconds, then zaps a mugful in the microwave until heated through.

Paula Zsiray, Logan, Utah

- 1-1/2 cups frozen peas, thawed
- 1-1/4 cups milk, *divided*
- 1/4 teaspoon salt
- 1/8 teaspoon pepper

Place the peas and 1/4 cup of milk in a blender; cover and process until pureed. Pour into a saucepan; add salt if desired, pepper and remaining milk. Cook and stir for 5 minutes or until heated through. **Yield:** 2 servings.

Golden Squash Soup

pictured below

This special recipe from my mother-in-law is one that I enjoy making as part of our fall meals. The soup is so pretty that it dresses up the table.

Maryann Klein, Washington Township, New Jersey

    3 leeks (white portion only), sliced
    4 medium carrots, chopped
    5 tablespoons butter
    3 pounds butternut squash, peeled and
      cubed
    6 cups chicken broth
    3 medium zucchini, peeled and sliced
    2 teaspoons salt
  1/2 teaspoon dried thyme
  1/4 teaspoon white pepper
    1 cup half-and-half cream
  1/2 cup milk
Grated Parmesan cheese and chives, optional

In a Dutch oven or soup kettle over medium heat, saute the leeks and carrots in butter for 5 minutes, stirring occasionally.

Add squash, broth, zucchini, salt, thyme and pepper; bring to a boil. Reduce heat; cover and simmer until vegetables are tender, about 30 minutes. Cool until lukewarm.

In a blender or food processor, puree soup in small batches until smooth; return to kettle. Add cream and milk; mix well and heat through (do not boil). Garnish with Parmesan cheese and chives if desired. **Yield:** 12-14 servings (3-1/2 quarts).

Curry Carrot Leek Soup

This recipe comes from an old Yorkshire cookbook I picked up in England, where leeks are very popular. The curry powder lends just the right amount of zip.

Valerie Engel, San Jose, California

    1 pound leeks, thinly sliced
    1 pound carrots, coarsely chopped
    2 teaspoons butter
    1 medium potato, peeled and diced
  1/2 teaspoon curry powder
    4 cups chicken broth
  1/4 teaspoon salt
  1/4 teaspoon pepper

In a large saucepan, saute leeks and carrots in butter until leeks are tender. Add potato and curry powder; cook and stir for 2 minutes. Add broth, salt and pepper; bring to a boil.

Reduce heat; cover and simmer for 15-20 minutes or until the vegetables are very tender. Cool slightly.

Process in batches in a food processor or blender until pureed. Return to the pan; heat through. **Yield:** 6 servings.

Creamy Red Pepper Soup

pictured below

Everyone loves this soup's taste, but no one guesses that pears are the secret ingredient.

Connie Summers, Augusta, Michigan

- 2 large onions, chopped
- 4 garlic cloves, minced
- 1/4 cup butter
- 2 large potatoes, peeled and diced
- 2 jars (7 ounces *each*) roasted red peppers, drained, patted dry and chopped
- 5 cups chicken broth
- 2 cans (15 ounces *each*) pears in juice
- 1/8 teaspoon cayenne pepper
- 1/8 teaspoon black pepper

In a Dutch oven, saute onions and garlic in butter until tender. Add potatoes, red peppers and broth. Bring to a boil. Reduce heat; cover and simmer for 15-20 minutes or until vegetables are tender. Remove from the heat. Add pears; let cool.

In a blender, cover and puree in batches. Return to the pan. Stir in cayenne and black pepper. Cook until heated through. **Yield:** 12 servings (3 quarts).

Favorite Fennel Soup

pictured above

For an interesting first course, try this delicate soup. The light broth has a mild fennel taste.

Nanette Cheramie, Oklahoma City, Oklahoma

- 4 fennel bulbs, sliced
- 1 large onion, chopped
- 2 tablespoons butter
- 2 cans (14-1/2 ounces *each*) vegetable *or* chicken broth
- 2 cups milk
- 1 bay leaf
- Salt and pepper to taste
- 2 egg yolks
- 1/2 cup half-and-half cream

In a large saucepan, saute fennel and onion in butter until tender. Add the broth, milk and seasonings. Cover and simmer for 30 minutes. Strain, reserving broth. Discard fennel, onion and bay leaf.

In a small bowl, beat egg yolks and cream. Gradually add a small amount of hot soup. Return all to the pan. Cook and stir until slightly thickened. Simmer 10-15 minutes longer (do not boil). **Yield:** 5 servings.

special CREAMED SOUPS *&* BISQUES

"Good **soup** is one of
the **prime** ingredients of **good** living."

wholesome
BEAN & LENTIL

Tortilla Soup
pictured above

Chock-full of ingredients, this tasty soup makes a warming lunch or dinner. Plus, it's so quick and easy to fix.

Sharon Adams, Columbus, Ohio

- 1 can (16 ounces) refried beans
- 1 can (15 ounces) black beans, rinsed and drained
- 1 can (14-1/2 ounces) chicken broth
- 1-1/2 cups frozen corn
- 3/4 cup chunky salsa
- 3/4 cup cubed cooked chicken breast
- 1/2 cup water
- 2 cups (8 ounces) shredded cheddar cheese, *divided*
- 28 baked tortilla chips, *divided*

In a large saucepan, combine the first seven ingredients. Bring to a boil. Reduce heat; cover and simmer for 10 minutes.

Add 1 cup cheese; cook and stir over low heat until melted. Crumble half of the tortilla chips into soup bowls. Ladle soup over chips.

Top each serving with two crumbled chips; sprinkle with remaining cheese. **Yield:** 7 servings.

Beef Barley Lentil Soup

It's easy to fill up your slow cooker and forget about supper...until the kitchen is filled with a wonderful aroma, that is! I've served this soup often to family and friends on cold nights, along with homemade rolls and a green salad. For variety, substitute jicama (a starchy root vegetable found in the produce department of many grocery stores) for the potatoes.

Judy Metzentine, The Dalles, Oregon

- 1 pound ground beef
- 1 medium onion, chopped
- 2 cups cubed red potatoes (1/4-inch pieces)
- 1 cup chopped celery
- 1 cup diced carrots
- 1 cup dried lentils, rinsed
- 1/2 cup medium pearl barley
- 8 cups water
- 2 teaspoons beef bouillon granules
- 1 teaspoon salt
- 1/2 teaspoon lemon-pepper seasoning
- 2 cans (14-1/2 ounces *each*) stewed tomatoes

In a nonstick skillet, cook beef and onion over medium heat until meat is no longer pink; drain. Transfer to a 5-qt. slow cooker.

Layer with the potatoes, celery, carrots, lentils and barley. Combine the water, bouillon, salt and lemon-pepper; pour over vegetables.

Cover and cook on low for 6 hours or until vegetables and barley are tender. Add the tomatoes; cook 2 hours longer. **Yield:** 10 servings.

Sixteen-Bean Soup

Count on this pleasingly seasoned, hearty soup to satisfy the whole family. My husband and kids say brimming bowls of it are flavorful and filling. I also love the fact that I can make a big pot from a handy bean mix.

Laura Prokash, Algoma, Wisconsin

- 1 package (12 ounces) 16-bean soup mix
- 1 large onion, chopped
- 2 garlic cloves, minced
- 1 teaspoon salt
- 1 teaspoon chili powder
- 1/4 teaspoon pepper
- 1/8 teaspoon hot pepper sauce
- 1 bay leaf
- 2 quarts water
- 1 can (14-1/2 ounces) stewed tomatoes
- 1 tablespoon lemon juice

Set seasoning packet from beans aside. Place beans in a Dutch oven or soup kettle; add water to cover by 2 in. Bring to a boil; boil for 2 minutes. Remove from the heat; cover and let stand for 1 hour. Drain and rinse beans, discarding liquid.

Return beans to the pan. Add contents of bean seasoning packet, onion, garlic, salt, chili powder, pepper, hot pepper sauce, bay leaf and water. Bring to a boil. Reduce heat; cover and simmer for 2-1/2 to 3 hours or until beans are tender.

Add tomatoes and lemon juice. Simmer, uncovered, until heated through. Discard bay leaf before serving. **Yield:** 10 servings (2-1/2 quarts).

Split Pea Soup

Bay leaves add great flavor to this recipe. Just remember to always remove them before serving!

Holly Dow, Chapman, Maine

- 1 small onion, diced
- 1 tablespoon vegetable oil
- 4 cups water
- 1 can (14-1/2 ounces) chicken broth
- 1-1/2 cups dried split peas, rinsed
- 1 cup cubed fully cooked ham
- 3 bay leaves
- 1-1/2 teaspoons salt
- 1/2 teaspoon dried rosemary, crushed
- 1/4 teaspoon dried thyme
- 1/4 teaspoon pepper

In a large saucepan, saute onion in oil until tender. Add remaining ingredients. Bring to a boil; reduce heat.

Cover and simmer for 1 hour or until peas are tender. Discard bay leaves. **Yield:** 6 servings.

Campfire Bean 'n' Ham Soup

pictured below

These are the best beans and ham you'll ever taste—bar none! Friends rave about this hearty soup that I serve hot off the grill. For easy cleanup, consider covering the outside of your Dutch oven with heavy-duty foil first.

Tom Greaves, Carrollton, Illinois

    1 pound dried navy beans
    2 small onions
    8 cups water
    2 cups chopped celery
    2 smoked ham hocks
    4 cups cubed fully cooked lean ham
      (1-1/2 pounds)
    1 cup chopped carrots
  1/2 teaspoon dried basil
  1/2 teaspoon pepper

Place beans in an ovenproof Dutch oven; add enough water to cover by 2 in. Bring to a boil; boil for 2 minutes. Remove from the heat; cover and let stand for 1 hour. Chop one onion; slice the second onion and separate into rings.

Drain and rinse beans, discarding liquid. Return beans to the pan. Add onions and remaining ingredients. Cover pan and place on the grill rack over indirect medium heat. Cover grill; cook for 1 hour or until beans are almost tender. Uncover grill and pan; cook 30 minutes longer or until beans are tender. Discard ham hocks. **Yield:** 12 servings (3 quarts).

Lentil and Brown Rice Soup

The first time I made this soup, I thought our teenage son would turn up his nose. Much to my delight—and surprise—he loved every bite! I know you will, too.

Janis Plourde, Smooth Rock Falls, Ontario

    2 quarts water
  3/4 cup dried lentils, rinsed
  1/2 cup uncooked brown rice
    1 envelope onion soup mix
    1 can (14-1/2 ounces) diced tomatoes,
      undrained
    1 medium carrot, diced
  1/2 cup diced celery
    1 tablespoon minced fresh parsley
    4 chicken bouillon cubes
  1/2 teaspoon dried basil
  1/2 teaspoon dried oregano
  1/2 teaspoon salt
  1/2 teaspoon pepper
  1/4 teaspoon dried thyme
    1 tablespoon cider vinegar, optional

In a Dutch oven or soup kettle, combine first 14 ingredients; bring to a boil. Reduce heat; cover and simmer for 35-45 minutes or until lentils and rice are tender, stirring occasionally. Stir in vinegar if desired. **Yield:** 12-14 servings (3-1/2 quarts).

Big-Batch Bean Soup

This is one of my most cherished recipes from my days in the service. I learned a lot from the cooks in the galley, and I still use those skills today!

Jene Cain, Northridge, California

6 pounds dried white beans (about 3-1/2 quarts)
7 gallons ham *or* chicken stock
8 ham bones
2-3/4 cups shredded carrots (about 1 pound)
4-1/2 cups finely chopped onion (about 2 pounds)
2 teaspoons pepper
2 cups all-purpose flour
3 cups cold water

Rinse beans. Place in a large kettle with stock and ham bones; bring to a boil. Reduce heat; cover and simmer for 2-3 hours or until the beans are tender. Stir in carrots, onion and pepper; cover and simmer for 30 minutes.

Combine flour and cold water until smooth; gradually stir into soup. Cook for 10 minutes. If too thick, add additional water. **Yield:** 100 servings (6-1/4 gallons).

White Bean Fennel Soup
pictured above

This filling soup is a favorite with our family and is often requested for company dinners. A hint of fennel accents the flavor of this quick-to-fix bean soup...and spinach and tomatoes add color.

Donna Quinn, Salem, Wisconsin

1 large onion, chopped
1 small fennel bulb, thinly sliced
1 tablespoon olive oil
5 cups chicken broth *or* vegetable broth
1 can (15 ounces) white kidney *or* cannellini beans, rinsed and drained
1 can (14-1/2 ounces) diced tomatoes, undrained
1 teaspoon dried thyme
1/4 teaspoon pepper
1 bay leaf
3 cups shredded fresh spinach

In a large saucepan, saute onion and fennel in oil until tender. Add broth, beans, tomatoes, thyme, pepper and bay leaf; bring to a boil.

Reduce heat; cover and simmer for 30 minutes or until fennel is tender. Discard bay leaf. Add spinach; cook 3-4 minutes longer or until spinach is wilted. **Yield:** 5 servings.

Lentil Vegetable Soup

Here is one good-for-you dish that our kids really enjoy. Serve this tasty soup as a hearty meatless entree...or pair it with a favorite sandwich.

Joy Maynard, St. Ignatius, Montana

1/2 cup dried lentils, rinsed
3 cans (14-1/2 ounces *each*) vegetable broth
1/2 cup uncooked long grain brown rice
1 medium onion, chopped
1/2 cup tomato juice
1 can (5-1/2 ounces) spicy tomato juice
1 tablespoon soy sauce
1 tablespoon canola oil
1 medium potato, peeled and diced
1 medium tomato, diced
1 medium carrot, sliced
1 celery rib, sliced

In a saucepan, combine the first eight ingredients. Bring to a boil. Reduce heat; cover and simmer for 30 minutes.

Add the potato, tomato, carrot and celery; simmer 30 minutes longer or until rice and vegetables are tender. **Yield:** 6 servings.

Peasant Soup
pictured above

Don't let the name fool you! This soup is anything but meager. The hearty vegetable broth really satisfies.

Bertha McClung, Summersville, West Virginia

  1 pound dried great northern beans
  3 carrots, sliced
  3 celery ribs, sliced
  2 medium onions, chopped
  2 garlic cloves, minced
  2 bay leaves
  1 can (14-1/2 ounces) diced tomatoes, undrained
  1 teaspoon dried basil
1/2 teaspoon pepper
  2 tablespoons olive oil

Place the beans in a Dutch oven and cover with water; bring to a boil. Boil for 2 minutes. Remove from heat; cover and let stand for 1 hour. Drain and rinse beans; return to Dutch oven.

Add 6 cups water, carrots, celery, onions, garlic, bay leaves, tomatoes, basil and pepper; bring to a boil. Reduce heat; cover and simmer for 1-1/2 hours or until the beans are tender. Discard the bay leaves. Add oil and heat through. **Yield:** 12 servings (3 quarts).

Neighborhood Bean Soup

Even though I cook for one, I make multiple servings of everything. That has helped me get to know my neighbors, who volunteer to be guinea pigs when I try out new recipes.

Cheryl Trowbridge, Windsor, Ontario

  2 cups dried great northern beans
  5 cups chicken broth
  3 cups water
  1 large meaty ham bone
  2 to 3 tablespoons chicken bouillon granules
  1 teaspoon dried thyme
1/2 teaspoon dried marjoram
1/2 teaspoon pepper
1/4 teaspoon rubbed sage
1/4 teaspoon dried savory
  2 medium onions, chopped
  3 medium carrots, chopped
  3 celery ribs, chopped
  1 tablespoon vegetable oil

Place beans in a Dutch oven or soup kettle; add water to cover by 2 in. Bring to a boil; boil for 2 minutes. Remove from the heat; cover and let stand for 1 hour. Drain.

Add broth, water, ham bone, bouillon and seasonings; bring to a boil. Reduce heat; cover and simmer for 2 hours. Saute onions, carrots and celery in oil; add to soup.

Cover and simmer 1 hour longer. Debone ham and cut into chunks; return to soup. Skim fat. **Yield:** 10 servings (2-3/4 quarts).

Corn and Bean Soup

For lunch or dinner on a chilly day, this fresh-tasting colorful vegetable soup really hits the spot. It's so quick and easy to make.

Betty Andrzejewski, Chino, California

  1 can (10-1/2 ounces) chicken broth
  2 medium carrots, diced
  2 celery ribs, diced
  1 small potato, peeled and diced
  1 small onion, chopped
1-1/2 cups frozen corn

1 can (15 ounces) white kidney *or* cannellini beans, rinsed and drained
1 cup milk
1 teaspoon dried thyme
1/4 teaspoon garlic powder
Pepper to taste

In a large saucepan, combine the broth, carrots, celery, potato and onion. Bring to a boil. Reduce heat; cover and simmer for 10-12 minutes or until vegetables are tender.

Stir in the remaining ingredients; simmer 5-7 minutes longer or until corn is tender. **Yield:** 5 servings.

U.S. Senate Bean Soup
pictured below

Chock-full of ham, beans and celery, this hearty soup makes a wonderful meal at any time of year. Freeze the bone from a holiday ham until you're ready to make soup. Plus, once prepared, it freezes well for a great make-ahead supper!

Rosemarie Forcum, White Stone, Virginia

1 pound dried great northern beans
1 meaty ham bone *or* 2 smoked ham hocks
3 medium onions, chopped
3 garlic cloves, minced
3 celery stalks, chopped
1/4 cup chopped fresh parsley

1 cup mashed potatoes *or* 1/3 cup instant potato flakes
Salt and pepper to taste
Parsley *or* chives for garnish

Place beans and enough water to cover in a saucepan; bring to a boil and boil for 2 minutes. Remove from the heat and soak for 1 hour. Drain and rinse beans.

In a large kettle, place beans, ham bone or hocks and 3 qts. water. Bring to boil. Reduce heat; cover and simmer for 2 hours. Skim fat if necessary.

Add onions, garlic, celery, parsley, potatoes, salt and pepper; simmer 1 hour longer. Remove meat and bones from the soup.

Remove meat from the bones; dice and return to kettle. Heat through. Garnish with parsley or chives. **Yield:** 8-10 servings (2-1/2 quarts).

Sausage Lentil Soup

My family loves when I serve hot bowls of this with sourdough bread.

Kathy Anderson, Casper, Wyoming

1/2 pound bulk Italian sausage
1 large onion, chopped
1 medium green pepper, chopped
1 large carrot, chopped
2 cans (10-1/2 ounces *each*) chicken broth
1 can (14-1/2 ounces) diced tomatoes, undrained
1 cup water
1 garlic clove, minced
1 teaspoon salt
1/2 teaspoon pepper
3/4 cup dried lentils, rinsed

In a Dutch oven or soup kettle, cook sausage over medium heat until no longer pink; drain. Add the next nine ingredients; bring to a boil. Add lentils.

Reduce heat; cover and simmer for 60-70 minutes or until the lentils are tender. **Yield:** 6-8 servings (2 quarts).

Vegetable Bean Soup

pictured below

This is a great soup that tastes good and is good for you. It features hearty beans and veggies as well as satisfying barley. I hope you enjoy it!

Laura Letobar, Livonia, Michigan

        2 cups chopped onion
        1 cup chopped carrots
        1 cup chopped celery
        6 cups water
        3 beef bouillon cubes
        1 can (28 ounces) diced tomatoes,
          undrained
        1 can (15 ounces) black beans, rinsed
          and drained
        1 cup quick-cooking barley
        1 teaspoon garlic powder
      3/4 teaspoon pepper
        1 package (10 ounces) frozen chopped
          spinach, thawed

In a large saucepan or Dutch oven coated with nonstick cooking spray, saute onion, carrots and celery over medium heat until onion is soft, about 8 minutes. Stir in water, bouillon, tomatoes, beans, barley, garlic powder and pepper; bring to a boil.

Reduce heat; cover and simmer for 10 minutes. Add spinach; cover and simmer for 10-15 minutes or until the vegetables are tender. **Yield:** 14 servings.

Black Bean Soup

Here's an economical meal that doesn't skimp on flavor. Hearty black beans make up for the meat, and the peppers add just the right splash of color.

Audrey Thibodeau, Mesa, Arizona

        1 pound dried black beans
    1-1/2 quarts chicken broth
        1 quart water
    1-1/2 cups chopped onion
        1 cup thinly sliced celery
        1 large carrot, chopped
      1/2 cup *each* chopped green, yellow
          and sweet red peppers
        2 garlic cloves, minced
        3 tablespoons olive oil
      1/4 cup tomato paste
        3 tablespoons minced fresh
          parsley
        1 tablespoon chopped fresh
          oregano *or* 1 teaspoon dried
          oregano
        1 tablespoon chopped fresh
          thyme *or* 1 teaspoon dried
          thyme
    1-1/2 teaspoons ground cumin
        1 teaspoon pepper
      3/4 teaspoon salt
        3 bay leaves
   Chopped tomato, optional

In a Dutch oven or soup kettle, combine beans, broth and water; bring to a boil. Reduce heat; cover and simmer for 1-1/2 hours or until beans are tender.

Meanwhile, in a large skillet, saute onion, celery, carrot, peppers and garlic in oil until tender. Add the next seven ingredients; mix well. Add to beans along with bay leaves; bring to a boil.

Reduce heat; cover and simmer for 1 hour. Remove bay leaves before serving. Garnish with chopped tomato if desired. **Yield:** 12 servings (3 quarts).

Fast Fiesta Soup

pictured above

This spicy soup was served at a very elegant lunch, and the hostess was deluged with requests for the recipe. The colorful combination is a snap to throw together...just open the cans and heat.

Patricia White, Monrovia, California

2 cans (10 ounces *each*) diced tomatoes and green chilies

1 can (15-1/4 ounces) whole kernel corn, drained
1 can (15 ounces) black beans, rinsed and drained
Shredded cheddar cheese and sour cream, optional

In a saucepan, combine tomatoes, corn and beans; heat through. Garnish servings with shredded cheese and sour cream if desired.
Yield: 4 servings.

celery, barley, 1/4 cup parsley, bay leaves, salt, thyme and pepper. Bring to a boil. Reduce heat; cover and simmer for 1 hour or until beans are tender.

Add the tomatoes; heat through. Discard bay leaves. Sprinkle with remaining parsley. **Yield:** 9 servings.

Hearty Black-Eyed Pea Soup
pictured below

I had eaten this soup countless times at a small restaurant in our town. When the owner finally retired, he said I deserved the secret recipe and passed it along.

Alice Jarrell, Dexter, Missouri

> 1 pound bulk pork sausage
> 1 pound ground beef
> 1 large onion, diced
> 4 cups water
> 3 cans (15 ounces *each*) black-eyed peas, rinsed and drained
> 1 can (28 ounces) diced tomatoes, undrained

White Bean 'n' Barley Soup
pictured above

A friend of mine gave me this recipe, and it's delicious.

Stephanie Land, Sudbury, Ontario

> 1-1/2 cups dried great northern beans
> 1 large onion, chopped
> 2 garlic cloves, minced
> 1 tablespoon olive oil
> 4 cups chicken *or* vegetable broth
> 4 cups water
> 3 medium carrots, sliced
> 2 medium sweet red peppers, diced
> 2 celery ribs, chopped
> 1/2 cup medium pearl barley
> 1/2 cup minced fresh parsley, *divided*
> 2 bay leaves
> 1 teaspoon salt
> 1/2 teaspoon dried thyme
> 1/2 teaspoon pepper
> 1 can (28 ounces) diced tomatoes, undrained

Place beans in a Dutch oven or soup kettle; add enough water to cover beans by 2 in. Bring to a boil; boil for 2 minutes. Remove from the heat; cover and let stand for 1 hour.

Drain and rinse beans, discarding liquid. In a Dutch oven, saute onion and garlic in oil. Add the broth, water, beans, carrots, red peppers,

1 can (10 ounces) diced tomatoes and
  green chilies, undrained
1 can (4 ounces) chopped green chilies
4 beef bouillon cubes
4 teaspoons molasses
1 teaspoon Worcestershire sauce
3/4 teaspoon garlic salt
1/2 teaspoon salt
1/4 teaspoon pepper
1/4 teaspoon ground cumin

In a Dutch oven or soup kettle, cook sausage, beef and onion over medium heat until meat is no longer pink; drain.

Add remaining ingredients; bring to a boil. Reduce heat; cover and simmer for 45 minutes. **Yield:** 12-16 servings (4 quarts).

Lentil Soup

This hearty soup can be easily doubled. My family likes it topped with cheese.

Joyce Pyra, North Battleford, Saskatchewan

    1 cup dried lentils, rinsed
    6 cups chicken broth
    2 cups chopped onion
    1 garlic clove, minced
    1 tablespoon vegetable oil
2-1/2 cups chopped fresh tomatoes
    1 cup sliced carrots
  1/2 teaspoon dried thyme
  1/4 teaspoon dried marjoram

In a large saucepan, bring lentils and chicken broth to a boil. Reduce the heat; simmer for 30 minutes.

Meanwhile, in a skillet, saute onion and garlic in oil; add to saucepan. Add tomatoes, carrots, thyme and marjoram.

Cook 30 minutes longer or until the lentils and vegetables are tender. **Yield:** about 8 servings (2 quarts).

Basil Tortellini Soup

pictured below

This soup is tasty, colorful and quick. I keep the ingredients on hand for a fast meal with a loaf of crusty bread.

Jayne Dwyer-Reff, Fort Wayne, Indiana

4-1/2 cups chicken broth
    1 package (9 ounces) refrigerated
      cheese tortellini
    1 can (15 ounces) white kidney *or*
      cannellini beans, rinsed and
      drained
    1 cup chopped fresh tomato
1/3 to 1/2 cup shredded fresh basil
    1 to 2 tablespoons balsamic
      vinegar
  1/4 teaspoon salt
1/8 to 1/4 teaspoon pepper
  1/3 cup shredded Parmesan cheese

In a large saucepan, bring broth to a boil. Add tortellini; cook until tender, about 6 minutes. Stir in the beans, tomato and basil.

Reduce heat; simmer, uncovered, for 5 minutes. Add the vinegar, salt and pepper. Serve with cheese. **Yield:** 6 servings.

Hearty Split Pea Soup

pictured below

For a different spin on traditional split pea soup, try this recipe. The flavor is peppery rather than smoky, and the corned beef is an unexpected, tasty change of pace.

Barbara Link, Alta Loma, California

    1 package (1 pound) dried split peas
    8 cups water
    2 medium potatoes, peeled and cubed
    2 large onions, chopped
    2 medium carrots, chopped
    2 cups cubed cooked corned beef *or* ham
    1/2 cup chopped celery
    5 teaspoons chicken bouillon granules
    1 teaspoon dried marjoram
    1 teaspoon poultry seasoning
    1 teaspoon rubbed sage
    1/2 to 1 teaspoon pepper
    1/2 teaspoon dried basil
    1/2 teaspoon salt

In a Dutch oven or soup kettle, combine all ingredients; bring to a boil. Reduce heat; cover and simmer for 1-1/4 to 1-1/2 hours or until peas and vegetables are tender. **Yield:** 12 servings (3 quarts).

Lemon Lentil Soup

Loaded with protein-rich lentils, this hearty soup is rooted in the old-fashioned goodness of leeks, parsnips, celery and carrots. The addition of lemon juice transforms what might otherwise be an everyday soup into something out of the ordinary.

Jean Rawlings, Saskatoon, Saskatchewan

    1 cup chopped leeks (white portion only)
    2 tablespoons canola oil
    1 can (15 ounces) tomato puree
    1 cup chopped celery
    1 cup chopped carrots
    1/4 cup chopped peeled parsnips
    2 tablespoons dried basil
    8 cups water
    1-1/2 cups lentils, rinsed
    2 bay leaves
    1 tablespoon grated lemon peel
    1-1/2 teaspoons salt
    1 teaspoon dill weed
    1/2 teaspoon pepper
    2 to 3 tablespoons lemon juice

In a large saucepan, saute leeks in oil until tender. Add the next five ingredients; saute for 3-4 minutes. Add water; bring to a boil. Add lentils and bay leaves.

Reduce heat; cover and simmer for 30 minutes. Stir in lemon peel, salt, dill and pepper; simmer 30 minutes longer or until lentils are tender. Discard bay leaves. Stir in lemon juice. **Yield:** 6 servings.

White Bean 'n' Ham Soup

pictured above right

I rely on convenience items that hurry along preparation for my meals. I look forward to cooking speedy dishes, like this one, that my family enjoys.

Bissy Crosby, Yazoo City, Mississippi

    2 cans (15-1/2 ounces *each*) great northern beans, rinsed and drained
    2 medium carrots, diced
    1 small onion, chopped
    2 tablespoons butter
    2-1/4 cups water

1-1/2 cups cubed fully cooked ham
1/2 teaspoon salt
1/8 to 1/4 teaspoon white pepper
1 bay leaf

Mash one can of beans; set aside. In a large saucepan, saute the carrots and onion in butter. Stir in the water, ham, seasonings, and whole and mashed beans.

Cook over medium heat until heated through. Discard the bay leaf before serving. **Yield:** 6 servings.

Lucky Bean Soup
pictured at right

This recipe is from a bean soup gift pack I developed as a fund-raiser for our church. We provide it along with the beans and a packet containing all the spices. The recipient just adds water and a can of tomatoes for a delicious pot of savory soup.

Doris Cox, South Orange, New Jersey

1/4 cup *each* dried yellow split peas, lentils, black beans, great northern beans, pinto beans, baby lima beans and kidney beans

1/2 cup *each* dried green split peas, black-eyed peas and navy beans
2 quarts water
1/3 cup dried minced onion
1 tablespoon salt
1 teaspoon dried thyme
1 teaspoon dried rosemary, crushed
1 teaspoon garlic powder
1/2 teaspoon celery seed
1/2 teaspoon dried basil
1/4 to 1/2 teaspoon crushed red pepper flakes
2 bay leaves
1 can (28 ounces) crushed tomatoes

Place peas, lentils and beans in a Dutch oven; add enough water to cover. Bring to a boil; boil for 2 minutes. Remove from the heat; let stand for 1 hour. Drain and discard liquid.

Add 2 qts. water and seasonings; bring to a boil. Reduce heat; cover and simmer for 1-1/2 to 2 hours or until beans are just tender.

Stir in tomatoes; increase heat to medium. Cook, uncovered, for 15-30 minutes. Discard bay leaves. **Yield:** 14 servings (3-1/2 quarts).

Texas Black Bean Soup
pictured below

This hearty soup made with convenient canned items is perfect for spicing up a family gathering on a cool day. It tastes great and requires so little time and attention.

Pamela Scott, Garland, Texas

    2 cans (15 ounces *each*) black beans,
      rinsed and drained
    1 can (14-1/2 ounces) stewed tomatoes
      or Mexican stewed tomatoes, cut up
    1 can (14-1/2 ounces) diced tomatoes *or*
      diced tomatoes with green chilies
    1 can (14-1/2 ounces) chicken broth
    1 can (11 ounces) Mexicorn, drained
    2 cans (4 ounces *each*) chopped green
      chilies
    4 green onions, thinly sliced
    2 to 3 tablespoons chili powder
    1 teaspoon ground cumin
  1/2 teaspoon dried minced garlic

In a slow cooker, combine all ingredients. Cover and cook on high for 4-5 hours or until heated through. **Yield:** 8-10 servings (about 2-1/2 quarts).

Prairie Bean Soup

This soup started out as an "end-of-the-month" meal, a creative way to use up items that were on hand. We liked it so well that I now prepare it even when the pantry is full. My twin daughters and I enjoy cooking...and my husband reaps the benefits!

Katherine VanDeraa, South Bend, Indiana

    1 pound ground beef
    1 pound bulk pork sausage
    2 large onions, chopped
  1/2 cup packed brown sugar
    1 tablespoon ground cumin
  1/2 teaspoon garlic powder
    1 tablespoon prepared mustard
    1 cup ketchup
  1/2 cup water
  1/3 cup vinegar
    4 cups cooked and drained pinto beans
    2 cans (15 ounce *each*) chili beans
    2 cans (16 ounce *each*) pork and beans
    1 tablespoon salt
1-1/2 teaspoons pepper

In a large Dutch oven or soup kettle, cook ground beef with pork sausage and onions over medium heat until the meat is no longer pink and the onions are tender; drain well.

Stir in the next seven ingredients; mix well. Stir in beans, salt and pepper. Bring to a boil; reduce heat and simmer for about 2 hours. **Yield:** 12-16 servings (4 quarts).

Southwestern Bean Soup

pictured below

When a friend needs a night off from cooking, I throw together this one-pot meal. I deliver it with tortilla chips, shredded cheese and sour cream for garnish. The pepper sauce can be ranged to suit individual tastes, and the broth can be eliminated for a thicker batch.

Jackie Hacker, Seville, Ohio

   1 large onion, chopped
   1 teaspoon vegetable oil
   2 cans (15 ounces *each*) black beans, rinsed and drained
   2 cans (14-1/2 ounces *each*) diced tomatoes with garlic and onion, undrained
   2 cans (14-1/2 ounces *each*) chicken broth
   1 can (16 ounces) kidney beans, rinsed and drained
   1 can (15 ounces) cannellini *or* white kidney beans, rinsed and drained
1-1/2 cups fresh *or* frozen corn
   4 garlic cloves, minced
1-1/2 teaspoons ground cumin
1-1/2 teaspoons chili powder
 1/8 to 1/4 teaspoon hot pepper sauce

In a Dutch oven or soup kettle, saute the onion in oil until tender. Stir in the remaining ingredients; bring to a boil. Reduce heat; simmer, uncovered, for 5 minutes or until heated through. **Yield:** 12 servings (3 quarts).

Wisconsin Split Pea Soup

pictured above

Marjoram, garlic salt, potatoes and carrots blend nicely with peas in this hearty and economical soup. I like to plant peas, so I can freeze and enjoy them all winter.

Linda Rock, Stratford, Wisconsin

   1 pound dried split peas
2-1/2 quarts water
   1 meaty ham bone
1-1/2 cups chopped onion
   1 cup *each* diced celery, carrots and potatoes
   1 teaspoon dried parsley flakes
 1/2 teaspoon pepper
 1/4 teaspoon garlic salt
 1/4 teaspoon dried marjoram
Salt to taste

In a Dutch oven or soup kettle, place the peas, water and ham bone; bring to a boil. Reduce heat; cover and simmer for 2 hours, stirring occasionally. Stir in the remaining ingredients. Bring to a boil. Reduce heat; cover and simmer for 30 minutes or until vegetables are tender.

Remove ham bone; when cool enough to handle, remove meat from the bone. Chop ham and return to the soup; heat through. **Yield:** 12 servings (3 quarts).

Curried Lentil Soup

pictured below

Curry gives a different taste sensation to this chili-like soup. It's delicious with a dollop of sour cream. My family welcomes it with open arms—and watering mouths.

Christina Till, South Haven, Michigan

4 cups hot water
1 can (28 ounces) crushed tomatoes
3 medium potatoes, peeled and diced
3 medium carrots, thinly sliced
1 large onion, chopped
1 celery rib, chopped
1 cup dried lentils
2 garlic cloves, minced
2 bay leaves
4 teaspoons curry powder
1-1/2 teaspoons salt

In a slow cooker, combine all ingredients; stir well. Cover and cook on low for 8 hours or until vegetables and lentils are tender. Discard the bay leaves before serving. **Yield:** 10 servings (2-1/2 quarts).

In a slow cooker, combine the first 10 ingredients. Cover and cook on high for 4-5 hours. For dumplings, combine the flour, cheese, cornmeal, sugar and baking powder in a bowl. In another bowl, combine the egg, milk and oil; add to dry ingredients just until moistened (batter will be stiff). Drop by heaping tablespoons onto soup.

Cover and cook on high 30 minutes longer (without lifting cover) or until a toothpick inserted in a dumpling comes out clean. **Yield:** 6 servings.

Tangy Bean Soup

pictured above

This soup has great southwestern flavors. I love having it cooking in my slow cooker while I'm at work and then I can quickly make dumplings and fix dinner once I get home.

Joan Hallford, North Richland Hills, Texas

- 2 cans (14-1/2 ounces *each*) chicken broth
- 1 package (16 ounces) frozen mixed vegetables
- 1 can (15 ounces) black beans, rinsed and drained
- 1 can (15 ounces) pinto beans, rinsed and drained
- 1 can (14-1/2 ounces) diced tomatoes, undrained
- 1 medium onion, chopped
- 1 tablespoon chili powder
- 1 tablespoon minced fresh cilantro
- 4 garlic cloves, minced
- 1/4 teaspoon pepper

CORNMEAL DUMPLINGS:
- 1/2 cup all-purpose flour
- 1/2 cup shredded cheddar cheese
- 1/3 cup cornmeal
- 1 tablespoon sugar
- 1 teaspoon baking powder
- 1 egg
- 2 tablespoons milk
- 2 teaspoons vegetable oil

Rosemary Split Pea Soup

This zesty soup is great served with warm rolls or French bread. Rosemary adds a nice, distinctive flavor.

Diane Hixson, Niceville, Florida

- 3 celery ribs, finely chopped
- 1 cup finely chopped onion
- 1 garlic clove, minced
- 1 tablespoon fresh rosemary, minced *or* 1 teaspoon dried rosemary
- 3 tablespoons butter
- 6 cups chicken broth
- 1-1/4 cups dried split peas, rinsed
- 1 teaspoon salt

MEATBALLS
- 1/2 pound ground pork *or* turkey
- 1-1/2 teaspoons fresh rosemary, minced
- 1/2 teaspoon dried rosemary
- 1/4 teaspoon pepper

In a large kettle or Dutch oven, saute celery, onion, garlic and rosemary in butter until tender. Add broth, peas and salt if desired; bring to a boil. Reduce heat; cover and simmer for 1-1/2 hours or until peas are soft. Remove from the heat and allow to cool.

For meatballs, combine pork or turkey, rosemary and pepper. Shape into 1/2-inch balls. In a skillet, brown meatballs until no pink remains, about 5 to 10 minutes.

Ladle half of the cooled soup into a blender or food processor; puree. Return soup to the kettle along with the meatballs and heat through. **Yield:** 5 servings.

"Chowder breathes reassurance and steams consolation."

chock-full
CHOWDERS

In a skillet over medium heat, cook bacon until crisp. Remove bacon; drain and discard all but 2 tablespoons drippings. Saute carrots, onion and asparagus in drippings over medium heat until crisp-tender.

Add to kettle along with potatoes, salt, thyme and pepper; return to a boil. Reduce heat; cover and simmer for 20 minutes or until potatoes are tender.

Combine flour and reserved broth; stir into soup. Bring to a boil; cook and stir for 2 minutes. Debone chicken and cut into thin strips; add to soup along with cream and parsley.

Heat through (do not boil). Sprinkle with bacon just before serving. **Yield:** 16-18 servings (4-1/2 quarts).

Editor's Note: If fresh asparagus is unavailable, a 10-ounce box of frozen cut asparagus (thawed) may be used. Add it with the chicken, cream and parsley.

Asparagus Chicken Chowder
pictured above

It makes me feel great to prepare a delicious soup like this one and set it on the table in my favorite soup tureen. Even my three children love it. The next day, we scramble for the leftovers...if there are any.

Jona Fell, Appleton, Wisconsin

       1 broiler/fryer chicken (3 to 3-1/2 pounds)
 3-1/2 quarts water
       2 teaspoons chicken bouillon granules
       5 bacon strips, diced
       2 medium carrots, chopped
       1 medium onion, chopped
   1/2 pound fresh asparagus, cut into 1/2-inch pieces
       2 cups cubed peeled potatoes
       1 tablespoon salt
 1-1/2 teaspoons dried thyme
   1/2 teaspoon pepper
   1/2 cup all-purpose flour
 1-1/2 cups heavy whipping cream
       2 tablespoons chopped fresh parsley

Place chicken, water and bouillon in a Dutch oven or soup kettle. Cover and bring to a boil; skim fat.

Reduce heat; cover and simmer for 1 to 1-1/2 hours or until chicken is tender. Remove chicken; cool. Remove 1 cup broth and set aside.

Mushroom and Potato Chowder

Its rich broth, big mushroom taste and medley of vegetables make this chowder a little different from ordinary mushroom soup.

Romaine Wetzel, Lancaster, Pennsylvania

   1/2 cup chopped onion
   1/4 cup butter
       2 tablespoons all-purpose flour
       1 teaspoon salt
   1/2 teaspoon pepper
       3 cups water
       1 pound fresh mushrooms, sliced
       1 cup chopped celery
       1 cup diced peeled potatoes
   1/2 cup chopped carrots
       1 cup half-and half cream
   1/4 cup grated Parmesan cheese

In a large kettle, saute onion in butter until tender. Add flour, salt and pepper; stir to make a smooth paste. Gradually add water, stirring constantly. Bring to a boil; cook and stir for 1 minute.

Add the mushrooms, celery, potatoes and carrots. Reduce heat; cover and simmer for 30 minutes or until vegetables are tender. Add cream and Parmesan cheese; heat through. **Yield:** 4-6 servings.

Clam Chowder

I make this chowder for our annual Souper Bowl luncheon at work, and everyone loves it. To slim it down, I use reduced-fat margarine and mushroom soup. Tender chunks of red potatoes add color and texture to this thick chowder.

Chris Sheetz, Olmsted Falls, Ohio

> 2 cups sliced fresh mushrooms
> 4 celery ribs with leaves, chopped
> 1 medium onion, chopped
> 2 tablespoons butter
> 2 cans (10-3/4 ounces *each*) condensed cream of mushroom soup, undiluted
> 1 bottle (8 ounces) clam juice
> 1/2 cup white wine *or* chicken broth
> 6 medium unpeeled red potatoes, cubed
> 1/2 teaspoon salt
> 1/4 teaspoon white pepper
> 3 cans (6-1/2 ounces each) minced clams, undrained

In a Dutch oven or soup kettle, saute the mushrooms, celery and onion in butter until tender.

In a bowl, whisk the soup, clam juice and wine or broth; stir into vegetable mixture. Add the potatoes, salt and pepper. Bring to a boil. Reduce the heat; cover and simmer for 25 minutes.

Add the clams; cover and simmer for 5-15 minutes or until the potatoes are tender. **Yield:** 10 servings.

Zippy Corn Chowder

pictured at right

This thick colorful chowder was so well received the first time I made it that some of us had to go without seconds. Now I make this hearty soup often.

Kera Bredin, Vancouver, British Columbia

> 1 medium onion, chopped
> 1 medium green pepper, chopped

> 2 tablespoons butter
> 1 can (14-1/2 ounces) chicken broth
> 2 large red potatoes, cubed
> 1 jalapeno pepper, chopped
> 2 teaspoons Dijon mustard
> 1 teaspoon salt
> 1/2 teaspoon paprika
> 1/4 to 1/2 teaspoon crushed red pepper flakes
> 3 cups frozen corn
> 4 green onions, chopped
> 3 cups milk, *divided*
> 1/4 cup all-purpose flour

In a large saucepan, saute onion and green pepper in butter until tender. Add broth and potatoes. Bring to a boil.

Reduce heat; cover and simmer for 15 minutes or until potatoes are almost tender. Stir in jalapeno, mustard, salt, paprika and red pepper flakes.

Add the corn, green onions and 2-1/2 cups milk. Bring to a boil. Combine flour and remaining milk until smooth; gradually add to soup.

Bring to a boil. Cook and stir for 2 minutes or until thickened and bubbly. **Yield:** 8 servings (2 quarts).

Editor's Note: When cutting or seeding hot peppers, use rubber or plastic gloves to protect your hands. Avoid touching your face. Leave the seeds in for spicier flavor.

chock-full CHOWDERS

Zesty Corn 'n' Chicken Chowder

This chowder needs no simmering—it goes from stovetop to table in just minutes. So it's perfect when time is short and your family is hungry.

Jan Ecklor, Souderton, Pennsylvania

1-1/2 cups milk
1 can (10-3/4 ounces) condensed cream of potato soup, undiluted
1 can (10-3/4 ounces) condensed cream of chicken soup, undiluted
1 cup chicken broth
2 cups cubed cooked chicken
1 can (11 ounces) Mexican-style corn, undrained
1 can (4 ounces) chopped green chilies
1/2 cup sliced fresh mushrooms
1-1/2 cups (6 ounces) shredded cheddar cheese

In a 3-qt. saucepan, combine the milk, soups and broth; blend well. Add the next four ingredients.

Heat through, stirring occasionally. Remove from the heat. Stir in cheese until melted. **Yield:** 6-8 servings (2 quarts).

Sausage Bean Chowder

When the first hint of cooler weather appears at the end of summer, my husband always asks if it is time to make some soup. It's his subtle hint for me to make this special chowder!

Phyllis Heberger, Fishers Landing, New York

1 pound bulk pork sausage
2 cans (16 ounces *each*) kidney beans, rinsed and drained
1 can (28 ounces) diced tomatoes, undrained
1 can (32 ounces) tomato juice
1 cup chopped onion
1 cup chopped green pepper
1 cup diced peeled potatoes
1 teaspoon seasoned salt
1/2 teaspoon garlic salt

1/2 teaspoon dried thyme
1/8 teaspoon pepper
1 bay leaf

In a Dutch oven or soup kettle, cook sausage over medium heat until no longer pink; drain. Add remaining ingredients; bring to a boil.

Reduce heat; cover and simmer for 2 hours. Remove bay leaf. **Yield:** 12-14 servings (about 3 quarts).

Country Fish Chowder

pictured above

You'll think you're on Cape Cod when you taste this thick, wholesome chowder. It's made from a recipe that I've treasured for many years.

Linda Lazaroff, Hebron, Connecticut

1 cup chopped onion
1/2 cup finely chopped salt pork
3 tablespoons butter
3 cans (12 ounces *each*) evaporated milk
1 can (15-1/4 ounces) whole kernel corn, undrained
1 can (6-1/2 ounces) chopped clams, undrained
3 medium potatoes, peeled and cubed
1 teaspoon salt

3/4 teaspoon pepper
1 pound fish fillets (haddock, cod *or* flounder), cooked and broken into pieces
Cooked crumbled bacon, optional
Snipped chives, optional
Additional butter, optional

In a large saucepan, cook onion and salt pork in butter until onion is tender. Add the milk, corn, clams, potatoes, salt and pepper.

Cover and cook over medium heat, stirring occasionally, until potatoes are tender, about 20 minutes. Stir in fish and heat through.

Ladle into bowls. If desired, top with bacon, chives and/or a pat of butter. **Yield:** 8-10 servings (2-1/2 quarts).

New England Clam Chowder

pictured above right

I wasn't satisfied with other recipes I came across for clam chowder, so I devised this one. Everyone who's tried it raves about it. The dish is great on a cold day.

Rachel Nydam, Uxbridge, Massachusetts

> " Parsley makes a pretty garnish, but its fresh flavor makes it a great ingredient as well. Parsley keeps its flavor and color best when frozen. When using parsley, add it during the last minutes of cooking. "
>
> —*Eunice Stoen*
> *Decorah, Iowa*

4 medium potatoes, peeled and cubed
2 medium onions, chopped
1/2 cup butter
3/4 cup all-purpose flour
2 quarts milk
3 cans (6-1/2 ounces *each*) chopped clams, undrained
2 to 3 teaspoons salt
1 teaspoon ground sage
1 teaspoon ground thyme
1/2 teaspoon celery salt
1/2 teaspoon pepper
Minced fresh parsley

Place potatoes in a saucepan and cover with water; bring to a boil. Cover and cook until potatoes are tender.

Meanwhile, in a Dutch oven, saute onions in butter until tender. Add flour; mix until smooth. Stir in milk. Cook over medium heat, stirring constantly, until thickened and bubbly.

Drain potatoes; add to Dutch oven. Add clams and remaining ingredients; heat through. **Yield:** 10-12 servings (3 quarts).

Seafood Chowder

pictured above

My husband, Chad, is an avid fisherman. When a family party was planned and we had to bring something, we created this recipe using fish from our freezer. The chowder got rave reviews!

Heather Saunders, Belchertown, Massachusetts

1/2 pound sliced bacon, diced
2 medium onions, chopped
6 cups diced peeled potatoes
4 cups water
1 pound bay *or* sea scallops, quartered

1 pound fresh *or* frozen lobster, cut into 1-inch pieces
1 pound uncooked medium shrimp, peeled and deveined
1 pound cod, cut into 1-inch pieces
1 pound haddock, cut into 1-inch pieces
1/2 cup butter, melted
4 teaspoons salt
4 teaspoons minced fresh parsley
1/2 teaspoon curry powder
2 quarts milk
1 can (12 ounces) evaporated milk

In a large soup kettle or stockpot, cook bacon over medium heat until crisp. Remove with a slotted spoon to paper towels; reserve drippings. Saute onions in drippings until tender. Add potatoes and water; bring to a boil. Cook for 10 minutes.

Add the scallops, lobster, shrimp, cod and haddock. Cook for 10 minutes or until scallops are opaque, shrimp turn pink and fish flakes easily with a fork. Add the butter, salt, parsley and curry powder. Stir in milk and evaporated milk; heat through. Garnish with bacon. **Yield:** 32 servings (8 quarts).

> Vegetable soups and chowders are so versatile! I often substitute combinations of ingredients that suit my family's tastes for those listed in recipes.
>
> —*Mary Nell Ruhenkoenig*
> *Burleson, Texas*

Corn Chowder

When I was growing up, my grandmother would often serve steaming bowls of corn chowder. I tried to capture that wonderful flavor and came up with this recipe.

Bonnie Miller, Devils Lake, North Dakota

    1 quart water
    4 cups diced peeled potatoes
    1 cup chopped celery
  1/2 cup chopped onion
  1/2 cup shredded carrot
    1 can (15-1/4 ounces) whole kernel corn, drained
    1 can (15 ounces) cream-style corn
    1 can (10-3/4 ounces) condensed cream of mushroom soup, undiluted
    2 cups chopped fully cooked ham
    1 jar (4-1/2 ounces) sliced mushrooms, drained

1-1/4 cups milk
  1/2 teaspoon salt
  1/2 teaspoon pepper
    6 bacon strips, cooked and crumbled

In a soup kettle or Dutch oven, combine the first five ingredients; bring to a boil. Reduce heat; cover and simmer for 12-15 minutes or until vegetables are tender.

Add the corn, soup, ham, mushrooms, milk, salt and pepper; heat through, stirring occasionally. Stir in bacon just before serving. **Yield:** 12-14 servings (about 3 quarts).

Wild Rice and Ham Chowder

The rich taste of this chowder appeals to everyone who tries it. I have my younger sister to thank for sharing this recipe with me.

Elma Friesen, Winnipeg, Manitoba

  1/2 cup chopped onion
    2 garlic cloves, minced
  1/4 cup butter
    6 tablespoons all-purpose flour
  1/2 teaspoon salt
  1/4 teaspoon pepper
    4 cups chicken broth
1-1/2 cups cubed peeled potatoes
  1/2 cup chopped carrots
    1 bay leaf
  1/2 teaspoon dried thyme
  1/4 teaspoon ground nutmeg
    3 cups cooked wild rice
2-1/2 cups cubed fully cooked ham
    2 cups half-and-half cream
    1 can (15-1/4 ounces) whole kernel corn, drained
Minced fresh parsley

In a Dutch oven or soup kettle over medium heat, saute onion and garlic in butter until tender. Add flour, salt and pepper; stir to form a smooth paste. Gradually add broth. Bring to a boil; boil and stir for 2 minutes.

Add potatoes, carrots, bay leaf, thyme and nutmeg; bring to a boil. Reduce heat; cover and simmer for 30 minutes or until vegetables are tender. Add rice, ham, cream and corn; heat through (do not boil). Remove bay leaf. Sprinkle with parsley just before serving. **Yield:** 8-10 servings (2-3/4 quarts).

Cheesy Chicken Chowder

pictured at right

I like to serve this hearty chowder with garlic bread and a salad. It's a wonderful dish to prepare when company drops in.

Hazel Fritchie, Palestine, Illinois

  3 cups chicken broth
  2 cups diced peeled potatoes
  1 cup diced carrots
  1 cup diced celery
  1/2 cup diced onion
  1-1/2 teaspoons salt
  1/4 teaspoon pepper
  1/4 cup butter
  1/3 cup all-purpose flour
  2 cups milk
  2 cups (8 ounces) shredded cheddar cheese
  2 cups diced cooked chicken

In a 4-qt. saucepan, bring chicken broth to a boil. Reduce heat; add potatoes, carrots, celery, onion, salt and pepper. Cover and simmer for 15 minutes or until vegetables are tender.

Meanwhile, melt butter in a medium saucepan; add flour and mix well. Gradually stir in milk; cook over low heat until slightly thickened.

Stir in cheese and cook until melted; add to broth along with the chicken. Cook and stir over low heat until heated through. **Yield:** 6-8 servings.

New England Fish Chowder

This is an old recipe handed down through the years. It always tasted best when made by a friend of mine who was a fisherman. There was nothing quite like sitting down with friends on a cold snowy night, enjoying this hot chowder.

Diane Vachon, Berwick, Maine

  1/4 pound salt pork *or* bacon
  3 medium onions, sliced
  4 cups diced uncooked peeled potatoes
  9 cups water, *divided*
  2 cups milk
  1 tablespoon butter
  1-1/2 teaspoons salt

  1 teaspoon pepper
  2 to 3 pounds haddock fillets, cut into large chunks
Minced fresh parsley

Fry salt pork or bacon in a large soup kettle or Dutch oven. Remove and set aside. Add the onions, potatoes and 5 cups of water to drippings. Cook until potatoes are tender. Add milk, butter, salt and pepper.

Meanwhile, in a large saucepan, cook fish in remaining water until it flakes easily with a fork, about 10 minutes. Add fish and 2 cups of cooking liquid to potato mixture.

Heat through. Garnish with parsley and salt pork or bacon. **Yield:** 16-18 servings (about 5 quarts).

Corn 'n' Spicy Pepper Chowder

Here in the Cornhusker State, we make lots of dishes with corn! Even my kids love this soup.

Marci Ingram, Omaha, Nebraska

  6 ears fresh corn
Milk
  1 small onion, chopped
  1 small green pepper, chopped
  1 celery rib, chopped

1 jalapeno pepper, seeded and chopped
1 tablespoon vegetable oil
3 medium tomatoes, peeled and chopped
2 medium potatoes, peeled and chopped
1 bay leaf
1 teaspoon salt
1/4 teaspoon pepper
1/4 teaspoon sugar
1/8 teaspoon ground allspice
2 cups half-and-half cream
Chopped fresh parsley, optional
Additional pepper, optional
6 bacon strips, cooked and crumbled, optional

Cut corn off cob (you'll need about 3-1/2 cups for this recipe). Rub the edge of a knife over each cob to milk it; add enough milk to cob juice to equal 1 cup. Set corn and liquid aside.

In a large saucepan, saute the onion, green pepper, celery and jalapeno in oil until soft. Add the next seven ingredients; bring to a boil.

Reduce heat; add cream, and the reserved corn and milk mixture. Simmer for 30-40 minutes. Discard bay leaf. Garnish with parsley, pepper and bacon if desired. **Yield:** 6-8 servings (2 quarts).

Editor's Note: When cutting or seeding hot peppers, use rubber or plastic gloves to protect your hands. Avoid touching your face.

Salmon Chowder
pictured below

When you live near some of the best salmon fishing in the world, you're always searching for imaginative ways to serve it. I came up with this chowder that uses salmon in place of shellfish.

Mary Lou Pearce, Victoria, British Columbia

2 cups diced peeled potatoes
1-1/2 cups fresh *or* frozen mixed vegetables
1 large onion, chopped
1/2 teaspoon celery seed
2 cups water
6 plum tomatoes, peeled, seeded and chopped
3 tablespoons butter
3 tablespoons all-purpose flour
1/4 teaspoon salt
Dash pepper
2 cups milk
2 cups cubed cooked salmon

In a Dutch oven or soup kettle, combine the potatoes, vegetables, onion, celery seed and water. Bring to a boil.

Reduce heat; cover and simmer for 20 minutes or until vegetables are tender. Add the tomatoes; simmer 5 minutes longer.

In a saucepan, melt butter. Stir in the flour, salt and pepper until smooth. Gradually add milk. Bring to a boil; cook and stir for 2 minutes or until thickened. Add to the vegetable mixture with salmon; heat through. **Yield:** 8 servings.

179

Chunky Veggie Chowder

pictured below

We enjoy this colorful chowder year-round. The light but flavorful soup is chock-full of vegetables and pleasantly seasoned with thyme.

Diane Molberg, Emerald Park, Saskatchewan

      2 medium onions, finely chopped
      2 garlic cloves, minced
      2 tablespoons butter
      3 medium carrots, chopped
      2 celery ribs, sliced
      2 medium potatoes, cubed
      1 small zucchini, cubed
      2 cans (10-1/2 ounces *each*) condensed
        chicken broth, undiluted
  1/4 cup minced fresh parsley
  3/4 teaspoon dried thyme
      1 cup frozen peas
      1 cup frozen corn
  1/4 cup all-purpose flour
      3 cups milk
Salt and pepper to taste

In a large saucepan or soup kettle, saute onions and garlic in butter until tender. Add the carrots, celery, potatoes, zucchini, broth, parsley and thyme. Bring to a boil. Reduce heat; cover and simmer until vegetables are tender, about 20 minutes. Stir in peas and corn.

In a bowl, combine flour, milk, salt if desired and pepper until smooth; gradually add to soup. Bring to a boil; cook and stir for 2 minutes or until thickened. **Yield:** 8 servings (2 quarts).

Cheesy Clam Chowder

I never thought I'd be able to duplicate the excellent taste of hearty clam chowders found in many restaurants, but this recipe proved me wrong. The dill makes it extra-special.

Laurie Jolliffe, Fort Morgan, Colorado

      2 cups chicken broth
      2 cans (6-1/2 ounces *each*) chopped
        clams, undrained
      3 medium potatoes, peeled and cubed
      4 medium carrots, sliced
      4 celery ribs, sliced
      1 medium onion, chopped
      1 tablespoon lemon juice
      1 tablespoon minced fresh dill *or* 1
        teaspoon dill weed
      1 garlic clove, minced
  1/2 teaspoon ground nutmeg
      1 teaspoon salt
  1/2 teaspoon pepper
      2 cups half-and-half cream
      1 cup cubed process cheese (Velveeta)
      1 cup (4 ounces) shredded Monterey
        Jack cheese
      6 bacon strips, cooked and crumbled

In a soup kettle or Dutch oven, combine the first 12 ingredients; bring to a boil. Reduce heat; simmer for 20 minutes or until the vegetables are tender.

Add cream and cheeses; heat through until cheese is melted. Stir in bacon just before serving. **Yield:** 8 servings (about 2 quarts).

Corn and Pepper Chowder

Chunks of potato, kernels of corn and flecks of red pepper punctuate the creamy broth of this hearty chowder. Cilantro and cumin lend a Southwestern flavor. I got this recipe from someone I work with. It's quick and tasty.

Donna Hackman, Huddleston, Virginia

      1 large onion, chopped
      1 medium sweet red pepper, chopped
      1 teaspoon canola oil
      3 tablespoons all-purpose flour
  1/2 teaspoon ground cumin
      2 cups water

1-1/3 cups cubed potatoes
1 teaspoon chicken bouillon granules
3/4 teaspoon salt
1/4 teaspoon white pepper
2 cups frozen corn
1 can (12 ounces) evaporated milk
1/4 cup minced fresh cilantro

In a saucepan, saute onion and red pepper in oil until tender. Stir in flour and cumin until blended. Gradually stir in water.

Bring to a boil; cook and stir for 2 minutes or until thickened. Reduce heat; add the potatoes, bouillon, salt and pepper.

Cover and cook for 10 minutes or until potatoes are tender. Add corn and milk. Cook, uncovered, 5 minutes longer or until heated through. Garnish with cilantro. **Yield:** 6 servings.

Clam Chowder for 60

When you're feeding a crowd, pick up this recipe. It makes a big batch that's loaded with clams, potatoes and cheese.

Gretchen Draeger, Santa Cruz, California

30 cans (6-1/2 ounces *each*) minced clams
8 cups diced onions
1-1/2 pounds butter
2 cups all-purpose flour
3 quarts milk
3 bunches celery, sliced
3 cups minced fresh parsley
12 pounds potatoes, peeled and cubed
3 pounds sharp cheddar cheese, shredded
Salt and pepper to taste

Drain and rinse clams, reserving juice; set aside. In a large kettle, saute onions in butter until tender.

Add flour; stir to form a smooth paste. Gradually add the milk, stirring constantly until slightly thickened (do not boil). Add celery, parsley and potatoes and cook until tender, about 45 minutes.

Add the clams and cheese; cook until cheese is melted and soup is heated through. Add reserved clam juice and salt and pepper. **Yield:** 60 servings (15 quarts).

Creole Fish Soup
pictured above

You can serve up a pot of this hearty soup in under an hour. The recipe calls for convenient frozen mixed veggies, so there's not a lot of peeling and chopping.

Ruby Williams, Bogalusa, Louisiana

1 can (28 ounces) diced tomatoes, undrained
1 can (15 ounces) tomato sauce
1/2 cup chopped onion
1/2 teaspoon garlic powder
1/2 teaspoon celery salt
1/4 teaspoon dried thyme
1/8 to 1/4 teaspoon cayenne pepper
2 bay leaves
1 package (16 ounces) frozen mixed vegetables
1 pound fresh *or* frozen cod, cut into 3/4-inch pieces

In a soup kettle, combine the first eight ingredients; cover and simmer for 10 minutes. Add vegetables; cover and simmer for 10 minutes.

Add fish; cover and simmer for 8-10 minutes or until the fish flakes easily with a fork. Discard the bay leaves. **Yield:** 8 servings (2 quarts).

chock-full CHOWDERS

Tomato Corn Chowder

pictured above

Five common ingredients are all you'll need to prepare this hearty full-flavored chowder. It's a terrific soup, particularly as the cooler season sets in.

Sue McMichael, Redding, California

- 4 bacon strips, diced
- 1 large onion, chopped
- 2 cans (15-1/4 ounces *each*) whole kernel corn, undrained
- 2 cans (14-1/2 ounces *each*) diced tomatoes, undrained
- 4 medium potatoes, peeled and diced

In a large saucepan, cook bacon over medium heat until crisp. Remove to paper towels. Drain, reserving 1 tablespoon drippings. In the drippings, saute onion until tender.

Add the corn, tomatoes and potatoes. Cook over medium heat for 25-30 minutes or until potatoes are tender. Sprinkle with bacon. **Yield:** 9 servings.

Slow-Cooked Chowder

The hectic holidays often leave little time for cooking. That's why this slow cooker recipe is a favorite. I just combine the ingredients, flip a switch and forget it!

Pam Leonard, Aberdeen, South Dakota

        5 cups water
        5 teaspoons chicken bouillon granules
        8 medium potatoes, cubed
        2 medium onions, chopped
        1 medium carrot, thinly sliced
        1 celery rib, thinly sliced
     1/4 cup butter, cubed
        1 teaspoon salt
     1/4 teaspoon pepper
        1 can (12 ounces) evaporated milk
        1 tablespoon minced fresh parsley

In a 5-qt. slow cooker, combine the first nine ingredients. Cover and cook on high for 1 hour. Reduce heat to low; cover and cook for 5-6 hours or until vegetables are tender. Stir in milk and parsley; heat through. **Yield:** 12 servings (about 3 quarts).

Sweet Pepper Chowder

Packed with potatoes, carrots and sweet peppers, this soup is nicely seasoned but not too spicy. My friend's mother made this soup for years.

Beverly Leveque, Fireside, British Columbia

        6 cups chicken broth
        6 medium potatoes, peeled and shredded
        4 medium carrots, shredded
        4 celery ribs, diced
        1 large onion, chopped
        1 large green pepper, diced
        1 large sweet red pepper, diced
        1 small sweet yellow pepper, diced
     1/2 cup all-purpose flour
  1-1/2 teaspoons salt
        1 teaspoon Italian seasoning
     1/4 to 1/2 teaspoon pepper
        1 cup water
        4 cups milk

In a Dutch oven or soup kettle, combine the broth, potatoes, carrots, celery and onion; bring to a boil. Reduce heat; cover and simmer for 20 minutes. Add peppers; return to a boil. Reduce heat; cover and simmer for 10-15 minutes or until vegetables are tender.

In a bowl, combine the flour, salt, Italian seasoning, pepper and water until blended. Stir into the vegetable mixture.

Bring to a boil; cook and stir for 2 minutes until thickened. Reduce heat. Stir in milk; heat through (do not boil). **Yield:** 20 servings.

Pantry-Shelf Salmon Chowder

pictured below

If you can open a can, you can make this soup! It's great for those running-all-day nights when you need something fast.

Kathryn Awe, International Falls, Minnesota

        1 small onion, thinly sliced
        1 tablespoon butter
        1 can (10-3/4 ounces) condensed cream of celery soup, undiluted
  1-1/3 cups milk
        1 can (7-1/2 ounces) salmon, drained, skin and bones removed
        1 can (15 ounces) cream-style corn
        1 tablespoon minced fresh parsley

In a large saucepan, saute onion in butter until tender. Stir in all of the remaining ingredients; heat through. **Yield:** 4 servings.

Creamy Corn Chowder

pictured above

The corn really stars in this delectable recipe. It hits the spot whenever you crave a hearty soup. I make it each year for a luncheon at our church's flea market.

Carol Sundquist, Rochester, New York

    2 chicken bouillon cubes
    1 cup hot water
    5 bacon strips
    1 cup chopped green pepper
  1/2 cup chopped onion
  1/4 cup all-purpose flour
    3 cups milk
1-1/2 cups fresh or frozen whole kernel corn
    1 can (14-3/4 ounces) cream-style corn
1-1/2 teaspoons seasoned salt
  1/4 teaspoon salt
  1/8 teaspoon white pepper
  1/8 teaspoon dried basil

Dissolve bouillon in water; set aside. In a 5-qt. Dutch oven, cook bacon until crisp. Remove bacon; crumble and set aside.

In the drippings, saute green pepper and onion until tender. Add flour; cook and stir until bubbly. Cook 1 minute longer. Gradually stir in milk and dissolved bouillon; bring to a boil.

Reduce heat; cook and stir until thickened. Add corn and seasonings. Cook for 10 minutes or until heated through. Sprinkle with bacon. **Yield:** 6-8 servings (2 quarts).

Chicken and Bacon Chowder

The original recipe for this chowder called for ground beef. One day I decided to use chicken instead. Everyone agreed they liked it even better.

Nancy Schmidt, Delhi, California

    1 pound sliced bacon
    3 cups diced celery
  1/2 cup diced onion
    4 cups diced peeled potatoes
    3 cups chicken broth
    2 cups diced carrots
    3 cups diced cooked chicken
    2 cans (10-3/4 ounces *each*) condensed
      cream of mushroom soup, undiluted
    2 cups half-and half cream
  1/2 teaspoon salt
  1/2 teaspoon pepper

In a soup kettle or Dutch oven, cook bacon until crisp. Drain, reserving 2 tablespoons drippings. Crumble bacon and set aside.

Saute celery and onion in drippings until tender. Add the potatoes, broth and carrots; bring to a boil.

Reduce heat; cover and simmer for 20 minutes or until vegetables are tender. Stir in remaining ingredients and heat through. **Yield:** 12 servings (3 quarts).

Shrimp Chowder

Pretty pink shrimp and green parsley dot this golden chowder. It's a rich and satisfying first course or main meal.

Anne Bennett, Hockessin, Delaware

    2 large onions, cut into thin wedges
  1/4 cup butter
    3 cups cubed peeled potatoes
    1 cup water
    2 teaspoons salt
  1/2 teaspoon seasoned pepper
    2 pounds uncooked small shrimp,
      peeled and deveined
    6 cups milk
    2 cups (8 ounces) shredded sharp
      cheddar cheese
  1/4 cup minced fresh parsley

In a soup kettle or Dutch oven, saute onions in butter until tender. Add potatoes, water, salt and pepper; bring to a boil.

Reduce heat; cover and simmer for 15-20 minutes or until potatoes are tender (do not drain). Add shrimp; cook until shrimp turn pink, about 5 minutes.

In a large saucepan over low heat, heat the milk. Stir in cheese until melted (do not boil). Add to potato mixture; heat through (do not boil). Stir in the parsley. **Yield:** 12 servings (about 3 quarts).

Sweet Potato Chowder
pictured below

My husband came up with this spicy soup that's a snap to make. Creamy bowls of it are warm and winning on a cool night.

Kathy Whitford, Oscoda, Michigan

- 1 celery rib, chopped
- 2 tablespoons butter
- 2 cans (14-1/2 ounces *each*) chicken broth
- 2 cups water
- 2 teaspoons chicken bouillon granules
- 4 medium potatoes, peeled and cubed
- 1 large sweet potato, peeled and cubed
- 2 cups cubed fully cooked turkey ham
- 2 tablespoons dried minced onion

- 1/2 teaspoon *each* garlic powder, seasoned salt, dried oregano and parsley flakes
- 1/4 teaspoon *each* pepper and crushed red pepper flakes
- 1/4 cup all-purpose flour
- 2 cups milk

In a large saucepan, saute celery in butter until tender. Stir in broth, water and bouillon. Add potatoes, sweet potato, turkey ham and seasonings. Bring to a boil.

Reduce heat; cover and simmer for 12 minutes or until potatoes are tender. Combine flour and milk until smooth; gradually stir into soup.

Bring to a boil; cook and stir for 2 minutes or until thickened and bubbly. **Yield:** 11 servings.

Potato Clam Chowder

I ran across this recipe in one of my antique cookbooks. It's a timeless classic I like to prepare for friends and family throughout the year.

Betty Ann Morgan, Upper Marlboro, Maryland

- 2 bacon strips, diced
- 1 cup chopped onion
- 2 tablespoons all-purpose flour
- 2 cans (6-1/2 ounces *each*) minced clams
- 1 cup water
- 1/2 teaspoon salt
- 1/4 to 1/2 teaspoon dried thyme
- 1/4 teaspoon dried savory
- 1/8 teaspoon pepper
- 4 medium potatoes, peeled and cubed
- 2 cups milk
- 2 tablespoons minced fresh parsley

In a 3-qt. saucepan or Dutch oven, cook bacon until crisp. Remove bacon; set aside. Saute onion in drippings until tender. Add flour; stir until smooth.

Drain clams, reserving juice; set clams aside. Gradually add water and clam juice to pan; cook and stir over medium heat until smooth and bubbly. Add salt, thyme, savory, pepper and potatoes; bring to a boil.

Reduce heat; cover and simmer for 25 minutes or until potatoes are tender, stirring often. Add bacon, clams, milk and parsley; heat through. **Yield:** 6 servings.

Crab and Corn Chowder

I started cooking at a local restaurant when I was 16 years old. This creamy chowder was one of the soups we made. The recipe had been passed from cook to cook and was finally written down.

Susanna Bellany, Cremona, Alberta

1 medium onion, chopped
5 tablespoons butter
1/3 cup all-purpose flour
3-1/2 cups milk
4 bacon strips, cooked and crumbled
2 cans (6 ounces *each*) crabmeat, drained
2 medium potatoes, diced
1 small green pepper, chopped
1 celery rib, chopped
1 can (8-1/4 ounces) whole kernel corn, drained
1 cup half-and-half cream
1 bay leaf
1 tablespoon chopped fresh parsley
1 teaspoon salt
1/4 to 1/2 teaspoon ground nutmeg
1/4 teaspoon white pepper

In a large saucepan, saute onion in butter until tender. Add flour; cook and stir until thick and bubbly. Gradually add milk; cook and stir until thickened. Add remaining ingredients.

Cover and simmer until vegetables are tender, about 35-40 minutes. Remove bay leaf before serving. **Yield:** 6 servings (1-1/2 quarts).

Cheesy Potato Chowder

This chowder was invented by my niece, who took a basic potato soup recipe and added some of her own ingredients. I was a cook at the time, and I tried her recipe at work. It was the hit of the season!

Carol Traxler, Philo, Illinois

8 to 12 medium potatoes, peeled and cubed
3 carrots, diced
2 cans (14-1/2 ounces *each*) chicken broth
1 pound process cheese (Velveeta), cubed
1 teaspoon dill weed
1/4 teaspoon salt
1/4 teaspoon pepper
1/2 pound bacon, cooked and crumbled, *divided*
3 cups milk

In a large kettle or Dutch oven, cook potatoes and carrots in chicken broth until tender, about 10 minutes. Add cheese, dill weed, salt and pepper. Cook and stir until cheese is melted.

Reserve some of the bacon for garnish; add the rest to chowder with milk. Heat through. Top individual bowls with reserved bacon. **Yield:** 10-12 servings (3 quarts).

Quick Clam Chowder

Not only is this soup a quick fix, but it's oh-so-tasty. Dressing up canned soups allows you to enjoy the comfort of clam chowder with a fraction of the work.

Judy Jungwirth, Athol, South Dakota

1 can (10-3/4 ounces) condensed cream of celery soup, undiluted
1 can (10-3/4 ounces) condensed cream of potato soup, undiluted
2 cups half-and-half cream
2 cans (6-1/2 ounces *each*) minced clams, drained
1/2 teaspoon ground nutmeg
Pepper to taste

In a large saucepan, combine all ingredients. Cook and stir over medium heat until heated through. **Yield:** 5 servings.

> " Add a dollop of sour cream to Cheeseburger Chowder, and you have another great flavor topper to this recipe. "
>
> *—Lori Risdal*
> *Sioux City, Iowa*

Cheeseburger Chowder
pictured above

After tasting a wonderful chowder at a restaurant, I dressed up a can of cheese soup to see if I could capture the same flavors. I then took things a step further by adding chilies and Southwestern spices. I hope you enjoy it as much as I do.

Lori Risdal, Sioux City, Iowa

1/2 **pound ground beef**
1 **can (10-3/4 ounces) condensed cheddar cheese soup, undiluted**
1-3/4 **cups milk**
1 **cup frozen shredded hash brown potatoes**
1 **can (4 ounces) chopped green chilies**
1 **tablespoon taco seasoning**
1 **tablespoon dried minced onion**
1/2 **teaspoon chili powder**
Coarsely crushed corn chips, shredded Monterey Jack cheese and chopped green onions, optional

In a large saucepan, cook beef over medium heat until no longer pink; drain. Stir in the soup, milk, potatoes, chilies, taco seasoning, onion and chili powder until blended.

Bring to a boil. Reduce heat; simmer, uncovered, for 5 minutes or until heated through. Garnish with corn chips, cheese and green onions if desired. **Yield:** 4 servings.

187

Cauliflower Ham Chowder

Soup is always good for warming the tummy and the heart, and this is one of our family's favorites. With a busy household, it's a simple but nutritious meal to have on hand!

Lois Buch, Clarinda, Iowa

- 2 cups cubed peeled potatoes
- 2 cups fresh cauliflower florets
- 1 small onion, finely diced
- 1 cup chicken broth
- 3 cups milk
- 2-1/2 cups cubed fully cooked ham
- 1 teaspoon salt
- 1/2 teaspoon pepper
- Dash ground nutmeg
- 1/2 to 1 cup instant potato flakes
- Minced fresh parsley

In a saucepan, cook the potatoes, cauliflower and onion in chicken broth until tender. Stir in the milk, ham, salt, pepper and nutmeg; heat through.

Stir in potato flakes; simmer for 5-10 minutes or until soup is as thick as desired. Sprinkle with parsley. **Yield:** 6-8 servings (2 quarts).

Autumn Chowder
pictured above right

When the weather gets chilly, we enjoy comfort foods like this hearty chowder. It's easy to prepare, and the aroma of it as it simmers makes my mouth water.

Sheena Hoffman
North Vancouver, British Columbia

- 2 bacon strips, diced
- 1/4 cup chopped onion
- 1 medium red potato, diced
- 1 small carrot, halved lengthwise and thinly sliced
- 1/2 cup water
- 3/4 teaspoon chicken bouillon granules
- 1 cup milk
- 2/3 cup frozen corn
- 1/8 teaspoon pepper
- 2-1/2 teaspoons all-purpose flour
- 2 tablespoons cold water
- 3/4 cup shredded cheddar cheese

In a saucepan, cook bacon over medium heat until crisp; remove to paper towels. Drain, reserving 1 teaspoon drippings.

In the drippings, saute onion until tender. Add the potato, carrot, water and bouillon. Bring to a boil. Reduce heat; cover and simmer for 15-20 minutes or until the vegetables are almost tender.

Stir in the milk, corn and pepper. Cook 5 minutes longer. Combine the flour and cold water until smooth; gradually whisk into soup. Bring to a boil; cook and stir for 1-2 minutes or until thickened.

Remove from the heat; stir in the shredded cheddar cheese until melted. Sprinkle with bacon. **Yield:** 2 servings.

Bean Counter Chowder

pictured below

This wonderfully seasoned chowder is always a hit at my table. Basil, oregano and celery flakes give it just the right flavor.

Vivian Haen, Menomonee Falls, Wisconsin

1/2 cup chopped onion
  2 garlic cloves, minced
  1 tablespoon vegetable oil
  1 medium tomato, chopped
  2 cans (14-1/2 ounces *each*) chicken broth
1-3/4 cups water
1/2 teaspoon *each* dried basil, oregano and celery flakes
1/4 teaspoon pepper
  3 cans (15-1/4 ounces *each*) great northern *or* pinto beans, rinsed and drained
  1 cup uncooked elbow macaroni
  1 tablespoon minced parsley

In a large saucepan, saute onion and garlic in oil until tender. Add tomato; simmer for 5 minutes. Add the broth, water and seasonings. Bring to a boil; cook for 5 minutes.

Add beans and macaroni; return to a boil. Reduce heat; simmer, uncovered, for 15 minutes or until macaroni is tender. Sprinkle with parsley. **Yield:** 8 servings (2 quarts).

cumin; bring to a boil. Reduce heat; cover and simmer for 5 minutes.

Add cream, cheese, corn, chilies and hot pepper sauce. Cook and stir over low heat until the cheese is melted. Stir in tomato. Serve immediately; garnish with cilantro if desired. **Yield:** 6-8 servings (2 quarts).

Mexican Chicken Corn Chowder

pictured above

I like to make this smooth, creamy soup when company comes to visit. Its zippy flavor is full of Southwestern flair.

Susan Garoutte, Georgetown, Texas

  1-1/2 pounds boneless skinless chicken breasts
    1/2 cup chopped onion
      1 to 2 garlic cloves, minced
      3 tablespoons butter
      2 chicken bouillon cubes
      1 cup hot water
    1/2 to 1 teaspoon ground cumin
      2 cups half-and-half cream
      2 cups (8 ounces) shredded Monterey Jack cheese
      1 can (16 ounces) cream-style corn
      1 can (4 ounces) chopped green chilies, undrained
    1/4 to 1 teaspoon hot pepper sauce
      1 medium tomato, chopped
Fresh cilantro, optional

Cut chicken into bite-size pieces. In a Dutch oven, brown chicken, onion and garlic in butter until chicken is no longer pink. Dissolve the bouillon in hot water. Add to pan along with

Clam Chowder For a Crowd

Bacon makes the difference in this potluck-pleaser. It's very popular at church camp and our family reunion. It has a thinner broth than most chowders, but it is very flavorful.

Lynn Richardson, Bauxite, Arkansas

   10 quarts water
    3 tablespoons salt
    8 pounds red potatoes, peeled and cubed
    6 large onions, chopped
    1 cup butter
    4 large carrots, grated
   16 cans (6-1/2 ounces *each*) minced clams
    3 cans (12 ounces *each*) evaporated milk
  1/2 cup minced fresh parsley
    1 to 2 tablespoons pepper
    2 pounds bacon, cooked and crumbled

> "Mexican Chicken Corn Chowder is perfect for dipping homemade bread. My family likes to soak up every bit of this chowder."
>
> *—Susan Garoutte Georgetown, Texas*

In several large kettles, bring water and salt to a boil. Add potatoes; cook until tender (do not drain). In another large pan, saute onions in butter until tender. Add onions and carrots to potato mixture; heat through.

Drain clams if desired. Stir the clams, milk, parsley and pepper into the vegetable mixture; heat through. Just before serving, stir in the bacon. **Yield:** 60-65 servings (about 15 quarts).

Hearty Ham and Cabbage Chowder

Ketchup and brown sugar add an appealing sweetness to this chowder. I make this frequently throughout the year, but my family especially looks forward to it on winter evenings.

Sharyl Mathis, Byron, Michigan

   1 **cup thinly sliced celery**
1/2 **cup chopped onion**
   2 **garlic cloves, minced**
   2 **tablespoons vegetable oil**
   3 **cups shredded cabbage**
   2 **cups (1 pound) cubed fully cooked ham**
   1 **can (28 ounces) diced tomatoes, undrained**
   1 **can (15-1/4 ounces) whole kernel corn, drained**
   1 **can (15 ounces) whole potatoes, drained and quartered**
   1 **can (10-1/2 ounces) condensed chicken broth, undiluted**
   1 **cup water**
1/2 **cup ketchup**
1/4 **cup packed brown sugar**

In a Dutch oven or soup kettle over medium heat, saute celery, onion and garlic in oil for 2 minutes, stirring constantly.

Add remaining ingredients; bring to a boil. Reduce heat; cover and simmer for 1-1/2 hours. **Yield:** 8-10 servings (2-3/4 quarts).

Favorite Fish Chowder
pictured below

Economics had a lot to do with what we ate when I was growing up in New Hampshire during the Depression. Money may have been scarce, but fish was plentiful and affordable, so that's how we began eating this dish.

Fran Gustafson, Bethesda, Maryland

     1 **large onion, chopped**
   1/2 **cup butter**
     4 **cups water**
     6 **cups diced peeled potatoes**
     2 **pounds fresh** *or* **frozen cod fillets, cut into large chunks**
     3 **tablespoons lemon juice**
     2 **cups milk**
     2 **cans (12 ounces** *each***) evaporated milk**
2-1/2 **teaspoons salt**
     2 **teaspoons pepper**
Chopped fresh parsley

In a Dutch oven or soup kettle, saute onion in butter. Add water and bring to a boil. Add the potatoes; cook for 10 minutes.

Add fish and lemon juice; reduce heat and simmer for 10 minutes or until the fish flakes easily with a fork. Add milk, evaporated milk, salt and pepper. Heat through but do not boil. Garnish with parsley. **Yield:** 16 servings (4 quarts).

Southwestern Corn Chowder

pictured below

A family friend gave me this spicy chowder recipe years ago. We usually take a batch along when we go camping. It's a fast, filling meal that satisfies all appetites.

Nancy Winters, Moorpark, California

> 4 boneless skinless chicken breast halves, cut into 3/4-inch cubes
> 1 medium onion, cut into thin wedges
> 1 tablespoon vegetable oil
> 2 teaspoons ground cumin
> 2 cans (14-1/2 ounces *each*) chicken broth
> 1 package (10 ounces) frozen whole kernel corn
> 3/4 cup picante sauce
> 1/2 cup chopped sweet red pepper
> 1/2 cup chopped green pepper
> 2 tablespoons finely chopped fresh cilantro
> 2 tablespoons cornstarch
> 2 tablespoons water
> Shredded Monterey Jack cheese, optional

In a 3-qt. saucepan, cook chicken and onion in oil until chicken juices run clear. Stir in cumin.

Add broth, corn and picante sauce; bring to a boil. Reduce heat; cover and simmer for 15 minutes. Stir in peppers and cilantro.

Combine cornstarch and water; stir into soup. Bring to a boil. Cook, stirring constantly, for 3 minutes or until slightly thickened. Spoon into bowls; top with cheese if desired. **Yield:** 6 servings (about 2 quarts).

Chunky Fish Chowder

Our kids refused to try this soup when I first served it, but then they saw how much their father and I were enjoying it! I serve it with salad and bread for a complete meal.

Cyndi Reason, Ruidoso, New Mexico

> 3 bacon strips, diced
> 1 large onion, chopped
> 1 garlic clove, minced
> 1 can (14-1/2 ounces) stewed tomatoes
> 1 quart water
> 3/4 teaspoon ground cumin
> 1/2 teaspoon salt
> 1/4 teaspoon ground turmeric
> Dash pepper
> 2 medium potatoes, peeled and diced
> 1 pound frozen cod, thawed and cut into 3/4-inch pieces
> 1 package (10 ounces) frozen whole kernel corn, thawed
> 1 tablespoon cider vinegar
> GARLIC BUTTER:
> 1/2 cup butter, softened
> 2 tablespoons chopped fresh parsley
> 2 tablespoons lemon juice
> 2 garlic cloves, minced
> Fish-shaped crackers, optional

In a 3-qt. saucepan, cook bacon until crisp. Remove with a slotted spoon and set aside. Saute onion and garlic in the reserved bacon drippings until tender.

Add tomatoes, water, cumin, salt, turmeric and pepper; bring to a boil. Add potatoes; simmer for 15 minutes or until tender. Add fish, corn and vinegar; cook for 10 minutes or until fish is opaque and flakes easily. Stir in bacon.

For garlic butter, beat butter, parsley, lemon juice and garlic in a small mixing bowl until fluffy. Top each serving of soup with a dollop of garlic butter; garnish with crackers if desired. **Yield:** 8 servings (2 quarts).

Ham and Corn Chowder

pictured at right

I'm always on the lookout for easy soups because my husband and I love them, particularly in the winter months. This creamy chowder gets a little kick from cayenne and chopped jalapeno pepper. Extra servings freeze very well.

Sharon Price, Caldwell, Idaho

> 2 celery ribs, chopped
> 1/4 cup chopped onion
> 1 jalapeno pepper, seeded and chopped
> 2 tablespoons butter
> 2 tablespoons all-purpose flour
> 3 cups milk
> 2 cups cubed fully cooked ham
> 2 cups cubed cooked potatoes
> 1-1/2 cups fresh *or* frozen corn
> 1 can (14-3/4 ounces) cream-style corn
> 3/4 teaspoon minced fresh thyme *or* 1/4 teaspoon dried thyme
> 1/8 to 1/4 teaspoon cayenne pepper
> 1/8 teaspoon salt

In a large saucepan, saute the celery, onion and jalapeno in butter until vegetables are tender. Stir in flour until blended. Gradually add milk. Bring to a boil; cook and stir for 2 minutes or until thickened.

Stir in the remaining ingredients. Bring to a boil. Reduce heat; cover and simmer for 10 minutes or until heated through. **Yield:** 8 servings (2 quarts).

Editor's Note: When cutting or seeding hot peppers, use rubber or plastic gloves to protect your hands. Avoid touching your face.

Christmas Seafood Chowder

For as long as I can remember, we always had this wonderful soup on Christmas Day. When winters are long and cold, this sure warms us up.

Sue Bridley, Dennison, Minnesota

> 2 cans (6-1/2 ounces *each*) chopped clams
> 2 cups diced peeled potatoes
> 2 cups chopped celery
> 2 cups diced carrots
> 1/2 cup water
> 2 cups milk
> 1 package (5 ounces) frozen cooked shrimp, thawed
> 4 bacon strips, cooked and crumbled
> 2 teaspoons minced fresh parsley

Salt and pepper to taste

Drain the clams, reserving juice; set clams aside. In a large saucepan or Dutch oven, combine clam juice, potatoes, celery, carrots and water. Bring to a boil.

Reduce heat; cover and cook for 15 minutes or until vegetables are tender. Add the milk, shrimp, bacon, parsley, salt, pepper and reserved clams; heat through. **Yield:** 7 servings.

Potato Bacon Chowder

pictured below

This chowder is like a bacon-topped baked potato in a bowl. On cold winter days, my family is thrilled to see this meal on the table.

Jacque Manning, Burbank, South Dakota

      2 cups cubed peeled potatoes
      1 cup water
      8 bacon strips
      1 cup chopped onion
  1/2 cup chopped celery
      1 can (10-3/4 ounces) condensed cream
         of chicken soup, undiluted
1-3/4 cups milk
      1 cup (8 ounces) sour cream
  1/2 teaspoon salt
Dash pepper
      1 tablespoon minced fresh parsley

In a covered 3-qt. saucepan, cook potatoes and water until tender. Meanwhile, cook bacon in a skillet until crisp; remove to paper towel to drain.

In the same skillet, saute onion and celery in drippings until tender; drain. Add to undrained potatoes. Stir in soup, milk, sour cream, salt and pepper. Cook over low heat for 10 minutes or until heated through (do not boil).

Crumble bacon; set aside 1/4 cup. Add remaining bacon to soup along with parsley. Sprinkle with reserved bacon. **Yield:** 6 servings.

Taste of Home's BIG BOOK *of* SOUP

Colby Corn Chowder

This comforting, cheesy soup is perfect for chilly winter nights—and it doesn't have to simmer for hours. The creamed corn adds a nice touch of sweetness. My family enjoys it with dill pickle spears and crusty fresh-from-the-oven bread.

Darlene Drane, Fayette, Missouri

> 6 large potatoes, peeled and cubed
> 1 teaspoon salt
> 1 large onion, chopped
> 1/4 cup butter
> 2 cans (14-3/4 ounces *each*) cream-style corn
> 4 bacon strips, cooked and crumbled
> 3 cups milk
> 8 ounces Colby cheese, cubed

Place potatoes in a Dutch oven or soup kettle; sprinkle with salt and cover with water. Bring to a boil. Reduce heat; cover and simmer until potatoes are tender.

Meanwhile, in a skillet, saute onion in butter until tender. Stir in corn and bacon; heat through.

Drain potatoes. Add milk; heat through. Stir in corn mixture and cheese. Serve immediately. **Yield:** 12-14 servings (about 3 quarts).

Surprise Clam Chowder

When family and friends first sampled this stew over 40 years ago, they were pleasantly surprised by the combination of ingredients. Now it's a dish they frequently request.

Evelyn Whalin, Denver, Colorado

> 1 can (14-1/2 ounces) diced tomatoes, undrained
> 1 cup water
> 1/2 cup diced peeled potato
> 1/4 cup diced green pepper
> 1/4 cup diced onion
> 1/4 teaspoon garlic salt
> 1/4 teaspoon chili powder
> 1 cup diced fully cooked ham
> 1 can (7-1/2 ounces) minced clams, undrained

In a saucepan, combine the first seven ingredients. Cover and simmer for 25-30 minutes or until vegetables are tender. Add ham and clams; heat through. **Yield:** 4 servings.

Herbed Fish Chowder

My husband loves fish prepared in variety of ways, so it's no surprise this soup has become one of his most-requested meals. I think you'll also enjoy its comforting flavor.

Geraldine De Iure, Calgary, Alberta

> 1 pound frozen fish fillets (cod, haddock, etc.), partially thawed
> 2 bacon strips, diced, optional
> 1 cup diced carrots
> 1 cup sliced fresh mushrooms
> 1 medium onion, sliced
> 1 garlic clove, minced
> 2 tablespoons vegetable oil
> 1/2 cup all-purpose flour
> 1/4 teaspoon dried thyme
> 1/4 teaspoon dill weed
> Dash pepper
> 4 cups chicken broth
> 1 bay leaf
> 1-1/2 cups frozen cut green beans

Cut fish into bite-size pieces; set aside. Cook bacon in a 3-qt. saucepan until crisp. Remove to paper towels to drain. Discard drippings.

In the same pan, saute carrots, mushrooms, onion and garlic in oil until onion is tender. Stir in flour, thyme, dill and pepper until smooth. Stir in broth; bring to a boil. Add bay leaf. Reduce heat; cover and simmer for 12-15 minutes or until carrots are tender. Add fish and beans.

Simmer, uncovered, for 5 minutes or until fish is opaque and flakes easily. Remove bay leaf. Garnish individual servings with bacon. **Yield:** 7 servings (about 2 quarts).

Sausage Corn Chowder

This hearty soup is a meal in itself when served with a salad and bread. For a spicier flavor, I sometimes substitute Mexicorn for the whole kernel corn.

Sharon Wallace, Omaha, Nebraska

    2 packages (7 ounces *each*) pork
        or turkey breakfast sausage
    2 cans (10-3/4 ounces *each*) condensed
        cream of chicken soup, undiluted
2-1/2 cups milk
    2 cups fresh corn
    2/3 cup sliced green onions
    1/2 teaspoon hot pepper sauce
    1 cup (4 ounces) shredded Swiss cheese

Crumble sausage into a large saucepan or Dutch oven; brown over medium heat. Drain. Add the soup, milk, corn, green onions and hot pepper sauce.

Cook until corn is tender. Reduce heat to low; add cheese and heat until melted. **Yield:** 6-8 servings (2 quarts).

Potato Chowder

pictured at right

One of the ladies in our church quilting group brought this savory potato soup to a meeting. It's easy to assemble in the morning, then cook all day. Cream cheese and a sprinkling of bacon provide richness.

Anna Mayer, Ft. Branch, Indiana

    8 cups diced potatoes
    1/3 cup chopped onion
    3 cans (14-1/2 ounces *each*) chicken
        broth
    1 can (10-3/4 ounces) condensed cream
        of chicken soup, undiluted
    1/4 teaspoon pepper
    1 package (8 ounces) cream cheese,
        cubed
    1/2 pound sliced bacon, cooked and
        crumbled, optional
Snipped chives, optional

In a slow cooker, combine the first five ingredients. Cover and cook on low for 8-10 hours or until potatoes are tender. Add cream cheese; stir until blended. Garnish with bacon and chives if desired. **Yield:** 12 servings (3 quarts).

Confetti Chowder

My mom always had flavorful soups simmering on the stove during a long workday on our cattle ranch. She inspired me to create my own rib-sticking recipes like this.

Donna Valen, Stonewall, Manitoba

    4 cups water
1-1/2 cups diced fully cooked ham
1-1/2 cups frozen *or* canned whole kernel
        corn
    1/2 cup diced celery
    1/2 cup shredded carrot
    1/4 cup diced cabbage
    1/4 cup diced onion
    2 tablespoons chicken bouillon granules
    1/4 cup cornstarch
    2 cups milk, *divided*

In a 3-qt. saucepan, combine the first eight ingredients; bring to a boil over medium heat. Reduce heat; cover and simmer for 10-12 minutes or until vegetables are tender.

Combine cornstarch with 1/2 cup milk until smooth; gradually add to soup, stirring constantly. Bring to a boil; boil and stir for 2 minutes. Add remaining milk; heat through, stirring frequently. **Yield:** 6-8 servings (2 quarts).

Combine flour and corn; stir into soup. Heat, but do not boil, until slightly thickened. Gently stir in salmon and heat through. **Yield:** 6-8 servings (2 quarts).

Salmon and Corn Chowder

pictured above

Chowders and stews are my specialty, because I enjoy making use of the wonderful variety of seafood from the cold waters of the North Atlantic. I devised this recipe years ago, and it remains one of my favorites.

Fred Johnson, Tyngsboro, Massachusetts

    2 medium potatoes, peeled and cubed
    1 large onion, chopped
    1 cup chopped celery
    1 can (14-1/2 ounces) chicken broth
    1 garlic clove, minced
1-1/4 teaspoon salt
  1/2 teaspoon dried marjoram
    2 cups half-and-half cream
    1 cup milk
  1/4 cup butter
    2 tablespoons all-purpose flour
    1 can (16 ounces) cream-style corn
    1 can (16 ounces) salmon, drained
      and flaked

In a large saucepan, combine the potatoes, onion, celery, chicken broth, garlic, salt and marjoram. Bring to a boil; reduce heat and simmer, covered, about 10 minutes of until vegetables are tender. Stir in cream, milk and butter.

Haddock Clam Chowder

Our Test Kitchen home economists modified a recipe to take advantage of leftover cooked fish. This seafood soup is wonderful served with warm homemade bread.

    4 strips bacon, diced
    3 tablespoons sliced green onions
    2 celery ribs, chopped
    2 cups diced peeled potatoes
    1 can (14-1/2 ounces) chicken broth
    1 teaspoon dill weed
    1 teaspoon celery seed, crushed
1-1/4 teaspoons salt
  1/4 teaspoon pepper
    3 cups milk, *divided*
    3 tablespoons all-purpose flour
2-1/2 cups cubed cooked haddock
    1 cup heavy whipping cream
    1 package (10 ounces) frozen chopped
      spinach, thawed
    1 can (6-1/2 ounces) minced clams

In a Dutch oven or large saucepan, cook bacon until crisp. Remove to paper towels. In the drippings, saute onions and celery for 5 minutes or until crisp-tender.

Add the potatoes, broth, dill, celery seed, salt and pepper. Bring to a boil. Reduce heat; cover and simmer for 15 minutes or until potatoes are tender. Add 2-1/2 cups of milk.

Combine flour and remaining milk; stir into soup. Bring to a boil; cook and stir for 2 minutes or until thickened.

Add the haddock, cream, spinach and clams. Cook and stir until heated through. Garnish with bacon. **Yield:** 8 servings.

chock-full CHOWDERS

Zippy Shrimp Chowder

pictured above

This chowder is chock-full of shrimp and vegetables, so it satisfies hearty appetites. You can also use skim milk and reduced-sodium broth to help keep fat and calories to a minimum. It tastes even better the next day, after the flavors have melded overnight.

Michelle Conley, Evanston, Wyoming

    1 pound red potatoes, peeled and
      cubed
2-1/2 cups chicken broth
    3 celery ribs, chopped
    8 green onions, chopped
  1/2 cup chopped sweet red pepper
1-1/2 cups milk
  1/4 cup all-purpose flour
  1/2 cup evaporated milk
1-1/2 pounds uncooked medium shrimp,
      peeled and deveined
    2 tablespoons minced fresh parsley
  1/2 teaspoon paprika
  1/2 teaspoon Worcestershire sauce
  1/8 teaspoon cayenne pepper
  1/8 teaspoon pepper

In a large saucepan, bring potatoes, broth, celery, onions and red pepper to a boil. Reduce heat; cover and simmer for 13-15 minutes or until vegetables are tender. Stir in milk. Gently mash vegetables with a potato masher, leaving some chunks of potatoes.

Combine flour and evaporated milk until smooth; gradually stir into potato mixture. Bring to a boil; cook and stir for 2 minutes or until thickened. Stir in the remaining ingredients. Return to a boil. Cook and stir for 2-3 minutes or until shrimp turn pink. **Yield:** 8 servings.

Panfish Chowder

pictured below

With my husband being an avid hunter and fisherman, I can never have enough new fish and wild game recipes. We especially enjoy this rich chowder. It's a hearty dish with big chunks of fish, potatoes and bacon.

Cyndi Fliss, Bevent, Wisconsin

    6 bacon strips, cut into 1-inch pieces
2/3 cup chopped onion
1/2 cup chopped celery
    3 medium potatoes, peeled and cubed
    2 cups water
1/2 cup chopped carrots
    2 tablespoons minced fresh parsley
    1 tablespoon lemon juice
1/2 teaspoon dill weed
1/4 teaspoon garlic salt
1/8 teaspoon pepper
    1 pound panfish fillets (perch, sunfish or crappie), cut into 1-inch chunks
    1 cup half-and-half cream

In a 3-qt. saucepan, cook the bacon until crisp. Remove bacon and set aside; discard all but 2 tablespoons of drippings. Saute onion and celery in drippings until tender.

Add the next eight ingredients. Simmer until vegetables are tender, about 30 minutes.

Add fish and bacon; simmer for 5 minutes or just until fish flakes with a fork. Add cream and heat through. **Yield:** 4-6 servings.

Garden Chowder

My family loves to eat, so I'm encouraged to spend lots of time in the kitchen! Featuring garden-fresh produce, this chowder quickly disappears whenever I serve it.

Betty Kuhlber, Slippery Rock, Pennsylvania

1/4 cup chopped onion
1/2 cup chopped celery
1/4 cup butter
1/4 cup all-purpose flour
1/2 teaspoon salt
1/4 teaspoon pepper
    2 cups chicken broth
    1 medium tomato, peeled and diced
    1 cup broccoli florets
    1 cup chopped carrots
    1 cup frozen corn
    1 cup thinly sliced zucchini
    2 cups half-and-half cream
1/4 cup grated Parmesan cheese

In a 3-qt. saucepan over medium heat, saute onion and celery in butter for 5 minutes. Add the flour, salt and pepper; stir to form a smooth paste. Gradually add broth, stirring constantly. Bring to a boil; boil and stir for 2 minutes or until thickened.

Add tomato, broccoli, carrots, corn and zucchini; return to a boil. Reduce heat; cover and simmer for 40 minutes or until vegetables are tender. Add cream and cheese; heat through. **Yield:** 4-6 servings.

"Nothing **lifts** the spirit and **strengthens** the soul more than a good bowl of **chili**."

heart-warming CHILI

Bulgur Chili

pictured above

*This vegetarian chili offers a hint of sweetness.
Because it doesn't have to simmer for hours, it's
ideal for serving to drop-in visitors.*

Jeraldine Hall, Ravenden Springs, Arkansas

   3/4 cup bulgur
     2 cups boiling water
1-1/2 cups finely chopped green peppers
     1 large onion, chopped
     2 teaspoons canola oil
     2 cups tomato juice

     1 can (16 ounces) kidney beans, rinsed
       and drained
     1 can (15 ounces) ranch-style beans,
       undrained
     1 can (14-1/2 ounces) diced tomatoes,
       undrained
     1 can (8 ounces) tomato sauce
     1 cup water
     2 to 3 tablespoons chili powder
     2 garlic cloves, minced
   1/2 teaspoon ground cumin
   1/8 to 1/4 teaspoon cayenne pepper
   3/4 cup shredded cheddar cheese

Place bulgur in a bowl; stir in boiling water. Cover and let stand for 30 minutes or until most of the liquid is absorbed. Drain; squeeze dry.

In a large saucepan, saute green peppers and onion in oil until tender. Stir in the bulgur, tomato juice, beans, tomatoes, tomato sauce, water and seasonings. Bring to a boil. Reduce heat; cover and simmer for 20-25 minutes or until heated through. Garnish with cheese. **Yield:** 9 servings.

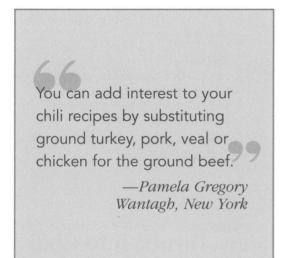

> "You can add interest to your chili recipes by substituting ground turkey, pork, veal or chicken for the ground beef."
>
> —*Pamela Gregory*
> *Wantagh, New York*

Steak Chili

I took traditional chili and made my version more satisfying using steak and V8 juice. It gets a little kick from hot pepper sauce.

DeAnn Hill, Indianapolis, Indiana

1-1/2 pounds lean round steak, cut into 1/2-inch cubes
   1 cup chopped onion
   3 garlic cloves, minced
   1 can (15 ounces) tomato sauce
1-1/4 cups water, *divided*
   1 cup V8 juice
  1/2 teaspoon hot pepper sauce
   1 tablespoon chili powder
   1 tablespoon paprika
1-1/2 teaspoons ground cumin
   1 teaspoon pepper
   2 tablespoons all-purpose flour

In a large saucepan, brown steak. Drain, discarding all but 2 tablespoons drippings. Set the meat aside. Saute onion and garlic in drippings for 3 minutes.

Return meat to pan. Add tomato sauce, 1 cup water, V8 juice, hot pepper sauce, chili powder, paprika, cumin and pepper. Bring to a boil.

Reduce heat; cover and simmer 2-1/2 hours. Combine flour with remaining water; whisk into chili. Cook 10 minutes. **Yield:** 6 servings.

Chili Verde
pictured below

Leftover pork adds heartiness to this zippy chili. It's great on a cool night with a stack of tortillas. I've taken it to many gatherings, and it's always gone when the party's over.

Jo Oliverius, Alpine, California

   2 cups cubed cooked pork (about 1 pound)
   1 can (16 ounces) kidney beans, rinsed and drained
   1 can (15 ounces) pinto beans, rinsed and drained
   1 can (15 ounces) chili with beans, undrained
   1 can (14-1/2 ounces) stewed tomatoes
1-1/2 to 2 cups green salsa
   1 large onion, chopped
   2 cans (4 ounces *each*) chopped green chilies
   2 garlic cloves, minced
   1 tablespoon minced fresh cilantro
   2 teaspoons ground cumin

In a large saucepan, combine all ingredients. Bring to a boil. Reduce heat; simmer, uncovered, for 10 minutes. **Yield:** 8 servings.

Buffalo Chili Con Carne
pictured above

This classic recipe of the American frontier is so meaty you can almost eat it with a fork. The zippy combination of ingredients is a perfect complement to the buffalo.

Donna Smith, Victor, New York

- 1 pound cubed *or* coarsely ground buffalo meat
- 2 tablespoons vegetable oil
- 1 to 2 cups diced onion
- 1 to 2 cups diced green pepper
- 2 cans (16 ounces *each*) diced tomatoes, undrained
- 1-1/2 to 2 cups tomato juice
- 1 can (16 ounces) dark red kidney beans, rinsed and drained
- 1 can (15 ounces) pinto beans, rinsed and drained
- 1 can (4 ounces) chopped green chilies
- 2 teaspoons chili powder
- 1 teaspoon salt
- 1/2 teaspoon pepper

In a large kettle or Dutch oven, brown meat in oil; drain. Add onion and green pepper; saute for 5 minutes. Stir in remaining ingredients and bring to a boil.

Reduce heat; cover and simmer 1-1/2 to 2 hours or until the meat is tender. **Yield:** 6 servings (1-1/2 quarts).

Five-Can Chili

Who says a thick hearty chili has to simmer all day on the stove? With five canned goods and zero prep time, a warm pot of this zesty specialty is a snap to whip up.

Jo Mann, Westover, Alabama

- 1 can (15 ounces) chili with beans
- 1 can (15 ounces) mixed vegetables, drained
- 1 can (11 ounces) whole kernel corn, drained
- 1 can (10-3/4 ounces) condensed tomato soup, undiluted
- 1 can (10 ounces) diced tomatoes and green chilies

In a saucepan, combine all ingredients; heat through. **Yield:** 6 servings.

Stew Turned into Chili

A big pot of this versatile blend can be enjoyed two ways. As is, it's a satisfying stew brimming with tender chunks of beef, tomato and two kinds of beans. Or add picante sauce and chili powder to create a spicier chili.

Don Trumbly, Paola, Kansas

- 5 pounds beef stew meat, cut into 3/4-inch cubes
- 5 garlic cloves, minced
- 3 tablespoons vegetable oil
- 4 cans (14-1/2 ounces *each*) diced tomatoes with green pepper and onion, undrained
- 2 teaspoons salt
- 1 teaspoon pepper
- 2 cans (16 ounces *each*) kidney beans, rinsed and drained
- 2 cans (15-1/2 ounces *each*) great northern beans, rinsed and drained

ADDITIONAL INGREDIENTS (for each batch of chili):
- 1 jar (16 ounces) picante sauce
- 1 to 2 teaspoons chili powder

Sour cream and chopped green onions, optional

In a Dutch oven, brown beef and garlic in oil; drain. Add tomatoes, salt and pepper. Bring to a boil. Reduce heat; cover and simmer for 1-1/4 hours. Stir in the beans.

Cover and simmer 30-45 minutes longer or until meat is tender. Serve immediately, or cool slightly and freeze in 4-cup portions. May be frozen for up to 3 months. **Yield:** 4 batches of stew (16 cups total).

To prepare chili: Thaw one batch of stew in the refrigerator. Place in a saucepan; add picante sauce and chili powder. Cook over medium heat until hot and bubbly. Garnish servings with sour cream and green onions if desired. **Yield:** 4 servings per batch.

Cowpoke Chili
pictured below

Many friends and relatives have requested my chili recipe, which I've been using for over 25 years. It actually won first place in a local contest, chosen from among 10 other entries. It always comes out delicious. Try it and enjoy!

Ramona Nelson, Fairbanks, Alaska

- 1 pound ground beef
- 1 small onion, chopped
- 1 garlic clove, minced
- 1 can (10-1/2 ounces) condensed beef broth, undiluted
- 1 can (8 ounces) tomato sauce
- 1 can (6 ounces) tomato paste
- 1 can (15-1/2 ounces) hot chili beans
- 1 can (15 ounces) black beans, rinsed and drained

- 2 tablespoons sugar
- 1 tablespoon butter
- 1 teaspoon chili powder
- 1/4 teaspoon salt
- 1/4 teaspoon dried oregano
- 1/8 teaspoon ground cumin
- 1/8 teaspoon crushed red pepper flakes
- Dash cayenne pepper
- 2 cups frozen lima beans, thawed
- Cherry tomatoes, fresh oregano and small chili peppers, optional

In a large saucepan, cook beef, onion and garlic over medium heat until meat is no longer pink; drain. Stir in the broth, tomato sauce and paste until blended. Add the next 10 ingredients, Bring to a boil. Reduce heat; cover and simmer for 30 minutes.

Add lima beans; cook 5-10 minutes longer or until beans are tender. Garnish with cherry tomatoes, oregano and peppers if desired. **Yield:** 7 servings.

Sausage Onion Chili

Sausage and beef give this chili its flavor. The French onion soup makes it different, too!

Denise VonStein, Shiloh, Ohio

- 1 pound bulk pork sausage
- 1 pound ground beef
- 1 can (10-1/2 ounces) condensed French onion soup, undiluted
- 2 tablespoons chili powder
- 1 teaspoon ground cumin
- 1/2 teaspoon salt
- 1/2 teaspoon pepper
- 1 can (16 ounces) kidney beans, rinsed and drained
- 1 can (8 ounces) tomato sauce
- 1 can (6 ounces) tomato paste
- 1/2 cup water

In a large saucepan, cook sausage and beef over medium heat until no longer pink; drain. Add remaining ingredients and mix well; bring to a boil.

Reduce heat; cook and stir for 10-15 minutes or until thickened. **Yield:** 6 servings (about 1-1/2 quarts).

Walk-Along Chili

pictured above

Satisfying young ones' after-school appetites is a cinch with this recipe. Not only is it filling, serving it in a chip bag makes it fun. Plus, you can use the leftover chili for a meal later.

Joyce vonStempa, Jeffersontown, Kentucky

2 pounds ground beef
1 small onion, chopped
2 garlic cloves, minced
1 can (28 ounces) diced tomatoes, undrained
1 can (8 ounces) tomato sauce
1 can (6 ounces) tomato paste
2 to 3 tablespoons chili powder
1 tablespoon paprika
1 tablespoon dried oregano
1-1/2 teaspoons salt
1 teaspoon ground cumin
16 bags (1-1/4 ounces *each*) corn chips
Shredded cheddar cheese

In a large saucepan or Dutch oven over medium heat, cook meat until no longer pink; drain. Add onion and garlic; cook and stir for 5 minutes. Add the next eight ingredients and mix well; bring to a boil. Cover and simmer for 1 hour.

To serve, split open bags of chips at the back

seam or cut an X in the bag; add 1/2 cup of chili to each and top with cheese. **Yield:** 16 servings.

Editor's Note: For a faster snack, heat canned chili and spoon into bags of chips, omitting the first 11 ingredients.

Quick Chicken Chili

Loaded with hearty beans and chicken, this zippy chili really warms us up on chilly winter nights.

Lisa Goodman, Bloomington, Minnesota

4-1/2 cups chicken broth
    2 cans (15 ounces *each*) black beans, rinsed and drained
  1/2 cup *each* chopped green, yellow and sweet red pepper
  1/4 cup chopped onion
    1 tablespoon chili powder
1-1/2 teaspoons paprika
    1 to 1-1/2 teaspoons pepper
    1 to 1-1/2 teaspoons crushed red pepper flakes
    1 to 1-1/2 teaspoons ground cumin
  1/2 teaspoon salt
Dash cayenne pepper
    2 cups cubed cooked chicken
Shredded cheddar cheese, optional

In a 3-qt. saucepan, bring broth to a boil. Reduce heat; add beans, peppers, onion and seasonings. Cover and simmer 15 minutes. Add chicken; simmer for 30 minutes. Garnish with cheese if desired. **Yield:** 7 servings.

Sausage Corn Chili

Italian sausage and corn distinguish this thick chili from usual offerings. My daughter won a national contest with this zesty recipe.

Rhea Lease, Colman, South Dakota

    1 pound bulk Italian sausage
    1 tablespoon dried minced onion
    1 can (16 ounces) kidney beans, rinsed and drained
    1 can (15-1/4 ounces) whole kernel corn, drained

    1 can (15 ounces) tomato sauce
  2/3 cup picante sauce
  1/3 to 1/2 cup water
    1 teaspoon chili powder

In a large saucepan, cook sausage and onion over medium heat until meat is no longer pink; drain. Stir in the remaining ingredients. Simmer, uncovered, for 5-10 minutes or until heated through. **Yield:** 6 servings.

Baked Bean Chili
pictured below

Who says a good chili has to simmer all day? This chili—with a touch of sweetness from the baked beans—can be made on the spur of the moment. It's an excellent standby when unexpected guests drop in. Served with bread and a salad, it's a hearty dinner.

Nancy Wall, Bakersfield, California

    2 pounds ground beef
    3 cans (28 ounces *each*) baked beans
    1 can (46 ounces) tomato juice
    1 can (11-1/2 ounces) V8 juice
    1 envelope chili seasoning

In a Dutch oven, cook beef over medium heat until no longer pink; drain. Stir in remaining ingredients. Bring to a boil. Reduce heat; simmer, uncovered, for 10 minutes. **Yield:** 24 servings.

for 4-5 hours or until vegetables are tender. Serve desired amount. Cool the remaining chili; transfer to freezer bags or containers. Freeze for up to 3 months.

To use frozen chili: Thaw in the refrigerator; place in a saucepan and heat through. Add water if desired. **Yield:** 3 quarts (12 servings).

Corn and Bean Chili

My favorite things are added to this recipe to make it special. Corn gives it flavor and color.

Mary Pitts, Powder Springs, Georgia

> 2 pounds ground beef
> 1 small onion, finely chopped
> 1 envelope chili seasoning mix
> 3 cans (15-1/2 ounces *each*) chili beans, undrained
> 1 can (46 ounces) V8 juice
> 1/2 teaspoon salt
> 1 can (16 ounces) cream-style corn
> Shredded cheddar cheese

In a 5-qt. kettle or Dutch oven, brown beef and onion. Stir in seasoning mix, beans, V8 juice and salt. Simmer, uncovered, for 15 minutes. Stir in corn. Cook and stir over low heat for 15 minutes. Garnish with cheese. **Yield:** 14-16 servings (4 quarts).

Slow-Cooked Chunky Chili
pictured above

Pork sausage, ground beef and plenty of beans make this chili a hearty meal-starter. I keep the versatile mixture in serving-size containers in my freezer at all times. I can quickly warm up bowls of it on cold days—or use it to fix chili dogs, chili tacos and more.

Margie Shaw, Greenbrier, Arkansas

> 1 pound ground beef
> 1 pound bulk pork sausage
> 4 cans (16 ounces *each*) kidney beans, rinsed and drained
> 2 cans (14-1/2 ounces *each*) diced tomatoes, undrained
> 2 cans (10 ounces *each*) diced tomatoes and green chilies, undrained
> 1 large onion, chopped
> 1 medium green pepper, chopped
> 1 envelope taco seasoning
> 1/2 teaspoon salt
> 1/4 teaspoon pepper

In a skillet, cook beef and sausage over medium heat until meat is no longer pink; drain. Transfer to a 5-qt. slow cooker. Stir in the remaining ingredients. Cover and cook on high

Easy Chicken Chili

We have lots of visitors on our 10-acre farm, so I like to make down-home dishes. Whenever I serve this chili, I'm asked for the recipe, which I'm happy to share.

Nancy Maxey, Rogue River, Oregon

> 1/2 cup chopped onion
> 1 tablespoon vegetable oil
> 2 cans (14-1/2 ounces *each*) chicken broth
> 2 cans (15-1/2 ounces *each*) great northern beans, rinsed and drained

   1 can (4 ounces) chopped green chilies
   2 cups cubed cooked chicken
   2 garlic cloves, minced
   2 tablespoons minced fresh cilantro
   1 teaspoon salt
   1 teaspoon dried oregano
   1 teaspoon ground cumin
1/8 to 1/4 teaspoon cayenne pepper

In a 3-qt. saucepan over medium heat, saute onion in oil until tender. Add remaining ingredients; bring to a boil.

Reduce the heat; cover and simmer for 10-15 minutes or until heated through. **Yield:** 6-8 servings.

White Bean Turkey Chili
pictured at right

Looking for a satisfying but healthy chili for your crew? Well, look no further. This robust meal keeps them coming back for more. Chock-full of ground turkey, white kidney beans and diced tomatoes, it's so tasty, your family won't even miss the ground beef!

Dorothy Muenzer, Perry, New York

1-1/2 pounds ground turkey
   2 medium onions, chopped

1-1/2 teaspoons dried oregano
1-1/2 teaspoons ground cumin
   1 can (28 ounces) diced tomatoes, undrained
   3 cups beef broth
   1 can (8 ounces) tomato sauce
   1 tablespoon chili powder
   1 tablespoon baking cocoa
   2 bay leaves
   1 teaspoon salt
1/4 teaspoon ground cinnamon
   3 cans (15 ounces *each*) white kidney *or* cannellini beans, rinsed and drained

In a Dutch oven or kettle, cook the turkey and onions over medium heat until meat is no longer pink; drain. Add oregano and cumin; cook and stir 1 minute longer.

Stir in the tomatoes, broth, tomato sauce, chili powder, cocoa, bay leaves, salt and cinnamon. Bring to a boil.

Reduce heat; cover and simmer for 45 minutes. Add beans; heat through. Discard bay leaves before serving. **Yield:** 12 servings.

Quick Chili

pictured below

Using the microwave to cook the beef makes this a quick-to-fix meal.

Betty Ruenholl, Syracuse, Nebraska

1 pound ground beef
1 large onion, chopped
1 garlic clove, minced
2 cans (8 ounces *each*) tomato sauce
1 tablespoon chili powder
1 tablespoon red wine vinegar
2 teaspoons baking cocoa
1/4 teaspoon ground cinnamon
Dash ground allspice
1 can (16 ounces) kidney beans, rinsed and drained
Hot cooked macaroni, shredded cheddar cheese and sliced green onions, optional

In a microwave oven, cook beef, onion and garlic on high for 3 minutes in a covered 2-qt. microwave-safe dish; stir to crumble meat. Cover and cook for 3 minutes; drain.

Add the next six ingredients; cover and cook on high for 6 minutes. Stir in the beans. Cover and cook 4 minutes more.

210

Let stand 3-5 minutes. If desired, serve over macaroni and top with cheese and onions. **Yield:** 4 servings (about 1 quart).

Editor's Note: Recipe was tested using a 700-watt microwave.

Zippy Pork Chili
pictured at right

In addition to eating this chili the traditional way (with a spoon!), my family likes to scoop bites onto tortilla chips. The leftovers are great rolled in tortillas and reheated, too.

Michelle Beran, Claflin, Kansas

   1 **boneless pork roast (3 to 4 pounds), cut into 1-inch cubes**
   1 **medium onion, chopped**
   1 **garlic clove, minced**
   2 **tablespoons vegetable oil**
   2 **cans (15-1/2 ounces *each*) chili beans**
   2 **cans (10 ounces *each*) diced tomatoes and green chilies, undrained**
   1 **can (14-1/2 ounces) diced tomatoes, undrained**
   1 **cup water**
   1 **teaspoon beef bouillon granules**
Chili powder, pepper and cayenne pepper to taste
Sour cream, tortilla chips and shredded cheddar cheese, optional

In a Dutch oven, cook pork, onion and garlic in oil over medium heat until meat is browned. Add the beans, tomatoes, water, bouillon and seasonings. Bring to a boil.

Reduce heat; cover and simmer for 2 hours or until meat is tender. If desired, serve with sour cream, tortilla chips and cheese. **Yield:** 10 servings.

Vegetable Beef Chili

Folks who like their chili hot really get a kick out of this zippy recipe. I serve steaming bowls of it with oven-fresh corn bread. It's so chock-full of garden goodness—with two kinds of squash, tomatoes, green chilies, black beans, etc.—that you can leave out the meat altogether and not miss it a bit.

Amy Baxter, Bishop, California

   1 **pound ground beef**
   1 **large onion, chopped**
   1 **medium zucchini, diced**
   1 **medium yellow summer squash, diced**
   1 **medium sweet red pepper, chopped**
   1 **can (15-1/2 ounces) hominy, drained**
   1 **can (15 ounces) black beans, rinsed and drained**
   1 **can (14-1/2 ounces) diced tomatoes with green peppers and onions, undrained**
   1 **cup beer *or* beef broth**
   1 **can (4 ounces) chopped green chilies**
   1 **tablespoon minced fresh parsley**
   2 **garlic cloves, minced**
   2 **teaspoons ground cumin**
   2 **teaspoons dried coriander**
   1 **teaspoon minced fresh cilantro**
   1 **teaspoon chili powder**
1/4 teaspoon cayenne pepper

In a large saucepan, cook beef and onion over medium heat until meat is no longer pink; drain. Add the zucchini, yellow squash and red pepper; cook and stir until crisp-tender. Stir in the remaining ingredients. Bring to a boil.

Reduce heat; cover and simmer for 20 minutes or until the vegetables are tender. **Yield:** 8 servings (2 quarts).

Spicy Turkey Chili

pictured above

This peppery chili is not for the faint of stomach. It's saucy and satisfying—according to my daughter, it's the one thing she can taste when she has a cold. It also freezes very well.

Margaret Shauers, Great Bend, Kansas

2 pounds ground turkey *or* turkey sausage
1 large onion, chopped
4 garlic cloves, minced
2 cans (15-1/2 ounces *each*) chili beans, undrained
2 cans (15 ounces *each*) tomato sauce
1 can (28 ounces) crushed tomatoes
1-1/2 cups beef broth *or* beer
2 to 3 tablespoons chili powder
2 teaspoons Italian seasoning
1/4 to 1/2 teaspoon ground cinnamon
1 jalapeno pepper, finely chopped
Dash cayenne pepper

In a large kettle, cook turkey, onion and garlic over medium heat until meat is no longer pink; drain. Add remaining ingredients.

Bring to a boil; reduce heat. Simmer, uncovered, for 45 minutes, stirring occasionally. **Yield:** 12-14 servings (3-1/2 quarts).

Editor's Note: When cutting or seeding hot peppers, use rubber or plastic gloves to protect your hands. Avoid touching your face.

Vegetarian Chili

With the abundance of beans, vegetables and flavor in this spicy chili, you'll never miss the meat! My family has been enjoying this meal for many years.

Polly Habel, Monson, Massachusetts

1/2 cup chopped onion
1 garlic clove, minced
1 tablespoon vegetable oil
1 cup chopped carrot
1 cup chopped celery
3/4 cup chopped green pepper
1/4 cup chopped green onions
1 cup chopped fresh mushrooms
1 can (6 ounces) pitted ripe olives, drained and chopped
1 can (6 ounces) tomato paste
4-1/2 cups water
1 can (16 ounces) kidney beans, rinsed and drained
1 can (15 ounces) tomato sauce
1 medium tomato, chopped
1 can (4 ounces) chopped green chilies
3 tablespoons chili powder
1 teaspoon ground cumin
1 teaspoon salt
1/2 teaspoon crushed red pepper flakes, optional
1/4 teaspoon cayenne pepper, optional

In a Dutch oven or soup kettle, saute onion and garlic in oil for 5 minutes. Add carrot, celery, green pepper and green onions; cook for 7 minutes or until crisp-tender.

Add mushrooms, olives and tomato paste; blend well. Add all of the remaining ingredients; bring to a boil. Reduce heat; cover and simmer for at least 3 hours. **Yield:** 8-10 servings (2-1/2 quarts).

Red, White and Blue Chili

pictured below

Instead of the usual picnic fare, I surprised family and guests with this mild-flavored dish one Independence Day. They were delighted!

Dotty Parker, Christmas Valley, Oregon

    1 medium green pepper, diced
 1/4 cup diced onion
    2 garlic cloves, minced
    1 tablespoon vegetable oil
    2 cans (14-1/2 ounces *each*) Mexican
       diced tomatoes, undrained
    2 cans (14-1/2 ounces *each*) chicken
       broth
    2 cups shredded cooked chicken
    2 cans (15-1/2 ounces *each*) great
       northern beans, rinsed and drained
    1 can (16 ounces) kidney beans, rinsed
       and drained
    1 envelope chili seasoning
    1 tablespoon brown sugar
    1 teaspoon salt
 1/4 teaspoon pepper
Blue tortilla chips

In a Dutch oven or soup kettle, saute the green pepper, onion and garlic in oil until tender. Stir

in the tomatoes, broth, chicken, beans, chili seasoning, brown sugar, salt and pepper.

Bring to a boil. Reduce heat; cover and simmer for 45 minutes. Serve with tortilla chips. **Yield:** 8 servings (about 2 quarts).

Zippy Vegetable Chili

Pinto beans lend protein while vegetables provide homegrown goodness and pretty color to this chunky chili recipe. Green chilies and salsa add a spicy kick to the broth.

Patricia Gibson, Ferguson, North Carolina

 1-1/2 cups chopped onions
   3/4 cup chopped sweet red pepper
   3/4 cup chopped green pepper
     1 can (14-1/2 ounces) vegetable
        broth
     2 cans (10 ounces *each*) diced
        tomatoes and green chilies
   1/2 cup salsa
     1 tablespoon chili powder
     1 teaspoon ground cumin
   3/4 teaspoon garlic powder
     1 can (15 ounces) pinto beans, rinsed
        and drained
     1 cup fresh *or* frozen corn
     1 cup (4 ounces) shredded cheddar
        cheese

In a large saucepan, bring the onions, peppers and broth to a boil. Reduce heat; cover and simmer for 5 minutes.

Add the tomatoes, salsa and seasonings; return to a boil. Reduce heat; simmer, uncovered, for 12-15 minutes.

Add beans and corn; simmer 5 minutes longer or until heated through, stirring occasionally. Garnish each serving with cheese. **Yield:** 7 servings.

Salsa Chili

pictured above

You'll need just five ingredients to stir up this quick-and-easy chili. We like to use medium salsa for more flavor, but sometimes I use half mild and half medium. Sprinkle hearty servings with shredded cheddar cheese and other tasty toppings.

Jane Bone, Cape Coral, Florida

> 1 pound ground beef
> 1 medium onion, chopped
> 1 jar (16 ounces) salsa
> 1 can (15 ounces) pinto beans, rinsed and drained
> 1 can (5-1/2 ounces) tomato juice
> Shredded cheddar cheese, diced peppers, sour cream and sliced green onions, optional

In a saucepan, cook beef and onion over medium heat until meat is no longer pink; drain. Stir in the salsa, beans and tomato juice; heat through.

If desired, garnish with cheese and peppers and serve with sour cream and onions. **Yield:** 5 servings.

White Chili
With Chicken
pictured at left

Folks who enjoy a change from traditional tomato-based chilies will enjoy this version. The flavorful blend has tender chunks of chicken, white beans and just enough zip.

Christy Campos, Richmond, Virginia

- 1 medium onion, chopped
- 1 jalapeno pepper, seeded and chopped, optional
- 2 garlic cloves, minced
- 1 tablespoon vegetable oil
- 4 cups chicken broth
- 2 cans (15-1/2 ounces *each*) great northern beans, rinsed and drained
- 2 tablespoons minced fresh parsley
- 1 tablespoon lime juice
- 1 to 1-1/4 teaspoons ground cumin
- 2 tablespoons cornstarch
- 1/4 cup cold water
- 2 cups cubed cooked chicken

In a large saucepan, cook onion, jalapeno if desired and garlic in oil until tender. Stir in broth, beans, parsley, lime juice and cumin; bring to a boil. Reduce heat; cover and simmer for 10 minutes, stirring occasionally.

Combine cornstarch and water until smooth; stir into chili. Add chicken. Bring to a boil; cook and stir for 2 minutes or until thickened. **Yield:** 6 servings.

Editor's Note: When cutting and seeding hot peppers, use rubber or plastic gloves to protect your hands. Avoid touching your face.

Hearty Black Bean Chili

Featuring beans, ground beef and chicken, this chili is perfect for those with big appetites.

Colleen Hilliker, Stevens Point, Wisconsin

- 1 pound dried black beans
- 1 pound ground beef
- 2 boneless skinless chicken breast halves, cubed
- 3/4 cup chopped onion
- 3 cups water
- 1 can (15 ounces) tomato sauce
- 1 can (14-1/2 ounces) diced tomatoes, undrained
- 1 tablespoon chili powder
- 2-1/4 teaspoons salt
- 1-1/2 teaspoons ground cumin
- 1/4 teaspoon garlic powder
- 1/4 teaspoon pepper
- Shredded cheddar cheese and thinly sliced green onions, optional

Place beans in a saucepan and cover with water; bring to a boil and boil for 2 minutes. Remove from the heat; soak for 1 hour. Drain and rinse beans.

Meanwhile, in a Dutch oven or soup kettle over medium heat, cook beef, chicken and onion until meats are no longer pink and onion is tender; drain. Add water, tomato sauce, tomatoes and seasonings; mix well. Add beans; bring to a boil.

Reduce heat; cover and simmer for 3-1/2 to 4 hours or until beans are tender. Garnish with cheese and green onions if desired. **Yield:** 6-8 servings (2-1/2 quarts).

Margie's Chili

I came up with this recipe to give my chili a little more heat. You can adjust the chili sauce and chili powder based on your own taste.

Margaret Ganzel, Mankato, Minnesota

- 1 pound ground beef
- 2 small onions, chopped
- 1 can (10-3/4 ounces) condensed tomato soup, undiluted
- 1 can (16 ounces) kidney beans, rinsed and drained
- 3/4 cup chili sauce
- 2 teaspoons chili powder
- 1/4 teaspoon salt
- 1/4 teaspoon pepper

In a medium saucepan, cook beef and onions over medium heat until meat is no longer pink; drain. Add all of the remaining ingredients; bring to a boil.

Reduce the heat; simmer, uncovered, for 5-10 minutes or until thickened. **Yield:** 4 servings (about 1 quart).

Heartwarming Chili

pictured below

This meaty meal-in-one is very versatile. Sometimes I make it without beans and serve it on hot dogs or over rice as a main dish.

Christine Panzarella, Buena Park, California

>   1 pound ground beef
>   1 pound ground pork
>   1 medium onion, chopped
> 1/2 cup chopped green pepper
> 1-1/2 to 2 cups water
>   1 can (15 ounces) tomato sauce
>   1 can (15 ounces) pinto beans, rinsed
>   and drained
>   1 can (14-1/2 ounces) diced tomatoes,
>   undrained
>   1 envelope chili seasoning mix
> 1/4 teaspoon garlic salt
> Shredded cheddar cheese, sour cream,
>   chopped green onions *and/or* hot
>   pepper slices, optional

In a large saucepan or Dutch oven, cook beef, pork, onion and green pepper over medium heat until meat is no longer pink and vegetables are tender; drain.

Add the water, tomato sauce, beans, tomatoes, chili seasoning and garlic salt. Bring to a boil. Reduce heat; simmer, uncovered, until heated through. Garnish with cheese, sour cream, green onions and/or hot peppers if desired. **Yield:** 8-10 servings.

Cincinnati Chili

pictured at right

Cinnamon and cocoa give a rich brown color to this hearty chili. This dish will warm you up on a cold day.

Edith Joyce, Parkman, Ohio

>   1 pound ground beef
>   1 pound ground pork
>   4 medium onions, chopped
>   6 garlic cloves, minced
>   2 cans (16 ounces *each*) kidney beans,
>   rinsed and drained
>   1 can (28 ounces) crushed tomatoes
> 1/4 cup vinegar
> 1/4 cup baking cocoa
>   2 tablespoons chili powder
>   2 tablespoons Worcestershire sauce
>   4 teaspoons ground cinnamon
>   3 teaspoons dried oregano
>   2 teaspoons ground cumin
>   2 teaspoons ground allspice
>   2 teaspoons hot pepper sauce
>   3 bay leaves
>   1 teaspoon sugar
> Salt and pepper to taste
> Hot cooked spaghetti
> Shredded cheddar cheese, sour cream,
>   chopped tomatoes and green onions

In a Dutch oven or soup kettle, cook beef, pork, onions and garlic over medium heat until meat is no longer pink; drain. Add the beans, tomatoes, vinegar, cocoa and seasonings; bring to a boil. Reduce heat; cover and simmer for 1-1/2 hours or until heated through.

Discard bay leaves. Serve over spaghetti. Garnish with cheese, sour cream, tomatoes and onions. **Yield:** 6-8 servings.

Sweet 'n' Snappy Chili

I created this dish by combining two different recipes and some of my own ideas. Folks are pleasantly surprised to see this chili brimming with ground pork instead of beef.

Joanne Withers, Osakis, Minnesota

- 2 pounds ground pork
- 2 celery ribs, diced
- 1 medium onion, chopped
- 1 small green pepper, chopped
- 2 garlic cloves, minced
- 2 cans (15-1/2 ounces *each*) chili beans, undrained
- 1 can (28 ounces) diced tomatoes, undrained
- 1 can (4 ounces) chopped green chilies
- 3 cups water
- 1/4 cup packed brown sugar
- 3 tablespoons chili powder
- 2 teaspoons ground cumin
- 3/4 teaspoon ground ginger

In a Dutch oven or soup kettle, cook pork until no longer pink; drain. Remove and set aside. In the same kettle, saute the celery, onion, green pepper and garlic until vegetables are tender; drain.

Add pork and remaining ingredients; bring to a boil. Reduce heat; cover and simmer for 45 minutes. **Yield:** 6-8 servings (2-1/4 quarts).

Easy Low-Fat Chili

This zesty chili really hits the spot on cool fall days. It is nourishing and satisfying, and it fills you right up.

Janet Moore, Ogdensburg, New York

- 1 medium onion, chopped
- 1/4 cup chopped green pepper
- 2 cups water, *divided*
- 1 can (15-1/2 ounces) great northern beans, rinsed and drained
- 1 can (15 ounces) navy beans, rinsed and drained
- 1 can (6 ounces) tomato paste
- 1 can (14-1/2 ounces) diced tomatoes, undrained
- 2 to 4 teaspoons chili powder
- 1 teaspoon salt
- 1/2 teaspoon pepper

In a large saucepan, cook the onion and green pepper in 1/2 cup water until tender. Add beans, tomato paste and tomatoes. Stir in chili powder, salt, pepper and remaining water; bring to a boil. Reduce the heat; cover and simmer for 20 minutes. **Yield:** 7 servings.

> 66 Be creative with roast beef! Cube any that's left over and add all your favorite chili ingredients. To turn it into my version of Cincinnati Chili, top with cooked spaghetti, shredded cheese and lettuce, chopped red onion and tomato. 99
>
> —*Marie Hollada*
> *Danville, Indiana*

Green Chili

We like this as a meal in itself but also use it to top our favorite Mexican foods like burritos.

Sharon Malleis, Parker, Colorado

    1 pork shoulder roast (3-1/2 to 4 pounds)
  1/2 cup all-purpose flour
  1/2 teaspoon salt
  1/4 teaspoon pepper
    1 tablespoon vegetable oil
    4 cans (4 ounces *each*) chopped green chilies
    2 cans (28 ounces *each*) stewed tomatoes
    2 garlic cloves, minced
    1 medium onion, chopped
    1 jalapeno pepper, seeded and chopped
    1 to 2 teaspoons minced fresh cilantro
  1/2 teaspoon ground cumin
Warm flour tortillas, optional

Trim pork and cut into 1/2-in. cubes. In a large bowl or resealable plastic bag, combine flour, salt and pepper. Add pork and toss to coat.

In a Dutch oven or soup kettle over medium heat, brown pork in oil; drain. Add the chilies, tomatoes, garlic, onion, jalapeno, cilantro and cumin; bring to a boil.

Reduce heat; cover and simmer for 1-1/2 to 2 hours or until pork is tender. Serve with tortillas if desired. **Yield:** 10-12 servings (3 quarts).

Editor's Note: When cutting and seeding hot peppers, use rubber or plastic gloves to protect your hands. Avoid touching your face.

Barley Chicken Chili

pictured above

I was looking for a new recipe for chicken when I discovered a dish I thought my husband might like. After making a few changes and additions to fit our preferences, I had this zesty chili simmering on the stovetop. It was great! Leftovers store well in the freezer.

Kayleen Grew, Essexville, Michigan

    1 cup chopped onion
  1/2 cup chopped green pepper
    1 teaspoon olive oil
2-1/4 cups water
    1 can (15 ounces) tomato sauce
    1 can (14-1/2 ounces) chicken broth
    1 can (10 ounces) diced tomatoes and green chilies, undrained
    1 cup quick-cooking barley
    1 tablespoon chili powder
  1/2 teaspoon ground cumin
  1/4 teaspoon garlic powder
    3 cups cubed cooked chicken

In a large saucepan, saute onion and green pepper in oil until tender. Add the water, tomato sauce, broth, tomatoes, barley, chili powder, cumin and garlic powder; bring to a boil.

Reduce heat; cover and simmer for 10 minutes. Add chicken. Cover and simmer 5 minutes longer or until barley is tender. **Yield:** 9 servings (about 2 quarts).

> " For convenience, I simmer my chili con carne on low all day in my slow cooker after first browning the hamburger. I like to add a cup of shredded zucchini to my chili for additional bulk, nutrition and flavor. "
>
> —*Linda Sinclair Congress, Saskatchewan*

Spiced Chili in Bread Bowls

pictured below

My father was a cook in the Army and taught me the basics in the kitchen. My childhood baby-sitter inspired my love of cooking and gave me this recipe. I like to serve it in bread bowls.

Julie Brendt, Antelope, California

1-1/2 pounds ground beef
  1/2 cup chopped onion
    4 garlic cloves, minced
    2 cans (16 ounces *each*) kidney beans, rinsed and drained
    2 cans (15 ounces *each*) tomato sauce
    2 cans (14-1/2 ounces *each*) stewed tomatoes, cut up
    1 cup water
    2 bay leaves
  1/4 cup chili powder
    1 tablespoon salt
    1 tablespoon brown sugar
    1 tablespoon dried basil
    1 tablespoon Italian seasoning
    1 tablespoon dried thyme
    1 tablespoon pepper
    1 teaspoon dried oregano
    1 teaspoon dried marjoram
Shredded cheddar cheese and additional chopped onions, optional

In a large skillet, cook beef, onion and garlic over medium heat until meat is no longer pink; drain. Transfer to a 5-qt. slow cooker. Stir in the beans, tomato sauce, tomatoes, water and seasonings.

Cover and cook on low for 4-5 hours. Discard bay leaves. If desired, serve in bread bowls and garnish with cheese and onions. **Yield:** 12 servings (about 3 quarts).

White Chili

I enjoy experimenting with new recipes, like this change-of-pace chili.

Kaye Whiteman, Charleston, West Virginia

  1/2 cup chopped onion
    3 garlic cloves, minced
    2 tablespoons vegetable oil
2-1/2 teaspoons ground cumin
  1/2 pound ground turkey
    1 pound uncooked boneless skinless turkey breast, cubed
    3 cups chicken broth
    1 can (15 ounces) garbanzo beans, rinsed and drained
    1 tablespoon minced jalapeno pepper
  1/2 teaspoon dried marjoram
  1/4 teaspoon dried savory
    2 teaspoons cornstarch
    1 tablespoon water
Shredded Monterey Jack cheese, optional

In a 2-qt. saucepan, saute onion and garlic in oil for 5 minutes or until tender. Stir in cumin; cook for 5 minutes.

Add turkey; cook over medium heat until no longer pink. Add broth, beans, jalapeno, marjoram and savory; bring to a boil. Reduce heat; cover and simmer for 45 minutes, stirring occasionally. Uncover; cook 15 minutes more.

Dissolve cornstarch in water; stir into chili. Bring to a boil; cook and stir for 2 minutes. Serve topped with cheese if desired. **Yield:** 6 servings.

Editor's Note: When cutting and seeding hot peppers, use rubber or plastic gloves to protect your hands. Avoid touching your face.

Tangy Oven Chili

pictured below

Frankly, I never cared for chili. But my husband does, so I came up with this recipe for us both to enjoy.

Sue O'Connor, Lucan, Ontario

      1 pound dried red kidney beans
      2 pounds ground beef
      2 medium onions, chopped
      1 medium green pepper, chopped
      2 envelopes chili seasoning mix
1-1/2 teaspoons salt
1-1/2 teaspoons pepper
      1 teaspoon sugar
      2 cans (28 ounces *each*) diced tomatoes, undrained
      1 can (12 ounces) tomato paste
      2 cans (8 ounces *each*) crushed pineapple, undrained
      2 jars (4-1/2 ounces *each*) sliced mushrooms, drained
      3 to 5 fresh jalapeno peppers, seeded and minced
      3 cans (11-1/2 ounces *each*) V8 juice

Rinse beans and place in a large kettle or Dutch oven; cover with water. Bring to a boil; boil for 2 minutes. Remove from heat; let stand for 1 hour. Drain, discarding liquid; set beans aside.

In a skillet, cook beef, onions and green pepper over medium heat until meat is no longer pink; drain. Stir in seasoning mixes, salt and pepper. Pour into an ovenproof 8-qt. Dutch oven. Add beans and remaining ingredients; mix well.

Cover and bake at 350° for 1 hour. Reduce heat to 250°; bake for 5 hours or until beans are tender, stirring every 30 minutes. **Yield:** 18-20 servings (5 quarts).

Editor's Note: When cutting and seeding hot peppers, use rubber or plastic gloves to protect your hands. Avoid touching your face.

Thick Turkey Bean Chili

When our daughters wouldn't eat the spicy chili beans I prepared, I came up with this milder, slightly sweet version. They love eating the hearty chili as a dip with tortilla chips. I never have leftovers.

Keri Scofield Lawson, Fullerton, California

> 1 pound ground turkey
> 2 cans (16 ounces *each*) baked beans, undrained
> 1 can (16 ounces) kidney beans, rinsed and drained
> 1 can (15-1/2 ounces) sloppy joe sauce
> 1 can (14-1/2 ounces) diced tomatoes, undrained
> 1 tablespoon brown sugar
> 1/4 teaspoon *each* garlic powder, salt and pepper

Shredded cheddar cheese, sour cream and tortilla chips, optional

In a large saucepan, cook turkey over medium heat until no longer pink; drain. Stir in beans, sloppy joe sauce, tomatoes, brown sugar and seasonings.

Simmer, uncovered, for 30 minutes or until heated through. Serve with shredded cheddar cheese, sour cream and tortilla chips if desired. **Yield:** 8-10 servings.

Slow-Cooked Chili
pictured above

This heart-warming chili can cook for up to 10 hours on low. It's so good to come home to after a long day away.

Sue Call, Beech Grove, Indiana

> 2 pounds ground beef
> 2 cans (16 ounces *each*) kidney beans, rinsed and drained
> 2 cans (14-1/2 ounces *each*) diced tomatoes, undrained
> 1 can (8 ounces) tomato sauce
> 2 medium onions, chopped
> 1 green pepper, chopped
> 2 garlic cloves, minced
> 2 tablespoons chili powder
> 2 teaspoons salt, optional
> 1 teaspoon pepper

Shredded cheddar cheese, optional

In a skillet, cook beef over medium heat until no longer pink; drain. Transfer to a slow cooker. Add the next nine ingredients.

Cover and cook on low for 8-10 hours or on high for 4 hours. Garnish individual servings with shredded cheddar cheese if desired. **Yield:** 10 servings.

Stir in tomatoes, picante sauce, bouillon and cumin; bring to a boil. Reduce heat; simmer, uncovered, for 30 minutes, stirring occasionally.

Add beans and olives; heat through. Garnish with cheese if desired. **Yield:** 9 servings (2-1/4 quarts).

Quick Zesty Chili

This chili always has everyone coming back for seconds—that's because I use fresh tomatoes in the recipe.

Laura Whitcomb, Wauseon, Ohio

- 1 pound ground beef
- 2 cans (16 ounces *each*) kidney beans, rinsed and drained
- 1 can (8 ounces) tomato sauce
- 2 cups chopped fresh tomatoes
- 1 cup water
- 2 tablespoons chili powder
- 1 tablespoon dried minced onion
- 1 to 2 teaspoons hot pepper sauce
- 1 teaspoon ground cumin
- 1/4 teaspoon ground cinnamon

In a large saucepan, cook beef over medium heat until no longer pink; drain. Add remaining ingredients. Bring to a boil; reduce heat and simmer for 15 minutes. **Yield:** 8 servings (2 quarts).

Vegetable Bean Chili

pictured above

Because it's so hearty, no one ever seems to miss the meat in this chili recipe. It's a favorite in my kitchen.

Rene Fry, Hampstead, Maryland

- 1 medium zucchini, sliced 1/4 inch thick
- 1 medium green pepper, chopped
- 1 cup chopped onion
- 1 cup shredded carrots
- 1/2 cup finely chopped celery
- 2 garlic cloves, minced
- 1/4 cup olive oil
- 1 can (28 ounces) diced tomatoes, undrained
- 1 jar (8 ounces) picante sauce
- 1 teaspoon beef bouillon granules
- 1-1/2 teaspoons ground cumin
- 1 can (15 ounces) garbanzo beans, rinsed and drained
- 1 can (15-1/2 ounces) chili beans, undrained
- 1 can (2-1/4 ounces) sliced ripe olives, drained
- 1 cup (4 ounces) shredded cheddar cheese

In a 4-qt. kettle or Dutch oven, saute zucchini, green pepper, onion, carrots, celery and garlic in oil until tender.

All-American Chili

Canned items make this traditional recipe more convenient. It cooks together in minutes!

Cheryl Groenenboom, Rose Hill, Iowa

- 1 pound ground beef
- 1 medium onion, chopped
- 1/4 teaspoon pepper
- 1 can (16 ounces) pork and beans, undrained
- 1 can (10-3/4 ounces) condensed tomato soup, undiluted
- 1 can (10-1/2 ounces) condensed vegetable beef soup, undiluted

Shredded mozzarella cheese

In a large saucepan, cook the beef, onion and pepper over medium heat until meat is no longer pink; drain. Stir in the beans and soups.

Simmer, uncovered, for 15 minutes. Garnish with cheese. **Yield:** 4-6 servings (1-1/2 quarts).

Super-Duper Chili

No one ever guesses the secret ingredient in this recipe that I created. A can of mushroom soup is what makes the chili so thick and creamy.

Elizabeth Mays, Nunnelly, Tennessee

  1 pound bulk pork sausage
  1 pound ground beef
  2 cans (15-1/2 ounces *each*) hot chili beans
  1 jar (16 ounces) salsa
  1 can (16 ounces) kidney beans, rinsed and drained
  1 can (15 ounces) pinto beans, rinsed and drained
  1 can (14-1/2 ounces) diced tomatoes, undrained
  1 can (10-3/4 ounces) condensed cream of mushroom soup, undiluted
  1 can (8 ounces) tomato sauce
  8 ounces process cheese (Velveeta), cubed
1-1/2 teaspoons chili powder
  1/2 teaspoon cayenne pepper

In a soup kettle or Dutch oven, cook the sausage and beef over medium heat until no longer pink; drain. Stir in the remaining ingredients. Bring to a boil. Reduce heat; cover and simmer for 30 minutes or until heated through. **Yield:** 14 servings (3-1/2 quarts).

Chicken Chili
pictured at right

This unique and delicious chicken chili is a much-requested meal around our house. I think you'll find it's a nice change of pace from the typical beef version.

Janne Rowe, Wichita, Kansas

  3 cups chopped onion
1-1/2 cups chopped green pepper

  4 garlic cloves, minced
  2 tablespoons vegetable oil
1-1/2 pounds boneless skinless chicken breasts, cut into 1/2-inch cubes
  2 to 4 tablespoons chili powder
  1 tablespoon ground cumin
  2 teaspoons ground coriander
  1/2 teaspoon cayenne pepper
  1/2 teaspoon salt
  2 cans (14-1/2 ounces *each*) diced tomatoes, undrained
  2 cans (10-1/2 ounces *each*) condensed chicken broth
  2 cups water
  1 can (6 ounces) tomato paste
  1 bay leaf
  2 cans (15 ounces *each*) garbanzo beans, rinsed and drained

In a 5-qt. Dutch oven, cook onion, green pepper and garlic in oil over medium-high heat for 10 minutes or until onion is tender.

Add chicken; cook and stir constantly for 4 minutes or until browned. Add the next 10 ingredients; bring to a boil.

Reduce heat; cover and simmer, stirring occasionally, for 40 minutes. Add beans; cook, uncovered, for 20 minutes, stirring occasionally. Remove bay leaf. **Yield:** 14 servings (3-1/2 quarts).

Chicken Chili with Black Beans

pictured below

My family was a little hesitant to try this dish at first. But thanks to full, hearty flavor, it's become a real favorite around our house.

Jeanette Urbom, Overland Park, Kansas

  3 whole skinless boneless chicken breasts (about 1-3/4 pounds), cubed
  2 medium sweet red peppers, chopped
  1 large onion, chopped
  4 garlic cloves, minced
  3 tablespoons olive oil
  1 can (4 ounces) chopped green chilies
  2 tablespoons chili powder
  2 teaspoons ground cumin
  1 teaspoon ground coriander
  2 cans (15 ounces *each*) black beans, rinsed and drained
  1 can (28 ounces) diced Italian plum tomatoes, undrained
  1 cup chicken broth *or* beer

In a Dutch oven, saute chicken, red peppers, onion and garlic in oil for 5 minutes or until chicken is no longer pink. Add green chilies, chili powder, cumin and coriander; cook for 3 minutes.

Stir in beans, tomatoes and broth or beer; bring to a boil. Reduce heat and simmer, uncovered, for 15 minutes, stirring often. **Yield:** 10 servings (3 quarts).

No-Fuss Vegetarian Chili

Hominy and garbanzo beans are interesting additions to this zippy chili. Serve it with corn bread or flour tortillas for a speedy meal.

Karen Hunt, Bellvue, Colorado

      2 cans (15 ounces *each*) pinto beans, rinsed and drained
      1 can (28 ounces) crushed tomatoes
      1 can (16 ounces) kidney beans, rinsed and drained
      1 can (15-1/2 ounces) hominy, rinsed and drained
      1 can (15 ounces) garbanzo beans, rinsed and drained
      1 can (6 ounces) tomato paste
      1 can (4 ounces) chopped green chilies
      2 small zucchini, halved and thinly sliced
      1 medium onion, chopped
  1-1/2 to 2 cups water
      1 to 2 tablespoons chili powder
      1 teaspoon ground cumin
      1 teaspoon salt
    1/2 teaspoon garlic powder
    1/2 teaspoon sugar
    1/2 cup shredded Monterey Jack cheese

In a large kettle or Dutch oven, combine the first 15 ingredients; mix well. Bring to a boil. Reduce heat; cover and simmer for 30-35 minutes. Sprinkle with cheese. **Yield:** 12 servings (about 3 quarts).

Chili with Potato Dumplings

pictured at right

Now that my husband has retired—we have two grown sons—we eat out a lot. If we stay home, though, he asks if we are going to have this chili!

Shirley Marshall, Michigantown, Indiana

      1 pound ground beef
      1 pound ground turkey
    1/2 cup chopped onion
      1 can (16 ounces) kidney beans, rinsed and drained
      1 can (15-1/2 ounces) mild chili beans, undrained
    1/2 cup chopped green pepper
      4 teaspoons chili powder
      1 teaspoon salt

1 teaspoon paprika
1 teaspoon cumin seed
1/2 teaspoon garlic salt
1/2 teaspoon dried oregano
1/4 teaspoon crushed red pepper flakes
3 cups V8 juice

DUMPLINGS:
1 cup mashed potato flakes
1 cup all-purpose flour
1 tablespoon minced fresh parsley
2 teaspoons baking powder
1/2 teaspoon salt
1 cup milk
1 egg, beaten

In a 5-qt. Dutch oven, cook beef, turkey and onion until meat is no longer pink; drain. Add the next 11 ingredients; bring to a boil. Reduce heat; cover and simmer for 30 minutes, stirring occasionally.

In a medium bowl, combine the first five dumpling ingredients. Add milk and egg; stir just until moistened. Let rest for 3 minutes.

Drop by tablespoonfuls into simmering chili. Cover and cook for 15 minutes. **Yield:** 8 servings (2 quarts).

" Simmering stew **warms** the heart
with savory **goodness**. "

savory
STEWS

to stew. Add parsley. Bring to a boil; cook and stir for 2 minutes or until thickened. **Yield:** 6 servings.

Sweet Potato Lentil Stew

Years ago, I fell in love with the spicy flavor and wonderful aroma of this slow-cooker recipe. You can serve the stew alone or as a topper for meat and poultry. It's great either way!

Heather Gray, Little Rock, Arkansas

     4 cups vegetable broth
     3 cups sweet potatoes, peeled and
       cubed (about 1-1/4 pounds)
 1-1/2 cups dried lentils, rinsed
     3 medium carrots, cut into 1-inch
       pieces
     1 medium onion, chopped
     4 garlic cloves, minced
   1/2 teaspoon ground cumin
   1/4 teaspoon ground ginger
   1/4 teaspoon cayenne pepper
   1/4 cup minced fresh cilantro
   1/4 teaspoon salt

In a slow cooker, combine the first nine ingredients. Cover and cook on low for 5-6 hours or until vegetables are tender. Stir in the cilantro and salt. **Yield:** 6 servings.

Irish Stew
pictured above

This satisfying stew is chock-full of potatoes, turnips, carrots and lamb. Served with Irish soda bread, it makes a hearty St. Patrick's Day meal.

Lois Gelzer, Cape Elizabeth, Maine

 1-1/2 pounds lamb stew meat
     2 teaspoons olive oil
     4 cups water
     2 cups sliced peeled potatoes
     1 medium onion, sliced
   1/2 cup sliced carrot
   1/2 cup cubed turnip
     1 teaspoon salt
   1/2 teaspoon *each* dried marjoram,
       thyme and rosemary, crushed
   1/8 teaspoon pepper
     2 tablespoons all-purpose flour
     2 tablespoons milk
   1/2 teaspoon browning sauce, optional
     3 tablespoons minced fresh parsley

In a Dutch oven, brown lamb in oil over medium-high heat. Add water; bring to a boil. Reduce heat; cover and simmer for 1 hour.

Add the potatoes, onion, carrot, turnip and seasonings. Bring to a boil. Reduce heat; cover and simmer for 30 minutes or until the vegetables are tender.

In a small bowl, combine the flour, milk and browning sauce if desired until smooth; stir in-

Stew-pendous Side Dishes...

Stews are a satisfying meal-in-one dish. However, when you'd like to serve something on the side, consider an add-on. Pick up a loaf of bread from your grocer's bakery. Or, if your stew has south-of-the-border appeal, consider serving corn bread or tortillas with it.

Salads are a natural with steaming bowls of stew. Throw together a simple salad with your favorite dressing, or serve a spinach salad with berry vinaigrette.

Shredded cheese, chives, chopped celery and sour cream are also great garnishes for most stews.

Vegetable Beef Stew

pictured below

Here is a variation of a beef stew that I came across. With sweet flavor from apricots and squash, we think it has South American or Cuban flair.

Ruth Rodriguez, Fort Myers Beach, Florida

     3/4 pound lean beef stew meat, cut
          into 1/2-inch cubes
       2 teaspoons canola oil
       1 can (14-1/2 ounces) beef broth
       1 can (14-1/2 ounces) stewed
          tomatoes, cut up
 1-1/2 cups cubed peeled butternut squash
       1 cup frozen corn, thawed
       6 dried apricot *or* peach halves,
          quartered
     1/2 cup chopped carrot
       1 teaspoon dried oregano
     1/4 teaspoon salt
     1/4 teaspoon pepper
       2 tablespoons cornstarch
     1/4 cup water
       2 tablespoons minced fresh parsley

In a nonstick skillet, brown beef in oil over medium heat. Transfer to a slow cooker. Add the broth, tomatoes, squash, corn, apricots, carrot, oregano, salt and pepper.

Cover and cook on high for 5-6 hours or until vegetables and meat are tender. Combine cornstarch and water until smooth; stir into stew. Cover and cook on high for 30 minutes or until gravy is thickened. Stir in parsley. **Yield:** 4 servings.

Pork and Pasta Stew

I like to make this stew in summer when I can use vegetables from my own garden. Because it doesn't simmer for hours, I often reach for this recipe when I need dinner in a hurry.

Margaret Bossuot, Carthage, New York

       1 pound lean boneless pork, cut
          into 1-inch strips
     1/2 teaspoon lemon-pepper seasoning
       1 tablespoon olive oil
       1 medium onion, sliced into thin wedges
       1 garlic clove, minced
       1 cup chicken broth
     3/4 cup salsa
       1 tablespoon brown sugar
       3 quarts water
       1 teaspoon salt
       1 package (8 ounces) spiral pasta
       1 cup fresh cut green beans (1-inch
          pieces)
       1 cup sliced yellow summer squash
       1 cup sliced zucchini
       1 cup sliced fresh mushrooms
       1 tablespoon cornstarch
       2 tablespoons cold water

Toss pork and lemon-pepper; brown in oil in a skillet over medium heat. Add onion and garlic; saute until tender. Stir in broth, salsa and brown sugar; bring to a boil. Reduce heat; cover and simmer for 15-20 minutes or until pork is tender.

Meanwhile, in a large saucepan over medium heat, bring water and salt if desired to a boil. Add pasta and beans; return to a boil. Cook, uncovered, for 7 minutes. Add the squash, zucchini and mushrooms. Cook, uncovered, 6-7 minutes more or until pasta and vegetables are tender. Drain; set aside and keep warm.

Combine cornstarch with cold water until smooth; add to the pork mixture and mix well. Bring to a boil; boil and stir for 2 minutes. To serve, place pasta and vegetables in a serving dish; top with pork mixture. **Yield:** 6 servings.

Mediterranean Seafood Stew

pictured above

The flavors in this dish make it special enough for company. Even people who don't like seafood ask for the recipe.

Virginia Anthony, Blowing Rock, North Caronlia

      1 medium onion, finely chopped
1-1/2 teaspoons minced garlic, *divided*
      1 tablespoon olive oil
   1/2 pound plum tomatoes, seeded and
          diced
      1 teaspoon grated lemon peel

   1/4 teaspoon crushed red pepper flakes
      1 cup clam juice
   1/3 cup white wine *or* additional clam
          juice
      1 tablespoon tomato paste
   1/2 teaspoon salt
      1 pound orange roughy *or* red snapper
          fillets, cut into 1-inch cubes
      1 pound uncooked large shrimp,
          peeled and deveined
   1/2 pound sea scallops
   1/3 cup minced fresh parsley
   1/3 cup mayonnaise

In a Dutch oven or large saucepan, saute onion and 1/2 teaspoon garlic in oil until tender. Add the tomatoes, lemon peel and pepper flakes;

cook and stir for 2 minutes. Add the clam juice, wine or additional clam juice, tomato paste and salt. Bring to a boil. Reduce heat; cover and simmer for 10 minutes or until heated through.

Add the fish, shrimp, scallops and parsley. Cover and cook for 8-10 minutes or until fish flakes easily with a fork, the shrimp turn pink and scallops are opaque. Combine mayonnaise and remaining garlic; dollop onto each serving. **Yield:** 6 servings.

Venison Vegetable Stew

My husband and sons see to it that we have venison every winter. So I came up with this stew to make good use of it.

Jennifer Whitaker, Winchendon, Massachusetts

3 bacon strips
2 pounds venison stew meat, cut into 1-inch cubes
2 large onions, chopped
3-1/2 cups water, *divided*
1 can (8 ounces) tomato sauce
1 envelope onion soup mix
2 teaspoons salt
1 bay leaf
2 teaspoons Italian seasoning
7 medium carrots, cut into 1-inch pieces
5 medium potatoes, peeled and cut into 1-inch cubes
4 celery ribs, sliced
3 tablespoons all-purpose flour
Cooked noodles

In a 4-qt. Dutch oven, cook bacon until crisp. Remove to a paper towel to drain; reserve drippings in pan. Crumble bacon; set aside.

Cook venison and onions in drippings until meat is lightly browned. Add 3 cups water, tomato sauce, soup mix, salt, bay leaf and Italian seasoning; bring to a boil.

Reduce heat; cover and simmer for 1-1/2 hours or until meat is almost tender. Add carrots, potatoes and celery; return to a boil. Reduce heat; cover and simmer 30-45 minutes or until meat and vegetables are tender.

Combine flour and remaining water; stir into stew. Cook and stir until boiling and slightly thickened. Stir in bacon. Remove bay leaf before serving. Serve over cooked noodles. **Yield:** 8 servings.

Editor's Note: If desired, beef stew meat or pork can be used in place of the venison.

Lima Bean Sunshine Stew

This fresh, flavorful stew features a nice light broth instead of a typical thickened base. My family has been regularly requesting this one-pot meal for as long as I can remember.

Mrs. Robert Scofield, Van Wert, Ohio

1-1/2 cups cubed fully cooked ham
2 medium potatoes, peeled and cut into 3/4-inch cubes
2 medium onions, cut into eighths
2 medium tomatoes, cut into 3/4-inch pieces
1 cup frozen lima beans
1 cup frozen whole kernel corn
1/4 cup diced green pepper
1 teaspoon sugar
1/2 teaspoon salt
1/4 teaspoon pepper

Combine all ingredients in an ungreased 2-qt. baking dish. Cover and bake at 350° for 50-60 minutes or until potatoes are tender. **Yield:** 6 servings.

> "For a sweeter venison stew, I soak the meat cubes in milk in the refrigerator overnight, then drain and discard the milk before browning the venison."
>
> —*Alma Zinth*
> *Fall Creek, Wisconsin*

well. Shape into 1-in. balls. In a Dutch oven over medium heat, cook meatballs in oil until no longer pink; drain and set aside.

In same pan, saute onion and garlic in oil until onion is tender. Blend in flour. Gradually add broth, stirring constantly; bring to a boil. Cook and stir 1-2 minutes or until thickened.

Add the tomatoes, paste, bay leaf, thyme and salt; mix well. Add meatballs and carrots; bring to a boil. Reduce the heat; cover and simmer 30 minutes.

Add zucchini and peppers; bring to a boil. Reduce heat; cover and simmer 10-15 minutes or until vegetables are tender. Add parsley and pasta; heat through. Remove bay leaf. **Yield:** 6-8 servings.

Pasta Meatball Stew
pictured above

This hearty stew is one of my favorites on cold winter nights.

Pat Jelinek, Kitchener, Ontario

   1 egg, lightly beaten
1/4 cup dry bread crumbs
1/4 cup milk
1/2 teaspoon dry mustard
1/2 teaspoon salt
1/2 teaspoon pepper
   1 pound ground beef
   1 tablespoon vegetable oil
SAUCE:
   1 cup chopped onion
   2 garlic cloves, minced
   1 tablespoon vegetable oil
   2 tablespoons all-purpose flour
1-1/2 cups beef broth
   1 can (14-1/2 ounces) diced tomatoes, undrained
   2 tablespoons tomato paste
   1 bay leaf
3/4 teaspoon dried thyme
1/2 teaspoon salt
1-1/2 cups sliced carrots
1-1/2 cups chopped zucchini
   1 cup chopped green pepper
   1 cup chopped sweet red pepper
   1 tablespoon minced fresh parsley
   2 cups cooked pasta

Combine egg, crumbs, milk, mustard, salt and pepper; crumble beef over mixture and mix

Turkey Noodle Stew
pictured below

My husband doesn't usually go for meal-in-one dishes, but he likes this savory stew.

Traci Maloney, Toms River, New Jersey

   2 turkey breast tenderloins (about 1/2 pound *each*), cut into 1/4-inch slices
   1 medium onion, chopped
   1 tablespoon vegetable oil
   1 can (14-1/2 ounces) chicken broth

1 can (10-3/4 ounces) condensed
  cream of celery soup, undiluted
2 cups frozen mixed vegetables
1/2 to 1 teaspoon lemon-pepper
  seasoning
3 cups uncooked extra wide egg
  noodles

In a large skillet, cook turkey and onion in oil until turkey is no longer pink, about 6 minutes; drain. Combine the broth, soup, vegetables and lemon-pepper. Add to the skillet; bring to a boil. Stir in noodles.

Reduce heat; cover and simmer for 10 minutes or until noodles and vegetables are tender. **Yield:** 6 servings.

Lentil Pepperoni Stew

Turkey pepperoni nicely spices this thick lentil stew. It's a mainstay at our house.

Diane Hixon, Niceville, Florida

    6 cups water
1-1/2 cups dried lentils, rinsed
    1 medium onion, chopped
    4 ounces turkey pepperoni, quartered
    1 can (6 ounces) tomato paste
1-1/2 teaspoons salt
  1/4 teaspoon dried oregano
  1/4 teaspoon rubbed sage
  1/8 teaspoon cayenne pepper
    2 medium tomatoes, chopped
    1 celery rib with leaves, chopped
    1 medium carrot, chopped

In a large saucepan or soup kettle, combine the first nine ingredients; bring to a boil. Reduce heat; cover and simmer for 30 minutes.

Add the tomatoes, celery and carrot; cover and simmer 35-45 minutes longer or until vegetables are tender. **Yield:** 6 servings.

Peasant Pasta Stew

pictured above right

When I was trying to duplicate a favorite restaurant recipe, I came up with this stew. Pork, pasta, vegetables and beans in a thick tomato broth make it warm and satisfying.

Eileen Snider, Cincinnati, Ohio

1-1/2 cups beef broth
    2 celery ribs, chopped
    2 large carrots, cut into 1/4-inch slices
    1 medium onion, chopped
    1 can (46 ounces) V8 juice
    1 can (14-1/2 ounces) Italian diced
      tomatoes, undrained
    2 cans (6 ounces *each*) Italian tomato
      paste
    1 tablespoon dried oregano
1-1/2 teaspoons pepper
  1/4 teaspoon garlic powder
  3/4 pound ground pork
  3/4 cup canned kidney beans, rinsed and
      drained
  3/4 cup canned great northern beans,
      rinsed and drained
    1 cup medium shell pasta, cooked and
      drained
Shredded Parmesan cheese

In a large saucepan, combine the broth, celery, carrots and onion. Bring to a boil. Reduce heat; cover and simmer for 5-7 minutes or until vegetables are crisp-tender.

Stir in the V8 juice, tomatoes, tomato paste, oregano, pepper and garlic powder. Cover and simmer for 40-45 minutes.

Meanwhile, in a skillet, cook pork over medium heat until no longer pink; drain. Add meat and beans to soup; cover and simmer 30-45 minutes longer or until heated through. Stir in pasta just before serving. Garnish with Parmesan cheese. **Yield:** 8 servings.

Green Chili Stew

I came up with this hearty pork stew when trying to duplicate the recipe we enjoyed at a local restaurant.

Doris Johns, Hurst, Texas

1-1/2 pounds boneless pork loin roast, cut into 3/4-inch cubes
   2 tablespoons olive oil
   1 large onion, diced
   1 to 2 jalapeno peppers, seeded and chopped
   3 garlic cloves, minced
1-1/2 teaspoons ground cumin
   1 teaspoon salt
 1/4 teaspoon white pepper
   1 bay leaf
   5 medium potatoes, peeled and cubed
   3 cups water
   1 can (14-1/2 ounces) diced tomatoes, undrained
   3 cans (4 ounces *each*) chopped green chilies

In a Dutch oven or large saucepan, brown pork in oil. Add the onion, jalapenos, garlic, cumin, salt, pepper and bay leaf; saute until onion is tender.

Add potatoes and water; bring to boil. Reduce heat; cover and simmer for 15-20 minutes or until potatoes are tender.

Add tomatoes and chilies; simmer 10 minutes longer. Discard bay leaf before serving. **Yield:** 8 servings.

Editor's Note: When cutting or seeding hot peppers, use rubber or plastic gloves to protect your hands. Avoid touching your face.

> "Leftover stew can become the makings of a meat pie. Simply fill an unbaked pie shell with stew and top with a crust. Cut a vent for steam. Bake at 350° until golden brown, about 45 minutes."
>
> —*Lynn McLuhan*
> *Consul, Saskatchewan*

Creamy Sausage Stew

pictured above

Depending on the time of year, I serve my stew with bread or sweet corn muffins and fresh butter. It tastes even better the next day.

Rosemary Jesse, Cabool, Missouri

  8 to 10 medium red potatoes, cut into 1-1/2-inch pieces
    2 large white onions, quartered
    1 large green pepper, cut into 1-inch pieces
    1 large sweet red pepper, cut into 1-inch pieces
    2 pounds smoked Polish sausage, cut into 1-inch slices
  1/3 cup vegetable oil
    1 tablespoon dried basil
    2 teaspoons salt
    1 teaspoon pepper
    1 pint heavy whipping cream
    3 tablespoons cornstarch
    3 tablespoons water

Place potatoes in a 5-qt. roasting pan. Add the onions, peppers and sausage; toss gently. Combine the oil, basil, salt and pepper. Pour over the meat and vegetables; toss well.

Cover and bake at 350° for 45 minutes; stir. Add cream; cover and bake 30-40 minutes longer or until potatoes are tender.

Combine cornstarch and water; stir into stew. Place on stovetop and bring to a boil, stirring constantly until thickened. **Yield:** 10-12 servings.

Lentil Barley Stew

You can have your comfort food and nutrition, too, when you stir up this scrumptious stew. We love this dish! Filled with wholesome barley, it's hearty and satisfying and the leftovers are excellent.

Sandy Starks, Amherst, New York

- 1/2 cup chopped celery
- 1/3 cup chopped onion
- 1 tablespoon butter
- 3 cups V8 juice
- 2-1/2 cups chopped seeded plum tomatoes (about 8)
- 1-1/2 cups water
- 3/4 cup dried lentils, rinsed
- 1/2 cup medium pearl barley
- 1/2 teaspoon salt
- 1/2 teaspoon pepper
- 1/2 teaspoon dried rosemary, crushed
- 1/2 cup shredded carrot
- 3/4 cup shredded cheddar cheese

In a large saucepan, saute celery and onion in butter until tender. Add the V8 juice, tomatoes, water, lentils, barley and seasonings. Bring to a boil. Reduce heat; cover and simmer for 45 minutes.

Add carrot; cook 10 minutes longer or until barley and lentils are tender. If desired, stir in additional water for a thinner stew. Sprinkle with cheese. **Yield:** 6 servings.

Tomato and Zucchini Stew

pictured at right

The town where I live is now considered a city. When my late husband and I moved here 40 years ago, though, it was country. He was an ex-farm boy and always had a large vegetable garden. We were well supplied for winter!

Helen Miller, Hickory Hills, Illinois

- 1-1/4 pounds bulk Italian sausage
- 1-1/2 cups sliced celery (3/4-inch pieces)
- 8 medium fresh tomatoes (about 4 pounds), peeled and cut into sixths
- 1-1/2 cups tomato juice
- 4 small zucchini, sliced into 1/4-inch pieces
- 2-1/2 teaspoons Italian seasoning
- 1-1/2 to 2 teaspoons salt
- 1 teaspoon sugar
- 1/2 teaspoon garlic salt
- 1/2 teaspoon pepper
- 3 cups canned *or* frozen corn
- 2 medium green peppers, sliced into 1-inch pieces
- 1/4 cup cornstarch
- 1/4 cup water
- Shredded mozzarella cheese

In a 4-qt. Dutch oven, cook sausage over medium heat. Add celery and cook for 15 minutes or until meat is no longer pink; drain.

Add the tomatoes, tomato juice, zucchini and seasonings; bring to a boil. Reduce heat; cover and simmer for 20 minutes. Add corn and peppers; cover and simmer for 15 minutes.

Combine cornstarch and water; stir into stew. Bring to a boil; cook and stir until the mixture thickens. Sprinkle with shredded cheese. **Yield:** 6-8 servings.

Editor's Note: Three 28-ounce cans of diced tomatoes (undrained) may be substituted for the fresh tomatoes and tomato juice.

Tangy Beef and Vegetable Stew

pictured below

How much does my husband like this stew? So much that he'll eat it cold!

Amberleah Holmberg, Calgary, Alberta

- 6 cups cubed peeled potatoes (1/2-inch pieces)
- 8 medium carrots, cut into 1/2-inch pieces
- 2 medium onions, cubed
- 4 pounds beef stew meat, cut into 1-inch pieces
- 1/3 cup vegetable oil
- 1/3 cup all-purpose flour
- 4 beef bouillon cubes
- 3 cups boiling water
- 1/3 cup vinegar
- 1/3 cup ketchup
- 3 tablespoons prepared horseradish
- 3 tablespoons prepared mustard
- 2 tablespoons sugar
- 2 cups *each* frozen peas and corn
- 2 cups sliced fresh mushrooms

Place the potatoes, carrots and onions in a large slow cooker. In a large skillet, brown beef in oil, a single layer at a time; place over the vegetables. Sprinkle with flour.

Dissolve bouillon cubes in boiling water. Stir in vinegar, ketchup, horseradish, mustard and sugar; pour over meat and vegetables.

Cover and cook on high for 5 hours. Add peas, corn and mushrooms. Cover and cook on high for 45 minutes. **Yield:** 12-16 servings.

Editor's Note: Cooking times may vary with slow cookers.

Seafood Stew

This flavorful stew is seasoned with chili powder and orange juice concentrate. They make a surprisingly good combination together. My husband really enjoys it, so I make it often.

Carolyn Hayes, Marion, Illinois

- 2-1/2 cups chicken broth
- 1/2 cup uncooked long grain rice
- 2 teaspoons chili powder
- 2 garlic cloves, minced
- 1 can (14-1/2 ounces) diced tomatoes, undrained
- 3/4 cup julienned green pepper
- 3/4 cup julienned sweet red *or* yellow pepper
- 1/2 cup thinly sliced onion
- 8 ounces orange roughy *or* red snapper fillets, cut into 1-inch pieces
- 4 ounces uncooked medium shrimp, peeled and deveined
- 3/4 cup orange juice concentrate

In a saucepan, bring broth to a boil. Add the rice, chili powder and garlic; return to a boil. Reduce heat; cover and simmer for 15-20 minutes or until rice is tender.

Add the tomatoes, peppers and onion. Cover and cook over medium heat until vegetables are tender.

Add fish, shrimp and orange juice concentrate. Cover and simmer for 2-4 minutes or until the fish flakes easily with a fork and the shrimp turn pink. **Yield:** 6 servings.

Southern Okra Bean Stew

When this spicy stew's simmering on the stove, my family has a hard time waiting for dinner. It's much like a thick tomato-based soup with a hearty mix of okra, brown rice and beans.

Beverly McDowell, Athens, Georgia

    4 cups water
    1 can (28 ounces) diced tomatoes, undrained
1-1/2 cups chopped green peppers
    1 large onion, chopped
    3 garlic cloves, minced
    1 teaspoon Italian seasoning
    1 teaspoon chili powder
  1/2 to 1 teaspoon hot pepper sauce
  3/4 teaspoon salt
    1 bay leaf
    4 cups cooked brown rice
    2 cans (16 ounces *each*) kidney beans, rinsed and drained
    3 cans (8 ounces *each*) tomato sauce
    1 package (16 ounces) frozen sliced okra

In a large Dutch oven or soup kettle, combine the first 10 ingredients. Bring to a boil. Reduce heat; simmer, uncovered, for 5 minutes.

Add the rice, beans, tomato sauce and okra. Simmer, uncovered, for 8-10 minutes or until the vegetables are tender. Discard bay leaf before serving. **Yield:** 11 servings.

Lumberjack Stew

pictured above right

I found this recipe many years ago in a brochure put out by the state of Wisconsin. This stew makes appearances on our table throughout the year, especially during hunting season.

Bonnie Tetzlaff, Scandinavia, Wisconsin

    2 pounds boneless pork, trimmed and cut into 1-inch cubes
    1 teaspoon salt
    1 teaspoon sugar
  1/2 teaspoon pepper
  1/2 teaspoon paprika
    2 tablespoons vegetable oil
    1 cup sliced onion
    1 garlic clove, minced
    3 cups water
    1 tablespoon lemon juice
    1 teaspoon Worcestershire sauce
    2 chicken bouillon cubes
    2 bay leaves
    6 medium carrots, cut into 1-inch pieces
    1 package (10 ounces) pearl onions, peeled
    3 cups frozen cut green beans
    3 tablespoons cornstarch
  1/2 cup cold water

Toss pork with salt, sugar, pepper and paprika; brown in oil in a Dutch oven or soup kettle over medium-high heat. Add sliced onion and garlic; cook over medium heat for 5 minutes.

Add water, lemon juice, Worcestershire sauce, bouillon and bay leaves; cover and simmer for 1 hour. Add the carrots and pearl onions; cover and simmer for 40 minutes. Add beans; cover and simmer for 10 minutes.

Combine cornstarch and cold water until smooth; stir into stew. Bring to a boil; boil and stir for 2 minutes. Remove bay leaves. **Yield:** 6 servings.

Sausage Stew

This stew is a flavorful way to get in your veggies. I hope your family likes it!

Sheila Murphy, Killdeer, North Dakota

- 1 pound bulk pork sausage
- 1 package (10 ounces) frozen corn
- 1 package (10 ounces) frozen peas and carrots
- 1-1/2 cups diced peeled potatoes
- 1 cup chopped tomato
- 1 can (11-1/2 ounces) condensed split pea with ham and bacon soup, undiluted
- 1-1/4 cups water
- 1/2 cup chopped celery
- 1/2 cup chopped onion
- 1/4 cup chopped green pepper
- 1-1/2 teaspoons dill weed
- 1-1/2 teaspoons chili powder

In a Dutch oven, cook sausage over medium heat until no longer pink; drain. Add remaining ingredients; cover and bring to a boil.

Reduce the heat; cover and simmer for 25-30 minutes or until the potatoes are tender. **Yield:** 4-6 servings.

Spinach Lentil Stew

pictured below

When my children requested more meatless dishes, this chunky stew became a favorite.

Alice McEachern, Surrey British Columbia

- 1/2 cup chopped onion
- 2 garlic cloves, minced
- 1 tablespoon canola oil
- 5 cups water
- 1 cup dried lentils, rinsed
- 4 teaspoons vegetable *or* chicken bouillon granules
- 3 teaspoons Worcestershire sauce
- 1/2 teaspoon salt
- 1/2 teaspoon dried thyme
- 1/4 teaspoon pepper
- 1 bay leaf
- 1 cup chopped carrots
- 1 can (14-1/2 ounces) diced tomatoes, undrained
- 1 package (10 ounces) frozen chopped spinach, thawed and squeezed dry
- 1 tablespoon red wine vinegar

In a large saucepan, saute onion and garlic in oil until tender. Add the water, lentils, bouillon, Worcestershire sauce, salt, thyme, pepper and bay leaf; bring to a boil. Reduce heat; cover and simmer for 20 minutes.

Add carrots, tomatoes and spinach; return to a boil. Reduce heat; cover and simmer 15-20 minutes longer or until lentils are tender. Stir in vinegar. Discard bay leaf before serving. **Yield:** 6 servings.

Beef Vegetable Stew

All kinds of root vegetables star in this hearty stew. A little hot pepper sauce also gives it some zip.

Donna Nannini, Caledonia, Michigan

2-1/2 pounds lean beef stew meat, cut into 1-inch cubes
   2 large onions, chopped
   2 garlic cloves, minced
1/2 cup water
   1 beef bouillon cube
   3 cans (14-1/2 ounces *each*) beef broth
   4 potatoes, peeled and cubed
   3 medium carrots, sliced
   2 medium green peppers, cut into 1/2-inch pieces
   2 celery ribs, sliced
   3 cups cubed rutabaga
1-1/2 cups cubed parsnips
1-1/2 cups cubed turnips
3/4 teaspoon dried marjoram
1/2 teaspoon pepper
1/4 teaspoon dried savory
1/4 teaspoon hot pepper sauce
   2 tablespoons cornstarch
   3 tablespoons water

In a Dutch oven, combine the beef, onions, garlic, 1/2 cup water, bouillon and enough of the broth to cover. Bring to a boil. Cover and simmer until meat is tender, about 2 hours.

Add vegetables, seasonings and remaining broth. Simmer 30-45 minutes or until vegetables are tender.

Combine cornstarch and water; gradually add to the boiling mixture. Cook and stir for 2 minutes. **Yield:** 16 servings.

Orzo Shrimp Stew

pictured above

Since we really enjoy seafood, I don't skimp on shrimp in this recipe! This mildly seasoned stew has other satisfying ingredients, too, like broccoli, tomatoes and pasta.

Lisa Stinger, Hamilton, New Jersey

2-1/2 cups chicken broth
   5 cups broccoli florets
   1 can (14-1/2 ounces) diced tomatoes, undrained
   1 cup uncooked orzo
   1 pound uncooked medium shrimp, peeled and deveined
3/4 teaspoon salt
1/4 teaspoon pepper
   2 teaspoons dried basil
   2 tablespoons butter

In a large nonstick skillet or saucepan, bring broth to a boil. Add the broccoli, tomatoes and orzo. Reduce heat; simmer, uncovered, for 5 minutes, stirring occasionally.

Add the shrimp, salt and pepper. Cover and cook for 4-5 minutes or until shrimp turn pink and orzo is tender. Stir in basil and butter. **Yield:** 4 servings.

Southwestern Meat And Potato Stew

pictured above

Even before it got cold outside one fall, my husband had asked me to make this stew twice. In fact, here at home, our name for it is Tom's Favorite Stew.

Linda Schwarz, Bertrand, Nebraska

>   2 pounds ground beef *or* chuck
>   1 large onion, chopped
>   1 cup water, *divided*
>   1 can (28 ounces) diced tomatoes, undrained
>   1 package (16 ounces) frozen corn
>   3 medium potatoes, peeled and cubed
>   1 cup salsa
>   1 teaspoon salt
>   1 teaspoon ground cumin
> 1/2 teaspoon garlic powder
> 1/2 teaspoon pepper
>   2 tablespoons all-purpose flour

In a Dutch oven or large kettle, cook beef and onion over medium heat until meat is no longer pink; drain. Add 3/4 cup water and the next eight ingredients. Bring to a boil; reduce heat. Cover and simmer for 1-1/2 hours.

Combine flour and remaining water; stir into stew. Cook and stir until boiling and slightly thickened. **Yield:** 6 servings.

Beef Mushroom Stew

Hearty beef and tasty mushrooms give my recipe just the right flavors.

Marilyn Schroeder, St. Paul, Minnesota

> 1/4 cup all-purpose flour
>   1 teaspoon salt
> 1/8 teaspoon pepper
> 2-1/2 to 3 pounds beef round steak, cut into cubes
>   2 tablespoons vegetable oil
>   1 cup burgundy *or* beef broth
> 3/4 cup water
>   1 jar (8 ounces) whole mushrooms, drained
> 1/2 cup chopped onion
>   2 bay leaves
>   1 garlic clove, minced
>   1 tablespoon dried parsley flakes
> Cooked rice *or* noodles

Place flour, salt and pepper in a plastic bag; add beef cubes and shake to coat on all sides. Brown beef in oil in a large saucepan. Stir in the next seven ingredients; bring to a boil.

Reduce heat; cover and simmer for 1-1/2 hours or until meat is tender. Thicken if desired. Serve over rice or noodles. **Yield:** 8-10 servings.

Hot Dog Stew

Kids will be thrilled with this change-of-pace stew. It's chock-full of hot dog bites and baked beans.

Dorothy Erickson, Blue Eye, Missouri

>   1 package (14 ounces) hot dogs, cut into 1/2-inch slices
>   1 can (11-1/2 ounces) condensed bean and bacon soup, undiluted
>   1 can (10-3/4 ounces) condensed tomato soup, undiluted
>   1 can (15 ounces) pork and beans
>   1 teaspoon chili powder
>   1 teaspoon dried minced onion
> 1/4 teaspoon pepper
> 1/4 teaspoon Liquid Smoke, optional
> 2/3 cup evaporated milk

In a large nonstick skillet, brown hot dogs over medium heat. Add the next six ingredients; add Liquid Smoke if desired. Cover and cook over low heat until heated through. Stir in milk; heat through. **Yield:** 6 servings.

Pinto Bean Stew

pictured below

This thick stew of beans and vegetables makes a wonderful supper on cold winter days. I sometimes serve it over rice for a fun change of pace. It also freezes well.

Gina Passantino, Arlington, Virginia

- 1 cup dried pinto beans
- 2 cups cold water
- 1/2 cup chopped carrot
- 2 garlic cloves, minced
- 3/4 teaspoon chili powder
- 1/2 teaspoon salt
- Dash cayenne pepper
- 1 package (16 ounces) frozen corn, thawed
- 1 large onion, chopped
- 1 medium green pepper, chopped
- 1 can (14-1/2 ounces) diced tomatoes, undrained
- 2 to 3 teaspoons balsamic vinegar
- 1/4 teaspoon sugar

Place beans in a large saucepan; add water to cover beans by 2 in. Bring to a boil; boil for 2 minutes.

Remove from the heat; cover and let stand for 1 hour. Drain and rinse beans, discarding liquid. Return beans to the pan.

Add the cold water, carrot, garlic, chili powder, salt and cayenne. Bring to a boil. Reduce heat; cover and simmer for 45 minutes or until beans are almost tender.

In a nonstick skillet coated with nonstick cooking spray; saute the corn, onion and green pepper until tender. Add to bean mixture.

Cover and cook for 45 minutes. Stir in the tomatoes, vinegar and sugar. Cook 5 minutes longer or until heated through. **Yield:** 6 servings.

Shortcut Brunswick Stew

Cooked chicken and condensed soup give me the jump start I need to get this satisfying dish on the table fast.

Eva Still, Crescent, Oklahoma

- 2 bacon strips
- 1/2 cup chopped onion
- 1 can (10-3/4 ounces) condensed tomato soup, undiluted
- 1-1/4 cups plus 1 tablespoon water, *divided*
- 1 teaspoon Worcestershire sauce
- 1/4 teaspoon pepper
- 1 package (10 ounces) frozen lima beans
- 1 package (10 ounces) frozen whole kernel corn
- 2 cups cubed cooked chicken
- 1 tablespoon cornstarch

In a large skillet, cook bacon until crisp; remove to paper towel to drain. In the drippings, cook onion until tender. Stir in the soup, 1-1/4 cups water, Worcestershire sauce and pepper; bring to a boil.

Add beans and corn; return to a boil. Reduce heat; cover and simmer for 20 minutes. Crumble bacon; add to stew with chicken.

Combine cornstarch with the remaining water; stir into stew. Bring to a boil, stirring constantly until thickened. **Yield:** 4 servings.

241

Irish Lamb Stew
pictured above

With our busy schedule, I cook lots of stews. This one was handed down to me by my mother-in-law. It's nice because you can prepare it on the weekend and reheat it during the week. For a great full-course meal, put out hard rolls and French bread and you're set.

Jeanne Dahling, Elgin, Minnesota

6 tablespoons all-purpose flour, **divided**

1 teaspoon salt
1/8 teaspoon pepper
1-1/2 pounds lamb stew meat, cut into 1-inch cubes
2 tablespoons vegetable oil
1/2 teaspoon dill weed
3 cups water
8 extra-small *or* boiling onions
3 medium carrots, cut into 1-inch pieces
2 large potatoes, peeled and cubed
1/2 cup half-and-half cream
Hot biscuits

Combine 4 tablespoons flour, salt and pepper in a plastic bag. Add lamb; shake to coat. In a 4-qt. Dutch oven, heat oil; brown the lamb on all sides.

Add dill and water; bring to a boil; Reduce heat; cover and simmer for 1-1/2 hours or until meat is almost tender. Add the onions, carrots and potatoes. Cover and simmer for 30 minutes or until the meat and vegetables are tender.

Combine cream and remaining flour; stir into stew. Cook and stir until boiling and slightly thickened. Serve over hot biscuits. **Yield:** 6 servings.

Maltese Stew

While growing up on the island of Malta, my mother ate this slightly spicy stew often. The recipe has been in the family for generations.

Jannet Sanden, Tempe, Arizona

> 1 **pork shoulder roast (1-1/2 to 2 pounds), trimmed and cut into 1-inch cubes**
> 2 **medium onions, quartered**
> 2 **tablespoons vegetable oil**
> 2 **cups chicken broth,** *divided*
> 3 **tablespoons tomato paste**
> 1 **tablespoon red wine vinegar**
> 1 **teaspoon browning sauce**
> 1/2 to 3/4 **teaspoon curry powder**
> 1/2 **teaspoon salt**
> 1/4 **teaspoon pepper**
> 1/4 to 1/2 **teaspoon ground allspice**
> 1/4 to 1/2 **teaspoon ground nutmeg**
> Pinch ground cloves
> 3 **medium potatoes, peeled and cut into 1-inch cubes**
> 1 **cup frozen peas**

In a Dutch oven or soup kettle over medium heat, cook pork and onions in oil for 10-12 minutes or until pork is browned and onions are soft.

In a bowl, combine 1 cup broth and tomato paste until smooth; add to pork mixture. Cook, uncovered, for 10 minutes. Stir in vinegar, browning sauce and seasonings; cook, uncovered, for 15 minutes.

Add potatoes, peas and remaining broth; bring to a boil. Reduce heat; cover and simmer for 50-60 minutes or until pork and potatoes are tender. **Yield:** 6-8 servings (2 quarts).

Skillet Chicken Stew
pictured below

It's been 30 years now since I adapted this from a recipe for beef stew. We like it so much that, in all that time, I have never changed any ingredients or amounts—unless it was to double them!

Valerie Jordan, Kingmont, West Virginia

> 1/3 **cup all-purpose flour**
> 1/2 **teaspoon salt**
> Dash pepper
> 1-1/2 **pounds boneless skinless chicken breasts, cut into 1-inch pieces**
> 3 **tablespoons butter**
> 1 **medium onion, sliced**
> 3 **celery ribs, sliced**
> 2 **medium potatoes, peeled and cut into 3/4-inch cubes**
> 3 **medium carrots, sliced 1/4 inch thick**
> 1 **cup chicken broth**
> 1/2 **teaspoon dried thyme**
> 1 **tablespoon ketchup**
> 1 **tablespoon cornstarch**

Combine flour, salt and pepper in a shallow bowl; coat chicken. In a large skillet, melt butter; brown chicken. Add onion and celery; cook for 3 minutes. Stir in potatoes and carrots.

Combine broth, thyme, ketchup and cornstarch; stir into skillet. Bring to a boil. Reduce heat; cover and simmer for 15-20 minutes or until the vegetables are tender. **Yield:** 4-6 servings.

Hodgepodge Stew

pictured above

This is a dish that I enjoyed as a child and still remember with pleasure. Mom's homemade bread made the perfect complement to this meal.

Julia Trachsel, Victoria, British Columbia

> 6 cups water
> 2 teaspoons salt, *divided*
> 1 pound green beans, cut into 1-inch pieces
> 6 carrots, cut into 1-inch pieces
> 3 medium potatoes, peeled and quartered
> 1 cup fresh *or* frozen corn
> 2 cups fresh *or* frozen peas
> 6 tablespoons butter
> 2 cups heavy whipping cream
> 2 tablespoons minced fresh chives
> 1/2 teaspoon pepper
> 1/4 teaspoon paprika

In a large saucepan or Dutch oven, bring water and 1 teaspoon salt to a boil. Add beans, carrots, and potatoes; cook 15 minutes. Add corn and peas; cook an additional 3-5 minutes or until tender. Drain, reserving 2 cups liquid. Set vegetables aside.

In the same saucepan, combine reserved liquid, butter, cream, chives, pepper, paprika and remaining salt. Add vegetables and heat through. **Yield:** 8-10 servings (3 quarts).

Okanagan Pork Stew

This stew gets its name from the area where my mom lives in British Columbia. She dries fruit from her orchards and sends it to me for my family to enjoy in this terrific recipe.

Monica Wilcott, Sturgis, Saskatchewan

> 2 packages (8 ounces *each*) dried mixed fruit
> 3 cups boiling water
> 3 pounds boneless pork, trimmed and cut into 3/4-inch cubes
> 3 tablespoons vegetable oil
> 3 large onions, chopped
> 2 garlic cloves, minced
> 2 tablespoons tomato paste
> 2 tablespoons honey
> 2 tablespoons vinegar
> 1 teaspoon ground ginger
> 1/2 teaspoon ground coriander
> 1/2 teaspoon salt
> 1/4 teaspoon pepper
> 1/4 cup slivered almonds, toasted

Combine fruit and water; cover and let stand 1 hour. Drain, reserving liquid; set aside. In an ovenproof Dutch oven or soup kettle over medium heat, brown pork in oil until no longer pink; drain.

Add onions and garlic; cook and stir until onions are tender. Add enough water to reserved fruit liquid to make 3 cups; add to kettle along with fruit, tomato paste, honey, vinegar and spices. Mix well.

Cover and bake at 325° for 1-1/2 hours or until pork is tender. Sprinkle with almonds. **Yield:** 8-10 servings (2-1/2 quarts).

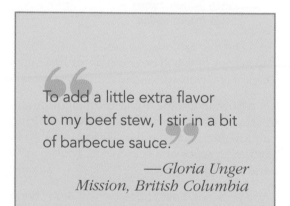

66 To add a little extra flavor to my beef stew, I stir in a bit of barbecue sauce. 99

—Gloria Unger
Mission, British Columbia

Old-Fashioned Venison Stew

Simmer a pot of satisfying stew, stirs plenty of garlic and herbs into the hearty meat-and-vegetable mixture. This stew tastes great right off the stove, but it's even better if you make it ahead and reheat it.

Rick Sullivan, Henryville, Indiana

    1 pound venison, cubed
    1 tablespoon olive oil
    2 cans (14-1/2 ounces *each*) beef
      broth
    2 teaspoons dried thyme
    2 teaspoons dried marjoram
    2 teaspoons dried parsley flakes
    2 garlic cloves, minced
  1/2 teaspoon salt
    6 to 8 whole peppercorns
    1 bay leaf
    2 cups cubed peeled potatoes
    1 large onion, chopped
    2 medium carrots, sliced
    2 celery ribs, chopped
    2 tablespoons all-purpose flour
    3 tablespoons water
  1/8 to 1/4 teaspoon browning
      sauce

In a Dutch oven, brown venison in oil over medium-high heat; drain. Stir in the broth, thyme, marjoram, parsley, garlic and salt.

Place peppercorns and bay leaf on a double thickness of cheesecloth; bring up corners of cloth and tie with kitchen string to form a bag. Add to pan. Bring to a boil. Reduce heat; cover and simmer for 30 minutes.

Add the potatoes, onion, carrots and celery; return to a boil. Reduce heat; cover and simmer for 30-35 minutes or until meat and vegetables are tender. Discard herb bag.

In a small bowl, combine the flour, water and browning sauce until smooth; stir into stew. Bring to a boil; cook and stir for 2 minutes or until thickened. **Yield:** 4 servings.

Beef Cabbage Stew
pictured below

This is one of my favorite meals since I don't have to stand over the stove or dirty a lot of pots and pans to prepare it. With six in the family, we have enough dishes to wash after each meal!

Lesa Swartwood, Fulton, Missouri

  1-1/2 pounds beef stew meat, cut
        into 1-inch pieces
      2 beef bouillon cubes
      1 cup hot water
      1 large onion, chopped
    1/4 teaspoon pepper
      1 bay leaf
      2 medium potatoes, peeled and cubed
      2 celery ribs, sliced
      4 cups shredded cabbage
      1 carrot, sliced
      1 can (8 ounces) tomato sauce
  Salt to taste

In a large saucepan or Dutch oven, brown stew meat; drain. Meanwhile, dissolve bouillon cubes in water; add to beef. Add onion, pepper and bay leaf. Cover; simmer 1-1/4 hours or until tender.

Add potatoes, celery, cabbage and carrot. Cover and simmer 30 minutes or until vegetables are tender. Stir in tomato sauce and salt. Simmer, uncovered, 15-20 minutes more. Remove bay leaf before serving. **Yield:** 6-8 servings.

245

Sausage Lentil Stew

pictured below

This hearty stew is chock-full of protein-packed lentils, vegetables and tasty turkey kielbasa.

Patti St.Antoine, Broomfield, Colorado

      1 pound fully cooked turkey kielbasa,
        thinly sliced
      2 medium carrots, sliced
      2 celery ribs, sliced
      1 medium onion, chopped
      2 garlic cloves, minced
      2 teaspoons canola oil
      3 cups water
      2 medium potatoes, diced
      1 can (14-1/2 ounces) chicken broth
      1 cup dried lentils
    3/4 teaspoon salt
    1/2 teaspoon ground cumin
    1/8 teaspoon cayenne pepper
      1 can (28 ounces) diced tomatoes,
        undrained
      1 can (4 ounces) chopped green chilies

In a Dutch oven, cook the kielbasa, carrots, celery, onion and garlic in oil until vegetables are almost tender, about 5 minutes. Stir in the water, potatoes, broth, lentils, salt, cumin and cayenne; bring to a boil.

Reduce heat; cover and simmer for 40 minutes or until potatoes are tender, stirring occasionally. Add tomatoes and chilies; heat through. **Yield:** 8 servings.

Pork Stew with Corn-Bread Dumplings

Corn-bread dumplings add down-home flavor to this truly country meal. I frequently make a double batch of this stew on Sunday so that we can have leftovers all week long.

Shelly Gresham, Dawson, Illinois

      2 pounds boneless pork, trimmed and
        cut into 3/4-inch cubes
      2 tablespoons vegetable oil
      1 can (28 ounces) stewed tomatoes
  1-1/4 cups chicken broth, *divided*
      1 medium onion, quartered
      2 bay leaves
      1 teaspoon Worcestershire sauce
      1 teaspoon dried thyme
    3/4 teaspoon sugar
    3/4 teaspoon salt
    1/4 teaspoon pepper
    1/4 teaspoon garlic powder
    1/8 teaspoon ground nutmeg
      2 tablespoons all-purpose flour
DUMPLINGS:
    1/2 cup all-purpose flour
    1/3 cup yellow cornmeal
  1-1/2 teaspoons baking powder
    1/4 teaspoon salt
Dash pepper
      1 egg
      3 tablespoons milk
      2 tablespoons vegetable oil
      1 can (8-3/4 ounces) whole kernel corn,
        drained

In a large skillet over medium heat, brown pork in oil; drain. Stir in tomatoes, 1 cup broth, onion and seasonings; bring to a boil. Reduce heat; cover and simmer for 60-70 minutes or until pork is tender.

Combine flour and remaining broth until smooth; gradually add to stew, stirring constantly. Bring to a boil; boil and stir for 2 minutes. Remove bay leaves.

For dumplings, in a bowl, combine flour, cornmeal, baking powder, salt and pepper. Beat egg, milk and oil; add to flour mixture and mix until just moistened. Stir in corn.

Drop by rounded tablespoonfuls into simmering stew. Cover and cook for 10-12 minutes or until dumplings are tender. (Do not lift lid while simmering.) **Yield:** 6 servings.

Italian Stew
pictured above

Spice up autumn evenings with this zippy stew. It has a blend of Italian turkey sausage, seasoned tomato broth, pasta and veggies.

Nancy Cox, Martinsville, Indiana

2 pounds turkey Italian sausage links, casings removed
1 cup chopped onion
3/4 cup chopped green pepper
3 garlic cloves, minced
1 can (28 ounces) diced tomatoes, undrained
1 can (15 ounces) Italian-seasoned tomato sauce
1/2 pound fresh mushrooms, sliced
1 cup water
1/2 cup beef broth
1/2 cup red wine or additional beef broth
1-1/2 cups cooked spiral pasta
1/2 cup shredded mozzarella cheese

In a large nonstick saucepan coated with non-stick cooking spray, cook the sausage, onion, green pepper and garlic until meat is no longer pink; drain. Add the next six ingredients; bring to a boil.

Reduce heat; cover and simmer for 1 hour. Add pasta; heat through. Top each serving with mozzarella cheese. **Yield:** 8 servings.

247

TOPPING:
  1/2 cup sour cream
  1/2 cup plain yogurt
  2 tablespoons snipped chives

In a Dutch oven, combine the first 15 ingredients. Bring to a boil. Reduce heat; cover and simmer for 35-40 minutes or until lentils and vegetables are tender. Stir in spinach; heat through.

Combine all of the topping ingredients; dollop about 1 tablespoon on each serving. **Yield:** 13 servings.

Vegetable Lentil Stew

pictured above

This delicious stew is nothing but good for you! This chunky mixture, seasoned with chili powder and cumin, is chock-full of beans, lentils and other veggies. Steaming bowls of it make a warm and satisfying supper.

Vi Toews, Bluffton, Alberta

  4 cups V8 *or* tomato juice
  2 cans (14-1/2 ounces *each*) Italian stewed tomatoes
  1 can (16 ounces) kidney beans, rinsed and drained
  1 can (15 ounces) garbanzo beans, rinsed and drained
  2 medium carrots, thinly sliced
  2 medium potatoes, cubed
  1 large onion, chopped
  1 green pepper, chopped
  1 sweet red pepper, chopped
  1 cup dried lentils, rinsed
  2 tablespoons minced parsley
  2 tablespoons chili powder
  2 teaspoons dried basil
  1 teaspoon garlic powder
  1 teaspoon ground cumin
  1 package (10 ounces) frozen chopped spinach, thawed

Moroccan Stew

Fragrant cinnamon, cumin and coriander give this hearty meatless medley its exotic Moroccan flavor.

Rita Reinke, Wauwatosa, Wisconsin

  2 cups cauliflowerets
  3 medium carrots, cut into 2-inch julienned strips
  1 medium onion, quartered and thinly sliced
  2 teaspoons olive oil
  1 cup sliced zucchini
  1/2 cup water
  1 teaspoon ground cumin
  1/2 teaspoon salt
  1/2 teaspoon ground coriander
  1/4 teaspoon ground cinnamon
  1/8 teaspoon cayenne pepper
  1/8 teaspoon pepper
  1 can (15 ounces) garbanzo beans *or* chickpeas, rinsed and drained
  1 can (14-1/2 ounces) diced tomatoes, undrained
Hot cooked rice, optional

In a large nonstick skillet, saute the cauliflower, carrots and onion in oil for 10 minutes. Add the zucchini, water, cumin, salt, coriander, cinnamon, cayenne and pepper. Bring to a boil.

Reduce heat; cover and simmer for 5 minutes. Stir in garbanzo beans and tomatoes; simmer 5 minutes longer. Serve over rice if desired. **Yield:** 5 servings.

Mexican Pork Stew

pictured below

I heat up cold nights by serving this thick and zesty stew with corn bread. I also like to spoon leftovers into corn tortillas with a little salsa.

Mickey Terry, Del Valle, Texas

- 1 pound boneless pork loin roast, cut into 3/4-inch cubes
- 3 teaspoons olive oil, *divided*
- 1 large onion, chopped
- 2 celery ribs, chopped
- 1 jalapeno pepper, seeded and chopped
- 1 garlic clove, minced
- 1-1/2 cups water
- 1 tablespoon chili powder
- 2 teaspoons brown sugar
- 1 teaspoon ground cumin
- 1/2 teaspoon salt
- 1/4 teaspoon pepper
- 1 can (6 ounces) tomato paste
- 1 can (16 ounces) kidney beans, rinsed and drained
- 1 can (15 ounces) pinto beans, rinsed and drained
- 1 can (14-1/2 ounces) diced tomatoes, undrained
- 2 teaspoons minced fresh cilantro

In a Dutch oven or large saucepan over medium-high heat, brown meat on all sides in 1 teaspoon oil; drain. Remove meat and keep warm. In the same pan, saute the onion, celery, jalapeno and garlic in remaining oil until tender. Stir in the water, chili powder, brown sugar, cumin, salt and pepper. Return meat to pan. Bring to a boil. Reduce heat; cover and simmer for 30 minutes.

Stir in the tomato paste, beans and tomatoes. Return to a boil. Reduce heat; cover and simmer 20 minutes longer or until meat is tender and beans are heated through. Garnish with cilantro. **Yield:** 5 servings.

Editor's Note: When cutting or seeding hot peppers, use rubber or plastic gloves to protect your hands. Avoid touching your face.

Tomato-Dill Shrimp Stew

Here in the Northwest, we have a seemingly endless supply of seafood, so we're always searching for creative new recipes. This thick stew was a big hit when I served it one year on Father's Day. My dad loved it! And so did everyone else.

Jennie Benjaminson, Renton, Washington

- 1 large onion, chopped
- 4 garlic cloves, minced
- 1 tablespoon olive oil
- 3 cups diced fresh tomatoes
- 1 can (8 ounces) tomato sauce
- 3 tablespoons minced fresh dill *or* 2 teaspoons dill weed
- 2 teaspoons Dijon mustard
- 1 teaspoon honey
- 1/2 teaspoon salt
- 1 pound cooked medium shrimp, peeled and deveined
- 4 ounces crumbled feta cheese
- 1 cup minced fresh parsley

In a large saucepan, saute onion and garlic in oil for 5 minutes. Stir in the tomatoes, tomato sauce, dill, mustard, honey and salt.

Bring to a boil. Reduce heat; simmer, uncovered, for 20 minutes. Add the shrimp, cheese and parsley; simmer 5 minutes longer. **Yield:** 4 servings.

Pork and Winter Squash Stew

pictured below

Here in the high desert area of California, we do get snow. So this stew's especially popular in winter!

Evelyn Plyler, Apple Valley, California

2 pounds lean boneless pork, cut into 1-inch cubes
2 tablespoons vegetable oil, *divided*
2 cups chopped onion
2 garlic cloves, minced
3 cups sliced fresh mushrooms
2-1/2 cups diagonally sliced carrots
2 cans (14-1/2 ounces *each*) Italian stewed tomatoes
2 teaspoons dried thyme
1/2 teaspoon pepper
1-1/2 teaspoons salt
4 cups cubed peeled butternut squash
Hot cooked noodles, optional

In a 4-qt. Dutch oven, brown pork in 1 tablespoon of oil. Remove from pan; drain and set aside. Heat remaining oil in the same pan over medium heat. Saute onion and garlic for 3 minutes.

Return pork to pan. Add the mushrooms, carrots, tomatoes and seasonings; bring to a boil.

Reduce heat; cover and simmer for 1 hour. Add squash; simmer, uncovered, for 30 minutes or until meat and vegetables are tender. Serve over noodles if desired. **Yield:** 8 servings.

Skier's Stew

This recipe is called Skier's Stew because you put it in the oven...and head for the slopes! It looks after itself for 5 hours.

Traci Gangwer, Denver, Colorado

2 pounds beef stew meat, cut into 1-inch cubes
6 large potatoes, peeled and cut into 1-inch cubes
8 to 10 carrots, sliced
1/2 cup water
1 can (15 ounces) tomato sauce
1 envelope dry onion soup mix

In a Dutch oven, place half of the meat, potatoes and carrots. Repeat layers. Add water and tomato sauce; sprinkle onion soup mix over the top. Do not stir. Cover and bake at 250° for 5 hours. **Yield:** 6-8 servings.

Irish Beef 'n' Carrot Stew

My husband was born on St. Patrick's Day, and this is the meal I make to celebrate that occasion. My family looks forward to it all year.

Marie Biggs, Anacortes, Washington

1 pound carrots, peeled and cut into 2-1/2-inch pieces
2 medium onions, chopped
3 tablespoons vegetable oil
3 tablespoons all-purpose flour
Salt and pepper to taste
1-1/2 pounds boneless beef chuck steak, cut into 1-inch strips
1/2 teaspoon chopped fresh basil
2/3 cup Guinness, other dark beer *or* beef broth
1 teaspoon honey
2/3 cup additional beef broth
Mashed *or* boiled potatoes

Place carrots in a greased shallow 2-qt. baking dish. In a skillet, saute onions in oil for 5 minutes or until tender. Using a slotted spoon, transfer onions to dish.

In a resealable plastic bag, combine the flour, salt and pepper. Add beef, a few pieces at a time, and shake to coat; reserve flour mixture. In the same skillet, brown meat in oil on all sides. Transfer to baking dish.

Stir reserved flour mixture into oil; cook and stir over medium heat for 1 minute. Add basil and beer or broth.

Bring to a boil; cook and stir for 1 minute or until thickened. Stir in honey and additional broth; return to a boil, stirring constantly. Pour over beef.

Cover and bake at 325° for 1-1/2 hours or until beef is tender. Serve with potatoes. **Yield:** 4-6 servings.

Easy Oven Stew

pictured above

Because I'd never entered a recipe contest before, I hesitated before sending in my stew recipe. I knew, though, it not only was so good but anybody could make it. You just throw the ingredients into a pot and stir!

Carol Smith, Stuart, Florida

- 2 pounds lean beef stew meat, cut into 1-inch cubes
- 4 large carrots, cut into 1-inch pieces
- 2 medium onions, cut into 1-inch pieces
- 2 celery ribs, cut into 1-inch pieces
- 2 medium parsnips, cut into 1-inch pieces
- 1 garlic clove, minced
- 1 can (14-1/2 ounces) Italian stewed tomatoes
- 1-1/2 cups beef broth
- 1 can (8 ounces) tomato sauce
- 1/2 cup quick-cooking tapioca
- 1 teaspoon instant coffee granules
- 1/2 teaspoon dried thyme
- 1/2 teaspoon dried oregano
- 1/2 teaspoon salt

In a 5-qt. Dutch oven, combine all ingredients. Cover and bake at 300° for 2-1/2 to 3 hours, stirring every hour, or until the meat and vegetables are tender. **Yield:** 8 servings.

Zippy Bean Stew

This bean stew is a staple for my co-workers and me once the weather turns cool.

Debbie Matthews, Bluefield, West Virginia

- 1 can (14-1/2 ounces) vegetable *or* chicken broth
- 1 can (16 ounces) kidney beans, rinsed and drained
- 1 can (15 ounces) pinto beans, rinsed and drained
- 1 can (14-1/2 ounces) diced tomatoes and green chilies
- 1 can (4 ounces) chopped green chilies, undrained
- 1 package (10 ounces) frozen corn, thawed
- 3 cups water
- 1 large onion, chopped
- 2 medium carrots, sliced
- 2 garlic cloves, minced
- 2 teaspoons chili powder

Combine all ingredients in a slow cooker. Cover and cook on high for 4-5 hours or until heated through and flavors are blended. **Yield:** 6 servings.

Herbed Beef Stew And Dumplings

pictured at right

With our supply of homegrown beef, I'm always searching for new ideas on how to cook it. Everyone loves this dish that I invented.

Madeleine DeGruchy, Antigonish, Nova Scotia

- 1 pound lean beef stew meat, cut into 1/2-inch cubes
- 2 tablespoons vegetable oil
- 2 medium onions, chopped
- 2 garlic cloves, minced
- 3-1/4 cups water, *divided*
- 1 teaspoon dried basil
- 3/4 teaspoon dried thyme
- 1/2 teaspoon rubbed sage
- 1/2 teaspoon ground cinnamon
- 1 to 2 teaspoons salt
- 1/4 teaspoon pepper
- 1 pound baby carrots
- 3 medium parsnips, cut into 1-inch pieces
- 1/2 teaspoon browning sauce, optional
- 2 tablespoons cornstarch

DUMPLINGS:
- 1-1/3 cups all-purpose flour
- 1 tablespoon baking powder
- 1 tablespoon chopped fresh parsley, optional
- 1/2 teaspoon salt
- 1 egg, beaten
- 1 tablespoon vegetable oil
- 1/2 cup water

In a 5-qt. Dutch oven, brown beef in oil. Add onions and garlic; continue to cook until onions are tender. Add 3 cups water and all of the seasonings.

Cover and simmer until the meat is tender, about 2 to 2-1/2 hours. Add carrots and parsnips; cover and simmer for 45 minutes or until vegetables are tender. Stir in browning sauce if desired.

Combine cornstarch and remaining water; gradually stir into stew. Bring to a boil, stirring constantly; boil for 1 minute.

For dumplings, combine flour, baking powder, parsley if desired and salt. Stir in egg, oil and water. Drop into six mounds onto boiling stew. Cover and cook 10-12 minutes or until done (do not lift cover while boiling). Serve immediately. **Yield:** 6 servings.

Sage 'n' Rosemary Pork Stew

This stew satisfies the appetites of my husband and son, who are real meat-and-potatoes men. It's easy on the family budget, yet is special enough to serve to guests.

Gail Dvorchak, Smock, Pennsylvania

- 3 to 4 pounds pork shoulder, trimmed and cut into 3/4-inch cubes
- 1 tablespoon vegetable oil
- 1 can (49-1/2 ounces) chicken broth
- 1-1/2 cups water
- 3/4 cup chopped onion
- 1-1/4 teaspoons dried rosemary, crushed
- 3/4 teaspoon salt
- 1/2 teaspoon dried sage
- 1/2 teaspoon pepper
- 4 cups cubed red potatoes
- 1 package (10 ounces) frozen cut green beans
- 1-1/2 cups frozen lima beans
- 1 teaspoon Dijon mustard
- 1/3 cup all-purpose flour
- 1/2 cup half-and-half cream

In a Dutch oven or soup kettle over medium heat, brown pork in oil; drain. Add the broth, water, onion, rosemary, salt, sage and pepper; bring to a boil. Reduce heat and simmer, uncovered, for 40-45 minutes or until the pork is almost tender. Add the potatoes, beans and mustard; mix well.

Return to a boil; reduce heat and simmer, uncovered, for 40-45 minutes or until vegetables and pork are tender.

Combine flour and cream; stir until smooth. Add to stew. Bring to a boil; boil for 2 minutes, stirring constantly. **Yield:** 10-12 servings (3 quarts).

Country Ham Stew

I've come to discover that everyone enjoys this chunky stew. Whenever I offer it to family and friends, I'm asked to share the recipe as well.

Paula Pelis, Rocky Point, New York

  1 jar (12 ounces) chicken gravy
  1 cup water
1-1/2 pounds fully cooked ham, cut
      into 1/2-inch cubes
  6 small red potatoes, quartered
  1 cup fresh sugar snap peas
  1 cup frozen lima beans
  1 cup fresh baby carrots *or* frozen tiny
      whole carrots
  1 cup frozen small whole onions

In a large saucepan over medium heat, stir gravy and water until smooth. Add remaining ingredients; mix well. Bring to a boil.

Reduce the heat; cover and simmer for 20-30 minutes or until vegetables are tender. **Yield:** 6 servings.

> 66 Oil your spoon before dropping dumplings into stew—it goes faster, it's less messy and the dumplings come out rounder. 99
>
> —*Ruby Felt*
> *Fenelon Falls, Ontario*

Chicken Mushroom Stew
pictured below

The flavors blend beautifully in this pot of chicken stew as it simmers slowly.

Kim Marie Van Rheenen, Mendota, Illinois

  6 boneless skinless chicken breast halves
      (1-1/2 pounds)
  2 tablespoons vegetable oil, *divided*
  8 ounces fresh mushrooms, sliced
  1 medium onion, diced
  3 cups diced zucchini
  1 cup diced green pepper
  4 garlic cloves, minced
  3 medium tomatoes, diced
  1 can (6 ounces) tomato paste
3/4 cup water
  2 teaspoons salt
  1 teaspoon *each* dried thyme, oregano,
      marjoram and basil

Cut chicken into 1-in. cubes; brown in 1 tablespoon oil in a large skillet. Transfer to a slow cooker. In the same skillet, saute the mushrooms, onion, zucchini, green pepper and garlic in remaining oil until crisp-tender.

Place in slow cooker. Add tomatoes, tomato paste, water and seasonings. Cover and cook on low for 4 hours or until the vegetables are tender. **Yield:** 6 servings.

Stir in pasta and beans. Add enough water to cover. Bring to a boil. Reduce heat; cover and simmer for 15 minutes or until pasta is tender. Sprinkle with cheese. **Yield:** 6 servings.

Tomato Sausage Stew
pictured above

When trying out new recipes, I modified one to combine my favorite sausage with fennel and garlic.

Jeanette Jones, Muncie, Indiana

- 1/2 pound turkey Italian sausage links, casings removed
- 1 large onion, chopped
- 2 garlic cloves, minced
- 3/4 cup chopped carrots
- 1 fennel bulb, chopped
- 1/3 cup chopped celery
- 1 can (14-1/2 ounces) chicken broth
- 3 medium tomatoes, peeled, seeded and chopped
- 1 teaspoon dried basil
- 1 teaspoon dried oregano
- 1/4 teaspoon salt
- 1 cup uncooked small pasta shells
- 1 can (15 ounces) navy beans, rinsed and drained
- 1/2 cup shredded Parmesan cheese

In a Dutch oven, cook the sausage, onion and garlic over medium heat until meat is no longer pink; drain. Add the carrots, fennel and celery; cook until vegetables are softened. Stir in broth to loosen any browned bits from pan.

Add tomatoes, basil, oregano and salt. Bring to a boil. Reduce heat; cover and simmer for 10 minutes or until vegetables are tender.

Sauerbraten Stew

Our kids can't get enough of this dish. I often put this stew on the stove before doing chores so we can come inside to a hearty meal.

Joanne Recker, West Point, Nebraska

- 2 pounds boneless pork, trimmed and cut into 1-1/2-inch cubes
- 2 tablespoons vegetable oil
- 1-1/2 quarts water
- 2 cups ketchup
- 1 large onion, chopped
- 2 medium potatoes, peeled and cubed
- 3 medium carrots, cut into 1/2-inch slices
- 1 cup fresh or frozen cut green beans (1-inch pieces)
- 1 cup shredded cabbage
- 2 celery ribs, cut into 1/2-inch slices
- 1/4 to 1/2 teaspoon ground allspice
- 1/4 teaspoon pepper
- 1 cup crushed gingersnaps (about 16 cookies)

In a Dutch oven or soup kettle, brown pork in oil. Add the next 10 ingredients. Cover and simmer for 1-1/2 hours. Stir in gingersnap crumbs; simmer, uncovered, for 30 minutes or until stew is thickened and pork is tender. **Yield:** 12-14 servings (3-1/2 quarts).

Smoked Sausage Stew

I like sharing dishes like this with others. It's a down-home one-pot dinner that appeals to all.

Ella Jay Tubbs, Fort Worth, Texas

- 2 cans (11-1/2 ounces each) condensed bean and bacon soup, undiluted
- 1 can (14-1/2 ounces) diced tomatoes, undrained
- 2 cups water
- 2 medium potatoes, diced
- 1 cup sliced carrots
- 1 cup sliced celery
- 1 teaspoon chili powder

12 ounces fully cooked smoked
  sausage, thinly sliced

In a saucepan, combine soup, tomatoes and water. Add potatoes, carrots, celery, and chili powder. Cover and bring to a boil; reduce heat and simmer for 20 minutes. Add sausage; simmer 40 minutes longer. **Yield:** 6-8 servings (2 quarts).

Savory Pork Stew

Dried herbs and fresh veggies combine in this stew. It's one of my favorites.

Jodi Bierschenk, Newhall, Iowa

  1 pound lean boneless pork, cut
    into 1-inch cubes
  1 cup chopped onion
  1 teaspoon dried basil
1/2 teaspoon dried rosemary
1/4 teaspoon pepper
1/2 cup water
  1 can (16 ounces) tomato sauce
  2 cups sliced carrots
  1 green pepper, chopped
1/2 pound fresh mushrooms, sliced

Place pork in a Dutch oven that has been sprayed with nonstick cooking spray. Cook over medium heat until browned. Add onion, seasonings, water and tomato sauce; bring to a boil.

Reduce heat; cover and simmer 1 hour or until meat is tender. Stir in remaining ingredients. Cover and simmer until the vegetables are tender, about 30 minutes. **Yield:** 5 servings.

Turkey Dumpling Stew

pictured at right

My mom made this stew when I was young, and it was always a hit.

Becky Mohr, Appleton, Wisconsin

  4 bacon strips, diced
1-1/2 pounds turkey tenderloin, cut
    into 1-inch pieces
  4 medium carrots, cut into 1-inch
    pieces

  2 cups water, *divided*
  1 can (14-1/2 ounces) chicken broth
  2 small onions, quartered
  2 celery ribs, cut into 1/2-inch pieces
1/4 teaspoon dried rosemary, crushed
  1 bay leaf
  3 tablespoons all-purpose flour
1/2 teaspoon salt
1/8 to 1/4 teaspoon pepper
  1 cup biscuit/baking mix
1/3 cup plus 1 tablespoon milk

In a Dutch oven or large saucepan, cook the bacon over medium heat until crisp. Remove to paper towels; drain, reserving 2 teaspoons drippings. Cook turkey in the drippings until no longer pink.

Add the carrots, 1-3/4 cups of water, broth, onions, celery, rosemary and bay leaf. Bring to a boil. Reduce heat; cover and simmer for 20-30 minutes or until vegetables are tender.

Combine flour and remaining water until smooth; stir into turkey mixture. Bring to a boil; cook and stir for 2 minutes or until thickened. Discard bay leaf. Stir in the salt, pepper and reserved bacon.

In a bowl, combine biscuit mix and milk. Drop batter in six mounds onto simmering stew. Cover and simmer for 15 minutes or until a toothpick inserted in a dumpling comes out clean (do not lift the cover while simmering). **Yield:** 6 servings.

Oven Beef Stew

pictured below

A thick flavorful sauce makes this hearty dish one that will be requested time and again.

Debbie Patton, Westchester, Illinois

- 2 pounds boneless beef round roast, cut into 1-1/2-inch cubes
- 2 medium potatoes, peeled and cut into 1/2-inch cubes
- 2 medium onions, cut into eighths
- 3 celery ribs, cut into 1-inch pieces
- 4 medium carrots, cut into 1-inch slices
- 1 can (11-1/2 ounces) tomato juice
- 1/3 cup dry sherry or water
- 1/3 cup quick-cooking tapioca
- 1 tablespoon sugar
- 1 teaspoon salt
- 1/2 teaspoon dried basil
- 1/4 teaspoon pepper
- 2 cups fresh green beans, cut into 1-inch pieces

In a Dutch oven, combine the beef, potatoes, onions, celery and carrots; set aside. In a bowl, combine the next seven ingredients. Let stand for 15 minutes. Pour over beef mixture.

Cover and bake at 325° for 2 to 2-1/2 hours or until meat is almost tender. Add beans; cook 30 minutes longer or until beans and meat are tender. **Yield:** 8 servings.

Southwestern Pork Stew

I grew tired of preparing the same old beef stew, so this pork variety was a welcome change.

Pam Gordon, Neptune Beach, Florida

    1 pound boneless pork, trimmed and
       cut into 3/4-inch cubes
1-1/2 teaspoons ground cumin
  1/4 teaspoon salt
  1/8 teaspoon cayenne pepper
    2 teaspoons vegetable oil
    2 medium green peppers, cut
       into 3/4-inch pieces
    2 small onions, quartered
    2 garlic cloves, minced
    2 medium potatoes, peeled and cubed
    1 can (14-1/2 ounces) Mexican-style
       stewed tomatoes
1-1/2 cups V8 juice
  1/2 cup water
    1 package (10 ounces) frozen whole
       kernel corn

In a large resealable plastic bag, combine pork, cumin, salt and cayenne; shake to coat evenly. In a Dutch oven or soup kettle over medium heat, brown pork in oil; drain.

Add green peppers, onions and garlic; saute for 3 minutes. Add potatoes, tomatoes, V8 and water; mix well. Bring to a boil. Reduce heat; cover and simmer for 45 minutes.

Add corn; cover and simmer for 10-15 minutes or until vegetables and pork are tender. **Yield:** 6-8 servings (2 quarts).

Veggie Black Bean Stew

pictured above right

The flavors in this stew work so well together that you'll never miss the meat. Cilantro, honey and garlic are an ideal match for the black beans and fresh vegetables.

Marilyn Waters, Outing, Minnesota

    2 large onions, chopped
  1/2 cup *each* chopped celery, carrot and
       sweet red pepper

    2 tablespoons minced garlic
  1/4 cup dry sherry *or* chicken broth
    1 tablespoon olive oil
    3 cans (15 ounces *each*) black beans,
       rinsed and drained
    1 can (14-1/2 ounces) chicken broth
    1 can (14-1/2 ounces) diced tomatoes,
       undrained
    2 tablespoons tomato paste
    2 tablespoons honey
    4 teaspoons chili powder
    2 teaspoons ground cumin
  1/2 teaspoon dried oregano
  1/4 cup minced fresh cilantro
    5 tablespoons shredded Monterey
       Jack cheese
    5 tablespoons sour cream
    2 tablespoons chopped green onion

In a Dutch oven or large saucepan, saute the onions, celery, carrot, red pepper and garlic in sherry or broth and oil until tender. Add the next eight ingredients.

Bring to a boil. Reduce heat; cover and simmer for 40 minutes. Stir in cilantro; simmer 5-15 minutes longer or until stew is thickened. Garnish with cheese, sour cream and green onion. **Yield:** 5 servings.

5-qt. slow cooker. Add water, spaghetti sauce, beans, summer squash, carrots, red pepper and onion; mix well. Cover and cook on low for 7-9 hours or until vegetables are tender.

Stir in the pasta, peas, sugar, salt and pepper; mix well. Cover and cook on high for 15-20 minutes or until the pasta is tender. **Yield:** 8 servings.

Sweet Potato Pork Stew

I'm an avid recipe collector and have fun trying new dishes. Fortunately, my family doesn't mind experimenting with new tastes. Everyone loves the blend of flavors in this stew.

Susan Klein, Waukesha, Wisconsin

    2 pounds boneless pork, trimmed and cut into 1-inch cubes
    3 tablespoons Dijon mustard
 1/2 cup all-purpose flour
    3 tablespoons brown sugar
    2 garlic cloves, minced
    3 tablespoons vegetable oil
2-1/3 cups chicken broth
    4 to 5 small onions, quartered
    2 medium sweet potatoes, peeled and cubed
 1/2 teaspoon salt
 1/4 teaspoon pepper
 1/4 cup minced fresh parsley

Toss pork and mustard. In a large resealable plastic bag, combine flour and brown sugar; add pork and shake to coat.

In a large skillet over medium-high heat, brown pork and garlic in oil. Add broth; bring to a boil. Scrape bottom of skillet to loosen any browned bits. Reduce the heat; cover and simmer for 30 minutes.

Add onions, sweet potatoes, salt and pepper; cover and simmer 30 minutes more or until the pork and potatoes are tender. Stir in parsley. **Yield:** 6-8 servings (2 quarts).

Sausage Pasta Stew

pictured above

I rely on my slow cooker to prepare this chili-like specialty. It's packed with turkey sausage, pasta and vegetables. My gang gobbles it up without realizing they're eating healthy.

Sara Bowen, Upland, California

    1 pound turkey Italian sausage links, casings removed
    4 cups water
    1 jar (26 ounces) meatless spaghetti sauce
    1 can (16 ounces) kidney beans, rinsed and drained
    1 medium yellow summer squash, halved lengthwise and cut into 1-inch pieces
    2 medium carrots, cut into 1/4-inch slices
    1 medium sweet red *or* green pepper, diced
 1/3 cup chopped onion
1-1/2 cups uncooked spiral pasta
    1 cup frozen peas
    1 teaspoon sugar
 1/2 teaspoon salt
 1/4 teaspoon pepper

In a nonstick skillet, cook sausage over medium heat until no longer pink; drain and place in a

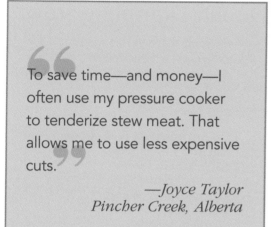

Corn and Ham Stew

When I was a little girl, my grandmother would use home-grown vegetables to prepare this old-fashioned stew. I was thrilled when she passed the family recipe on to me.

Lili Lanz, Coral Gables, Florida

- 1 medium onion, chopped
- 1 medium green pepper, chopped
- 1 cup cubed fully cooked ham
- 3 garlic cloves, minced
- 3 tablespoons vegetable oil
- 1/2 pound bulk pork sausage
- 2-1/2 cups water
- 1 can (8 ounces) tomato sauce
- 2 cups fresh, canned *or* frozen corn
- 1 cup cubed peeled butternut squash
- 1 cup cubed peeled potatoes
- 1 bay leaf
- 1/8 teaspoon pepper

In a 3-qt. saucepan, saute the onion, green pepper, ham and garlic in oil until vegetables are tender.

In a skillet, cook sausage over medium heat until no longer pink; drain and add to ham mixture. Add remaining ingredients; bring to a boil.

Reduce heat; cover and simmer for 30 minutes or until potatoes and squash are tender. Remove the bay leaf before serving. **Yield:** 4 servings.

Kielbasa Cabbage Stew
pictured below

If you like German potato salad, you'll love this sweet-and-sour stew. Caraway seeds, smoky kielbasa, tender potatoes and shredded cabbage make it a filling change of pace.

Valrie Burrows, Shelby, Michigan

- 1/2 pound smoked turkey kielbasa *or* Polish sausage, sliced
- 1 pound potatoes, peeled and cubed
- 2 cups shredded cabbage
- 1 large onion, chopped
- 1 can (14-1/2 ounces) chicken broth
- 3/4 cup water, *divided*
- 2 tablespoons sugar
- 1 teaspoon caraway seeds
- 1/4 teaspoon pepper
- 1 can (16 ounces) kidney beans, rinsed and drained
- 3 tablespoons cider vinegar
- 2 tablespoons all-purpose flour

In a large saucepan or nonstick skillet, brown sausage over medium heat. Add the potatoes, cabbage, onion, broth, 1/2 cup water, sugar, caraway and pepper. Bring to a boil. Reduce heat; cover and simmer for 15-18 minutes or until potatoes are tender, stirring occasionally.

Add beans and vinegar; cover and simmer 5-10 minutes longer. Combine flour and remaining water until smooth; stir into stew. Bring to a boil; cook and stir for 2 minutes or until thickened. **Yield:** 4 servings.

Southwest Beef Stew

pictured below

Add your family's favorite picante sauce to ground beef, black beans and corn, then watch how quickly they empty their bowls. This mixture freezes well, so I keep a batch on hand for quick nutritious meals.

Janet Brannan, Sidney, Montana

      2 pounds ground beef
1-1/2 cups chopped onions
      1 can (28 ounces) diced tomatoes, undrained
      1 package (16 ounces) frozen corn, thawed
      1 can (15 ounces) black beans, rinsed and drained
      1 cup picante sauce
   3/4 cup water
      1 teaspoon ground cumin
   3/4 teaspoon salt
   1/2 teaspoon garlic powder
   1/2 teaspoon pepper
   1/2 cup shredded cheddar cheese

In a Dutch oven, cook beef and onions over medium heat until meat is no longer pink; drain. Stir in the tomatoes, corn, beans, picante sauce, water, cumin, salt, garlic powder and pepper.

Bring to a boil. Reduce heat; cover and simmer for 15 minutes or until corn is tender. Garnish with cheese. **Yield:** 8 servings.

Dublin Dumpling Stew

I've come a long way with my cooking since getting married over 40 years ago...and the credit goes to my older sister. Through the years, she's passed on many delicious recipes like this.

Annette Fisher, Marion, Ohio

      1 pound boneless pork, trimmed and cut into 1-inch cubes
      2 tablespoons butter
   1/2 cup chopped onion
   1/2 cup chopped celery
      1 garlic clove, minced
      5 medium carrots
      3 cups water
      1 tablespoon beef bouillon granules
      1 teaspoon salt
   1/4 cup all-purpose flour
   1/2 cup cold water
      1 package (10 ounces) frozen mixed vegetables
DUMPLINGS:
1-1/2 cups all-purpose flour
      1 tablespoon sugar
      2 teaspoons baking powder
      1 teaspoon caraway seed
   1/2 teaspoon salt
   1/4 teaspoon ground mustard
      1 egg
   2/3 cup milk
      2 tablespoons vegetable oil

In a Dutch oven or soup kettle over high heat, brown pork in butter. Add onion, celery and garlic; reduce heat to medium and cook until vegetables are tender. Cut carrots into 2-in. pieces, then quarter lengthwise; add to pork mixture. Add water, bouillon and salt.

Reduce heat; cover and simmer for 45 minutes or until the meat and vegetables are tender. Combine flour and cold water until smooth; stir into stew. Bring to a boil; boil and stir for 2 minutes. Add the mixed vegetables; reduce heat to low.

In a bowl, combine the first six dumpling ingredients. Beat the egg, milk and oil; add to the dry ingredients all at once. Mix just until moistened.

Drop by tablespoonfuls into bubbling stew. Cover tightly and simmer for 25 minutes or until the dumplings are cooked through. **Yield:** 6-8 servings (2-1/2 quarts).

Cover and simmer until the vegetables are tender, about 30 minutes. If desired, thicken with cornstarch dissolved in water. **Yield:** about 8-10 servings (3-1/2 quarts).

Vegetable Stew

pictured above

This particular stew is so colorful you can bring the pot right to the table and serve it.

Kenneth Wrigley, Langley, British Columbia

1-1/2 pounds lean boneless lamb *or* pork, cut into 1-inch cubes
  2 tablespoons vegetable oil
  1 medium onion, chopped
  2 medium potatoes, peeled and cubed
  1 medium leek, sliced
  6 cups beef broth
  2 tablespoons tomato paste
  1 teaspoon salt
1/2 teaspoon dried thyme
1/4 teaspoon pepper
  4 cups chopped cabbage
  2 to 3 cups cauliflower florets
  3 carrots, sliced
  1 celery rib, sliced
  1 package (10 ounces) frozen green beans, thawed
Chopped fresh parsley
Cornstarch and water, optional

In a Dutch oven, brown meat in oil over medium-high. Add onion and cook until tender; drain. Add the next seven ingredients. Cover and simmer until the meat is tender, about 1 hour. Add cabbage, cauliflower, carrots, celery, beans and parsley.

Bologna and Sauerkraut Stew

This old-fashioned stew conveniently bakes in the oven, so I can put it together and forget about it.

Gladie Delaney, West Allis, Wisconsin

1 large onion, chopped
1 garlic clove, minced
1 tablespoon vegetable oil
1 can (14-1/2 ounces) diced tomatoes, undrained
1 can (14 ounces) sauerkraut, undrained
6 small potatoes, peeled and halved
1 teaspoon caraway seed
1 teaspoon sugar, optional
1 pound fully cooked ring bologna

In a skillet, saute onion and garlic in oil until tender. Transfer to a 2-1/2-qt. baking dish. Add tomatoes, sauerkraut, potatoes, caraway and sugar if desired; mix gently.

Cover and bake at 350° for 30 minutes. Cut bologna into 1-in. chunks; arrange over vegetables. Cover and bake 20 minutes longer or until potatoes are tender. **Yield:** 6-8 servings (2 quarts).

> 66 Since I like a thick stew, just before serving I add instant potato flakes (about 1/2 cup at a time) until the gravy's the right consistency for my taste. 99
>
> —*Lillian Child Omaha, Nebraska*

Microwave Meatball Stew

pictured above

This fast-to-fix dish is a sure-to-please favorite at my house!

Clara Goddard, Orillia, Ontario

    1 egg, beaten
1/2 cup dry bread crumbs
1/2 cup finely chopped onion
    2 tablespoons dry onion soup mix
    1 pound ground beef
    1 can (16 ounces) whole potatoes,
        drained and quartered
1-1/4 cups sliced frozen carrots

1-1/4 cups frozen peas
    1 can (10-3/4 ounces) condensed
        cream of mushroom soup, undiluted
    1 can (10-1/2 ounces) condensed
        beef broth, undiluted
1/2 teaspoon dried savory
1/4 teaspoon dried thyme
    2 tablespoons cornstarch
    2 tablespoons water
1/4 teaspoon browning sauce, optional

Combine egg, crumbs, onion and soup mix; crumble beef over mixture and mix well. Shape into 1-1/2-in. balls. Place in a microwave-safe baking dish. Cover and microwave on high for 5 minutes. Turn meatballs and microwave 5 minutes more or until no longer pink; drain.

Combine the next seven ingredients; spoon over meatballs and stir once. Combine corn-starch, water and browning sauce; stir into the stew. Microwave on high for 2 minutes or until thickened and bubbly. **Yield:** 4-6 servings.

Southwestern Beef Stew

This hearty stew is oh-so-tasty, with a good variety of vegetables and a spicy seasoning blend. My husband and I enjoy it often. It's the perfect way to warm up on a cool evening. Sometimes I add chopped green chilies for a little more heat.

Betty Jean Howard, Prineville, Oregon

1-1/2 pounds boneless beef round steak, cut into 1/2-inch cubes
  1 can (14-1/2 ounces) beef broth
  1 cup cubed peeled potatoes
  1 cup sliced carrots
  1 cup chopped onion
1/4 cup chopped sweet red pepper
  1 jalapeno pepper, seeded and chopped
  1 garlic clove, minced
1-1/2 teaspoons chili powder
1/2 teaspoon salt
  1 can (14-1/2 ounces) diced tomatoes, undrained
  2 tablespoons all-purpose flour
  2 tablespoons water
  2 tablespoons minced fresh cilantro

In a Dutch oven coated with nonstick cooking spray, brown meat on all sides over medium-high heat. Add the broth, potatoes, carrots, onion, red pepper, jalapeno, garlic, chili powder and salt. Bring to a boil.

Reduce heat; cover and simmer for 30 minutes or until potatoes and carrots are tender. Add tomatoes; cover and cook 1 hour longer or until meat is tender.

Combine flour and water until smooth; stir into pot. Stir in cilantro. Bring to a boil; cook and stir for 2 minutes or until thickened. **Yield:** 6 servings.

Editor's Note: When cutting or seeding hot peppers, use plastic gloves to protect your hands. Avoid touching your face.

Green Chili Pork Stew

pictured below

Now that we are empty nesters, my husband knows that I'm going to spring at least one new recipe on him each week. He's always brave!

Pat Henderson, Deer Park, Texas

  2 pounds lean boneless pork, cut into 1-1/2-inch cubes
  1 tablespoon vegetable oil
  4 cups chicken broth, *divided*
  3 cans (11 ounces *each*) whole kernel corn, drained
  2 celery ribs, diced
  2 medium potatoes, peeled and diced
  2 medium tomatoes, diced
  3 cans (4 ounces *each*) chopped green chilies
  2 teaspoons ground cumin
  1 teaspoon dried oregano
  1 teaspoon salt
  3 tablespoons all-purpose flour
Corn bread *or* warmed flour tortillas, optional

In a 5-qt. Dutch oven over medium-high heat, brown pork in oil. Add 3-1/2 cups broth, corn, celery, potatoes, tomatoes, chilies, cumin, oregano and salt; bring to a boil. Reduce heat; cover and simmer for 1 hour or until meat and vegetables are tender.

Combine flour and remaining broth; stir into stew. Bring to a boil; cook, stirring constantly, until thickened. Serve with corn bread or tortillas if desired. **Yield:** 8 servings.

Sausage Bean Stew

pictured below

One of the reasons I like quick dinners like this is our two sons. With boys, I am constantly on the go! With this recipe, I can still fix a good meal for my family.

Cheryl Nagy, Newark, Ohio

    4 cups chicken broth
    3 cans (16 ounces *each*) beans (kidney,
       butter, pinto *and/or* black-eyed peas,
       etc.), rinsed and drained
    3 medium carrots, diced
    3 celery ribs, diced
    1 pound smoked sausage, cut
       into 1/2-inch slices
    1 large onion, chopped
  1/2 cup medium pearl barley
  1/2 cup dried lentils, rinsed
    1 teaspoon hot pepper sauce
    1 cup chopped fresh spinach

In a 4-qt. Dutch oven, place the broth, beans, carrots, celery, sausage, onion, barley, lentils and hot pepper sauce.

Cover and cook over medium heat for 45-60 minutes or until the barley and lentils are tender. Stir in spinach and heat through. **Yield:** 6-8 servings.

Italian Hunters Stew

pictured at right

This is an all-time favorite because it combines meat and vegetables with pasta. My husband is a hunter besides, so on occasion I'll use elk or venison in place of the beef.

Ann Shorey, Sutherlin, Oregon

    2 pounds beef stew meat, cut
       into 1-1/2-inch cubes
    1 tablespoon all-purpose flour
    3 tablespoons vegetable oil
    2 garlic cloves, minced
    3 large onions, quartered
    1 cup beef broth
    2 tablespoons seasoned salt
    1 teaspoon chili powder
    1 teaspoon dried oregano
    1 teaspoon dried rosemary
    2 cans (14-1/2 ounces *each*) Italian
       stewed tomatoes
    1 can (6 ounces) tomato paste
  1/2 cup minced fresh parsley
    3 medium carrots, cut into 1-inch pieces
    8 ounces mostaccioli *or* penne pasta,
       cooked and drained
  1/3 cup shredded Parmesan cheese

Toss meat with flour; brown on all sides in oil in a 5-qt. Dutch oven. Add garlic and onions; saute until tender. Stir in broth, seasoned salt, chili powder, oregano and rosemary. Cover and simmer for 1-1/2 hours.

Add tomatoes, tomato paste, parsley and carrots. Cover and simmer for 1 hour or until meat and carrots are tender. Stir in pasta; heat through. Sprinkle with cheese. **Yield:** 8-10 servings.

Woodcutter's Stew

I found this recipe in one of my many cookbooks and modified it to suit my family's tastes. It's the one they regularly ask me to prepare.

Patricia Gunning, Highland, Illinois

    1 can (14-1/2 ounces) stewed
       tomatoes
    2 celery ribs, sliced
  1/2 chopped onion
    1 tablespoon butter

5 cups water
1 cup dried lentils, rinsed
2 medium potatoes, cubed
2 medium carrots, sliced
5 teaspoons chicken bouillon granules
1/2 teaspoon dried thyme
1/2 teaspoon pepper
1 bay leaf
8 ounces fully cooked Polish sausage

In a blender or food processor, process the tomatoes until smooth; set aside. In a large saucepan, saute celery and onion in butter until tender. Add the next eight ingredients; cover and bring to a boil. Reduce heat; simmer for 35-40 minutes or until lentils are tender.

Meanwhile, cut sausage into 1/2-in. slices; cut each slice into quarters. In a skillet over medium heat, brown sausage; drain. Add to lentil mixture with reserved tomatoes; heat through. Remove bay leaf. **Yield:** 6-8 servings (2-1/4 quarts).

Artichoke Beef Stew
pictured at right

This stew recipe was given to me by a dear friend. She served it with dumplings, but my husband prefers noodles.

Janell Schmidt, Athelstane, Wisconsin

1/3 cup all-purpose flour
1 teaspoon salt
1/2 teaspoon pepper
2-1/2 pounds lean beef stew meat, cut into 1-inch cubes
3 tablespoons vegetable oil
1 can (10-1/2 ounces) condensed beef consomme, undiluted
2 medium onions, halved and sliced
1 cup red wine *or* beef broth
1 garlic clove, minced
1/2 teaspoon dill weed
2 jars (6-1/2 ounces *each*) marinated artichoke hearts, drained and chopped
20 small fresh mushrooms, halved
Hot cooked noodles

In a shallow bowl or large resealable plastic bag, combine the flour, salt and pepper. Add the beef and toss to coat. In a skillet, brown beef in oil.

Transfer to a slow cooker with a slotted spoon. Gradually add consomme to the skillet. Bring to a boil; stir to loosen browned bits from pan. Stir in the onions, wine or broth, garlic and dill. Pour over beef.

Cover and cook on low for 7-8 hours or until the meat is nearly tender. Stir in the artichokes and mushrooms. Cook 30 minutes longer or until heated through. Serve over noodles. **Yield:** 6-8 servings.

savory STEWS

utes. Stir in the carrots, celery, water, bay leaves, bouillon, thyme and remaining pepper. Bring to a boil. Reduce the heat; cover and simmer for 1-1/4 hours.

Stir in pumpkin. Return to a boil. Reduce heat; cover and simmer for 20-25 minutes or until meat and pumpkin are tender. Discard bay leaves. **Yield:** 9 servings.

Country-Style Stew

I created this recipe when my husband and I were married over 20 years ago. As a new bride, I was delighted with the delicious results. This is still our favorite stew.

LaDonna Reed, Ponca City, Oklahoma

>   2 pounds ground beef
>   1 can (32 ounces) tomato juice
>   1 quart water
>   4 medium carrots, sliced
>   1 large onion, diced
>   2 cups frozen sliced okra
> 1-1/2 cups shredded cabbage
> 1-1/2 cups diced celery
>   1 cup frozen green beans
>   1 cup frozen peas
>   2 cans (14-1/2 ounces *each*) diced tomatoes, undrained
>   1 can (16 ounces) great northern beans, rinsed and drained
>   1 can (15-1/2 ounces) black-eyed peas, rinsed and drained
>   1 can (15-1/4 ounces) lima beans, rinsed and drained
>   1 can (11 ounces) Mexican-style corn
>   5 beef bouillon cubes
>   1 teaspoon seasoned salt
> 1/2 teaspoon dried oregano
> 1/2 teaspoon garlic powder
> 1/2 teaspoon pepper
> 1/4 teaspoon celery salt

In a Dutch oven or soup kettle, cook beef over medium heat until no longer pink; drain. Add remaining ingredients; bring to a boil.

Reduce the heat; cover and simmer for 2 hours or until the vegetables are tender. **Yield:** 18-22 servings (5-1/2 quarts).

Pumpkin Stew

pictured above

After our kids carve their Halloween pumpkins, I use the discarded pieces in this savory stew. My family eagerly looks forward to it every year.

Christine Bauer, Durand, Wisconsin

> 1/2 cup all-purpose flour
> 1/2 teaspoon salt
> 1/2 teaspoon pepper, *divided*
>   2 pounds beef stew meat, cut into 1-inch cubes
>   2 tablespoons vegetable oil
>   2 tablespoons butter
>   1 large onion, chopped
>   2 to 3 garlic cloves, minced
>   3 medium carrots, thinly sliced
>   2 celery ribs, thinly sliced
>   4 cups water
>   1 to 2 bay leaves
>   1 to 2 teaspoons beef bouillon granules
>   1 to 1-1/2 teaspoons dried thyme
>   3 cups cubed peeled pumpkin

In a large resealable plastic bag, combine the flour, salt and 1/4 teaspoon pepper. Add meat, a few pieces at a time, and shake to coat.

In a Dutch oven, brown meat in oil and butter. Add onion and garlic; cook and stir for 2-3 min-

Pioneer Stew
pictured below

I had no choice but to learn to cook some years ago while my wife recuperated from surgery. But I found I really enjoyed trying different recipes and adapting them to my own taste—that's how my now-famous venison stew recipe came to be!

Gene Pitts, Wilsonville, Alabama

- 2 tablespoons vegetable oil
- 2 pounds venison stew meat
- 3 large onions, chopped
- 2 garlic cloves, minced
- 1 tablespoon Worcestershire sauce
- 1 bay leaf
- 1 teaspoon dried oregano
- 1 tablespoon salt
- 1 teaspoon pepper
- 3 cups water
- 7 medium potatoes, peeled and quartered
- 1 pound carrots, cut into 1-inch pieces
- 1/4 cup all-purpose flour
- 1/4 cup cold water
- Browning sauce, optional

Heat oil in a Dutch oven. Brown meat on all sides. Add the onions, garlic, Worcestershire sauce, bay leaf, oregano, salt, pepper and water.

Cover and simmer 1-1/2 to 2 hours or until meat is tender. Add potatoes and carrots. Con-tinue to cook until vegetables are tender, about 30-45 minutes. Mix flour and cold water; stir into stew.

Cook and stir until thickened and bubbly. Add browning sauce if desired. Remove bay leaf. **Yield:** 8-10 servings.

Hot Pot Stew

This full-bodied stew is ideal for chilly rainy days. So I often try—unsuccessfully—to sneak some into the freezer before my family can eat it all! I hope you enjoy it, too.

Sandra Allen, Leadville, Colorado

- 1 cup cubed lean boneless pork (1/2-inch pieces)
- 1 cup cubed fully cooked ham
- 1 cup coarsely chopped green pepper
- 1/2 cup chopped onion
- 1/2 cup chopped celery
- 1 garlic clove, minced
- 3 cups cubed red potatoes
- 3 cups water
- 1 can (15 ounces) pinto beans, rinsed and drained
- 1 can (15-1/2 ounces) great northern beans, rinsed and drained
- 1-1/4 teaspoons sugar
- 1 teaspoon chicken bouillon granules
- 1 teaspoon beef bouillon granules
- 1/4 teaspoon ground nutmeg
- 1/4 teaspoon coarsely ground pepper
- 1 package (10 ounces) frozen chopped spinach *or* turnip greens *or* 1 can (14-1/2 ounces) spinach *or* turnip greens, drained

In a Dutch oven or soup kettle coated with non-stick cooking spray, brown pork over medium-high heat.

Add ham, green pepper, onion, celery and gar-lic. Reduce heat to medium; cook for 8-10 minutes or until vegetables are just tender, stirring occasionally.

Add the next nine ingredients. Reduce heat; cover and simmer for 20 minutes or until pota-toes are tender. Add spinach and cook until heated through. **Yield:** 8-10 servings (2-1/2 quarts).

"On the side or for dessert,
fruit soups sweeten any day."

favorite FRUIT SOUPS

Pipe two thin concentric circles 1/2 in. apart on top of each bowl of soup. Beginning with the center circle, gently pull a toothpick through both circles toward outer edge.

Wipe toothpick clean. Draw toothpick from outer edge of bowl back to center. Repeat to complete star pattern. **Yield:** 6 servings.

Succulent Strawberry Soup

This creamy fruit soup makes a perfect summertime treat for family and friends. The strawberry base with a hint of orange appeals to all palates!

Paula Pelis, Rocky Point, New York

> 2 quarts fresh strawberries, *divided*
> 1/2 cup water
> 5 tablespoons sugar
> 1 tablespoon all-purpose flour
> 1 teaspoon grated orange peel
> 1 cup heavy whipping cream
> Fresh mint and additional strawberries, optional

Starry Fruit Soup

pictured above

If you want to make a soup that your children will love, try this cool and refreshing summer blend. The impressive star design is simple to create with sweetened sour cream.

Edie DeSpain, Logan, Utah

> 1 can (15 ounces) sliced pears, undrained
> 1 package (10 ounces) frozen sweetened raspberries, thawed
> 1 can (6 ounces) frozen orange juice concentrate, thawed
> 2 medium ripe bananas, cut into chunks
> 1/4 cup lemon juice
> 1 to 2 teaspoons grated orange peel
> 1/8 to 1/4 teaspoon ground coriander, optional
> 1/2 cup sour cream
> 2 tablespoons confectioners' sugar

In a blender, combine the first seven ingredients; cover and process until smooth. Strain to remove seeds if desired. Chill until serving.

Combine sour cream and sugar until smooth; place in a heavy-duty resealable plastic bag. Cut a small hole in a corner of bag.

Sweet Facts on Fruit Soups

Fruit soups are refreshingly delicious and a snap to prepare. There are two varieties. One version requires precooking, then chilling. The other is simply whirred in a blender or food processor. Both can be prepared in advance and easily modified.

No matter what ingredients you choose, the perfect blend should be a balance of sweet and tart. Here are a few other souped-up suggestions:

- Fruit soups benefit from being chilled overnight. You might have to add more seasoning after the soup sits.
- Chilled soups should be almost too thick to pour.

Mash half of the strawberries with a potato masher or fork; set aside. In a blender, combine the remaining strawberries, water, sugar, flour and orange peel; process until smooth.

Pour into a 2-qt. saucepan. Bring to a boil over medium heat; boil for 2 minutes, stirring constantly. Add mashed strawberries. Reduce heat; simmer, uncovered, for 10 minutes, stirring constantly.

Chill for at least 1 hour. Stir in cream. Cover and chill overnight. Garnish with mint and strawberries if desired. **Yield:** 4 servings.

Pineapple Peach Soup

I like to take this one-of-a-kind soup along to potlucks and other get-togethers. It is usually different than what other people bring, and everyone raves about the flavors.

Teresa Lynn, Kerrville, Texas

   6 medium fresh peaches, peeled and
     sliced
   1 can (8 ounces) crushed unsweetened
     pineapple, undrained
1/4 cup white grape juice
1/4 cup lemon juice
   2 tablespoons honey
3/4 teaspoon ground cinnamon
1/4 teaspoon ground nutmeg
   1 medium cantaloupe, peeled, seeded
     and cubed
   1 cup orange juice
Fresh strawberries and whipped cream,
optional

In a 3-qt. saucepan, combine peaches, pineapple, grape juice, lemon juice, honey, cinnamon and nutmeg; bring to a boil over medium heat. Reduce heat and simmer, uncovered, for 10 minutes.

Remove from the heat; cool to room temperature. Add three-fourths of the cantaloupe and the orange juice; puree in batches in a blender.

Pour into a large bowl. Add remaining cantaloupe. Cover and refrigerate for at least 3 hours. Garnish with strawberries and whipped cream if desired. **Yield:** 8-10 servings (2-1/4 quarts).

Chilled Blueberry Soup
pictured below

My guests are always delighted when I serve this fruit soup on a warm summer evening. Compliments abound for this sweet and smooth meal starter.

Sue Tucker, Brush Prairie, Washington

   4 cups fresh *or* frozen blueberries
   3 cups water
2/3 cup sugar
1/4 teaspoon ground allspice
   1 carton (16 ounces) plain yogurt
Sour cream *or* additional yogurt, optional

In a large saucepan, combine the blueberries, water, sugar and allspice. Bring to a boil, stirring occasionally. Remove from the heat.

In batches, process blueberry mixture in a blender for 1-2 minutes or until pureed. Strain through a sieve; discard seeds. Cool completely.

In batches, process blueberry mixture and yogurt until smooth. Cover and refrigerate until chilled. Garnish servings with sour cream or yogurt if desired. **Yield:** 6 servings.

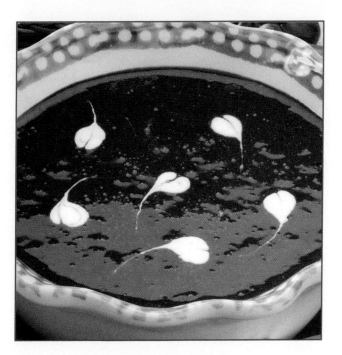

favorite FRUIT SOUPS

Chilled Berry Soup

pictured above

I sampled a cool strawberry soup while visiting Walt Disney World. I enjoyed it so much that the restaurant gave me the recipe, but I eventually found this combination, which I like even better. The ginger ale adds a special zing.

Lisa Watson, Sparta, Michigan

    1 **quart fresh strawberries, hulled**
1/3 **cup ginger ale**
1/4 **cup milk**

1/3 **cup sugar**
    1 **tablespoon lemon juice**
    1 **teaspoon vanilla extract**
    1 **cup (8 ounces) sour cream**

Place strawberries in a food processor or blender; cover and process until smooth. Add ginger ale, milk, sugar, lemon juice and vanilla; cover and process until blended.

Pour into a bowl; whisk in sour cream until smooth. Cover and refrigerate until thoroughly chilled, about 2 hours. **Yield:** 4 servings.

Taste of Home's BIG BOOK *of* SOUP

Cherry Dumpling Soup

My husband grew up with this dish, but his mother never wrote down the recipe. So when we got married, I had to create my own. Luckily, my husband deemed my version a success!

Sharon Skildum, Maple Grove, Minnesota

- 1 can (15 ounces) dark sweet cherries
- 2 cups water
- 1/3 cup plus 1 teaspoon sugar, *divided*
- 1/2 teaspoon ground cinnamon
- 1/2 cup all-purpose flour
- 1 teaspoon baking powder
- 1/4 cup milk
- 1 tablespoon vegetable oil
- 1 tablespoon cornstarch
- 1 tablespoon cold water

Drain cherries, reserving juice; set cherries aside. In a 2-qt. saucepan, combine juice, water, 1/3 cup sugar and cinnamon; bring to a boil over medium heat, stirring occasionally.

For dumplings, combine flour, baking powder and remaining sugar in a small bowl. Add milk and oil, stirring just until moistened. Drop by teaspoonfuls into boiling soup. Reduce heat; cover and simmer for 10 minutes.

Dissolve cornstarch in cold water; stir into soup. Add cherries. Bring to a boil; boil for 1-2 minutes. Reduce heat; cover and simmer for 3-4 minutes. **Yield:** 4-6 servings.

Ruby-Red Rhubarb Soup

Even folks who don't care for rhubarb can't resist the sweet, tangy taste of this soup. This dish is an attractive addition to any table.

Alice Hill, Lindon, Colorado

- 4 cups sliced fresh *or* frozen rhubarb
- 1 quart plus 1 tablespoon water, *divided*
- 2/3 cup sugar
- 1 tablespoon cornstarch
- 1/2 teaspoon red food coloring, optional
- 1 egg yolk, beaten
- 1/2 cup heavy whipping cream

In a 2-qt. saucepan, combine rhubarb, 1 qt. of water and sugar; bring to a boil. Reduce heat; cover and simmer for 20 minutes or until rhubarb is tender. Cool for 15 minutes.

Place in a blender; process until smooth. Return to pan. Dissolve cornstarch in remaining water; stir into rhubarb mixture. Bring to a boil; boil for 2 minutes, stirring constantly. Add food coloring if desired; mix well.

Add a small amount of soup to egg yolk, stirring constantly; return to pan. Chill. Just before serving, beat cream until very soft peaks form; fold into soup. **Yield:** 6 servings.

Hot Fruit Soup

Some fruit soups call for soaking dried fruit overnight. But my fast version conveniently uses canned fruits.

Rose Kammerling, Sun City, Arizona

- 1 can (21 ounces) cherry pie filling
- 1 can (20 ounces) pineapple tidbits, drained
- 1 can (15-1/4 ounces) apricot halves, drained and halved
- 1 can (15 ounces) sliced peaches, drained
- 1 can (15 ounces) sliced pears, drained
- 1 can (11 ounces) mandarin oranges, drained
- 1 cup golden raisins

In a large bowl, combine all ingredients; mix well. Pour into an ungreased 2-1/2-qt. baking dish. Bake, uncovered, at 350° for 25-30 minutes or until bubbly. **Yield:** 16-18 servings.

> If you like my Hot Fruit Soup, just wait until you try it as a side dish to ham. It gets raves at my table whenever I serve it!
>
> —*Rose Kammerling*
> *Sun City, Arizona*

Fresh Fruit Soup

pictured below

On a hot summer day, nothing can top the flavor of the season's finest fruits. This recipe is both fast and festive.

Beulah Goodenough, Belleville, New Jersey

> 2 cups water
> 2 tablespoons quick-cooking tapioca
> 1 can (6 ounces) frozen orange juice concentrate, thawed
> 1 to 2 tablespoons sugar
> 1 tablespoon honey
> 1/8 teaspoon almond extract
>
> Pinch salt
> 2-1/2 cups fresh fruit (blueberries, raspberries, sliced strawberries, halved grapes, etc.)

In a 2-qt. saucepan, combine water and tapioca; let stand for 10 minutes. Bring to a boil; boil for 2 minutes, stirring constantly.

Remove from the heat; stir in orange juice concentrate, sugar, honey, extract and salt. Chill. Add fruit; chill until ready to serve. **Yield:** 4 servings.

Christmas Soup

In addition to serving it as a summertime meal, I put this traditional Mennonite soup on our Christmas lunch table along with an assortment of cold sandwiches and salads.

Marg Peters, Hanley, Saskatchewan

> 4 quarts plus 1/2 cup water, *divided*
> 3 packages (8 ounces *each*) mixed dried fruit (4 cups)
> 1 cup raisins
> 1 cinnamon stick (3 inches)
> 1-1/2 cups sugar
> 6 tablespoons cornstarch
> 1 package (3 ounces) cherry gelatin
> 1 can (16 ounces) pitted tart cherries, undrained

In a Dutch oven or soup kettle, bring 4 qts. water, dried fruit, raisins and cinnamon stick to a boil. Reduce heat; cover and simmer for 30 minutes or until fruit is tender.

Combine sugar, cornstarch and remaining water; mix well. Add to kettle. Return to a boil; boil for 2 minutes, stirring constantly.

Remove from the heat; stir in gelatin until dissolved. Add cherries. Remove cinnamon stick. Chill. **Yield:** 12 servings (3 quarts).

Rhubarb Soup

Served warm or chilled, this thick fruit soup makes an interesting first course. It is also a refreshing dessert with a dollop of ice cream.

Linda Murray, Allenstown, New Hampshire

> 4 cups diced fresh *or* frozen rhubarb
> 1 cup plus 2 tablespoons water, *divided*
> 1/2 cup sugar
> 1 cinnamon stick (2 inches)
> 1 tablespoon cornstarch
> 1 cup white grape juice *or* white wine
>
> Toasted sliced almonds, optional

In a 3-qt. saucepan, combine the rhubarb, 1 cup of water, sugar and cinnamon; bring to a boil. Reduce heat; simmer, uncovered, for 15-20 minutes or until rhubarb is tender.

Combine cornstarch and remaining water until smooth; stir into rhubarb mixture. Bring to a boil; cook and stir for 2 minutes or until thickened.

Remove from the heat and discard cinnamon stick. Stir in grape juice. Serve warm or cover and refrigerate overnight. Garnish with almonds if desired. **Yield:** 4 servings.

Chilled Cantaloupe Soup
pictured below

A friend in New York shared the recipe for this chilled melon soup that's pleasantly spiced with cinnamon. Most people are skeptical when I describe it, but after one spoonful, they're hooked. It's easy to prepare, pretty to serve and so refreshing.

Margaret McNeil, Memphis, Tennessee

>   1 medium cantaloupe, peeled, seeded
>   and cubed
>   2 cups orange juice, divided
>   1 tablespoon lime juice
> 1/4 to 1/2 teaspoon ground cinnamon
> Fresh mint, optional

Place cantaloupe and 1/2 cup orange juice in a blender or food processor; cover and process until smooth. Transfer to a large bowl; stir in lime juice, cinnamon and remaining orange juice. Cover and refrigerate for at least 1 hour. Garnish with mint if desired. **Yield:** 6 servings.

Cold Raspberry Soup
pictured above

I received this recipe 20 years ago and improved upon it. I serve my friends this delightful soup for lunch, usually with a large tomato stuffed with chicken or shrimp salad and homemade rolls.

Nola Rice, Miami, Arizona

>   4 cups fresh or frozen unsweetened
>   raspberries, thawed
> 1/4 cup red wine *or* 1/4 cup white grape
>   juice plus 1 teaspoon red wine vinegar
> 1/2 to 3/4 cup sugar
>   1 cup (8 ounces) sour cream

In a blender or food processor, combine the first three ingredients; cover and process until pureed. Strain seeds if desired.

Transfer to a bowl; whisk in sour cream until blended. Cover and refrigerate for at least 1 hour. **Yield:** 4-6 servings.

Summertime Melon Soup

pictured above

Summertime soup always elicits a sweet response, and my guests never fail to request the recipe. To make it look even better, I often serve it in cantaloupe bowls.

Valerie Black, Fairfield Bay, Arkansas

    5 cups seeded cubed watermelon
    1 pint fresh strawberries
 1/4 cup sour cream
    2 tablespoons milk
    2 tablespoons sugar
    3 to 4 cantaloupes, optional

Additional fresh strawberries, optional

Combine watermelon and strawberries. Puree in batches in a blender, adding sour cream, milk and sugar to the last batch. Pour into a 2-qt. container; mix well. Cover; chill at least 3 hours.

To serve soup in cantaloupe bowls, cut cantaloupes in half; hollow out melon and seeds, leaving about a 1/2-in. shell.

Cut a decorative edge if desired. Add soup; garnish with a strawberry if desired. **Yield:** 6-8 servings.

Raspberry Orange Soup

If you're looking for a new and interesting recipe to offer company, you'll love this one. Not only is this soup delicious and easy, it's also impressive to serve.

Patti McPheeters, Gothenburg, Alabama

    2 cans (11 ounces *each*) mandarin
      oranges
    2 cups apple juice
    1 cup orange juice
    1/2 cup grape juice
    1/2 cup lemon juice
    1/4 cup quick-cooking tapioca
    2 packages (10 ounces *each*) frozen
      raspberries in syrup
Whipped cream and ground nutmeg,
  optional

Drain oranges, reserving syrup; set oranges aside. In a 2-qt. saucepan, combine syrup, juices and tapioca; let stand for 5 minutes.

Bring to a boil over medium heat; boil for 5 minutes, stirring occasionally. Remove from heat; stir in raspberries until thawed. Add oranges.

Chill for at least 8 hours. Garnish with whipped cream and a pinch of nutmeg if desired. **Yield:** 8 servings (2 quarts).

Chilled Peach Soup

Here's a peachy way to begin a lady's luncheon or brunch. The toasted almonds on top are a nice complement to the sweet-tart flavor. A serving of this fruit soup is surprisingly filling.

Lane McLoud, Perry, Georgia

    3 cups chopped peeled fresh peaches
    1 cup (8 ounces) plain yogurt
    1 teaspoon lemon juice
    1/8 to 1/4 teaspoon almond extract
    6 tablespoons sliced almonds, toasted
Fresh mint, optional

In a blender or food processor, combine the peaches, yogurt, lemon juice and extract; cover and process until smooth. Refrigerate until chilled. Garnish with almonds and mint if desired. **Yield:** 4 servings.

Swedish Fruit Soup

Our children expect me to make this sweet soup for the holidays. It's a delicious dessert served with pound cake and whipped cream.

Dolores Bean, Baldwinsville, New York

    4 cups cranberry-apple juice
    1/4 cup quick-cooking tapioca
    1 medium lemon, thinly sliced
    6 whole cloves
    1/4 teaspoon ground nutmeg
    1 can (20 ounces) pineapple chunks,
      drained
    1 can (11 ounces) mandarin oranges,
      drained
    1 package (10 ounces) frozen
      sweetened strawberries, thawed,
      undrained
    1/3 cup maraschino cherry juice *or*
      grenadine syrup, optional
    1/8 teaspoon salt

In a 3-qt. saucepan, combine the first five ingredients; let stand for 10 minutes. Bring to a boil over medium heat. Reduce heat; cook and stir for 15 minutes or until thickened and clear.

Remove from the heat; discard lemon slices and cloves. Stir in remaining ingredients. Cover and refrigerate for at least 4 hours. **Yield:** 6-8 servings.

> " My recipe for Swedish Fruit Soup is versatile since you can also serve it as a fruit compote for brunch. "
>
> —*Dolores Bean*
> *Baldwinsville, New York*

Raspberry-Cranberry Soup

pictured below

Served hot, this beautiful tangy soup helps beat the winter blahs. On a sunny day, it's refreshing cold. I have fun serving it because people are so intrigued with the idea of a fruit soup. Even doubters scrape their bowls clean when this is on the table.

Susan Stull, Chillicothe, Missouri

> 2 cups fresh *or* frozen cranberries
> 2 cups apple juice
> 1 cup fresh *or* frozen unsweetened raspberries, thawed
> 1/2 to 1 cup sugar
> 1 tablespoon lemon juice
> 1/4 teaspoon ground cinnamon
> 2 cups half-and-half cream, *divided*
> 1 tablespoon cornstarch
> Whipped cream, additional raspberries and mint, optional

In a 3-qt. saucepan, bring cranberries and apple juice to a boil. Reduce heat and simmer, uncovered, for 10 minutes.

Press through a sieve; return to the pan. Also press the raspberries through the sieve; discard skins and seeds.

Add to cranberry mixture; bring to a boil. Add sugar, lemon juice and cinnamon; remove from the heat. Cool 4 minutes. Stir 1 cup into 1-1/2 cups cream. Return all to pan; bring to a gentle boil.

Mix cornstarch with remaining cream; stir into soup. Cook and stir for 2 minutes. Serve hot or chilled. Garnish with whipped cream, raspberries and mint if desired. **Yield:** 4 servings.

Chilled Rhubarb Soup

I like to start a variety of my summer meals with this refreshing soup.

Laurel Anderson, Pinole, California

> 3 cups sliced fresh *or* frozen rhubarb (1/2-inch pieces)
> 1-1/4 cups orange juice
> 1 pint fresh strawberries, sliced
> 3/4 cup sugar

In a 3-qt. saucepan, bring rhubarb, orange juice and strawberries to a boil. Reduce heat; cover and simmer for 10 minutes. Remove from heat; stir in sugar.

In a blender or food processor, blend half the fruit mixture at a time until smooth. Chill. **Yield:** 4 servings.

Blueberry-Orange Soup

With 100 blueberry bushes in my garden, I'm always looking for recipes calling for this sweet-tart fruit. So I was delighted when my granddaughter shared this delicious recipe with me.

Edith Richardson, Jasper, Alabama

> 1/2 cup sugar
> 2 tablespoons cornstarch
> 2-3/4 cups water
> 2 cups fresh *or* frozen blueberries
> 1 cinnamon stick (3 inches)

1 can (6 ounces) frozen orange juice
   concentrate
Sour cream, optional

In a large saucepan, combine sugar and cornstarch. Gradually stir in water until smooth. Bring to a boil over medium heat; cook and stir for 2 minutes or until thickened. Add blueberries and cinnamon stick; return to a boil.

Remove from heat. Stir in orange juice concentrate until melted. Cover and refrigerate for at least 1 hour. Discard cinnamon stick. Garnish with sour cream if desired. **Yield:** 4 servings.

Cold Fruit Soup
pictured above

This soup is a great start to a Mexican meal, but I've also served it with butter cookies at a baby shower.

Jenny Sampson, Layton, Utah

   1 can (12 ounces) frozen orange juice
      concentrate, thawed
1-1/2 cups sugar

   1 cinnamon stick (2 inches)
   6 whole cloves
1/4 cup cornstarch
   2 tablespoons lemon juice
   2 cups sliced fresh strawberries
   2 bananas, sliced
   2 cups halved green grapes

In a large saucepan, mix orange juice with water according to package directions. Remove 1/2 cup of juice; set aside.

Add the sugar, cinnamon stick and cloves to saucepan; bring to a boil. Reduce heat and simmer for 5 minutes.

Blend cornstarch and reserved orange juice to form a smooth paste; stir into pan. Bring to a boil; cook and stir until thickened, about 2 minutes more. Remove from the heat and stir in lemon juice.

Pour into a large bowl; cover and chill. Just before serving, remove the spices and stir in fruit. **Yield:** 10 servings (2-1/2 quarts).

Berry Briefly Speaking

When shopping, choose unblemished berries in dry, unstained containers. Raspberries should be medium to bright red in color and should be free of surface moisture.

Store berries uncovered in the fridge as soon as possible after picking or purchasing. Arrange unwashed berries in a shallow pan lined with paper towels. Top them with a paper towel to absorb additional moisture.

Raspberries should be consumed within 2 to 3 days of purchase. Wash just prior to use. For fullest flavor, eat them at room temperature.

“ Hot days plus **chilled** soups equal
a **perfect** combination. ”

chilled
VEGGIE SOUPS

Black Bean Zucchini Gazpacho

pictured above

My family enjoys chilled soups during the hot summer months. I came up with this spicy blend when trying to use up our garden zucchini. It's a hit with friends whenever I serve it, too.

Julie Wilson, Grand Rapids, Ohio

- 3 cans (5-1/2 ounces *each*) spicy hot V8 juice
- 1 can (15 ounces) black beans, rinsed and drained
- 1 medium onion, chopped
- 2 large tomatoes, seeded and chopped
- 2 medium zucchini, chopped
- 2 tablespoons olive oil
- 2 tablespoons white wine vinegar
- 1 garlic clove, minced
- 1/4 teaspoon salt
- 1/4 teaspoon pepper
- 1/4 teaspoon cayenne pepper

In a large bowl, combine the V8 juice, beans, onion, tomatoes, zucchini, oil, vinegar, garlic, salt, pepper and cayenne.

Cover and refrigerate for 8 hours or overnight. **Yield:** 6 servings.

Icy Olive Soup

When summer turns up the heat, I reach for this cool, refreshing soup. The color of the olives contrasts nicely with the creamy yogurt base.

Theresa Goble, Muscatine, Iowa

> 2 cups (16 ounces) plain yogurt
> 2 cans (10-1/2 ounces *each*) condensed chicken broth, undiluted
> 2 cans (2-1/4 ounces *each*) sliced ripe olives, drained
> 1 cup coarsely chopped cucumber
> 1/2 cup chopped green onions
> 1/2 cup chopped green pepper
> 1/2 cup sliced stuffed olives
> 1/8 teaspoon white pepper
> Seasoned croutons, optional

In a large bowl, stir yogurt until smooth. Whisk in broth. Add the next six ingredients and mix well.

Cover and chill for 4 hours. Stir before serving. Garnish soup with croutons if desired. **Yield:** 6 servings.

Shrimp Blitz

On a summer day, this invigorating soup really hits the spot. I've made it for special-occasion luncheons as well as for casual dinners with friends.

Jeannette Aiello, Placerville, California

> 1 bottle (8 ounces) clam juice
> 1 package (8 ounces) cream cheese, softened
> 1 garlic clove
> 1 package (5 ounces) frozen cooked salad shrimp, thawed
> 1 bottle (32 ounces) tomato juice
> 1 medium ripe avocado, diced
> 1/2 cup chopped cucumber
> 1/3 cup chopped green onions
> 2 tablespoons red wine vinegar
> 2 teaspoons sugar
> 1 teaspoon dill weed
> 1/2 teaspoon salt
> 1/4 teaspoon hot pepper sauce
> 1/8 teaspoon pepper

In a blender, combine clam juice and cream cheese; process until smooth. Pour mixture into a large bowl.

Add remaining ingredients; mix well. Cover and chill for at least 4 hours. **Yield:** 8 servings (2 quarts).

Cold Cucumber Soup
pictured below

I love trying to duplicate restaurant dishes at home. Friends and family tell me they like the results!

Shirley Dufresne, Grants Pass, Oregon

> 2 large cucumbers, peeled and seeded
> 1-1/4 cups sour cream
> 1 cup chicken broth
> 1 small onion, cut into wedges
> 4 sprigs fresh parsley, stems removed
> 2 sprigs fresh dill, stems removed
>   or 1 teaspoon dill weed
> 1 tablespoon lemon juice
> 3/4 teaspoon salt
> 1/4 teaspoon white pepper

Cut cucumbers into large chunks; place in a blender with remaining ingredients. Puree; pour into a bowl. Cover and refrigerate for at least 8 hours. **Yield:** 4 servings.

chilled VEGGIE SOUPS

Cucumber Potato Soup

pictured at right

Served hot or cold, this soup never fails to delight the taste buds! It's simple to make, has a nice dill flavor and is a great way to use a few potatoes and a garden cucumber. It's one of my favorites.

Robert Breno, Strongsville, Ohio

     4 medium potatoes, peeled and diced
     1 teaspoon salt
     2 cups water
     1 medium cucumber, peeled, seeded
       and diced
   1/4 teaspoon white pepper
     1 cup heavy whipping cream *or* milk
   1/2 cup milk
     1 green onion, sliced
     1 teaspoon dried dill weed *or* 1
       tablespoon chopped fresh dill
Additional salt and pepper to taste

In a large saucepan, cook potatoes in salted water until very soft. Place sieve over a large bowl. Pour potatoes and liquid into sieve and force potatoes through.

Return to saucepan. Stir in cucumber, pepper, cream, milk and onion. Simmer gently for about 5 minutes or until cucumber is tender. Add dill, salt and pepper. Serve hot or cold. **Yield:** 4 servings.

In a 2-qt. saucepan, combine water, lemon juice, sorrel leaves and bundle of stems. Simmer for 20 minutes; discard stem bundle.

In a small bowl, beat egg yolks; add a small amount of sorrel mixture, stirring constantly. Return all to the pan. Cook and stir until soup thickens (do not boil). Cool; chill for several hours.

Chilled Sorrel Soup

This is a tart, refreshing soup with lovely spring green color. I especially like serving sorrel this way.

Sara Seltzer, Sacramento, California

   1/2 pound fresh sorrel
     4 cups water
     1 tablespoon lemon juice
     2 egg yolks
     1 teaspoon salt
   1/4 teaspoon pepper
Sour cream
Additional chopped fresh sorrel, optional

Remove center ribs and stems from sorrel; tie ribs and stems in a bundle and wrap in cheesecloth. Chop leaves into thin strips.

So What's Sorrel?

Sorrel is a spring plant with arrowhead-shaped leaves. Its distinctive sour flavor can add spark to salads, and it can also be cooked as greens.

If you don't find sorrel leaves growing wild in your area, you may be able to grow them. To order seeds, you'll want to check catalogs that carry herbs and more unusual plants.

As with any wild ingredient, make sure you know what you're picking. If you're unsure, check with your county Extension agent.

Add salt and pepper. Garnish with a dollop of sour cream and additional sorrel if desired. **Yield:** 4 servings (1 quart).

Gazpacho
pictured below

Nothing equals the taste of an ice-cold bowl of gazpacho on a hot summer day—I was hooked from the first spoonful! I found this recipe when I was looking for something to make with the abundance of tomatoes from my garden.

Robynn Shannon, Alexandria, Virginia

- 1 medium green pepper, finely chopped
- 2 celery ribs, finely chopped
- 1 medium cucumber, peeled, seeded and finely chopped
- 1/4 cup minced fresh parsley
- 1 tablespoon minced fresh chives
- 1 garlic clove, minced
- 1 green onion, thinly sliced
- 1/3 cup red wine vinegar

- 1/4 cup olive oil
- 1 teaspoon salt
- 1/2 teaspoon pepper
- 1/2 teaspoon Worcestershire sauce
- 3 cups chopped seeded peeled fresh tomatoes
- 1 can (46 ounces) tomato juice
Seasoned croutons

In a large bowl, combine the first 14 ingredients. Chill for several hours or overnight. Garnish each serving with croutons. **Yield:** about 10 servings (2-1/2 quarts).

Blue Cheese Tomato Soup

This recipe comes in handy when I want to serve a fancier soup without a lot of extra fuss. Because it's so rich and flavorful, you can enjoy this as a meal in itself.

Mary Stiner, Fremont, New Hampshire

- 1 bottle (32 ounces) tomato juice, *divided*
- 1 package (3 ounces) cream cheese, softened
- 2 to 4 ounces crumbled blue cheese, *divided*
- 1 small onion, coarsely chopped
- 1 tablespoon Worcestershire sauce
- 1 tablespoon sugar
- 2 teaspoons lemon juice
- 1/2 teaspoon pepper
- 1/4 teaspoon salt
Toasted garlic bread, optional

In a blender or food processor, combine 2 cups tomato juice, cream cheese, half of the blue cheese, onion, Worcestershire sauce, sugar, lemon juice, pepper and salt; process until smooth.

Pour into a large bowl; stir in remaining tomato juice. Chill at least 1 hour. Top with garlic bread if desired and remaining blue cheese. **Yield:** 6 servings.

Chilled Squash and Carrot Soup

pictured below

This smooth soup is colorful as well as nutritious and filling. Served chilled, it makes an elegant first course when entertaining. But it's also good served warm.

Elaine Sabacky, Litchfield, Minnesota

1-1/2	pounds butternut squash, peeled, seeded and cubed (about 3 cups)
1	can (14-1/2 ounces) chicken broth
2	medium carrots, sliced
1	medium onion, chopped
1/4	teaspoon salt
1/2	cup evaporated milk
3	tablespoons sour cream

In a large saucepan, combine the squash, broth, carrots, onion and salt. Bring to a boil. Reduce heat; cover and simmer for 15-20 minutes or until vegetables are very tender. Remove from the heat; cool.

In a blender or food processor, puree squash mixture in batches. Transfer to a bowl; stir in milk. Cover and chill until serving. Garnish with sour cream. **Yield:** 4 servings.

Chilled Potato Soup

It takes just minutes to blend together this unusual soup seasoned with basil. It's creamy, rich and so refreshing on a hot summer day.

Sandi Pichon, Slidell, Louisiana

1-1/3	cups milk
1	can (10-3/4 ounces) condensed cream of potato soup, undiluted
3/4	teaspoon snipped fresh basil or 1/4 teaspoon dried basil
1/4	teaspoon snipped fresh or dried chives
1	cup (8 ounces) sour cream
1/4	cup white wine or chicken broth

Place all the ingredients in a blender or food processor; cover and process until smooth. Transfer to a bowl; cover and chill until serving. **Yield:** 4 servings.

To serve soup warm: Process the milk, soup and herbs in a blender until smooth; transfer to a saucepan. Bring to a boil over medium heat, stirring constantly. Reduce the heat. Add sour cream and wine or broth; heat through (do not boil).

Low-Fat Gazpacho

This soup often appears on my menu when I'm cooking for guests. It's a real favorite because I can make it ahead.

Shirley McCabe, Grand Junction, Colorado

1	can (46 ounces) light and tangy V8 juice
2	large tomatoes, chopped and seeded
1	large cucumber, peeled, seeded and chopped
3	celery ribs, chopped
1	large green pepper, chopped
1/2	cup chopped green onions
1/3	cup red wine vinegar
1	tablespoon Worcestershire sauce
1	teaspoon salt, optional
1/2	teaspoon pepper

In a large bowl, combine all of the ingredients. Cover and chill overnight. **Yield:** 12 servings (3 quarts).

Zucchini Soup
pictured above

When there's an abundance of zucchini in our garden, I know it's time for this fresh-tasting soup.

Mrs. R.C. Friend, Lynden, Washington

- 1 cup chopped onion
- 1 cup thinly sliced celery
- 1 garlic clove, minced
- 1/4 cup chopped green pepper
- 1 tablespoon vegetable oil
- 2 pounds zucchini, chopped
- 2 medium tomatoes, chopped
- 3 cups chicken broth
- 1/2 teaspoon dried basil
- 1/4 teaspoon dried thyme
- 1 cup half-and-half cream *or* milk

In a large saucepan, saute onion, celery, garlic and green pepper in oil until tender. Add zucchini, tomatoes, broth, basil and thyme; bring to a boil.

Reduce heat; simmer, uncovered, for 20-30 minutes or until the vegetables are tender. Stir in cream; heat through. Serve hot or cold. **Yield:** 8 servings (2 quarts).

287

Chilled Asparagus Soup

pictured below

This is a delightful soup that's perfect for hot weather. The curry seasoning comes through just right.

Kim Gilliland, Simi Valley, California

- 1 pound fresh asparagus
- 5 cups chicken broth
- 1/2 cup water
- 1/4 cup butter
- 1/4 cup all-purpose flour
- 3 egg yolks, beaten
- 3/4 cup heavy whipping cream
- 1 teaspoon curry powder
- 1/8 teaspoon pepper
Dash lemon juice

Cut asparagus into 1-in. pieces; set tips aside. Place the remaining asparagus in a saucepan; add broth. Bring to a boil; reduce heat. Cover and simmer for 40-45 minutes.

Cool slightly. Process in batches in a blender or food processor until smooth; set aside.

In a small saucepan, bring water to a boil. Add the asparagus tips; cook for 2-3 minutes or until tender. Drain and chill until serving.

In a saucepan, melt butter. Stir in flour until smooth. Gradually add pureed asparagus. Bring to a boil; cook and stir for 2 minutes or until thickened.

Remove from the heat. Stir a small amount of hot soup into egg yolks; return all to the pan, stirring constantly. Cook over low heat for 5 minutes or until mixture is heated through and reaches 160°. Stir in the cream, curry powder, pepper and lemon juice.

Remove from the heat; cool slightly. Cover and chill until serving. Garnish with asparagus tips, gently adding to each bowl. **Yield:** 8-10 servings.

Chilled Cream of Cucumber Soup

We grow lots of cukes in North Carolina, and plenty are available from friends if you don't happen to have a garden. This is a good make-ahead summer soup that is so cool and refreshing. If people like cucumbers, they will enjoy this—even those who say they don't care for cold soup.

Doris Heath, Franklin, North Carolina

- 1 medium onion, chopped
- 2 tablespoons butter
- 2 pounds cucumbers, peeled
- 5 cups chicken broth
- 1/4 cup minced fresh dill *or* 1 tablespoon dill weed
- 1 tablespoon balsamic vinegar
- 1/4 teaspoon salt
- 1/4 cup quick-cooking farina
- 1 cup (8 ounces) sour cream, *divided*

In a large saucepan, saute onion in butter until tender. Slice 1/3 cup cucumbers; refrigerate. Chop the remaining cucumbers and add to onion mixture.

Add the broth, dill, vinegar and salt; bring to a boil. Gradually add farina, stirring constantly. Reduce heat; simmer, uncovered, for 20 minutes, stirring occasionally. Cool slightly.

In a blender or food processor, process soup in batches until pureed. Pour into a container;

refrigerate until chilled. Just before serving, whisk in 1/2 cup sour cream. Garnish each serving with reserved cucumber slices and 1 tablespoon sour cream. **Yield:** 8 servings.

Easy Gazpacho

pictured at right

There's plenty of garden goodness in every bowl of this fresh-tasting soup. Served chilled, it's perfect for a summer meal.

Marlene Muckenhirn, Delano, Minnesota

2-1/2 cups tomato juice
   3 tablespoons white vinegar
   3 tablespoons olive oil
   2 garlic cloves, minced
1/4 teaspoon salt
   2 to 3 drops hot pepper sauce
   4 large tomatoes, chopped and *divided*
   1 medium onion, chopped
   1 medium cucumber, peeled, seeded and chopped
   1 medium green pepper, chopped
1/4 cup croutons

In a blender or food processor, combine the tomato juice, vinegar, oil, garlic, salt, hot pepper sauce and half of the tomatoes; cover and process until smooth.

Transfer to a bowl. Add the onion, cucumber, green pepper and remaining tomatoes. Cover and refrigerate for 4 hours or until chilled. Garnish with croutons. **Yield:** 4 servings.

> In Chilled Cream of Cucumber Soup, the recipe calls for farina. This is a fine meal or flour made from wheat, nuts or cereal grains. It's much like Cream of Wheat.
>
> —*Doris Heath*
> *Franklin, North Carolina*

Beet Borscht

After a busy day, I like to unwind by creating something delicious for dinner. This recipe proves great meals can be quick.

Courtney Bird, Papillion, Nebraska

   2 cans (15 ounces *each*) diced beets
   1 can (10-3/4 ounces) condensed cream of chicken soup, undiluted
   1 can (10-1/2 ounces) condensed beef consomme, undiluted
   4 dill pickle spears
   1 cup (8 ounces) sour cream
   1 jar (16 ounces) shredded sweet-and-sour red cabbage, undrained

Drain one can of beets; place beets in a blender, Add soup, consomme, pickles and sour cream; process until smooth.

Pour into a large bowl. Add undrained can of beets and cabbage. Chill at least 4 hours. **Yield:** 8-10 servings (2-1/2 quarts).

289

Chilled Cucumber Soup

pictured above

This is a wonderful way to use up all those cucumbers that seem to be ready at the same time. It's so refreshing on hot summer days.

Shirley Kidd, New London, Minnesota

    2 medium cucumbers
    2 cups buttermilk
  1/2 cup sour cream
1-1/2 teaspoons sugar
    1 teaspoon dill weed
  1/2 teaspoon salt
  1/8 teaspoon white pepper
    2 green onions, chopped
Fresh dill, optional

Cut four thin slices of cucumber; set aside for garnish. Peel and finely chop the remaining cucumbers.

In a bowl, combine the buttermilk, sour cream, sugar, dill, salt, pepper, green onions and chopped cucumbers; mix well.

Refrigerate for 4 hours or overnight. Garnish with cucumber slices and fresh dill if desired. **Yield:** 4 servings.

Chilled Bean Soup

pictured below

Combine crunchy fresh veggies with black beans and a splash of hot pepper sauce to create this spicy chilled soup. I often serve this during the warm summer months, when tomatoes are in season. It tastes best when you let it mellow overnight in the refrigerator.

Betty Nickels, Tampa, Florida

> 4 cups chopped seeded tomatoes
> 2 cups picante V8 juice
> 1 can (15 ounces) black beans, rinsed and drained
> 1 cup chopped cucumber
> 1 cup chopped sweet red *or* yellow pepper
> 1/2 cup chopped red onion
> 2 tablespoons balsamic vinegar
> 1 teaspoon sugar
> 1/4 to 1/2 teaspoon hot pepper sauce
> 1/4 teaspoon ground cumin
> 1/4 teaspoon salt
> 1/4 teaspoon pepper
> 7 tablespoons sour cream
> Sliced cucumber, optional

In a blender or food processor, combine tomatoes and V8 juice; cover and process just until blended.

Transfer to a large bowl. Stir in the black beans, chopped cucumber, sweet pepper, onion, vinegar, sugar and seasonings.

Cover and refrigerate for at least 4 hours or overnight. Serve with sour cream. Garnish with sliced cucumber if desired. **Yield:** 7 servings.

Asparagus and Potato Soup

This is my version of a recipe I tasted while on vacation. When we got home, I tinkered around with ingredients until I came up with a winning combination.

Lisa Hagdohl, Walbridge, Ohio

> 1 medium potato, peeled and diced
> 1 medium onion, chopped
> 5 green onions, chopped
> 1 medium carrot, chopped
> 1 celery rib, chopped
> 1/4 cup butter
> 1/4 cup all-purpose flour
> 1 teaspoon salt
> 1/4 teaspoon pepper
> 1 can (49-1/2 ounces) chicken broth
> 1 pound fresh asparagus, trimmed and cut into 2-inch pieces
> 1/2 cup half-and-half cream
> 1 cup (8 ounces) sour cream
> 2 bacon strips, cooked and crumbled
> Additional sour cream
> Asparagus tips, optional

In a Dutch oven or soup kettle, saute potato, onions, carrot and celery in butter until onions and celery are tender. Stir in flour, salt and pepper until blended. Gradually add broth. Bring to a boil; cook and stir for 2 minutes.

Add asparagus; reduce heat. Cover and simmer for 20-25 minutes or until vegetables are tender. Cool to lukewarm.

In a blender, puree vegetable mixture in small batches until smooth. Pour into a large bowl; stir in cream and sour cream until smooth.

Serve warm, or cover and refrigerate for at least 2 hours and serve chilled. Garnish with bacon, sour cream and asparagus tips if desired. **Yield:** 8-10 servings.

"Giving soup mix shares the warmth of yourself."

pantry-pleasing
MIXES

Freezer Vegetable Soup

pictured at right

This wonderful soup tastes so fresh you'll never know it's been frozen. You can easily double the recipe when tomatoes are plentiful or toss in extra vegetables from your garden. For heartier fare, beef it up with ground beef, sausage or meatballs.

Elizabeth Moore, Frankfort, Kentucky

SOUP BASE:
- 1 quart chopped fresh tomatoes
- 1 cup diced celery
- 1 cup diced carrots
- 1 cup diced onion
- 1 teaspoon sugar
- 1/2 teaspoon salt
- 1/4 teaspoon pepper
- 1/4 teaspoon dill weed

ADDITIONAL INGREDIENTS (for each batch):
- 2 cups diced cooked potatoes
- 2 cups water

Combine soup base ingredients in a kettle or Dutch oven; bring to a boil over medium heat. Reduce the heat; cover and simmer for 45 minutes. Cool.

Place 2 cups each into freezer containers. May be frozen for up to 3 months. **Yield:** 2 batches (4 cups total).

To prepare soup: Thaw soup base in the refrigerator. Transfer to a kettle or Dutch oven. Add potatoes and water; simmer for 30-40 minutes. **Yield:** 4 servings per batch.

Jambalaya Mix

Keep this zippy jambalaya mix on hand and a full-flavored meal is never far away. Add shrimp, smoked sausage and a few other easy ingredients to the nicely seasoned rice mix to create a speedy skillet sensation.

Sybil Brown, Highland, California

- 3 cups uncooked long grain rice
- 3 tablespoons dried minced onion
- 3 tablespoons dried parsley flakes
- 4 teaspoons beef bouillon granules
- 1 tablespoon dried minced chives
- 1 tablespoon dried celery flakes
- 1-1/2 teaspoons pepper
- 3/4 teaspoon cayenne pepper
- 3/4 teaspoon garlic powder
- 3/4 teaspoon dried thyme

ADDITIONAL INGREDIENTS:
- 2 cups water
- 1/2 cup chopped green pepper
- 1 can (8 ounces) tomato sauce
- 1 pound fully cooked smoked sausage, cut into 1/4-inch slices
- 1 pound uncooked medium shrimp, peeled and deveined

In an airtight container, combine the first 10 ingredients. Store in a cool dry place for up to 6 months. **Yield:** about 3 batches (about 3-1/3 cups total).

To prepare jambalaya: In a saucepan, bring water and green pepper to a boil. Stir in 1 cup jambalaya mix; return to a boil. Reduce heat; cover and simmer for 18-20 minutes or until rice is tender.

In another saucepan, heat tomato sauce and sausage. Cook shrimp in boiling water until pink; drain. Stir into sausage mixture. Serve over rice mixture. **Yield:** 4-6 servings.

Classic Onion Soup Mix
pictured below

You can prepare soup, make dips and even season meats with this handy mix. It's an inexpensive alternative to the envelopes you get at the store.

June Mullins, Livonia, Missouri

3/4 cup dried minced onion
1/3 cup beef bouillon granules
1/4 cup onion powder
1/4 teaspoon sugar
1/4 teaspoon celery seed
FOR ROASTED POTATOES (shown below):
   6 medium potatoes (about 2 pounds),
     cut into 1/2-inch cubes
1/3 cup olive oil
FOR ONION SOUP:
   4 cups water
FOR ONION DIP:
   2 cups (16 ounces) sour cream
Assorted raw vegetables, chips *or* crackers

Combine the first five ingredients. Store in an airtight container in a cool dry place for up to 1 year. **Yield:** 4 batches (20 tablespoons total).

To prepare roasted potatoes: In a bowl, toss potatoes and oil. Sprinkle with 5 tablespoons onion soup mix; toss to coat. Transfer to an ungreased 15-in. x 10-in. x 1-in. baking pan. Bake, uncovered, at 450° for 35-40 minutes or until tender, stirring occasionally. **Yield:** 6 servings.

To prepare onion soup: In a saucepan, combine water and 5 tablespoons onion soup mix. Bring to a boil over medium-high heat, stirring occasionally. Reduce heat; simmer, uncovered, for 10 minutes, stirring occasionally. **Yield:** 3 servings.

To prepare onion dip: In a bowl, combine sour cream and 5 tablespoons onion soup mix; mix well. Refrigerate for at least 2 hours. Serve with assorted raw vegetables, chips or crackers. **Yield:** 2 cups.

Cream Soup Mix

This mix makes a great substitute for canned creamed soup in many recipes. Or, add leftover chicken, asparagus or mushrooms for a delicious soup!

Kay Beard, Vass, North Carolina

   2 cups instant nonfat dry milk powder
3/4 cup cornstarch
1/4 cup chicken bouillon granules
   1 teaspoon onion powder
1/2 teaspoon dried thyme
1/2 teaspoon dried basil
1/4 teaspoon pepper

Combine all ingredients; mix well. Store in an airtight container. **Yield:** 3 cups dry mix.

For a condensed cream soup substitute: Blend 1/3 cup mix and 1-1/4 cups water in a 1-qt. saucepan or microwave-safe dish until smooth. Bring to boil or microwave for 2-1/2 to 3 minutes. Stir occasionally; cool. Use as a substitute for one 10-3/4-ounce can condensed cream of chicken, celery or mushroom soup.

For 1-1/2 cups soup: Blend 1/3 cup of the mix and 1-1/2 cups water in 1-1/2-qt. saucepan or microwave safe dish until smooth. Boil or microwave for 3 to 3-1/2 minutes. Stir occasionally.

Bean Soup Mix

pictured above

An attractive bag of this savory mix makes a tasteful gift for a teacher or co-worker. Remember to attach the soup recipe with a decorative ribbon or cord.

Elizabeth Clayton Paul, Nepean, Ontario

BEAN MIX:
 1 cup *each* dried yellow split peas, green split peas, lentils, medium pearl barley, black-eyed peas, small lima beans, navy beans, great northern beans and pinto beans

SOUP:
 1-1/2 quarts water
 1 large onion, chopped
 1 large carrot, chopped
 2 teaspoons chili powder
 1-1/4 teaspoons salt
 1/4 teaspoon pepper
 1/8 teaspoon ground cloves
 1/2 pound fully cooked smoked sausage, sliced
 1 can (28 ounces) diced tomatoes, undrained
 1 tablespoon lemon juice

Combine mix ingredients. Divide into six batches (1-1/2 cups each); store in airtight containers.

To make one batch of soup: Place 1-1/2 cups bean mix in a Dutch oven or soup kettle; cover with water by 2 in. Bring to a boil; boil for 2 minutes. Remove from the heat; let stand for 1 hour. Drain, discarding liquid.

Return beans to kettle; add 1-1/2 qts. water. Bring to a boil. Reduce heat; cover and simmer for 1-1/2 to 2 hours or until the beans are tender.

Add onion, carrot, chili powder, salt, pepper and cloves. Return to a boil. Reduce heat and simmer, uncovered, for 30 minutes. Add sausage, tomatoes and lemon juice; simmer 15-20 minutes longer. **Yield:** 9 cups of mix (six batches of soup—each batch makes 2-1/2 quarts and serves 8-10).

Make-Ahead Squash Soup

I make a big batch of this soup when I have an abundance of zucchini from the garden. In winter, I just heat and serve it to be reminded of summer's goodness.

Suzanne McKinley, Lyons, Georgia

SOUP BASE:
   3 pounds zucchini, sliced
   2 cups water
   1 can (14-1/2 ounces) beef broth
   1 cup chopped onion
1-1/2 teaspoons salt
   1/8 teaspoon garlic powder
ADDITIONAL INGREDIENTS (for each batch):
   1 cup half-and-half cream
Grated Parmesan cheese and crumbled
   cooked bacon, optional

Combine soup base ingredients in a large kettle or Dutch oven; bring to a boil. Reduce heat; simmer for 20 minutes or until the zucchini is tender. Cool slightly. Puree in batches in a blender or food processor; cool.

Place 2 cups each into freezer containers. May be frozen for up to 3 months. **Yield:** 4 batches (8 cups total).

To prepare soup: Thaw soup base in the refrigerator. Transfer to a saucepan. Add cream; cook and stir over medium heat until heated through. Garnish with Parmesan cheese and bacon if desired. **Yield:** 3 servings per batch.

Classic Chili Mix
pictured below

This mix is on the mild side, which is nice for those who aren't partial to extra-spicy food.

Bernice Morris, Marshfield, Missouri

   1 cup plus 2 tablespoons all-purpose
      flour
3/4 cup dried minced onion
   4 to 6 tablespoons chili powder
1/4 cup paprika
   2 tablespoons salt
   1 tablespoon ground cumin
   1 tablespoon dried minced garlic
   1 tablespoon sugar
ADDITIONAL INGREDIENTS (for each batch):
   1 pound ground beef
   1 can (15 ounces) pinto beans, rinsed
      and drained
   1 small green pepper, chopped
   1 can (14-1/2 ounces) diced tomatoes,
      undrained
1/2 to 3/4 cup water

Combine the first eight ingredients; divide into six batches (a little less than 1/2 cup each). Store in airtight containers. **Yield:** 6 batches (2-3/4 cups total).

To prepare chili: Cook beef over medium heat in a large saucepan until no longer pink; drain. Stir in one batch of chili mix, beans, green pepper, tomatoes and water; bring to a boil. Reduce heat; simmer for 30 minutes. **Yield:** 4 servings per batch.

Five-Bean Soup
pictured at right

This tasty recipe was one I discovered years ago. With salad and bread, it makes a savory supper.

Lynne Dodd, Mentor, Ohio

> 5 packages (16 ounces *each*) dried beans: lima, great northern, kidney, pinto and split peas

ADDITIONAL INGREDIENTS (for *each* batch):
> 3 beef bouillon cubes
> 3 tablespoons dried chives
> 1 teaspoon dried savory
> 1 teaspoon salt
> 1/2 teaspoon ground cumin
> 1/2 teaspoon pepper
> 1 bay leaf
> 2-1/2 quarts water
> 1 can (14-1/2 ounces) stewed tomatoes

Combine beans; divide into four batches (about 3-3/4 cups each). **Yield:** 4 batches.

To make one batch of soup: Wash one batch of beans. Place in a large kettle; add enough water to cover. Bring to a boil; cook for 3 to 4 minutes. Remove from heat. Cover; let stand 1 hour.

Tie spices in a cheesecloth bag. Drain and rinse beans. Return to kettle; add bouillon, spices and water. Bring to a boil. Reduce heat; cover and simmer 1-1/2 hours or until beans are tender, stirring occasionally. Remove spices. Add tomatoes and heat through. **Yield:** 14 servings (3-1/2 quarts).

ADDITIONAL INGREDIENTS:
> 1 quart chicken broth
> 1/4 teaspoon pepper
> 1 cup cubed cooked chicken, optional

Combine the first seven ingredients. Store in airtight containers in a cool dry place for up to 1 year. **Yield:** 13 batches (13 cups total).

To prepare soup: In a large saucepan, combine 1 cup soup mix, broth, pepper and chicken if desired. Bring to a boil. Reduce heat; cover and simmer for 60-70 minutes or until peas and lentils are tender. **Yield:** about 4 servings per batch.

Split Pea Soup Mix

My mother sent me this dry blend and the recipe. This soup is thick with lentils, barley and peas.

Susan Ruckert, Tangent, Oregon

> 1 package (16 ounces) dried green split peas
> 1 package (16 ounces) dried yellow split peas
> 1 package (16 ounces) dried lentils
> 1 package (16 ounces) medium pearl barley
> 1 package (12 ounces) alphabet pasta
> 1 jar (1/2 ounce) dried celery flakes
> 1/2 cup dried parsley flakes

Chicken Rice Soup Mix

This mix calls for brown rice instead of white and is subtly seasoned with tarragon and pepper.

Iola Egle, McCook, Nebraska

> 2 cups uncooked long grain brown rice
> 1/2 cup chicken bouillon granules
> 4 teaspoons dried tarragon
> 4 teaspoons dried parsley flakes
> 1 teaspoon white pepper

ADDITIONAL INGREDIENTS:
3 cups water
1 tablespoon butter

In a bowl, combine the first five ingredients. Cover and store in a cool dry place for up to 6 months. **Yield:** 4 batches (about 2-2/3 cups).

To prepare soup: In a saucepan, bring water, butter and 2/3 cup mix to a boil. Reduce heat; cover and simmer for 30-35 minutes or until rice is tender. **Yield:** 2-3 servings per batch.

Friendship Soup Mix

I layer this pretty, delicious soup mix in glass jars to give as gifts or save for busy days.

Wendy Taylor, Mason City, Iowa

1/2 cup dried split peas
1/3 cup beef bouillon granules
1/4 cup medium pearl barley
1/2 cup dried lentils
1/4 cup dried minced onion
2 teaspoons Italian seasoning
1/2 cup uncooked long grain rice
1/2 cup alphabet macaroni *or* other small macaroni

ADDITIONAL INGREDIENTS:
1 pound ground beef
3 quarts water
1 can (28 ounces) diced tomatoes, undrained

In a 1-1/2-pint jar, layer the first eight ingredients in the order listed. Seal tightly. **Yield:** 1 batch.

To prepare soup: Carefully remove macaroni from top of jar and set aside. In a large saucepan or Dutch oven, cook beef over medium heat until no longer pink; drain.

Add the water, tomatoes and soup mix; bring to a boil. Reduce heat; cover and simmer for 45 minutes. Add the reserved macaroni; cover and simmer for 15-20 minutes or until macaroni, peas, lentils and barley are tender. **Yield:** 16 servings (4 quarts) per batch.

Wild Rice and Barley Soup Mix

pictured below

Warm up with this stick-to-the-ribs soup mix from our Test Kitchen. Include prep instructions when you give this away.

1 tablespoon brown sugar
2 teaspoons Italian seasoning
1/2 teaspoon dried minced garlic
1/2 teaspoon ground celery seed
1/2 teaspoon pepper
1/2 cup medium pearl barley
1/3 cup dried vegetable flakes
3 tablespoons chicken bouillon granules
1/2 cup uncooked wild rice
1/2 cup dried minced onion

ADDITIONAL INGREDIENTS:
8 cups water
Real bacon bits

In a small bowl, combine first five ingredients. In a pint-size jar with a tight-fitting lid, layer the barley, vegetable flakes, brown sugar mixture, bouillon, rice and onion, packing each layer tightly (do not mix). Cover and store in a cool dry place for up to 4 months.

To prepare soup: Pour soup mix into a large saucepan. Add 8 cups of water; bring to a boil. Reduce heat. Cover; simmer for 1 hour or until rice is tender. Garnish with bacon bits. **Yield:** 6 servings.

Spicy Chili Seasoning Mix

pictured below

Having the seasonings mixed up in advance makes stirring up a batch of chili a breeze. It's a bold but pleasant blend. I like the round steak and ground beef combination.

Mary Henderson, Opelika, Alabama

> 4 tablespoons chili powder
> 2-1/2 teaspoons ground coriander
> 2-1/2 teaspoons ground cumin
> 1-1/2 teaspoons garlic powder
> 1 teaspoon dried oregano
> 1/2 teaspoon cayenne pepper

ADDITIONAL INGREDIENTS:
> 1 pound boneless round steak, cut into 1-inch pieces
> 2 teaspoons vegetable oil
> 1 pound lean ground beef
> 1 medium onion, chopped
> 1 can (28 ounces) diced tomatoes, undrained
> 2 cans (15 ounces *each*) chili beans, *divided*

Combine the first six ingredients. Store in an airtight container in a cool dry place. **Yield:** 4 batches (20 teaspoons total).

To prepare chili: Lightly brown steak in oil in a Dutch oven; add 3 teaspoons of the seasoning mix and toss to coat. Add ground beef; cook over medium heat until meat is no longer pink. Add onion; cook until tender. Add tomatoes and 2 more teaspoons of mix.

Stir in one can of chili beans. Place the other can in a blender; cover and process until smooth. Add to chili. Cook on low for 30-40 minutes or until meat is tender. **Yield:** 10 servings (2-1/2 quarts) per batch.

Confetti Bean Soup Mix

With its colorful variety of beans and delicious flavor, this soup is tempting. I like to give it to friends each Christmas.

Rebecca Lambert, Staunton, Virginia

> 1 pound *each* dried navy beans, great northern beans, red kidney beans, pinto beans and green split peas

SEASONING MIX:
> 12 beef bouillon cubes
> 3/4 cup dried minced chives
> 6 teaspoons salt
> 4 teaspoons dried savory
> 2 teaspoons ground cumin
> 2 teaspoons coarsely ground pepper
> 4 bay leaves

ADDITIONAL INGREDIENTS FOR SOUP:
> 12 cups water, *divided*
> 1 can (14-1/2 ounces) stewed tomatoes
> 1/4 teaspoon hot pepper sauce, optional

Combine beans and peas; place 3-1/4 cups each in four large resealable plastic bags. Set bags aside.

In four snack-size resealable plastic bags or on four squares of plastic wrap, place 3 bouillon cubes, 3 tablespoons chives, 1-1/2 teaspoons salt, 1 teaspoon savory, 1/2 teaspoon cumin, 1/2 teaspoon pepper and 1 bay leaf. Seal bags or tie plastic wrap with ribbon if desired.

To prepare soup: Place the contents of one bag of beans in a Dutch oven; add 7 cups water. Bring to a boil; boil for 2 minutes. Remove from the heat; cover and let stand for 1 hour. Drain beans and discard liquid.

Add remaining water and contents of one seasoning bag. Bring to a boil. Reduce heat; cover and simmer for 1 hour or until beans are tender, stirring occasionally. Add tomatoes and hot pepper sauce if desired. Simmer, uncovered, for 20 minutes. Discard bay leaf before serving. **Yield:** 4 batches, 9 servings (2-1/4 quarts) per batch.

Calico Soup Mix

pictured at right

This colorful medley cooks up into a satisfying soup that'll stand by itself or serve as a side dish.

Rhonda Letendre, Epsom, New Hampshire

BEAN MIX:
1-1/2 cups *each* dried lentils, baby lima beans, yellow split peas, red kidney beans, great northern beans, pinto beans, green split peas and navy beans

ADDITIONAL INGREDIENTS (for each batch):
2-1/4 quarts water
    2 cups cubed fully cooked ham
    1 can (14-1/2 ounces) stewed tomatoes
    1 medium onion, sliced
    1 medium green pepper, chopped
    1 garlic clove, minced
    2 teaspoons salt
    1 teaspoon *each* dried marjoram, oregano, parsley flakes and Italian seasoning

Combine beans; divide into six batches (2 cups each). Store in airtight containers. **Yield:** 6 batches (12 cups total).

To prepare soup: Place one batch of bean mix in a Dutch oven or soup kettle; add water to cover by 2 in. Bring to a boil and boil for 2 minutes. Remove from the heat; cover and let stand for 1 hour. Drain. Add 2-1/4 qts. water; bring to a boil.

Reduce heat; cover and simmer for 1-1/2 to 2 hours or until beans are tender. Add the ham, tomatoes, onion, green pepper, garlic and seasonings; return to a boil. Reduce heat; simmer for 45-50 minutes. **Yield:** 16 servings (about 4 quarts) per batch.

Country Bean Soup

I like to give this mix as a gift, layering the beans in a clear pint jar. You'll find it's perfect to serve year-round.

Donna Higbee, Sandy, Utah

    1 cup *each* dried yellow split peas, green split peas, lentils, black-eyed peas, pinto beans, black beans, kidney beans and great northern beans

ADDITIONAL INGREDIENTS:
1-1/2 quarts water
    1 large onion, chopped
    2 medium carrots, chopped
    1 celery rib, chopped
    1 garlic clove, minced
    1 to 2 teaspoons salt
    1 teaspoon chili powder
1/4 teaspoon pepper
    1 smoked ham hock
    1 can (8 ounces) tomato sauce

Combine peas, lentils and beans; divide into four equal batches, 2 cups each. Store in an airtight container.

To make one batch of soup: Place one batch of beans in a large saucepan. Add remaining ingredients; bring to a boil over medium-high heat. Reduce heat; cover and simmer for 3 hours or until beans are tender. Remove ham hock; cut meat into bite-size pieces and return to pan. Heat through. **Yield:** 4 batches, 8-10 servings (2-1/2 quarts per batch).

Index of Tips

Index by Chapter

Bountiful Beef & Ground Beef

Appealing Pork

303

Index by Major Ingredient & Cooking Method

Taste of Home's BIG BOOK *of* SOUP